The Small Firm Owner-Manager

John Deeks

The Small Firm Owner-Manager

Entrepreneurial Behavior and Management Practice

PRAEGER SPECIAL STUDIES IN INTERNATIONAL BUSINESS, FINANCE, AND TRADE

Praeger Publishers   New York   Washington   London

Library of Congress Cataloging in Publication Data

Deeks, John.
   The small-firm owner-manager.

   (Praeger special studies in international business,
finance, and trade)
   Bibliography: p.
   Includes index.
   1. Small business--Management. 2. Furniture industry
and trade--Great Britain--Management. 3. Entrepreneur.
I. Title.
HD69.S6D43   658'.022   75-19773
ISBN 0-275-55550-X

PRAEGER PUBLISHERS
111 Fourth Avenue, New York, N.Y. 10003, U.S.A.

Published in the United States of America in 1976
by Praeger Publishers, Inc.

Printed in the United States of America

ACKNOWLEDGMENTS

This book grew from a research programme on the management of small companies financed by the Furniture and Timber Industry Training Board in High Wycombe, Buckinghamshire, England. The launching of that programme was due to the far-sightedness of the Board's first Chairman, Lawrence Neal, and to the energy and enthusiasm of its Director, James Saddler, who provided, together with Ian Finlator, Alec Grassby and Roy Wilkie, much-appreciated encouragement during the subsequent course of the research. My thanks also to more than two hundred owners and managers of small enterprises in the United Kingdom for the time made available to me and for the interest shown in my work.

In addition, financial assistance was received from the Department of Employment and Productivity in London, research assistance from James Young, computational assistance from Peter Laycock, and secretarial assistance from Ingrid Arman, Annette Charlton, and Jane Jones. I also wish to thank Roger Boshier, Pat Deeks, and Jack Lambert for ideas and comments on portions of the manuscript; I hope they will not be disappointed in the final product.

Acknowledgment is gratefully extended to the following for permission to use material from their publications:

Basil Blackwell Ltd.: from "Educational and Occupational Histories of Owner-Managers and Managers" by John Deeks, The Journal of Management Studies 9, no. 2 (May 1972).

Doubleday & Co. Inc.: from Without Marx or Jesus: The New American Revolution Has Begun by Jean-Francois Revel, translated by Jack Bernard. Translation © 1971 by Doubleday Co., Inc. Used by permission of the publisher. U.K. and Commonwealth rights by permission of MacGibbon and Kee, London.

Estate of H. G. Wells: from The World of William Clissold by H. G. Wells.

H.M. Stationery Office: from Report of the Committee of Inquiry on Small Firms, Cmnd. 4811, 1971, Table 1.I, para. 1.9, and para. 19.5, used with the permission of the Controller of Her Majesty's Stationery Office.

CONTENTS

Page

ACKNOWLEDGMENTS   v

LIST OF TABLES AND FIGURES   ix

INTRODUCTION   xii

PART I: BACKGROUND PERSPECTIVES

Chapter

1   THE ECONOMICS OF THE ENTREPRENEUR   3

2   THE PSYCHOLOGY OF THE ENTREPRENEUR   16

3   THE ENTREPRENEUR IN LITERATURE   27

4   THE SMALL FIRM IN AN ADVANCED INDUSTRIAL
    SOCIETY   56

PART II: RESEARCH FINDINGS

5   SMALL COMPANIES IN THE FURNITURE INDUSTRY   73

6   FAMILY AND KINSHIP IN THE SMALL FIRM   92

7   EDUCATIONAL AND OCCUPATIONAL HISTORIES
    OF OWNER-MANAGERS   104

8   THE TRAINING AND DEVELOPMENT OF THE
    OWNER-MANAGER   128

9   THE OWNER-MANAGER AND HIS WORK   151

PART III: FURTHER CONSIDERATIONS

10 THE MOTIVATION AND GOALS OF THE
    OWNER-MANAGER   185

Chapter   Page

11 THE MANAGERIAL PROCESS IN THE SMALL FIRM 209

12 THE OWNER-MANAGER AND ORGANIZATION
    THEORY 230

13 EDUCATION, TRAINING, AND DEVELOPMENT
    PROCESSES AND THE SMALL FIRM 253

14 SOCIAL AND ECONOMIC POLICIES FOR SMALL
    BUSINESS 289

APPENDIX: RESEARCH METHODS 313

BIBLIOGRAPHY 326

INDEX 353

ABOUT THE AUTHOR 361

LIST OF TABLES AND FIGURES

Table		Page
4.1	Size of U.S. Companies, 1963 and 1967	61
4.2	Distribution of U.S. Companies by Number of Employees and of Employees by Size of Company, 1967	62
4.3	U.K. Small-Firm Sector as Defined by the Bolton Committee	62
5.1	U.K. Furniture Firms with Sales Turnovers of under £500,000 Per Annum	76
5.2	Small Firms and the U.K. Furniture Industry	76
5.3	U.K. Furniture Establishments, 1969 and 1970	77
5.4	Backgrounds of the Founders	78
5.5	Financial and Cost Structures	83
6.1	Kinship by Management Category	93
6.2	The Employment of Owner-Managers' Relatives	94
7.1	Educational Backgrounds of Managers	106
7.2	Schooling of Managers by Age	108
7.3	Part-Time Further Education of Managers by Schooling	110
7.4	First Full-Time Occupations of Managers	113
7.5	Interfirm Mobility of Managers	117
7.6	Length of Service of Managers	119
7.7	Ages of Managers	124
8.1	Training Involvement of Managers with Their Employing Companies	130

Table   Page

8.2   Managers' External Training Activities   132

9.1   Managerial Specialization in the Small Firm   152

9.2   Distribution of Owner-Managers' Time and
          Work Episodes by Activities   158

9.3   Distribution of Owner-Managers' Time and Work
          Episodes by Interpersonal Contacts   159

9.4   Distribution of Owner-Managers' Time and Work
          Episodes by Initiation of Activity   160

10.1   Work Satisfactions and Dissatisfactions of
          Owner-Manager Founders and Inheritors   200

11.1   Small- and Large-Firm Management Processes:
          Summary   227

A.1   Descriptive Survey Population and Sample
          Interviewed   315

Figure

6.1   Management Structures in Small Firms   98

8.1   The Training Framework   137

9.1   Distribution of Managerial Time by Functions   155

9.2   Distribution of Work Episodes by Functions   157

11.1   Managerial Skills Taxonomy   228

13.1   Structure for Defining Training and Development
          Content   262

13.2   Managerial Skills: Job Relevance and Training
          Need by Managerial Group   263

13.3   Managerial Techniques: Job Relevance and
          Training Need by Managerial Group   265

Figure   Page

13.4   Suitability of Training and Development Methods
       to Various Managerial Groups   267

13.5   Suitability of Methods to Entrepreneurial
       Skills Training   268

13.6   Suitability of Methods to Administrative
       Skills Training   269

13.7   Suitability of Methods to Common Managerial
       Skills and Managerial Techniques Training   270

13.8   Matching Training Needs to Training Methods:
       An Example   271

The overthrow of the Allende government in Chile, election campaign fund scandals in the United States and in Japan, the oil crisis, and Watergate and its aftermath have refocused attention on the power of corporations to influence both the internal political processes in democratic countries and the development of international relations. The bogey of Big Business has once again taken hold of the public imagination. The 1960s' fear of domination by an ill-defined military-industrial complex has been displaced in the 1970s by a growing awareness of the operations of corporate-political cabals in local, state, and national government. While the United States has been purging itself of the kleptocrats in the bloodstream of its body politic, the United Kingdom has been faced with a number of uncomfortable insights into corporate practices: the Poulson case with its evidence of local government corruption, the disclosures about the employment policies of British subsidiaries in South Africa, the Lonhro affair, which led a Conservative prime minister to talk about the "ugly and unacceptable face of capitalism."

Such events have brought into perspective a variety of questions concerning the behavior of managers and entrepreneurs and have added urgency to demands that corporations should exercise their social and political powers in a responsible and ethical manner. The invasion of annual general meetings by "concerned shareholders," the preparation by employers' associations of booklets on how to handle protests at company meetings, concern with the minority group employment records of companies, with corporate responsiveness to ecological and environmental issues, with the internal democratic processes of companies, and with the physiological and psychological demands that they make on their employees are all symptomatic of the increasing pressure on organizations, and on their owners and managers, to recognize that social needs provide the primary rationale for their economic activities and that economic activities cannot be pursued regardless of social consequences. Suggestions as to how organizations are to be made accountable for the exercise of these social responsibilities vary. At one extreme are proposals to change company law provisions in such a way as to diminish the legal dominance of shareholders in corporate affairs and to establish legal rights for the various other parties that have a vested interest in the activities of a company--its employees, its customers, the local community. At an intermediate point are proposals that companies should be required to submit an annual social audit along with audited statements of their financial affairs. At the other extreme are vague hopes that exhortations to businessmen to monitor their own ethical and social practices, with a weather eye open to the changing ideological climate, will be sufficient.

Not unnaturally, in view of recent events and the greater public visibility of large enterprises, questions concerning the social responsibilities of business have been debated in a forum largely confined to reviewing the practices of big business and the attitudes and behavior of senior executives in major corporations. But such questions are of equal importance and concern in the context of the small firm. How, for example, do the myriad of owner-managers view their business and social responsibilities? Are the values espoused by owner-managers changing to accommodate new perspectives on the relationship between business and society and are any such shifts in values accompanied by changes in the business behavior of owner-managers? Or are owner-managers immune from the potential crises of conscience facing many large-company executives? Do traditions of probity survive in small enterprises with owner-managers being the last surviving torchbearers for the hard-working God-fearing artisan virtues of piety, honesty, and frugality advocated by Benjamin Franklin? Or is the small business owner-manager cast now in the predatory entrepreneurial mode, the mode of the money-maker rather than the goods-maker, surviving by wit and native cunning in the jungle of the capitalist system? Who are the owner-managers and what are their origins? Are they, like Franklin, self-taught, philanthropic, innovative, and inventive people whose business ventures provide an outlet for their creative energies? Or are they redundant aerospace engineers and technicians, the fallout of the technological revolution? Does the small business sector provide a haven for eccentrics, misfits, the socially displaced, a last opportunity for upward occupational and social mobility for those without formal educational qualifications? How many owner-managers adopt the whimsical business practices of the small company in Newcastle, England, which, whenever it received an order that its warehouse found difficult to supply, simply tore the order up, burnt it, or threw it away? To what extent are the business goals pursued by owner-managers a response to their psychological needs for achievement, autonomy, money, status, or power, rather than a response to particular economic and cultural conditions? Is it really necessary, as one psychologist has claimed, that if we wish to increase the supply of entrepreneurial talent in our societies we must look to changes in our child-rearing practices?

These, then, are some of the wider issues that form the framework for this book. More specifically the book examines the available empirical data on the characteristics and behavior of small-business owner-managers and, in doing so, highlights the gap that exists between theories about entrepreneurial behavior and the management practices of owner-managers. The book attempts to bridge this gap by challenging a number of traditional viewpoints and developing alternative theories. The principal new empirical data are presented in Part II, which summarizes the findings of small furniture firm studies carried out in the United Kingdom between 1968 and 1972. To put the research findings of Part II into context, however, it is necessary to examine traditional perspectives on small companies and their owner-managers. This is the purpose of Part I of the book, which describes theories concerning the functions and behavior of the entrepreneur. Chapter 1 outlines the different functions ascribed to the entrepreneur by economists, considers the place of the entrepreneur in economic theories of the firm, and looks at the impact of cultural factors on the social status of the owner-manager. Chapter 2 summarizes theories about the psychological attributes of the entrepreneur and attempts by psychologists to identify the secrets of entrepreneurial success and to develop general theories of entrepreneurial behavior. Chapter 3 examines the treatment of the entrepreneur by British and American novelists and relates changes in the portrayal of the entrepreneur in fiction to social and economic developments during the period from 1850 to 1950. Chapter 4 tackles the question of definition of a small firm, examines the numerical and economic importance of small firms, and looks at their future prospects within advanced industrial societies.

In Part III a number of these traditional perspectives are reexamined in the light of the data set out in Part II and of the findings of other European and American studies. Chapter 10 reconsiders the stereotypes that exist about the motivation of entrepreneurs in the light of data on the attitudes, expectations, and work satisfactions expressed by owner-managers, and examines the problem of differentiating organizational goals in the small firm. Chapter 11 describes the ways in which the management process in the small firm differs from the management process in the large company, and looks at the implications of these differences for an improved understanding of the abilities and skills required in the management of a small enterprise. Chapter 12 develops the arguments presented in Chapters 10 and 11 by attempting to construct a theoretical model, related to systems theories of organization, that can be used to describe the organizational processes and objectives of small companies. Chapter 13 looks at educational processes in the small firm, at the management training and development needs of small companies, suggests means of defining appropriate training methods, and considers the functions that can most usefully be filled by training agencies. Finally Chapter 14 relates small firms to their broader social context, discusses the problems involved in establishing, from a national or governmental point of view, the place of small businesses in the social and economic structure of a country, and outlines the kinds of policy objectives that governments might pursue in respect to small enterprises. Throughout Part III we are conscious that there is a need to achieve a better integration of theoretical perspectives on the small business sector with the realities revealed by research data.

It was Mark Twain who suggested that the fascination of science is that one gets such wholesale returns in conjecture from such trifling investment in fact. While our investment in fact in Part II is a fairly substantial investment, nevertheless our further considerations in Part III not only challenge prevalent assumptions, myths, and stereotypes about owner-management of small enterprises but also raise a variety of questions that we hope will provide a stimulus to additional research. Our approach is deliberately eclectic, drawing freely from the work of economists, psychologists, sociologists, and novelists in an attempt to integrate a number of different perspectives on small business management and the behavior of owner-managers. We trust, however, that the broad spectrum of issues that we touch upon will help to identify those aspects of the subject that require a more penetrating focus.

*   *   *

This book grew out of a research program sponsored by the United Kingdom Furniture and Timber Industry Training Board over the four years from 1968 to 1972. The board was established in December 1965 under the provisions of the 1964 Industrial Training Act. Early in its life it became apparent that a major feature of the board's work would be the creation and development of training policies and programs geared to the needs of the numerous small firms that the board was designed to serve. In this context the board set up an area training advisory service in 1967 and established its first group training schemes early in 1968. By the autumn of 1968 these services had begun to identify a number of difficulties in tackling management training and development problems in small companies. Up to that time much of what had been offered in the United Kingdom in the way of management training and development for the small firm was merely large-firm practice adapted and watered down. Very few of the solutions proposed to meet the management training needs of small firms had stemmed from systematic analysis of what those needs were, and there was insufficient knowledge to indicate clearly what the content of management training and development programs for small firms should be. Consequently in October 1969 the Furniture and Timber Industry Training Board, after a number of preliminary studies, launched two complementary research projects, both designed to throw greater light on the management training and development problems of small companies and to help the board ensure that its management training activities were tuned to the needs and requirements of the small firms within its scope.

The first of these two projects, which was carried out by the board's research division, was a general survey to obtain a better understanding of the qualifications and experience of the existing managerial labor force in the board's small firms. The specific objectives of this descriptive survey were:

1. To identify variations in the structure, organization, and growth, or otherwise, of a sample of small firms within the scope of the Furniture and Timber Industry Training Board.

2. To provide information on the control of such firms, the extent of the delegation within them, and on their use of specialist managerial staff.

3. To describe the qualifications, experience, and past training of managers in small firms.

4. To probe managers' perceptions of their problem areas and of consequent management training needs, and to clarify attitudes toward the investment of resources in training.

The second of the two projects, which was carried out by the Department of Administration at the University of Strathclyde, was a survey in depth of the work of a number of owner-managers and managers of small companies in the furniture and timber industries with a view to building up a clear picture of how small firms are managed and of the abilities and skills of their owner-managers and managers. The specific objectives of this depth study were:

1. To describe the activities and tasks carried out by managers in a number of small firms.

2. To indicate how frequently such activities and tasks occur and the degree of difficulty experienced by managers in handling them.

3. To identify the problems that arise in the course of the managers' working day, and to examine the methods by which managers deal with such problems.

4. To analyze the skills used by the managers of small firms and to identify those skills that most contribute to successful achievement of the firms' objectives.

5. On the basis of such descriptive and analytical study, to make recommendations on the appropriate aims and content of management training and development policies and programs for small firms within the scope of the Furniture and Timber Industry Training Board.

Findings from these two projects form the bulk of Part II of this book. Chapter 5 describes the furniture industry in Britain, the importance of small firms within it, and the founding, development, profitability, and growth of the sample of small companies studied. Chapter 6 examines the extent of family ownership and control of small furniture companies, the impact of kinship on organization structures, and some of the common problems that family relationships create in the management of small enterprises. Chapter 7 details the educational and occupational histories of owner-managers and contrasts the career profiles of the managers of small furniture firms with the career profiles of large firm executives. Chapter 8 analyzes the training and development of owner-managers and identifies a variety of management training and development needs that exist within small enterprises. Chapter 9 considers the work activities of owner-managers, the degree of managerial specialization within small firms, and characteristic styles of small firm management. The methods used in the two research projects are described in the Appendix.

Three groups of managers are dealt with in the analysis and discussion set out in Part II: "owner-managers," that is, those managers who were shareholders or partners in their company or who were sole proprietors; nonshareholding "managers," that is, managers who were fully engaged with managerial responsibilities, whether of a general or specialist character, but who had no stake in the ownership of the enterprises where they worked; and "supervisors," a category that included full-time supervisors and those working foremen who were estimated to spend 50 percent or more of their time in supervisory duties. Throughout the book fictitious names are used when reference is made to specific companies and their managers.

PART

I

**BACKGROUND
PERSPECTIVES**

1

THE ECONOMICS
OF THE ENTREPRENEUR

This chapter outlines the different functions ascribed to the entrepreneur by economists, considers the place of the entrepreneur in economic theories of the firm, and looks at the impact of cultural factors on the social status of the owner-manager. The chapter is essentially a broad overview of a complex field and is designed to summarize the viewpoints of others, primarily economists, in order to provide some perspective to the presentation of research data in Part II of the book. The theories of the economists are set out with little comment at this stage. It will become increasingly clear later in the book that these theoretical models do not adequately describe or account for the behavior of many small-firm owner-managers. The implications of these discrepancies are discussed in Part III.

HISTORICAL PERSPECTIVE

The word "entrepreneur" has had a variety of meanings. In Victorian England the entrepreneur was the manager of a public musical institution or one who directed or organized entertainments, especially musical performances. This latter description of the entrepreneur's function is now more likely to be subsumed under the mantle of the "impresario" or the "promoter" of public entertainments. In France, in the fifteenth and sixteenth centuries, champions at arms and the leaders of military expeditions were sometimes referred to as entrepreneurs. This adventuring spirit of the word was carried over in the eighteenth century to the undertakers of construction and public works contracts, particularly road and bridge builders. From there it was a short step to bring the word into the orbit of the political economists. By the middle of the eighteenth century, individuals who bought labor and materials at variable prices and sold their products at fixed prices were described as entrepreneurs. There were, however, different views as to the precise functions of the entrepreneur in the economic system.

The classical British economists, insofar as they used the word entrepreneur at all, considered that the entrepreneur was one who created a business by providing the necessary capital. Adam Smith, for example, made no distinction between the profits of the entrepreneur and the interest of the capitalist:

> Both with Smith and his successors the word
> "profit" signified a twofold revenue, and this was
> perfectly correct so long as the entrepreneur was
> also a capitalist. The word "interest" was re-
> served for the income of that person who lent
> capital but who did not himself produce anything.
> The revenue "derived from stock, by the person
> who manages or employs it, is called profit.
> That derived from it by the person who does not
> employ it himself, but lends it to another, is
> called the interest or the use of money."
> [Wealth of Nations, Book 1, chapter vi][1]

Much of Adam Smith's thinking revolved around the economics of agriculture. Jean Baptiste Say, in contrast, who popularized Adam Smith's work on the continent of Europe, was more interested in the pubescent manufacturing industry of early nineteenth-century France, where he was a master spinner. Although the entrepreneur had an important place in Cantillon's Essai sur la nature du commerce, written in the middle of the eighteenth century, it was Say who first established a distinct role in economic theory for the entrepreneur by distinguishing between the entrepreneur and the capitalist: "At the beginning of the nineteenth century the principal agent of economic progress was the industrious, active, well-informed individual, either as ingenious inventor, a progressive agriculturist, or an experienced businessman. This type became quite common in every country where mechanical production and increasing markets became the rule. It is he rather than the capitalist so called, the landed proprietor, or the workman, . . . who directs production and superintends the distribution of wealth."[2] Say's entrepreneur was a middleman between the productive potential of capital, labor, and physical resources and the demands of the consumer. The return to those who furnished capital was interest, to those who furnished labor it was wages, to those who furnished land it was rent. The return to the key figure of the entrepreneur, whether as a merchant, manufacturer, or agriculturist, was profit.

While Say's distinction between the functions and kinds of remuneration of the capitalist and the entrepreneur was a useful one, in practice in many enterprises the roles of capitalist and entrepreneur were carried by the same person or persons, enterprises being owner or investor managed or dominated by the owning family. Consequently early British economists, following Adam Smith's example, made little effort to define or allow for entrepreneurship as part of any overall economic theory. In family enterprises confusion between the payment of profit to the owner as entrepreneur, salary to the owner as manager, and interest to the owner as investor of capital remains to this day. What the economists were faced with, therefore, having made some distinction between capitalist and entrepreneur, was the question as to what the entrepreneur's profit was payment <u>for</u>.

For Saint-Simon and his followers the entrepreneur's profit was payment for the work of directing the enterprise. Nassau Senior, the incumbent for a time of the first chair of economics to be established in England, at Oxford University in 1825, conceived of profits as remuneration for the entrepreneur's exceptional skill. Similarly John Stuart Mill treated the entrepreneur's profit as a kind of rent for ability, "the extra gains which any producer or dealer obtains through superior talents for business or superior business arrangements."[3] This conception of profits as remuneration for the entrepreneur's skill was further developed by the American economist Francis Walker:

> By the term "profit" Walker understands the special remuneration of the entrepreneur, omitting any interest which he may draw as the possessor of capital. This distinguishes him from the majority of English economists who, contrary to Continental practice, have always persisted in confusing the functions of the entrepreneur and the capitalist. Neither is he content to regard his work as confined to simple business arrangement and superintendence, which would result in his being paid a salary equal to that of a managing director. His work is altogether of a more dignified character, and consists largely in anticipating the fluctuations of the market and in organising production to meet them--in a word, in adapting supply to demand.[4]

The entrepreneur's duties, says Walker, are "to furnish also technical skill, commercial knowledge, and powers of administration; to
assume responsibilities and provide against contingencies; to shape
and direct production, and to organise and control the industrial
machinery."[5]

Some economists, most notably Alfred Marshall, thought that
additional elements, such as insurance against risk and payment for
the expense of training the entrepreneur, should also be considered
as part of the rationale for the entrepreneur's profit. Others saw
risk-taking as the distinguishing feature of the entrepreneur's role
and his profit as compensation or reward for risks taken. The key
activity of the entrepreneur then becomes the exploration of uncertainty: "As a key factor in entrepreneurial decisions, 'uncertainty'
provides a technique for exploring various environments in which
choices are made and resources are committed to diverse uses.
Then the entrepreneur, creative or adaptive, supplies the dynamics
of change; and 'uncertainty' is a means of systematically examining
the interaction between man and the conditions, opportunities and
pressures to which he responds."[6] Here too is the notion developed
by Joseph Schumpeter, but attributed by him to the American economist John B. Clark, that entrepreneurial profits were to be associated with the successful introduction of technological, commercial,
and organizational improvements. According to Schumpeter the
social function of the entrepreneur was "not only to introduce something new into economic development, to invent, to discover, and to
diversify products, but also to spread new methods of organisation
and manufacture, and to adopt and popularise the inventions of others.
He does not confine himself to the efficient management of the existing economic system according to the traditional rules, but at each
moment, by his initiative and bold faith in the future, he 'threatens'
the habits and customs and therefore the sources of profit of his
more conservative competitors."[7] Schumpeter judged, however,
that innovation was being reduced to routine by the growth of large
corporations and public bodies employing teams of trained specialists whose sole function was to improve existing methods of work
and that, consequently, the entrepreneurial function itself was declining in importance.

Economists have, then, ascribed a variety of functions to the
entrepreneur and developed a number of theories designed to relate
his contribution to an enterprise to the rewards he derives from the
profits of that enterprise. He has been viewed as a kind of alchemist
transmuting the unrealized potential of land, labor, and capital into
the gold of satisfied consumer demand; as a go-between or broker
between capital and labor; as an organizer of production and captain
of industry with onerous responsibilities for the direction of an

enterprise; as the risk-taking promoter prepared to put his energies
behind the creativity and ability of others; and as a focal point for
innovation in economic enterprises. Economists do not, then, provide a consistent body of theory about the economic functions of the
entrepreneur, nor a consistent definition as to the role of the entrepreneur in an enterprise. Some of the complexity in functions and
roles ascribed to the entrepreneur is also apparent in economists'
theories of business behavior and it is to these that we now turn.

THE ENTREPRENEUR AND THE THEORY OF THE FIRM

"The entrepreneur is at the same time one of the most in-
triguing and one of the most elusive characters in the cast that constitutes the subject of economic analysis. He has long been recognized as the apex of the hierarchy that determines the behavior of
the firm and thereby bears a heavy responsibility for the vitality of
the free enterprise society."[8] So writes William Baumol in a paper
presented to the eightieth annual meeting of the American Economic
Association. Baumol differentiates the entrepreneur from the manager, defining the manager as "the individual who oversees the on-
going efficiency of continuing processes" and the entrepreneur as

> the Schumpeterian innovator and some
> more. . . . It is his job to locate new ideas
> and to put them into effect. He must lead,
> perhaps even inspire; he cannot allow things
> to get into a rut and for him today's practice is
> never good enough for tomorrow. . . . He is
> the individual who exercises what in the busi-
> ness literature is called "leadership." And it
> is he who is virtually absent from the received
> theory of the firm. . . . The theoretical firm
> is entrepreneurless--the Prince of Denmark
> has been expunged from the discussion of
> Hamlet.[9]

The traditional economic theory of the firm emphasizes that
the firm has a clear-cut goal in the form of profit maximization, a
goal that will be collectively pursued by the members of the firm in
a rational manner given the nature of the cultural, political, and
legal environment within which the firm operates. The entrepreneur
as a person is irrelevant to this theory and yet the entrepreneurial
role, in the form of the profit maximization assumption, is central
to the theory. The classical economist assumes that the firm is the

entrepreneur and this enables him to discuss the behavior of the firm as though it consisted of the actions of a single rational organism. Many economists have of course been highly critical of this traditional theory on a number of counts. The most fundamental criticisms have revolved around four related points: (1) that the theory is not applicable to large-scale enterprises; (2) that the theory is oversimple and cannot illuminate the real-life complexities of the decision-making behavior of an enterprise; (3) that firms, in reality, do not maximize profits; (4) that, because of environmental uncertainty and lack of the necessary information, firms cannot maximize profits.

J. K. Galbraith, for example, points out that "with the rise of the modern corporation, the emergence of the organisation required by modern technology and planning, and the divorce of the owner of the capital from control of the enterprise, the entrepreneur no longer exists as an individual person in the mature industrial enterprise. Everyday discourse, except in the economics textbooks, recognises this change. It replaces the entrepreneur, as the directing force of the enterprise, with management."[10] But not only does the person of the entrepreneur disappear in the large organization, but the entrepreneurial role of profit maximization is, suggests Galbraith, "inconsistent with the behaviour of the technostructure in the mature corporation."[11] The goals of the technostructure include survival, the preservation of the autonomy on which its decision-making power depends, and, consequently, prevention of loss will take precedence over maximum profits. But "once the safety of the technostructure is insured by a minimum level of earnings, there is then a measure of choice as to goals. Nothing is so compelling as the need to survive. However, there is little doubt as to how, overwhelmingly, this choice is exercised: It is to achieve the greatest possible rate of corporate growth as measured in sales."[12] Secondary goals of the technostructure include, says Galbraith, technological virtuosity and a progressive rise in the dividend rate. Other and lesser goals may include such things as building a better community, improved education, and political and religious goals.

Other economists, too, have emphasized the need for a theory of business behavior that allows for a wider range of goals than are assumed in the rational profit-maximizing model. It has been argued, for example, that the entrepreneur may not maximize profits at the expense of leisure, or at the expense of losing financial control over his firm, and that firms may place market share, sales maximization, growth, liquidity, and production efficiency targets above profit maximization goals. [13] None of these alternative goals of the economic revisionists have been widely accepted and "most of them resemble burned out Christmas-tree bulbs--their brief and transitory moment of glory lost in the glow of the star of profit maximization which remains bright and secure at the top of the tree."[14]

Observations of the activities of businessmen have suggested that business firms do not maximize profits, not that they might not wish to, but that they simply do not or cannot equate marginal revenue and marginal cost in the sense in which some economists have asserted that this is essential profit-maximizing behavior.[15] As long ago as 1939, R. F. Harrod pointed out the devastating completeness of entrepreneurs' uncertainty about matters usually assumed by economists to be known. The profit motive he suggested was not to be challenged; the knowledge of the entrepreneur perhaps could be.[16] More recently a study of company pricing policies carried out by the Centre for Business Research at the Manchester Business School found that "profit maximisation, which in economic theory is assumed to be the major objective of pricing, was not a pricing objective in any case studied. In a few cases firms suggested that profit maximisation was a long-term over-all objective, but short-run market share was usually regarded as the best guarantee of long-run profit."[17] Economists who have emphasized the uncertainties surrounding the decision-making behavior of the entrepreneur or businessman have further suggested that businessmen cannot maximize their profits, except by chance, even if this is their motive.

> Firms do not maximize except in those rare instances when coincidence or luck intervenes. Even if the theory is interpreted more properly to be that businessmen try to--rather than necessarily do--maximize profits, uncertainty critics would state that this has had little utility as a description, prescription, or predictive device for business behavior. Businessmen do not know, it is argued, which of the limited number of alternative courses of action which they perceive open to them will maximize profits, or what the probability of success of any decision will be. Under such conditions the notion of maximization becomes meaningless.[18]

Economists and others, recognizing the limited predictive value of the traditional theory of the firm, have sought to modify the theory or to develop alternative theories in such a way as to provide some link with the actual behavior of businessmen. One such behavioral theory of the firm is that developed by R. M. Cyert and J. G. March, who attempt to describe the ways in which the business firm makes decisions on such matters as the price and output of its

products.[19] They argue that economic theories are frequently based
on the notion of the individual entrepreneur as decision-maker,
whereas in reality decision-making processes take place within complex large-scale organizations pursuing multiple goals. Neither the
entrepreneur nor the entrepreneurial role have any place within the
theory put forward by Cyert and March. Whereas the traditional
economic theory of the firm was, therefore, bound up with a theory
of entrepreneurial behavior, subsequent attempts to modify or qualify
the theory in order to encompass large-scale organizations and managerial behavior have tended to eliminate the entrepreneur entirely.
Nevertheless it has to be recognized that economic decisions on such
matters as price, output, product mix, and resource allocation are
still being made by individual entrepreneurs. The question then
arises as to whether or not the traditional profit-maximizing theory
of the firm is appropriate in explaining and predicting the decision-
making processes of individual entrepreneurs. Just as Cyert and
March were able to review the classical economic theory of the firm
in the light of studies of decision-making behavior in large-scale
enterprises, so it is necessary to review the theory in the light of
studies of decision-making behavior in small businesses. This is a
subject to which we return in Part III of this book.

CULTURAL DIFFERENCES

The assumption of many economists is, then, that whereas
managers and executives of large organizations are likely to pursue
goals other than the goal of profit maximization, the owner-manager
or entrepreneur is still cast in an older classical mold. Indeed
managerial decision-making and managerial goals are frequently
contrasted with the assumed decision-making behavior and goals of
the entrepreneur. Thus, for example, Robert Gordon, in developing
a distinction between the executive and the owner-entrepreneur,
pointed out that "our reasoning about the working of a private enterprise system has long been predicated on the assumption that the
business decisions entering into the leadership function are made by
owner-entrepreneurs seeking to maximize profits for their firms
and thus for themselves--or at least, if concerns are not managed
by their owners, that business leaders will make exactly the same
decisions as profits-maximizing owner-entrepreneurs would have
made in similar circumstances."[20] It may be, however, that, because of certain emphases in American culture, the notion of the
entrepreneur as self-reliant, "individualistic, with a trace of justifiable arrogance, fiercely competitive and with a desire to live
dangerously"[21] survived longer, or took root more firmly, in the

United States than in Europe. It has been suggested that in Europe the business subculture is radically different from that of the United States, that it is more closely linked to the culture as a whole, that there is more carryover from the social to the business setting, and that, in Europe, the profit motive is in general very much weaker. Indeed, French writers such as Pierre Bize have suggested that the profit motive is absent from much entrepreneurial activity. [22]

In this context, therefore, it is interesting to look at the study by David Granick of the European executive and in particular his description of the cultural factors surrounding the roles of the manager and the entrepreneur in Germany. It was in Germany that Granick found the greatest resistance to the nonowner-manager: "The very term 'manager' traditionally carries a negative tone. There is something shady about the activities of a 'manager'; for the term is still close to its original meaning in Germany, a promoter of boxing matches, circuses, and the like. The manager is a man without a solid base, a fly-by-night who cannot be trusted. In contrast an 'entrepreneur' (Unternehmer)--risking his own money--is a socially reputable person. "[23] Granick reports a strong ambivalence toward nonowner top managers in the large German companies:

> On the one hand, they are envied for their power--
> and often for their income. After all, they are
> among the great names of industry. But linked
> with envy is scorn. No matter what their power
> and living standard, these executives do not base
> their careers on the foundation stone of personal
> ownership of the means of their power. They are
> still lightweights in terms of security over the
> generations. As to social position, they are viewed
> in somewhat the same fashion as nouveaux riches.
> Their stature represents a change in business
> society, a movement away from the time-honoured
> family firm. As such, it has not earned the respect
> due to established values. [24]

One of the consequences is that many top managers of large German companies own their own small businesses on the side, thereby enabling them to combine entrepreneurial status with the power and salary of top corporate executives.

Casting the cross-cultural net wider, Granick suggests that the American businessman and the Soviet industrial manager are entrepreneurs, in the sense of risk-takers, in a way that is quite foreign to their British, French, and Belgian counterparts whose main tendency is to play for safety in the business game. By risk-taking, however, Granick appears to mean primarily a willingness to act outside the law, a rather limited conception of entrepreneurship but nevertheless useful in providing a focus for cultural differences in the relationship between business and society: "Thus bankruptcy in Britain is not just a misfortune which could happen to anyone; it is a moral failure and a disgrace. British business success stories are not of the American brand; they do not tell of the man who failed in one business after another until he finally chose the right one and made a million--or became General of the Army and then President, as did Ulysses S. Grant."[25] The French owner-manager is also far removed from the daring innovating type of entrepreneur, the goals of the French family firm being security for the firm and unchallenged control over it by the family, rather than efficiency, expansion, or profits: "Add to the major emphasis on family security a disdain for business as a whole on the part of many members of the important business-owning families. One man to whom I wrote asking for introductions answered that he could not help me because the French businessmen he knew were not much interested in business."[26]

To describe cultural differences purely in terms of national stereotypes is, however, to distort the complexity and variability of the different cultural influences that may exist within any society. Stephen Aris' study of the Jews in business illustrates how cultural values sustained early Jewish immigrants in alien societies. He suggests that "the Jews, by reason of their history and their culture, have inherited a whole system of values which when combined with the environment in which they have found themselves has led them to behave in quite specific and identifiable ways. And the more hostile and unfriendly the environment, the more marked this characteristic behaviour becomes."[27] Aris suggests four reasons why the Jews who arrived in late Victorian Britain as refugees from the Russo-Polish empire had such an overriding desire to control their own destinies by becoming self-employed. First, it was common sense to try to escape from the suffocating squalor of ghetto life in London's East End, "to drag themselves up out of the ranks of the lumpenproletariat and gain admission to middle-class society." Second, "the Jews were so low on the economic scale that they could afford to take risks" and their history had been so punctuated by tragedies and disasters that they had learned to grasp such opportunities as existed. Third, there was Jewish optimism: "The out-worker with the tumbledown shed and a couple of ancient Singer machines in some East End backstreet may know in his heart of hearts that he will never be Sir Montague Burton, but as long as he is his own boss there is always a chance; anyway he will keep on trying." Fourth is a desire for independence and a consciousness of their own cultural identity:

> The Jews have been persecuted for so long,
> forced to move from one place to another, that
> they have in self-defence constructed their own
> survival kit . . . at the back (and sometimes at
> the forefront) of every Jew's mind lies the fear,
> no matter how secure or how well-regarded he
> and his fellow Jews might be, that anti-semitism
> might rear its head. . . . And if, as Sir John
> Cohen put it, "we have to take up our bundle and
> run" the knowledge that one's bundle is of a use-
> ful size is infinitely comforting. The need to set
> out on one's own and acquire that bundle might
> not seem so pressing now, but to the immigrants
> of the 1880s the pressures were very strong. [28]

And the unusual energy, stamina, and self-reliance needed to succeed under the conditions of the time were supported by a self-
conscious and highly knit community of family and kinship networks
in which "furniture men married the daughters of other furniture
men," in which business was carried out on a direct and personal
basis, and in which the cutthroat competition was "tempered by a
certain charity; by the willingness of one Jew to help another, if
only because he knew that circumstances might change and that one
day he might himself need a helping hand." Underpinning the economic behavior of the Jewish community, rather as Calvinism sanctioned the enterprise of the thriving sixteenth-century tradesman,
was a religious ethic that "plays down the importance of the afterlife
and stresses that it is what a man does in his lifetime that determines his future happiness."

It seems a far cry from the heroic entrepreneur of economic
theory to the ghetto manufacturer whose lot was almost as harsh
and precarious as that of the sweated labor he employed. One of
the characteristics of economic theory is its effort to apply to a
variety of diverse situations, situations with different historical
antecedents and different cultural nuances, all-embracing generalizations about the goals of a business enterprise and the nature of the
entrepreneurial function: "The very attempt of economic analysis
to build a theory of universal validity, to avoid any and all psychological and sociological commitments takes it into the path of operational meaninglessness. . . . We should extricate ourselves from
the shackles of economic universalism and experiment with less general but often more useful construction." [29]

NOTES

1. C. Gide and C. Rist, A History of Economic Doctrines (first published, France 1909), 2nd ed., trans. R. Richards (London: George G. Harrap, 1948).

2. Ibid., p. 128.

3. J. S. Mill, Principles, Book III, chapter v, para. 4 (1848).

4. Gide and Rist, op. cit., pp. 575, 576.

5. F. Walker, The Wages Question (1876), p. 245.

6. W. T. Easterbrook, "The Entrepreneurial Function in Relation to Technological and Economic Change," in Industrialisation and Society, B. F. Hoselitz and W. E. Moore, eds. (Paris: UNESCO, 1963).

7. Gide and Rist, op. cit., p. 717.

8. W. J. Baumol, "Entrepreneurship in Economic Theory," American Economic Review 58, no. 2 (May 1968): 64-71.

9. Ibid., pp. 65, 66.

10. J. K. Galbraith, The New Industrial State (London: Hamish Hamilton, 1967), p. 71.

11. Ibid., p. 129.

12. Ibid., p. 171.

13. For discussion of these points, see J. W. McGuire, Theories of Business Behavior (Englewood Cliffs, N.J.: Prentice-Hall, 1964), pp. 75ff., and Chapter 5: Alternative Economic Theories.

14. Ibid., p. 79.

15. See R. L. Hall and C. J. Hitch, "Price Theory and Business Behaviour," Oxford Economic Papers, No. 2 (May 1939). A summary of what became known as "the marginal controversy" is set out in McGuire, op. cit., pp. 80ff.

16. R. F. Harrod, "Price and Cost in Entrepreneur's Policy," Oxford Economic Papers, No. 2 (May 1939).

17. "Blindfold Pricing," article in The Financial Times, April 30, 1968.

18. McGuire, op. cit., p. 83.

19. R. M. Cyert and J. G. March, A Behavioral Theory of the Firm (Englewood Cliffs, N.J.: Prentice-Hall, 1963).

20. R. A. Gordon, "The Executive and the Owner-Entrepreneur," in Reader in Bureaucracy, ed. R. K. Merton et al. (Glencoe, Ill.: The Free Press, 1952).

21. Galbraith, op. cit., p. 92.

22. See the article by D. Graves, "Vive la Management Difference," Management Today, April 1971.

23. D. Granick, The European Executive (London: Weiden-feld and Nicolson, 1962).

24. Ibid. , pp. 61, 62.

25. Ibid. , p. 132.

26. Ibid. , p. 148.

27. S. Aris, The Jews in Business (London: Jonathan Cape, 1970). All extracts are from Chapter 11.

28. Ibid. , p. 234.

29. A. Papandreou, "Economics and the Social Sciences," The Economic Journal 60 (1950): 721.

2

THE PSYCHOLOGY
OF THE ENTREPRENEUR

Just as economists have searched for some general theory of the entrepreneurial function that will assist in predicting and analyzing the behavior of individual entrepreneurs, so too have psychologists sought some general theory to describe the personality characteristics of entrepreneurs. In this chapter we summarize some of the studies of entrepreneurial motivation carried out by psychologists and others, a subject to which we will return in Chapter 10.

THE PHILOSOPHER'S STONE

The attempt to discover the secret of the businessman's success has preoccupied writers and analysts from a variety of disciplines both in the social sciences and in the humanities. Biographies of successful entrepreneurs and businessmen, for example, reflect the tendency of the subjects of such studies to explain their success in terms of simple Smilesian virtues of thrift, hard work, and clean living or in terms of some succinct catchword, like "Think," that is the touchstone to riches.[1] A study of the biographies of American businessmen born between 1771 and 1920, however, qualified the self-sufficient, independent, struggling-against-all-the-odds image of the successful businessman. Throughout the period studied about two-thirds of each generation of successful businessmen had enjoyed a very favorable family background with the result that the recruitment of the American business elite had remained remarkably stable. The evidence, then, is at variance with the popular impression that during the early industrial development of the United States opportunities for spectacular upward social mobility were readily available, and the authors of the study

question the validity of a doctrine which draws its
strength from the folk-lore of the American frontier
and from the thriving business civilization of the
late nineteenth century. For, according to this
amalgam of classical economic liberalism with a
popularised Darwinian doctrine, the successful
businessman had proved himself to be the fittest
in the struggle for survival. Such a doctrine
could have carried little conviction if it had been
widely known that economic success was greatly
facilitated in most cases by the influence of a
favourable family background. Instead, selected
instances of the "rags to riches" story, liberally
embellished by wishful thinking, were fashioned
into a symbol of American society in keeping with
its ideological equalitarianism. [2]

As an alternative to the homespun biographical models are
those studies that turn the entrepreneur into a mastermind manipulating the complexities of an uncertain world with a sure and omnipo-
tent touch. Thus emerges the notion of the "genius entrepreneur"
whose success "is in large measure caused by his unswerving dedi-
cation to setting high goals and to reaching for them. He has vision
on which he bases his own objectives and sets his own goals. And he
does this not simply on the basis of last year's results plus some
growth factor, but on the basis of his own perception of his own
capabilities and the drive to satisfy his own needs."[3] Tagged on
behind as other distinguishing attributes of entrepreneurship are a
willingness to assume risk; a sense of acquisitiveness or unceasing
curiosity; insight into the relationships between concepts, objectives,
needs, and needs satisfaction; an ability to make sound value judgments as to what is central and peripheral to attaining his objectives;
creativity; problem-solving ability; ability to marshall the resources
needed to achieve his objectives and goals; and the administrative
ability to organize those resources to accomplish his goals and satisfy his minor needs.[4]
    More penetrating theoretical studies have stressed the impor-
tance of the interplay between the successful executive's personal
skills and abilities and the business environment within which he
operates and from which he learns. David Braybrooke, for example,
suggests that it may be a mistake to seek any peculiar factors or any
special skills or techniques as the common denominator of successful executives: "The reason why the intellectual operations of the
man in power seem mysterious and elusive, like his other activities,
may be that we are continually tempted to adopt unhappy ways of

describing them. In particular, we may be inclined to attribute to
him as a detached individual what belongs to him only as features of
his special social role, hedged about with peculiar controls, advantages and disadvantages."[5] The executive has a number of personal
resources, such as his energy, perseverance, and skill in bargaining, that are relatively transferable from situation to situation, and
a number, such as his trade knowledge or his local connections,
that are relatively untransferable. For Braybrooke a number of key
questions about executive success revolve around the way in which
the businessman uses information. Does the successful executive,
for example, have special skill in dealing with information? How
does he reduce his stock of information to effective "rules of thumb"
that can be applied, perhaps unconsciously, to practical situations?
Why does he trust and act upon some information cues from his environment and not others? Braybrooke is interested too in the
processes of innovation, that distinctive function of Schumpeter's
entrepreneur. He hypothesizes that executives who have to operate
in a flux of changing conditions, where flexibility and innovation are
essential, evolve new decision-making stratagems in a number of
ways; they partly modify old stratagems in the very course of imi-
tating them, they partly combine old stratagems or features of old
stratagems, they partly imitate stratagems of others that they have
observed or been told of, and they partly work out the likely consequences of different courses of action. "We can completely account
for all the features of a stratagem by showing how some are chosen
because they are explicitly held to be capable of achieving certain
effects, while others, introduced spontaneously or by imitation of
the behavior of others, survive partly because they have not been
condemned as the causes of any past disasters. The stratagem as
a whole . . . is selected on the basis of pragmatic success, although
the tests of success are not always stringent."[6] The place of
strategies and tactics in the work of owner-managers, the use that
owner-managers make of the information available to them, and the
incremental learning behavior of owner-managers are subjects to
which we shall return in Part III.

In spite of the legion of theories about what makes individual
businessmen, entrepreneurs, or owner-managers successful, however, there are very few empirical studies that attempt to relate
the success of specific groups of businessmen to their personality
characteristics. One such attempt, that by Hal Pickle, had somewhat inconclusive findings. Pickle set out to determine whether or
not successful small business managers do have certain character-
istics--such as thinking ability, human relations ability, drive,
communications ability, and technical knowledge--that are partially
or wholly lacking in unsuccessful managers. Successful firms were

defined as those that were able to provide a high degree of satisfaction to their various "parties-at-interest," that is, to their owners, employees, customers, suppliers, and communities; unsuccessful firms those that provided only a relatively low degree of satisfaction for their parties-at-interest. Successful managers were defined as those who worked for successful firms and unsuccessful managers as those who worked for unsuccessful firms, all the firms studied being firms employing only one major level of management. In the state of Texas, 97 businesses were the subject of study, 54 of them being retail establishments, 26 service establishments, 8 wholesale establishments, and 3 oil and gas extraction businesses. The main sources of data for each business were standardized and specially constructed surveys were administered to the owners, employees, customers, and suppliers of the business, informal interviews with creditors and competitors, and special surveys and standardized psychological testing devices were administered to their managers. The satisfaction of each party-at-interest was ranked, weighted, and reranked and then correlated with measurements of the five personality characteristics of thinking ability, human relations ability, drive, communications ability, and technical knowledge, and their component traits.

> Only 45.5 percent of the variance in the measure of success is explained by the five characteristics. The remaining 54.5 percent of the variance comes from unknown causes--probably because the measuring devices for parties-at-interest and characteristics do not provide highly accurate measures. Another causal factor probably would be the differences in business environment among the businesses surveyed. A small business manager who operates in an environment of intensive competition would encounter more difficulties in satisfying his parties-at-interest than would a manager meeting less competition. [7]

The Pickle study illustrates some of the methodological complexities of trying to establish relationships between psychological variables, such as the personality characteristics of entrepreneurs, and economic aspects of business performance. There are few writers about small business enterprise, however, who are not prepared to take a stab at describing what they see as the characteristic motivation of entrepreneurs, almost all such descriptions being couched in terms of the active aspirations of the entrepreneur rather than in terms of any analysis of the realities of his occupational or

economic situation. Thus entrepreneurs are seen to be motivated by
desire for high financial rewards, by aspirations for upward social
mobility, or by the personal achievement, autonomy, self-expression,
or independence available to the self-employed: "The 'go-it-alone'
small businessman is often the man whose psychological make-up
and mixture of skills and abilities made him a round peg in a square
hole while working for other people. This situation makes him willing to put his future at risk by taking the big step into business by
himself."[8]

PARACELSUS

The arch-priest of the simple psychological explanation for
complex economic behavior, however, is David McClelland. In his
startling and influential book, The Achieving Society, he sets out,
"rigorously by quantitative scientific methods," to test the hypothesis
that a particular psychological factor, the need for achievement, is
responsible for economic growth and decline. Just as others have
looked for some general explanation of entrepreneurial or executive
success, so McClelland searches for some general explanation of
the rise and fall of civilizations.

Three types of study were carried out to test the hypothesis.
The first type dealt with the relationship between group measures of
the need for achievement and overall rates of economic development.
Thus, for example, folk tales from primitive cultures were analyzed
to see whether the tales containing large amounts of achievement
imagery came from tribes that showed a higher level of economic
activity. The cultures were rated in terms of sophistication and
methods of property ownership but the principal measure of economic
growth was an estimate of the percentage of adult males in any given
culture who received 75 percent or more of their income from entrepreneurial activities, the presumed mechanism by which a high
need for achievement in any culture generates economic growth being the activities of an entrepreneurial class. An entrepreneur was
defined as

> someone who exercises some control over the
> means of production and produces more than he
> can consume in order to sell (or exchange) it for
> individual (or household) income. . . . In prac-
> tice such people turned out to be traders (who do
> not produce, but acquire for resale or rental,
> rather than subsistence or use), independent
> artisans (shoemakers, smiths, carpenters, and

the like, when they control the means of production rather than when they work for a wage) and
firm operators (for example, innkeepers, export
houses, fisheries, sheep raisers).[9]

In spite of the fact that cultures such as the Winnebago, Koryak, and
Tenetehara did not keep occupationally classified manpower records,
in spite of the fact that there is no guarantee that the folk tales analyzed for need achievement imagery belonged to the same period in
a culture's history as the ratings of entrepreneurial activity, despite
all the admittedly obvious flaws in the data, the admittedly crude
methodology, the admitted probability of errors in measurement,
the admitted difficulties of cross-cultural comparisons, McClelland
concludes that his data "confirm the hypothesis that the n Achievement level of a society is a variable significantly related to entrepreneurial economic activity in a culture, despite wide variations
in social structure, in climate, means of subsistence, and level of
technological development."[10] Apparently one of the favorite games
of the Mandans, the tribe with the highest need achievement level in
McClelland's sample, "was to see who could shoot the most arrows
into the air before the first one hit the ground--a typical activity
for people high in n Achievement."[11]

To test whether a rise in achievement motivation preceded
economic growth in various countries in the past and a fall in such
motivation preceded economic decline, McClelland further analyzed
the relationship between achievement imagery in imaginative literature and indicators of economic growth and decline for a range of
historical epochs--Ancient Greece, Spain in the late Middle Ages,
England from the late Middle Ages to the Industrial Revolution, the
United States from the Industrial Revolution to modern times, and
pre-Incan Peru. Thus, for example, samples of the works of
Hesiod, Homer, Aeschylus, Xenophon, Aristotle, Demosthenes,
and others were scored for achievement imagery, the location of
the remains of earthenware jars used for the transport of olive oil
and wine were mapped out to provide an index of economic development, and the two sets of data were related to the periods of growth,
climax, and decline of Greek civilization. Even the decorative designs on Greek vases and Peruvian urns come under McClelland's
microscope. For England the need for achievement levels reflected
in English literature between 1550 and 1800 were compared with the
rates of gain in coal imports at the Port of London. For more
modern times children's stories in school readers were collected
from around the world and analyzed for, among other things, evidence of the need for achievement. The derived need achievement
levels for each country were then related to such economic growth

indicators as per capita national income, per capita production of electricity in kilowatt-hours, rates of growth in electrical output, and, in the case of the United States, to the number of patents issued per million population for the period from 1800 to 1950. The interpretation of the associations revealed by these many comparisons is that they confirm the hypothesis that "$\underline{n}$ Achievement is a key factor in the rise and fall of the economic base of civilizations."[12]

The second type of study carried out by McClelland traced the origins of the need for achievement by studying the transmission of parental values and attitudes (exclusively from mothers to sons, a peculiarly American view of the processes of socialization?), and by studying the relationships between the occupational interests of adolescent boys, their performance under various incentives, and their levels of need for achievement. Thus "the mothers of sons with high $\underline{n}$ Achievement tended to expect 'self-reliant mastery' at earlier ages than mothers of sons with low $\underline{n}$ Achievement. They also placed fewer restrictions on their sons than did the mothers of the 'lows,' but the restrictions they did insist on were to be observed at an earlier age."[13] Attempts were made to generalize these findings through cross-cultural studies of the association between various child-rearing practices and the need for achievement levels reflected by folk tales, and through testing groups of mothers and sons drawn from different social classes and from various countries. The importance of these studies, in our context, is in their relation to the third type of study carried out by McClelland, which dealt with the entrepreneurial role and the motives and behaviors of actual business entrepreneurs.

McClelland suggests that the link between high levels of the need for achievement in a nation and the rapid economic development of that nation "is obviously the entrepreneur--the man who organizes the firm (the business unit) and/or increases its productive capacity."[14] McClelland suggests that the key components of the entrepreneurial role, as distinct from what entrepreneurs do in practice, are moderate risk-taking in which the outcome depends more on skill than on chance; energetic, innovating activity; individual responsibility for generating and choosing among alternative courses of action; concrete knowledge of the results of individual actions or decisions; and long-range planning and organizational abilities. McClelland goes on to say that there are a number of aspects of the entrepreneurial role that provide a working situation suitable to individuals with high need achievement levels. Thus the strongly achievement motivated tend to perform well under conditions of moderate uncertainty where their efforts or skills can make a difference in the outcome; tend to believe that their probability of success is high, particularly when there are no facts to justify their self-confidence;

tend to work harder when there is some challenge in a situation or where some degree of originality or a new angle of approach is necessary in order to find a successful solution; tend to perform better in situations where they can obtain some sense of personal achievement and where the criteria of achievement are explicit and tangible; tend to think ahead more, to anticipate a future event before it occurs and to prefer experts to friends as working partners in a problem-solving task:

> High n Achievement leads people to behave in most
> of the ways they should behave if they are to fulfill
> the entrepreneurial role successfully as it has
> been defined by economists, historians and soci-
> ologists. The achievement motive should lead
> individuals to seek out situations which provide
> moderate challenge to their skills, to perform
> better in such situations, and to have greater
> confidence in the likelihood of their success.
> It should make them conservative when things
> are completely beyond their control, as in games
> of chance, and happier where they have some op-
> portunity of influencing the outcome of a series
> of events by their own actions and of knowing
> concretely what those actions have accomplished.
> Contrary to the expectations of extreme economic
> individualists, the achievement motive should not
> lead them to perform better when they are work-
> ing for themselves than when they are working
> for a group. And finally, it should encourage
> them to value money not for itself but as a
> measure of success.[15]

The entrepreneur's interest in profitability, suggests McClelland, "can now be understood, not in terms of the naive psychology of the 'profit motive,' but in terms of a need for Achievement which is interested in profitability precisely because it gives definite knowledge of how competent one is,"[16] that is, profit and personal money income become symbols of achievement rather than goals in themselves.

It is then necessary to explain, in order to substantiate the thesis that the entrepreneur is the link between high achievement motivation and economic development, the social processes or mechanisms by which persons with a high need for achievement become entrepreneurs, and successful entrepreneurs at that. Evidence provided by S. M. Lipset and R. Bendix on social mobility

and occupational career patterns in the United States illustrates the
instability of business ownership, the heterogeneity of the past experience of persons who own or manage small enterprises, the frequency of social mobility through shifts into self-employment, and
the high incidence of manual occupational backgrounds in the ranks
of the self-employed proprietors and owner-managers: "Self-
employment continues to be important as a career goal at the same
time that it proves to be unattainable on a permanent basis for the
overwhelming majority of Americans. Only 8 percent of the population are presently self-employed, but many more persons have been
in business for themselves at some time of their work history.
Every socioeconomic category contains a large group who have once
been self-employed."[17] While those from lower-income groups
often aspire to business ownership, those from higher-income groups
are more likely to seek professional careers. At one end of the social scale there exists, says McClelland, on the basis of studies
showing the antipathy of graduates and student elites toward a business career, a situation in which "those among the elite who are en-
dowed with more of the entrepreneurial spirit--with higher n Achieve-
ment--will seek the higher-prestige professional occupations even
more, with a net loss to the business community. . . . At the other
end of the income or social status scale, . . . as a middle-prestige
occupation which is easy to enter at a low level, business should get
the lion's share of the people with high n Achievement from lower-
status backgrounds."[18]

Unfortunately the evidence that McClelland presents on the
"characteristics of entrepreneurs" does not throw much light on the
issue at stake, namely the transmutation of high achievement motivation into successful entrepreneurship. The "entrepreneurs" whose
achievement imagery or motivation he describes are executives, including some executive engineers, from the M.I.T. Sloane Fellow
Program, executives from the Harvard Business School Middle Management Program, unit managers from the General Electric Company, junior and middle managers from various Italian companies
attending management training courses in Turin or Palermo, junior
managers in private companies attending the Middle Management
training programs of the Institute of Business Administration of the
University of Istanbul, managers from various Polish firms, and
salesmen and managers from a management course at Mexico City
College. No clear criteria are set up to distinguish how successful
or unsuccessful these managers and executives were in the entrepreneurial roles they were presumed to perform, high status in an
organization and the numbers of subordinates supervised being two
of the factors equated with successful entrepreneurship. Since no
instruments of job analysis were available to decide which managers

among the various groups studied were acting in entrepreneurial roles, the terms entrepreneur, executive, and manager were used interchangeably and no distinction was drawn between entrepreneurial and managerial success. One "pure case" of the small-time entrepreneur who has little or nothing to work with but his own skills is, however, described. Data were collected on the achievement motivation of 19 trainee mechanics in a rural Indian village. These were considered to be people who were potential small-time entrepreneurs and so a year later they were revisited to see to what extent they had used their training as a basis for setting themselves up as "more or less" independent artisans, that is, as mechanics, carpenters, or masons. Three of the four men with the highest achievement motivation scores were running "very active and successful shops for such a backward rural setting" and the six with lowest scores, two of whom were still studying, were "without exception not engaged in anything like full-time work related to their training."[19] It is on the basis of such inadequate research design and data, compounded by the conceptual confusion arising from inconsistent terminology, that McClelland is prepared to argue that the evidence he presents, both theoretical and practical, "makes such a strong case for the association between n Achievement and entrepreneurial success that when the association is not obtained, it can be considered prima facie evidence that one or more of the conditions defining the entrepreneurial role in the theoretical sense has not been met."[20]

Lord Bacon compared the alchemists of his time to a father, "who on his death-bed inform'd his lazy sons, of a sum of money which he had hid underground in his garden. After his death they went to digging, in hopes of finding the treasure, and tho' they missed their aim, for in reality there was none hid, yet they sufficiently enrich'd themselves, by the large crop which the ground, in consequence of this tillage, produced."[21] McClelland's impact is similar in that he provokes discussion, stimulates argument and explores a range of original hypotheses without finally bringing his speculations to a conclusive issue. The treatment of entrepreneurial behavior by psychologists ranges over a diversity of topics, from simple formulae for business success to characterizations of genius, from concern with the individual entrepreneur's response to economic opportunities and uncertainties to concern with his sense of social displacement and inferiority, and from the analysis of primitive folk-tales to the analysis of modern child-rearing practices. For the time being, however, we must conclude that the examination of empirical studies leaves the question of entrepreneurial motivation unresolved and that a clear link between the personality characteristics of entrepreneurs and the success of their business ventures has not been established.

NOTES

1. W. Rodgers, Think. A Biography of the Watsons and IBM (London: Weidenfeld and Nicolson, 1970).

2. R. Bendix and F. W. Howton, "Social Mobility and the American Business Elite," British Journal of Sociology, December 1957, pp. 357-69.

3. D. McConnell, "Entrepreneurial Planning," Management Decision 9, no. 1 (Spring 1971).

4. See ibid.

5. D. Braybrooke, "The Mystery of Executive Success Re-examined," Administrative Science Quarterly 8 (1963-64): 533-60.

6. Ibid.

7. H. B. Pickle, Personality and Success: An Evaluation of Personal Characteristics of Successful Small Business Managers, Small Business Research Series No. 4 (Washington, D.C.: Small Business Administration, 1964).

8. J. Stanworth and J. Curran, "Profile of the Small Business," Enterprise 1, no. 7 (1971).

9. D. C. McClelland, The Achieving Society (New York: The Free Press, 1967, paperback edition), p. 65.

10. Ibid.', p. 70.

11. Ibid., pp. 67, 68.

12. Ibid., p. 157.

13. Ibid., p. 342.

14. Ibid., p. 205.

15. Ibid., p. 238.

16. Ibid., p. 234.

17. S. M. Lipset and R. Bendix, "Social Mobility and Occupational Career Patterns," American Journal of Sociology, January and March 1952, pp. 366-74, 494-504.

18. McClelland, op. cit., p. 252.

19. Ibid., p. 271.

20. Ibid., pp. 270, 271.

21. From E. J. Holmyard, Alchemy (Harmondsworth, Middlesex: Penguin Books, 1957).

3

THE ENTREPRENEUR
IN LITERATURE

In this chapter we examine the treatment of the entrepreneur by some British and American novelists and try to relate the portrayal of the entrepreneur in fiction to social and economic changes consequent upon the development of industrial societies. In the United States, where it is possible to identify a distinct business culture that provides a focus for the culture as a whole, entrepreneurs and businessmen are quite frequently the chief characters in novels. The structure and story line of such novels will often revolve around the activities of the entrepreneur as entrepreneur--the development of his business, his financial speculations or trading activities, his relationships to competitors and to business colleagues. British novelists, however, appear to have less interest in, and less knowledge of, the mechanics of business enterprise and the drama of the entrepreneur's work activities. Their concern is more with the entrepreneur in his social context rather than in his economic context-- with the eccentricities of his behavior, with the moral and ethical problems he poses and faces, with his acceptability to and impact upon "society." The main structure of this chapter, therefore, looking at the treatment in fiction of the self-made man, the robber baron, the salesman, and the corporate executive, is based on discernible patterns in American business history into which we have slotted, perhaps in some cases inappropriately, examples from British fiction. Again, as in Chapters 1 and 2, we make no pretense of being exhaustive in our considerations but rather attempt to outline some of the major themes of the literature.

THE SELF-MADE MAN

The novels of Horatio Alger (1832-99) provide a useful point of entry to our first theme in the treatment of the entrepreneur in

literature: the self-made man. The titles of Alger's novels are indicative of the struggle for success of their heroes: <u>Facing the World</u>,
<u>The Odds Against Them</u>, <u>Strive and Succeed</u>, <u>Risen from the Ranks</u>,
<u>Struggling Upward</u>, <u>Bound to Rise</u>, <u>Helping Himself</u>, <u>Do and Dare</u>.
The progress of Richard Hunter through the three books, <u>Ragged</u>
<u>Dick</u>, <u>Fame and Fortune</u>, and <u>Mark, the Match Boy</u>, illustrates the
characteristic flavor of the Alger story. Ragged Dick is a bootblack,
an honest lad with the self-reliance born of his street education. In-
spired and encouraged to improve himself, he saves his money little
by little and with the help of his friend, Fosdick, studies hard. By
means of his "self-denial and judicious economy" and a stroke of
good fortune he is able to achieve the respectable status of counting-
room clerk and work up to the position of bookkeeper. Now as Richard
Hunter Esq. he can lend a helping hand to other young boys like Ragged
Dick. Stories such as these were expressions of the rags-to-riches
mythology of American culture, the tradition of log-cabin presidents,
the equation of success with "getting-on" in a material sense, and
with the accumulation of self-made wealth. Alger's heroes are relatives of Richard Johnson's <u>Nine Worthies of London</u> (1592), nine apprentices who rose to positions of honor through the exercise of personal virtue, and more closely of Benjamin Franklin. Franklin, in
<u>Poor Richard's Almanack</u> (1732-58), <u>The Way to Wealth</u> (1758), <u>Ad-</u>
<u>vice to a Young Tradesman</u> (1757), and in his <u>Memoirs</u> (1771-90),
stressed the character virtues of hard work, perseverance, frugality, and sobriety as part of a broad and humane ideal of self-improvement: "Where <u>The Way to Wealth</u> stressed industry, thrift and attention to business, the <u>Memoirs</u> continually emphasized the development of the mind, the achievement of self-discipline and wisdom, and
the assumption of responsibility towards one's fellow man."[1]
     The Alger hero, the Alger success story, and the Alger legend
still live on in American culture. Thus, for example, the Horatio
Alger awards, in the form of bronze plaques inscribed "Diligence,
Industry, Perseverance," continue to be given annually by the American Schools and Colleges Association to successful men who have
risen from humble circumstances. The myth that a young man of
good character who worked hard and saved his money could, and inevitably would, rise to a position of power and affluence, is at odds,
however, with the plot of most of Alger's novels:

> Although the self-help books insist that indi-
> vidual qualities of character are the key to suc-
> cess, in the novels one can hardly find a single
> instance where industriousness, frugality and
> piety are the operative factors in the hero's rise
> in society. Instead, the hero saves an elderly

> gentleman from a runaway horse and gains a
> wealthy patron; or falls in love with a charming
> young lady who turns out to be the governor's
> daughter; or discovers that he is the long-lost
> heir to a great fortune; or is simply favored
> by Providence.[2]

Alger's heroes are not only helped up the ladder by some deus ex machina or fairy godfather but the end product of their struggle is generally the respectability and moderate economic security of a white-collar job rather than the financial independence of the self-made businessman. As well as their character virtues, Alger's heroes display the employee virtues of punctuality, reliability, deference, and loyalty, and a willingness to take initiatives that are to the employer's advantage.

Alger's heroes tended to end up where Denry Machin, the creation of Arnold Bennett in The Card (1911), started out. For Denry the great moment comes when he can abandon his first job as a solicitor's clerk; he returns home that day,

> a young fellow obviously at peace with the world,
> a young fellow content with himself for the
> moment. No longer a clerk; one of the employed;
> . . . An independent unit, master of his own time
> and his own movements! In brief, a man! The
> truth was that he earned now in two days a week
> slightly more than Mr. Duncalf paid him for the
> labour of five and a half days. His income, as
> collector of rents and manager of estates large
> or small, totalled about a pound a week. But he
> walked forth in the town, smiled, joked, spoke
> vaguely, and said "Do you?" to such a tune that
> his income might have been guessed to be any-
> thing from ten pounds a week to ten thousand a
> year. And he had four days a week in which to
> excogitate new methods of creating a fortune.

From rent collector and estate agent Denry progresses to money-lender, property-owner (and giver away of property!), founder of the Five Towns Universal Thrift Club of which he becomes secretary and manager and subsequently managing director, a newspaper-owner for a short period, a town councillor, patron of the local football club, and, at the age of 34, the youngest mayor of Bursley. Denry is the opportunist entrepreneur par excellence, surprising everyone including himself by his ability to take the

out-of-ordinary course of action, turning a shipwreck into a successful boat excursion business at Llandudno during one summer season,
turning his temporary imprisonment in Sneyd Hall, the district manor
house, into a series of articles for the local newspaper: "Denry . . .
was not by nature a business man at all, but an adventurous spirit
who happened to be in a business which was much too good to leave."

Denry's hatred of paperwork and the routine of accounting,
bookkeeping, and the mechanics of business management preclude
his developing a large business enterprise. He remains the successful individualist, wedded to the idiosyncratic or eccentric gesture,
"a card, . . . identified with the great cause of cheering us all up."
The hero of William Dean Howells' The Rise of Silas Lapham (1885),
however, finds difficulty in expanding his paint business for other
reasons. On his return from the American Civil War Silas Lapham
tries to revive his small business:

> But I found that I had got back to another world.
> The days of small things was past, and I don't
> suppose it will ever come again in this country.
> My wife was at me all the time to take a partner--
> somebody with capital; but I couldn't seem to bear
> the idea. That paint was like my own blood to me.
> To have anybody else concerned in it was like--
> well, I don't know what. I saw it was the thing to
> do; but I tried to fight it off, and I tried to joke it
> off. . . . Well, I had to come to it. I took a
> partner. . . . He had money enough . . . but he
> didn't know anything about paint. We hung on to-
> gether for a year or two. And then we quit. . . .
> [And since then] I've played it alone.

And very lonely it is, too, for the man who believes that his paint
is a blessing to the world, a paint that "was something more than a
business to him; it was a sentiment, almost a passion. He could
not share its management and its profit with another without a measure of self-sacrifice far beyond that which he must make with
something less personal to him. It was the poetry of that nature,
otherwise so intensely prosaic."

It was Lapham's sense of guilt toward the partner he had dis-
carded that subsequently involved him in his ex-partner's speculations and brought about his own financial downfall. Lapham's loneliness is highlighted when his financial difficulties accumulate: "He
grew thin and old, and both at home and at his office he was irascible
to the point of offense. In these days Penelope shared with her
mother the silence or the petulance of the gloomy, secret man who
replaced the presence of jolly prosperity there."

The intrusion of business affairs into family relationships is a theme common to a number of novels. Samuel Butler in The Way of All Flesh (1903) writes of the impact on George Pontifex of rapid financial success:

> Money came pouring in upon him, and the faster it came the fonder he became of it, though, as he frequently said, he valued it not for its own sake, but only as a means of providing for his dear children.
>
> Yet when a man is very fond of his money it is not easy for him at all times to be very fond of his children also. The two are like God and Mammon. . . . George Pontifex felt this as regards his children and his money. His money was never naughty, his money never made noise or litter, and did not spill things on the table- cloth at meal times, or leave the door open when it went out. His dividends did not quarrel among themselves, nor was he under any uneasiness lest his mortgages should become extravagant on reaching manhood and run him up debts which sooner or later he should have to pay. . . . His children might, perhaps, have answered, had they known what was in their father's mind, that he did not knock his money about as he not infre- quently knocked his children. He never dealt hastily or pettishly with his money, and that was perhaps why he and it got on so well together.

But more important than the impact of business affairs on family relationships is the dependence of the family's position in society on the financial state of father's business, and the oppor- tunity that business success provides for upward social mobility. The Rise of Silas Lapham is not solely a novel about the success and failure of Lapham's business but also a novel about the attempts of the Lapham family, at Silas' instigation, to enter Boston society. Howells was himself a Boston resident and would have been familiar with the history of the "Boston Associates," the 15 Boston families who by 1850 controlled 20 percent of America's cotton spindleage, 30 percent of Massachusetts railroad mileage, 39 percent of Massa- chusetts insurance capital, and 40 percent of Boston banking resources.

> Living sumptuously on Beacon Hill, admired by their neighbors for their philanthropy and their patronage of art and culture, these men traded

in State Street while overseers ran their factories, managers directed their railroads,
agents sold their water power and real estate.
They were absentee landlords in the most complete sense. Uncontaminated by the diseases of
the factory town, they were also protected from
hearing the complaints of their workers or suffering mental depression from dismal and
squalid surroundings. In the metropolis, art,
literature, education, science flowered in the
Golden Day; in the industrial towns children
went to work with their fathers and mothers,
schools and doctors were only promises, a bed
of one's own was a rare luxury. [3]

This was the kind of social elite that Lapham aspired, with disastrous consequences, to join. Howells himself, while he portrays
both the members of this society and the social-climbing Lapham
with some sympathy, nevertheless makes it clear that individual
economic advancement, the wealth of the self-made man, can be a
major cause both of social dislocation and personal unhappiness.
For the self-made Lapham, barriers of taste, education, and social
position cannot simply be eradicated by the profit from the sale of
paint.

The term "self-made man" was an American one. In Britain
the use of the French expressions parvenu and nouveau riche emphasized the newness of the individual's rise rather than the fact that
he had succeeded by his own exertions. They were frequently used
as expressions of condescension. Mrs. Trollope, indeed, who visited America in the 1830s, was apparently stupefied by the pride that
leading Americans took in the fact that they were self-taught and
self-made, which, as she acidly remarked, meant to her only that
they were badly taught and badly made. [4] It was an attitude that
would have been shared by many of her compatriots including the
young Margaret Hale, the heroine of Mrs. Gaskell's North and
South (1855):

"Gormans," said Margaret. "Are those the
Gormans who made their fortune in trade at
Southampton? Oh! I'm glad we don't visit
them. I don't like shoppy people. I think we
are far better off, knowing only cottagers and
labourers, and people without pretence."
"You must not be so fastidious, Margaret,
dear!" said her mother, secretly thinking of

a young and handsome Mr. Gorman whom she
had once met at Mr. Hume's.

"No! I call mine a very comprehensive
taste; I like all people whose occupations have
to do with the land; I like soldiers and sailors,
and the three learned professions, as they call
them. I'm sure you don't want me to admire
butchers and bakers, and candlestick-makers,
do you, mamma?"

"But the Gormans were neither butchers
nor bakers, but very respectable coach-
builders."

"Very well. Coach-building is a trade all
the same, and I think a much more useless one
than that of butchers or bakers."

Imagine Margaret's initial horror, therefore, on hearing that her
father has accepted a position as tutor to a manufacturer and the
family are to move from the rural peace of a Southern English ham-
let to Milton-Northern, the manufacturing town in Darkshire:

"A private tutor!" said Margaret, looking scorn-
ful: "What in the world do manufacturers want
with the classics, or literature, or the accom-
plishments of a gentleman?"

"Oh," said her father, "some of them really
seem to be fine fellows, conscious of their own
deficiencies, which is more than many a man at
Oxford is. Some want resolutely to learn, though
they have come to man's estate. Some want their
children to be better instructed than they themselves have been."

In the course of the novel, however, Margaret, for all her Southern
sensibility, comes to recognize the manufacturer, Thornton, as a
man of honesty and integrity and ultimately she marries the practical energetic Northerner.

THE ROBBER BARON

Thornton, like Lapham, eventually fails in business. Both
men, however, are consoled by the thought that their failures dam-
aged no one but themselves. Lapham is proud that he can pay off
all his debts and come out of the crisis with clean hands and a clear

conscience, and Thornton resists the temptation to save himself by speculating with his creditors' money. Such moral scruples were no object, however, to the accumulation of wealth of those entrepreneurs who were "money-makers" rather than "goods-makers."
I. G. Wyllie points out that before the American Civil War the self-help idea posed a threat to the security of the older privileged aristocratic classes and served the interests of a business class that had not yet completed its march to power.[5] After the Civil War, however, the business class had attained power and used the self-help rationale to maintain its superiority and consolidate its control. The democratic pressures of the self-made men began to give way to the oligarchic tendencies of the robber barons. One of the components of the self-help ideology was the doctrine of the stewardship of wealth. Many of the leading proponents of the nineteenth-century self-help cult were Protestant clergymen, like the Rev. Thomas P. Hunt, author of The Book of Wealth: in Which it is Proved from the Bible that it is the Duty of Every Man to Become Rich (1836). They believed that the rewards of spiritual virtue were economic success and that business stood high on God's list of approved vocations. They were not, however, indifferent either to the means whereby economic success was attained nor to the uses that the successful businessman made of his money, the expectation being that he would use it to the advantage of the community through the patronage of schools, libraries, museums, orphanages, hospitals, and, of course, churches. Horatio Alger's heroes reflected this religious version of the gospel of wealth with its accompanying doctrine of stewardship: "An Alger hero not only sought, found, and made the best use of opportunities, but he also possessed traits of character that kept him on the path of righteousness. Alger's image of the self-made man demanded more than the chance to be just lucky or shrewd. A self-made man also had to be deserving of good fortune, to be the kind of man whom the Lord could favor. . . . Alger stands for trying harder, wanting more, and contributing to the community chest."[6]

The Protestant Ethic represented, however, only one of four different stances toward individualism and economic success in nineteenth-century America.[7] There was also the dog-eat-dog philosophy that success and its prizes of wealth and power went to the swiftest and most ruthless; there was the Social Darwinist justification of the distribution of wealth and power along the lines that only the fittest survive to hold power and, therefore, those who hold power are the fittest; and there was the classical laissez-faire view that the pursuit of individual self-interest inevitably led to the general good. The spread of corporate stocks and bonds among a wider investing American public during the 1840s and 1850s, the speculations associated with the development of railways and the opening up

of the American West led to an increasing emphasis being placed on
money wealth rather than on landed wealth. By the 1850s, suggest
Cochran and Miller, money-making had become one of the virtues
and no longer something that was itself subject to any moral code.[8]
Whereas the self-help manuals had generally condemned the speculator and distinguished him from the investor, now the creators of economic wealth, like those railroad engineers who were eager to build
the best railroads, came into conflict with the manipulators of wealth,
like those financiers "who showed interest in traffic conditions only
as they affected the movement of securities."[9] It was the New York
Times description of the corporate manipulations of Cornelius Van-
derbilt in the 1860s that provided the robber baron tag:

> If ever there was a man who made his way in the
> world, it is Mr. Cornelius Vanderbilt. . . .
> Like those old German barons who, from their
> eyries along the Rhine, swooped down upon the
> commerce of the noble river, and wrung tribute
> from every passenger that floated by, Mr.
> Cornelius Vanderbilt, with all the steamers of
> the Accessory Transit Company held in his leash,
> has insisted that the Pacific Company should pay
> him toll, taken of all America that had business
> with California and the Southern Sea, and the
> Pacific Company have submitted to his demand.[10]

This was the world of Frank Cowperwood, the central figure
of Theodore Dreiser's novels The Financier (1912) and The Titan
(1914), and of Sam McPherson in Sherwood Anderson's novel Windy
McPherson's Son (1916). Frank Cowperwood, son of a bank-teller/
cashier father and a prim religious mother, received an early schooling in the philosophy of the survival of the fittest. Outside a store in
the local fish-market was a tank where the fishermen put odd speci-
mens of sea life taken up with their catches: One day Frank saw that
a squid and a lobster had been placed in the tank and over the succeeding days he returned at every opportunity to watch with fascination as the lobster pursued and progressively devoured the squid.
"The incident made a great impression on him. It answered in a
rough way that riddle which had been annoying him so much in the
past: 'How is life organized?' Things lived on each other--that was
it. Lobsters lived on squids and other things. What lived on lobsters? Men, of course! Sure, that was it! And what lived on men?
he asked himself. Was it other men?"
Cowperwood's socialization in the making of money starts at
the age of 12 when he enters into his first business venture, buying

seven cases of Castile soap at auction for $32, borrowed from his
father, and selling them to the family grocer for $62. "From the
very first young Cowperwood knew how to make money. He took
subscriptions for a boys' paper; handled the agency for the sale of a
new kind of ice-skate, and once organized a band of neighborhood
youths into a union for the purpose of purchasing their summer straw
hats at wholesale. It was not his idea that he could get rich by saving.
From the first he had the notion that liberal spending was better,
and that somehow he would get along."

Later in life, however, his liberal spending of money from the
Philadelphia city treasury for speculative ventures lands Cowperwood
in the State Penitentiary. A stock market depression subsequently
allows him to make another fortune and he moves to Chicago where
he establishes himself in the street railway business, becoming,
through the manipulation of securities and the bribery of city officials, a major figure in the Chicago business world. Cowperwood
learns that success is won by force and by fraud and he allows no
scruples and no emotional or family ties to stand in the way of doing
what he wants. For him the slave agitation, while no doubt well
founded in human rights, is exceedingly dangerous to trade and the
Civil War is a commercial opportunity to be exploited to the full.
Money, for Cowperwood, is not primarily a means to social acceptance but a means of power: "Few people have the sense of financial
individuality strongly developed. They do not know what it means to
be a controller of wealth, to have that which releases the sources of
social action--its medium of exchange. They want money, but not
for money's sake. They want it for what it will buy in the way of
simple comforts, whereas the financier wants it for what it will
control--for what it will represent in the way of dignity, force and
power. Cowperwood wanted money in that way."

Sam McPherson starts out in life with all the necessary attributes of a rags-to-riches hero. From an impoverished rural childhood in an Iowa village he leaves home and migrates to the metropolis
of Chicago in search of fame and fortune, confident in his own ability
to master the business game:

> Instinctively he looked upon business as a great
> game in which many men sat, and in which the
> capable, quiet ones waited patiently until a cer-
> tain moment and then pounced upon what they
> would possess. With the quickness and accuracy
> of a beast at the kill they pounced and Sam felt
> that he had that stroke, and in his deals with
> country buyers used it ruthlessly. He knew the
> vague, uncertain look that came into the eyes of

> unsuccessful business men at critical moments
> and watched for it and took advantage of it as a
> successful prize fighter watches for a similar
> vague, uncertain look in the eyes of an opponent.

The brute trader in Sam, intent upon personal gain, upon "I will get
what I can" soon stifles his adolescent sense of equity:

> He was in business, and young in business, in a
> day when all America was seized with a blind
> grappling for gain. The nation was drunk with
> it, trusts were being formed, mines opened;
> from the ground spurted oil and gas; railroads
> creeping westward opened yearly vast empires
> of new land. To be poor was to be a fool, thought
> waited, art waited, and men at their firesides
> gathered their children around them and talked
> glowingly of men of dollars, holding them up as
> prophets fit to lead the youth of the young nation.
> Sam had in him the making of the new, the com-
> manding man of business.

But the heroic entrepreneur soon becomes the robber baron. He
gains control of a finance company and then, through the suppression
of facts, the creation of illusions, the use of the newspapers "as a
whip to crack at the heels of congressmen, senators and legislators,
of the various states, when such matters as appropriation for firearms came before them," he successfully undertakes the consolidation of the Chicago firearms companies. Then, as head of "the
McPherson Chicago crowd," he embarks on a series of stock raids,
speculation, and manipulations that attract countrywide attention.
But in his heart, like many of Sherwood Anderson's heroes, he is
increasingly sickened by the whole charade: "The great forward
movement in modern industry of which he had dreamed of being a
part had for him turned out to be a huge meaningless gamble with
loaded dice against a credulous public," and most of the great financial leaders were not great men but merely "shrewd, greedy vul-
tures feeding upon the public or upon each other." He comes to look
upon his business years as a kind of nightmare, discontinues his entrepreneurial activities, and goes off to search in vain for peace of
mind and a meaning to his life.

    Increasingly, then, in late nineteenth-century America, for-
tunes were accumulated not by producing goods or supplying services
but by manipulating securities and diverting to personal uses the
capital that those securities nominally represented. Industrial

capitalism gave way to financial capitalism. The creation of industrial trusts was indicative of this shift, the Standard Oil Company setting the trust pattern in 1879 at which time J. D. Rockefeller controlled about 90 percent of America's refining industry. From the 1880s up to World War I a growing number of books appeared that looked behind the moral facade of business, discounted the self-acclaimed virtues of the self-made men, and examined actual business practices--books such as Henry George's Progress and Poverty (1879), T. A. Bland's How to Grow Rich (1881), the studies of Standard Oil by Henry Demarest Lloyd, Wealth Against Commonwealth (1894), and Ida Tarbell, History of the Standard Oil Company (1904), Gustavus Myer's History of the Great American Fortunes (1910), and Bouck White's Book of Daniel Drew (1910), Daniel Drew being a pillar of the Methodist Church whose business activities made his name a byword for financial chicanery. That there was a wide discrepancy between the beliefs and the behavior of businessmen was not a new discovery, "what was new was the documentation--concrete evidence that the greatest barons were robber barons, men who made their way by corrupting legislatures, appropriating resources, organizing monopolies, and crushing competitors."[11]

The self-made man and his self-help philosophy had, as we have seen, come under attack from the landed gentry and the aristocracies of letters and scholarship, but now he was under attack from those who denounced him as a fraud whose revealed morality was that of the jungle. The rags-to-riches myth was merely an opiate of the people, completely at odds with the reality of their socioeconomic status in American society, a status that was one of minimal opportunity for upward occupational or social mobility but where there was plenty of "room at the bottom" among the squalor of the factory town. This was the kind of reality portrayed in Upton Sinclair's novel The Jungle (1905). Sinclair was sent to Chicago by a socialist newspaper to study the meat-packaging industry, an industry already known in radical circles to represent all that was arrogant, crude, evil, and irresponsible in Big Business practice. His novel, the story of the struggle of a Lithuanian immigrant and his family to survive the moral, spiritual, and physical degradation of work in the Chicago stockyards, describes in detail the horrors of meat-handling practices in the Chicago slaughterhouses. Coinciding as it did with the embalmed beef scandals of the Spanish-American War, The Jungle had an immediate political impact that led, within the year, to the passage by Congress of Theodore Roosevelt's law to regulate the meat, food, and drug industries.

In Britain there were similar exposes of the realities of life in working-class communities, such as in Arthur Morrison's novels about London's East End, Tales of Mean Streets (1894) and A Child of the Jago (1896). The Ragged Trousered Philanthropists by Robert Tressell, first published in 1914, describes the life of a group of workmen employed in the small-town painting and decorating business of Rushton and Co. in around 1906:

> It would have been much better for them if, instead of being "Freemen," they had been slaves, and the property, instead of the hirelings, of Mr. Rushton. As it was, he would not have cared if one or all of them had become ill or died from the effects of exposure. It would have made no difference to him. There were plenty of others out of work, and on the verge of starvation who would be very glad to take their places. But if they had been Rushton's property, such work as this would have been deferred until it could be done without danger to the health and lives of the slaves; or at any rate, even if it were proceeded with during such weather, their owner would have seen to it that they were properly clothed and fed; he would have taken as much care of them as he would of his horse.

Here, too, as in the American novels, is depicted the corruption and hypocrisy of municipal government: "The town of Mugsborough was governed by a set of individuals called the Municipal Council. Most of these 'representatives of the people' were well-to-do or retired tradesmen. In the opinion of the inhabitants of Mugsborough, the fact that a man had succeeded in accumulating money in business was a clear demonstration of his fitness to be entrusted with the business of the town." The chief of the band of "brigands" was the mayor, Adam Sweater, managing director of a large drapery business, exploiter of female sweated labor under systems of indentured apprenticeship and homeworking, profiteer, by which means

> Adam Sweater had contrived to lay up for himself a large amount of treasure upon earth, besides attaining undoubted respectability; for that he was respectable no one questioned. He went to chapel twice every Sunday, his obese figure arrayed in costly apparel, . . . He was an official of some sort of the Shining Light Chapel. His name appeared in nearly every published list of charitable subscriptions. No starving wretch had ever appealed to him in vain for a penny soup ticket.

THE SALESMAN AS ROMANTIC HERO

Many big businessmen ignored the attacks made upon them.
Some, however, personally defended themselves and the system of
which they were a product, most notably Andrew Carnegie in his
book The Gospel of Wealth (1887). "The millionaires who are in active control," wrote Carnegie, "started as poor boys and were
trained in the sternest but most efficient of all schools--poverty."
Until World War I very little attempt was made by businessmen to
influence public opinion or indeed to reconsider the relationships of
business to society in the light of the criticisms of the "Muckrakers."
The war, however, demonstrated the possibilities of propaganda and
in the postwar period increasing numbers of company public relations departments and public relations agencies were established.
One of the central figures in John dos Passos' trilogy, U.S.A.
(1930-36), is a public relations executive and counsel, J. Ward
Moorehouse; his career development from advertising to public relations counseling is paralleled by that of Dickon, William Clissold's
brother in H. G. Wells' World of William Clissold (1926). Dickon
starts out as a free-lance advertising agent at the time when proprie-
tary brands were coming to dominate retailing patterns: "A great
light had come to him, and for a time he saw life wholly as a field of
action in which he was to create appetites in people for commodities
they had never in the least desired hitherto, or to direct their attention to the great superiority of common necessities when they are
labelled distinctly with a proprietor's name." In his early advertising ventures Dickon had a "cheerfully piratical spirit. It was to be
his way of 'getting on'--and that was all that mattered." But as his
enterprise grows, his interests spread and his wealth increases he
begins "to think of advertising less and less as an adventure, and
more and more as an integral social function, with obligations and
standards of its own." He becomes a prime mover in the organization of advertisers into a professional organization, helps to found
lectureships and establish examinations in advertisement, thinks up
schemes for making deliberate falsehood in advertising into a legal
offense:

> Here we have people making fortunes by keeping
> people ill, misinforming them about their symp-
> toms, inducing them to trust in misdescribed
> goods. Billy, it's a crime against the Empire.
> It fills the street with uncomfortable people.
> Poor mothers, induced to give the children they
> cared for innutricious muck, so that they grow
> up disappointing weeds. All these weedy people

> in the streets, in the buses, everywhere--just
> because you let advertisers say their muck is
> flesh-forming and frame-building and bone-
> making when every competent authority knows
> that it isn't. The poor mother isn't a competent
> authority. How can she be? She finds it out too
> late. Can't help herself. And in the long run
> it's bad for advertising. It's bad for advertis-
> ing. . . . For most people, flat statement in
> advertisements is warranty, absolute warranty.
> And it ought to be. They take it as they take
> the news in the adjacent columns. The voice
> of print, Billy, is the voice of God. To them
> it is. And it's up to us to see that they get it
> divine and true.

Dickon, much to the amusement of his brother, goes on to advocate
that the Public Prosecutor, at the instigation of a properly consti-
tuted Advertisement Society, should prosecute those who misdescribe
their products and send them to jail.

H. G. Wells' main characterization of the salesman-advertiser
as entrepreneur is in his novel Tono-Bungay (1909). The story of
the rise and fall of Edward Ponderevo, an Icarus borne on the wings
of the tonic Tono-Bungay and its complementary products, "Tono-
Bungay Thistle Brand," "Tono-Bungay Hair Stimulant," and others,
is told by Edward's nephew, George. At the outset uncle Ponderevo
seems to George to be a "very small shabby little man in a dirty
back street, sending off a few hundred bottles of rubbish to foolish
buyers . . . a busy blackbeetle in a crack in the floor," an eccentric retail chemist with absurd dreams of great achievements through
the cornering of supplies of particular drugs and the selling of patent
medicines. But uncle Ponderevo's formula, "that the quickest way
to get wealth is to sell the cheapest thing possible in the dearest
bottle," turns out to be a most successful one. George takes over
responsibility for the bottling and packing of Tono-Bungay, leaving
Ponderevo to pay attention to the aspects of the business he enjoyed
most, the advertising and selling of the product.

> We sold our stuff and got the money, and spent
> the money honestly in lies and clamour to sell
> more stuff. Section by section we spread it
> over the whole British Isles; first working the
> middle-class London suburbs, then the outer
> suburbs, then the home counties, then going
> (with new bills and a more pious style of "ad")

into Wales, a great field always for a new patent-
medicine, and then into Lancashire. My uncle
had in his inner office a big map of England, and
as we took up fresh sections of the local press
and our consignments invaded new areas, flags
for advertisements and pink underlines for orders showed our progress.

"The romance of modern commerce, George!" my uncle would say,
rubbing his hands together and drawing in air through his teeth.
"The romance of modern commerce, eh? Conquest. Province by
province. Like sogers [soldiers]."

For four and a half years the company boomed and Ponderevo
and George lived "a life of mingled substance and moonshine," underlying which "there was nothing but fictitious values as evanescent as
rainbow gold." George throughout is amazed at the supreme un-
reason of it all:

At the climax of his Boom, my uncle at the most
sparing estimate must have possessed in substance and credit about two million pounds'-
worth of property to set off against his vague
colossal liabilities, and from first to last he
must have had a controlling influence in the
direction of nearly thirty millions. This irra-
tional middle of a community in which we live
gave him that, paid him at that rate for sitting
in a room and scheming and telling it lies. For
he created nothing, he invented nothing, he
economised nothing. I cannot claim that a single
one of the great businesses we organised added
any real value to human life at all. . . .

You perceive now, however, the nature of
the services for which this fantastic community
gave him unmanageable wealth and power and
real respect. It was all a monstrous payment
for courageous fiction, a gratuity in return for
the one reality of human life--illusion. We gave
them a feeling of hope and profit; we sent a tidal
wave of water and confidence into their stranded
affairs. "We mint Faith, George," said my
uncle one day. "That's what we do. And by
Jove we got to keep minting! We been making
human confidence ever since I drove the first
cork of Tono-Bungay."

Ponderevo, however, is totally trapped in the illusion, his business enterprises becoming his whole life, giving him a buoyancy and sense of achievement: "He was on the whole a very happy man throughout all that wildly enterprising time. He made and . . . spent great sums of money. He was constantly in violent motion, constantly stimulated mentally and physically and rarely tired. About him was an atmosphere of immense deference, much of his waking life was triumphal and all his dreams. I doubt if he had any dissatisfaction with himself at all until the crash bore him down. Things must have gone very rapidly with him. . . . I think he must have been very happy." Ponderevo illustrates a number of the characteristics of the salesman entrepreneur; he has the energy, the initiative, the supreme self-confidence and refusal to contemplate the possibility of failure, and above all the will, especially the will to win, that characterize the self-made man of the "New Thought" movement. By the end of the nineteenth century in America self-help books were dominated by the ethos of this new movement with its emphasis on personal salesmanship and boosterism. The movement took on new energy with the large advertising campaigns, the growth in instalment selling and personal credit plans, the quest for goodwill and the greater emphasis on consumer relations and consumer service in the 1920s, and incorporates the discovery of the businessman's Jesus by Bruce Barton in his book The Man Nobody Knows (1924), Dale Carnegie's How to Win Friends and Influence People (1936), and Norman Vincent Peale's The Power of Positive Thinking (1952).

This was the world of Sinclair Lewis' novel Babbitt (1922) and the model that George F. Babbitt, Presbyterian, Republican, family man, and real estate broker earnestly sought to imitate. It was a membership boom-time for such organizations as Rotary, Kiwanis Lions, and Elks, organizations where "small business competitors felt the need to boost one another's morale."[12] George F. Babbitt belonged to one such organization:

> He serenely believed that the one purpose of the real-estate business was to make money for George F. Babbitt. True, it was a good advertisement at Boosters' Club lunches, and all the varieties of Annual Banquets to which Good Fellows were invited, to speak sonorously of Unselfish Public Service, the Broker's Obligation to Keep Inviolate the Trust of His Clients, and a thing called Ethics, whose nature was confusing but if you had it you were a High-class Realtor and if you hadn't you were a shyster, a piker, and a fly-by-night. These virtues awakened

Confidence, and enabled you to handle Bigger
Propositions. But they didn't imply that you
were to be impractical and refuse to take twice
the value of a house if a buyer was such an
idiot that he didn't jew you down on the asking-
price.

Babbitt spoke well--and often--at these
orgies of commercial righteousness about the
"realtor's function as a seer of the future development of the community, and as a prophetic
engineer clearing the pathway for inevitable
changes"--which meant that a real-estate broker
could make money by guessing which way the
town would grow. This guessing he called
Vision.

For Babbitt and his kind "the Romantic hero was no longer the
knight, the wandering poet, the cowpuncher, the aviator, nor the
brave young district attorney, but the great sales-manager, who had
an Analysis of Merchandising Problems on his glass-topped desk,
whose title of nobility was 'Go-getter,' and who devoted himself and
all his young samurai to the cosmic purpose of Selling--not of selling anything in particular, for or to anybody in particular, but pure
Selling." Sinclair Lewis depicts a world of small-minded nervous
men, anxious to reassure one another on the merits of their little
community and their own importance within it, indifferent to the
aesthetic, hostile to change, a group whose claustrophobic conform-
ity is even rejected, for a short time, by Babbitt himself. Even the
speculator in the novel is a timid man who, before he gambled, con-
sulted "bankers, lawyers, architects, contracting builders, and all
of their clerks and stenographers who were willing to be cornered
and give him advice," desiring "nothing more than complete safety
in his investments, freedom from attention to details, and the thirty
or forty per cent profit which, according to all authorities, a pioneer
deserves for his risks and foresight."

In Babbitt, too, is an indication of the race prejudice and in-
cipient fascism of the middle-class small-town establishment, a
theme that Sinclair Lewis was to develop in his novel Kingsblood
Royal (1947). Babbitt's antiintellectualism provides him with a
suitable finale for one of his oratorical efforts:

Before I close I must call your attention to a
problem we have to face, this coming year.
The worst menace to sound government is not
the avowed socialists but a lot of cowards who

work under cover--the long-haired gentry who
call themselves "liberals" and "radicals" and
"non-partisan" and "intelligentsia" and God only
knows how many other trick names! Irresponsible teachers and professors constitute the
worst of this whole gang, and I am ashamed to
say that several of them are on the faculty of
our great State University! The U. is my own
Alma Mater, and I am proud to be known as an
alumni, but there are certain instructors there
who seem to think we ought to turn the conduct
of the nation over to hoboes and roustabouts.

Those profs are the snakes to be scotched--
they and all their milk-and-water ilk! The American business man is generous to a fault, but one
thing he does demand of all teachers and lecturers
and journalists: if we're going to pay them our
good money, they've got to help us by selling
efficiency and whooping it up for national prosperity! And when it comes to these blab-mouth,
fault-finding, pessimistic, cynical University
teachers, let me tell you that during this golden
coming year it's just as much our duty to bring
influence to have those cusses fired as it is to
sell all the real estate and gather in all the
good shekels we can.

Not till that is done will our sons and
daughters see that the ideal of American man-
hood and culture isn't a lot of cranks sitting
around chewing the rag about their Rights and
their Wrongs, but a God-fearing, hustling, successful, two-fisted Regular Guy, who belongs to
some church with pep and piety to it, who belongs to the Boosters or the Rotarians or the
Kiwanis, to the Elks or Moose or Red Men or
Knights of Columbus or any one of a score of organizations of good, jolly, kidding, laughing,
sweating, upstanding, lend-a-handing Royal
Good Fellows, who plays hard and works hard,
and whose answer to his critics is a square-
toed boot that'll teach the grouches and smart
alecks to respect the He-man and get out and
root for Uncle Samuel, U.S.A.!

THE CORPORATE EXECUTIVE

The growth of large-scale business enterprises, the growing divorce between company ownership and control, is reflected in the self-help literature after World War I. Now the prescriptions for business success include exhortations on how to rise into the managerial elite. The independent aggressive entrepreneur is replaced by the man in the grey flannel suit, the organization man, Babbitt as a senior executive. Mr. Pritchard, a character in John Steinbeck's The Wayward Bus (1947) is one such. In his youthful folly he had once voted for Eugene Debs and visited a parlor house when he was twenty--"such things were, like a kid's acne, a part of the process of adolescence"--but subsequently he had given up his freedom and then forgotten what freedom was like:

> Mr. Pritchard was a businessman, president of a medium-sized corporation. He was never alone. His business was conducted by groups of men who worked alike, thought alike, and even looked alike. His lunches were with men like himself who joined together in clubs so that no foreign element or idea could enter. His religious life was again his lodge and his church, both of which were screened and protected. One night a week he played poker with men so exactly like himself that the game was fairly even, and from this fact his group was convinced that they were very fine poker players. Wherever he went he was not one man but a unit in a corporation, a unit in a club, in a lodge, in a church, in a political party. His thoughts and ideas were never subjected to criticism since he willingly associated only with people like himself. He read a newspaper written by and for his group. The books that came into his house were chosen by a committee which deleted material that might irritate him. He hated foreign countries and foreigners because it was difficult to find his counterpart in them. He did not want to stand out from his group. He would like to have risen to the top of it and be admired by it; but it would not occur to him to leave it. At occasional stags where naked girls danced on tables and sat in great glasses of wine, Mr. Pritchard howled with laughter and drank the wine, but five hundred Mr. Pritchards were there with him.

H. G. Wells' World of William Clissold gives a far more sympathetic treatment of the corporate executive. William Clissold,
newly married and struggling to make ends meet, gives up his pure
research studies at the Royal College of Science to join the metal-
lurgical and chemical firm of Romer, Steinhart, Crest & Co. He
does so with considerable misgivings: "For the rest of my life as I
saw it then, I should be nosing out artful ways for underselling mag-
nesium or making aluminium cheap. Fine fun! I was to be a scientific truffle-hunting dog for predacious business." But Romer,
Steinhart is a science-based company in which the antagonisms between employer and employed are minimal. The original Steinhart
was "a student of Robert Owen, and regarded his employees with an
amiable generosity of intention. His idea, and it is still a tradition
of the firm, was that there is a sort of moral partnership of the
business inherent in those who have been employed by it for some
time. But I won't pretend that our virtue has had to struggle against
our interests; old Steinhart's good intentions happen to have yielded
the very best policy possible for us." Romer, Steinhart's welfare
policies, its contented highly paid salaried employees, its absence
of strikes, its educational and training programs, its savings bank
organization, its investment system, its employee shareholding,
its "housing companies, recreation grounds, cricket clubs, swimming-
baths, two art museums, and a number of social clubs," and its two
weekly company newspapers are not without their critics, however.
To William Clissold all these things are "just sound modern business,"
made possible by the monopoly position the company enjoys in its industry. To some of the directors, however, notably Lord Crest,
all these paternalistic practices are a sure road to ruin. The Crests
are old established landed aristocracy, "great grabbers and savers
they have always been, a hard-fisted, firm-mannered race." Lord
Crest is

> as hard and mean as a French peasant and a
> British duke rolled into one. . . . When some
> unasked improvement in our workers' condition
> is in contemplation, Crest will still come to our
> board meeting with the clatter of rusty armour
> in his voice and demand where all this sort of
> pauperisation is to end. Where is the money to
> come from? he asks. Nothing will ever con-
> vince him that our dividends do not come out of
> the pockets of other people, nor that our profits
> are not abstracted from the wages of workers
> who have been held down while the abstraction
> is effected. He is equally persuaded that the
> object of foreign trade is to pauperise foreigners.

> He is not really an employer as we conceive it;
> he is a medieval robber baron who offers terms.
> He is always trying to force our people into rifle
> clubs and the Territorials because it would give
> them a sense of discipline, and once he wanted a
> man dismissed because he did not touch his hat
> to him outside the works.

"There are many ways," suggested Paul Baran, "to describe
the contrast between the tycoon and the modern manager. The former
was the parent of the giant corporation, the latter is its child. The
tycoon stood outside and above, dominating the corporation. The manager is an insider, dominated by it. The loyalty of the one was to himself and his family. . . the loyalty of the other is to the organization
to which he belongs and through which he expresses himself. To one
the corporation was merely a means to enrichment; to the other the
good of the company has become both an economic and ethical end.
The one stole from the company, the other steals for it."[13]

ENTREPRENEURIAL ETHICS

It is clear that a number of the changes in the economic and
social position of the entrepreneur, over the period from around
1850 to 1950, can be traced in the work of both British and American
novelists. The entrepreneur is portrayed at different times as self-
made man, as robber baron, as salesman, and as corporate executive. The dream of the self-made man, that the pursuit of success
will be a means to happiness and love, gives way to the rat race,
"run desperately by bright fellows who do not believe in it, because
they are afraid to stop."[14] The novelists reflect the social changes
of the period, illustrate the conflicts and struggles for power of different interest groups, analyze the impact of the newly rich on existing class structures and attitudes, and explore the individual
psychological effects of making the pursuit of economic success a
central life interest. The novelists also reflect the attitudes of the
intellectual world toward the values and ethics espoused by businessmen, and toward the values and ethics implicit in the behavior of
businessmen during the period. The increasingly apparent discrepancy between the attitudes of entrepreneurs and their behavior leads
to a growing hostility toward businessmen among novelists, so much
so that by 1948 one reviewer of business novels complains that "a
distilled malevolence, a cold and frightening spite, went into the
painting of practically every fictional businessman," and that Sherwood Anderson's novels, "in which businessmen suddenly flee their

offices in middle age as though menaced by the plague," are indicative of the novelists' lack of sympathy with the business world. [15]

Among the nineteenth-century novelists there is still some sympathy for the self-made man who becomes aware of the power that
his wealth gives him and who is concerned to recognize his responsibilities for a proper stewardship of that wealth and a just exercise of
that power. Mr. Thornton, in Mrs. Gaskell's North and South, for
example, is initially a manufacturer whose work-people "look upon
him as what the Bible called a 'hard man'--not so much unjust as un-
feeling; clear in judgment, standing upon his 'rights' as no human being ought to stand, considering what we and all our petty rights are
in the sight of the Almighty." Proud of his independence and his
scrupulous honesty, believing "that, in the great scheme of commerce, all dishonourable ways of acting were sure to prove injurious
in the long run," Thornton comes to recognize, through his own business failure, the dependence of others upon him and his own feelings
of responsibility toward them: "Until now, he had never recognised
how much and how deep was the interest he had grown of late to feel
in his position as manufacturer, simply because it led him into such
close contact, and gave him the opportunity of so much power,
among a race of people strange, shrewd and ignorant; but, above all,
full of character and strong human feeling."

The boorishness of the self-made man is a more common
theme, however, caricatured by Dickens, for example, in the person
of Josiah Bounderby of Coketown (Hard Times, 1854):

> A remarkable man, and a self-made man, and a
> commercial wonder more admirable than Venus,
> who had risen out of the mud instead of the
> sea. . . .
> He was a rich man: banker, merchant, manu-
> facturer, and what not. A big loud man, with a
> stare, and a metallic laugh. A man made out of
> a coarse material, which seemed to have been
> stretched to make so much of him. A man with
> a great puffed head and forehead, swelled veins
> in his temples, and such a strained skin to his
> face that it seemed to hold his eyes open, and
> lift his eyebrows up. A man with a pervading
> appearance on him of being inflated like a balloon,
> and ready to start. A man who could never suf-
> ficiently vaunt himself a self-made man. A man
> who was always proclaiming, through that brassy
> speaking-trumpet of a voice of his, his old ig-
> norance and his old poverty.

In fact Bounderby turns out to be a fraud, not a self-made man at all
as he claims, but merely a "self-made Humbug." The caricature of
the self-interested, aggressive and competitive entrepreneur is
summed up in Robert Tressell's description of the small businessman, Rushton: "Any profit that it was possible to make out of the
work, Rushton meant to secure for himself. He was a smart man,
this Rushton, he possessed the ideal character: the kind of character that is necessary for any man who wishes to succeed in business--
to get on in life. In other words, his disposition was very similar
to that of a pig--he was intensely selfish." Tressell contrasts Rushton's ethics of self-interest with the values adopted by

> a master decorator who was a man of a type that
> has now almost disappeared, being not merely an
> employer but a craftsman of a high order. . . .
> At one time he had had a good business in the
> town, and used to boast that he had always done
> good work, had found pleasure in doing it and
> had been paid well for it. But of late years the
> number of his customers had dwindled consider-
> ably, for there had arisen a new generation
> which cared nothing about craftsmanship or art,
> and everything for cheapness and profit.

Perhaps the strongest reaction of the novelists to the ethics of
entrepreneurship is to be seen in their response to the survival-of-
the-fittest ideologies that were popularized in the United States at
the end of the nineteenth century by the writing of the Englishman,
Herbert Spencer. Cochran and Miller point out that Spencer provided
a rationale and a vocabulary for the American businessman.[16]
Spencer "gave cosmic sanction to free competition," provided a sup-
posedly "scientific" justification for ceaseless exploitation, defended
the greed of businessmen as part of the inevitable universal struggle
for survival, and hallowed their wealth as a sign of their fitness. It
was a philosophy that sanctified almost any kind of business activity,
making "the lesser seem the greater good, the private seem the national profit." It was the initial philosophy of William Clissold and
his brother Dickon who see the world as a lawless and adventurous
place in which the only crime is being caught out: "Our father had
been careless, indifferent, and they had caught him. But he had
only done what everybody did. 'They don't catch me,' said Dickon,
gauging the realities of life. Neither of us believed that he was essentially worse than the run of business men. We contemplated a
brigand world."
This is the world of the "brigandish" Mr. Golspie in J. B.
Priestley's novel Angel Pavement (1930). Restless, opportunistic,

exploiting immediate short-term advantages, Golspie comes in and
out of the staid London firm of Trigg and Dersingham, brokers of
veneers and inlays, like a whirlwind.

> I've picked up a good many different sorts of busi-
> ness in my time, and I haven't finished yet, not by
> a long chalk. But I don't call this veneer trade a
> proper business. It's a side-line. There's no
> size to it. You might as well be selling sets o'
> chessmen or rocking-horses. No size to it, no
> chance of real growth, you see? It's all right
> for Dersingham--it's about his mark--but then
> he's not really in business. He's only got one leg
> in it instead of being up to the neck in it. He
> thinks he's a gentleman amusing himself. Too
> many of his sort in the City here. That's how the
> Jews get on, and the Americans. None of that
> nonsense about them.

This is the world that the hired public relations counsel must
justify, as does Howard Littlefield, Ph.D., in Babbitt:

> He was the employment-manager and publicity-
> counsel of the Zenith Street Traction Company.
> He could, on ten hours' notice, appear before the
> board of aldermen or the state legislature and
> prove, absolutely, with figures all in rows and
> with precedents from Poland and New Zealand,
> that the street-car company loved the Public and
> yearned over its employees; that all its stock was
> owned by Widows and Orphans; and that whatever
> it desired to do would benefit property-owners
> by increasing rental values, and help the poor
> by lowering rents. . . . But Littlefield's great
> value was as a spiritual example. Despite his
> strange learnings he was as strict a Presbyterian
> and as firm a Republican as George F. Babbitt.
> He confirmed the business men in the faith.
> Where they knew only by passionate instinct that
> their system of industry and manners was perfect,
> Dr. Howard Littlefield proved it to them, out of
> history, economics, and the confessions of re-
> formed radicals. . . . his Phi Beta Kappa key
> shone against a spotty black vest; he smelled of
> old pipes; he was altogether funereal and

archidiaconal; and to real estate brokerage
and the jobbing of bathroom-fixtures he added
an aroma of sanctity.

This is the world that George, the storyteller of <u>Tono-Bungay</u>,
could never quite believe was true, the world of "corners":

> The idea of cornering a drug struck upon my mind
> then as a sort of irresponsible monkey-trick that
> no one would ever be permitted to do in reality.
> It was the sort of nonsense one would talk to make
> Ewart laught and set him going on to still odder
> possibilities. I thought it was part of my uncle's
> way of talking. But I have learnt differently
> since. The whole trend of modern money-making
> is to foresee something that will presently be
> needed and put it out of reach, and then to haggle
> yourself wealthy. You buy up land upon which
> people will presently want to build houses, you
> secure rights that will bar vitally important de-
> velopments, and so on, and so on. Of course,
> the naive intelligence of a boy does not grasp the
> subtler developments of human inadequacy. He
> begins life with a disposition to believe in the
> wisdom of grown-up people, he does not realise
> how casual and disingenuous has been the develop-
> ment of law and custom, and he thinks that some-
> where in the state there is a power as irresistible
> as a head master's to check mischievous and fool-
> ish enterprises of every sort. I will confess that
> when my uncle talked of cornering quinine, I had
> a clear impression that any one who contrived to
> do that would pretty certainly go to jail. Now I
> know that any one who could really bring it off
> would be much more likely to go to the House of
> Lords! . . . It seems to me indeed at times that
> all this present commercial civilisation is no
> more than my poor uncle's career writ large, a
> swelling, thinning bubble of assurances; that its
> arithmetic is just as unsound, its dividends as
> ill-advised, its ultimate aim as vague and for-
> gotten; that it all drifts on perhaps to some
> tremendous parallel to his individual disaster. . . .

This is the world that had defeated Ernest Horton's father in
<u>The Wayward Bus</u>:

My old man had two faiths. One was that honesty
got rewarded some way or other. He thought
that if a man was honest he somehow got along,
and he thought if a man worked hard and saved
he could pile up a little money and feel safe.
Teapot Dome and a lot of stuff like that fixed
him on the first, and nineteen-thirty fixed him
on the other. He found out that the most ad-
mired people weren't honest at all. And he died
wondering, a kind of awful wondering, because
the two things he believed in didn't work out--
honesty and thrift. It kind of struck me that
nobody has put anything in place of those two.

and deluded Joe in <u>Windy McPherson's Son</u>:

The threshing outfit with which Sam worked was
owned by a man named Joe, who was in debt for
it to the maker and who, after working with the
men all day, drove about the country half the
night making deals with farmers for other days
of threshing. Sam thought that he looked constantly on the point of collapse through over-
work and worry, and one of the men, who had
been with Joe through several seasons, told
Sam that at the end of the season their employer
did not have enough money left from his season
of work to pay the interest on the debt for his
machines and that he continually took jobs for
less than the cost of doing them.
     "One has to keep going," said Joe, when
one day Sam began talking to him on the matter.
     When told to keep Sam's wage until the end
of the season he looked relieved and at the end
of the season came to Sam, looking more worried
and said that he had no money.
     "I will give you a note bearing good interest
if you can let me have a little time," he said.
     Sam took the note and looked at the pale,
drawn face peering out of him from the shadows
at the back of the barn.
     "Why do you not drop the whole thing and
begin working for some one else?" he asked.
     Joe looked indignant.
     "A man wants independence," he said.

And it is the world satirized by Mark Train in his short story, The International (Christian) Lightning Trust (1909). Two out-of-work printers, Jasper Hackett and Stephen Spaulding, set out with roguish good humor to trade "on the assfulness of the human race" in general and, more particularly, on the fear that people have of being struck by lightning and on their greed and gambling instincts. They devise a scheme offering, for a $1 premium, $5,000 death benefit on being struck by lightning, $35,000 benefit for a $5 premium, and $100,000 benefit for a $10 premium. Next they spread their circular "among the clergy, widows, orphans, holders of trust funds, and the other born speculators," justifying their attempt to recruit a potential 90 million policy-holders, when only 28 Americans a year are likely to be killed by lightning, with a belief in their role as public benefactors:

> What are we in this world for? To do good. If we do good, Providence will make everything right for us. Aren't we doing good? Who is doing more? We are providing fortunes for the poor; fortunes for poor bereaved families; and giving every one of them a chance. I love our mission. We are Benefactors; Benefactors of the stricken, the unfortunate, the bereaved; we are the stay and support and consolation of the desolate, we heal the broken heart, we are the pauper's only friend. Providence watches over us; Providence sees what we are doing; Providence will recompense us; . . .

But they are sensitive souls, conscience-stricken by some of their business practices. "I have no peace of mind these days," declares Steve, ". . . we do so much lying. Providence is noticing that, too, you may be sure, and it will do us damage." Jasper "realized, with shame, that every new circular he issued contained fresh lies--lies essential to prosperity and expansion in the business, it was true, but lies all the same; he realized that the size of these lies was getting bigger and bigger with every new output, and the thought of it made his cheek burn. He saw clearly that in contriving these unholy inventions he was imperiling his salvation, and he spoke up with decision, and said 'I stop it right here! I will no longer soil my soul with it; we must hire a liar.'"

NOTES

1. J. G. Cawelti, Apostles of the Self-Made Man (Chicago: University of Chicago Press, 1965), p. 14.

2. Ibid., p. 62.

3. T. C. Cochran and W. Miller, The Age of Enterprise (New York: Macmillan, 1958), p. 72.

4. See Cawelti, op. cit., p. 3.

5. I. G. Wyllie, The Self-Made Man in America (New Brunswick, N.J.: Rutgers College, 1954).

6. R. Fink, "Horatio Alger as a Social Philosopher," Introduction to H. Alger, Ragged Dick and Mark, the Match Boy (New York: Collier Books, 1962). The idea that Alger stood for contributing to the community chest is somewhat anachronistic since the first community chest was not established until 1914 (see Cochran and Miller, op. cit., p. 329).

7. See R. H. Gabriel, The Course of American Democratic Thought (New York: Ronald Press, 1940).

8. Cochran and Miller, op. cit.

9. Ibid., p. 67.

10. See T. C. Cochran, Basic History of American Business (Princeton, N.J.: Van Nostrand, 1959), pp. 174-75.

11. Wyllie, op. cit., p. 146.

12. Cochran and Miller, op. cit.

13. P. A. Baran, Monthly Review, July-August 1962, p. 146; quoted in R. L. Heilbroner, The Limits of American Capitalism (New York: Harper and Row, 1965), p. 28.

14. P. Goodman, Growing Up Absurd (New York: Random House, 1960).

15. J. Chamberlain, "The Businessman in Fiction," Fortune, November 1948.

16. Cochran and Miller, op. cit., p. 119.

4

THE SMALL FIRM IN
AN ADVANCED
INDUSTRIAL SOCIETY

WHAT IS A SMALL FIRM?

The term small is a relative one and the point at which any firm may justifiably be regarded as small will depend largely upon the distribution of firms of different size within its industry. British Census of Production information for 1958, for example, indicated that in the engineering industry 84 percent of the work force were employed in establishments of over 100 persons.* In such a context, therefore, it would be valid to regard a firm with less than 100 employees as a small firm. But in agriculture less than 5 percent of the work force were employed in establishments of over 100 persons and 64 percent were employed in establishments of less than 10 persons. In such a context a firm of less than 10 persons would necessarily need to be regarded as fairly typical of the industry.

While the engineering and agricultural industries may represent extreme cases, they do, nevertheless, reveal some of the pitfalls that await those who adopt definitions of a small firm independently of the industrial structure within which the firm operates. When such definitions are used as a basis for policy formulation and implementation they may lead to quite inappropriate policy applications. The work of the Bolton Committee in Britain provides a use-

---

*The problem of statistical measures of smallness is further complicated by the distinction in many official statistics between establishments and enterprises, an enterprise in British census data being "one or more firms under common ownership or control as defined in the Companies Act 1948" and an establishment generally being a single factory or plant.

ful example of the difficulties that can arise. The committee in its
report rightly pointed out that "a small firm could not be adequately
defined in terms of employment or assets, turnover, output or any
other arbitrary single quantity, nor would the same definition be
appropriate throughout the economy."[1] They therefore explored alternative ways of defining small firms, in terms of those market,
managerial, and institutional characteristics that were likely to differentiate small firms from large in terms of performance and problems. In practice, however, the committee was forced to accept the
arbitrary operational definitions used as a basis for the collection of
official statistics in different industries. These definitions varied
from industry to industry and yet were rarely referred to when the
committee came to make specific recommendations. Such recommendations were made in terms of "the small firm," an entity whose existence in such composite form had been seriously questioned by the
committee and its research unit. The committee's conclusions and
recommendations, therefore, effectively treat a manufacturing firm
with 200 employees, a wholesale company with a turnover of £200,000
per annum, and a road transport undertaking with five vehicles as
equal and similar units, something which at the outset the committee
had been anxious to avoid. The road to hell is paved with good intentions. We, too, particularly in this chapter and in Part III of the book,
will tread that road and generalize about the small firm without making reference to specific industrial contexts.

Ideally, then, our definition of a small firm might well be in
terms of criteria quite different from the various size categoriza-
tions used for collecting official statistics. The relative complexity
of a firm's management structure, for example, might be a useful
indicator of degrees of largeness or smallness. In Britain the Central Training Council suggested that the dividing line between a small
and large firm could conveniently be taken where the structure has
become sufficiently complex to call for "functional devolution at the
management level."[2] A small firm would then be one in which the
owner-manager or managing director or chief executive was able to
exercise overall control without the need to introduce functional
devolution. Yet it is questionable whether this is a useful distinction. Most firms have some degree of functional devolution, however slight, and the change from complete control by a single person
to a position where different people are responsible for different
parts of the operation of an enterprise is a gradual progression
rather than, as suggested by the Central Training Council, a single
turning point. These two positions, that of one-man control on the
one hand and of a complicated management structure on the other,
can be regarded as being at different ends of a continuum along
which there are a large number of possible variations. It is probable

that in modern industry most of these variations exist. In some
firms, one man may remain in overall charge of the enterprise but
he may be forced, by pressure of work, to delegate some of his
duties to other people. In other firms, a number of people, perhaps
three or four, may divide the many responsibilities of management
between themselves, each being responsible for a number of functions. The degree of functional differentiation will also depend on
the ability and industry of each managing director. A well-organized
man with a capacity for hard work may be able successfully to control a larger firm than a man with less ability and industry. The notion of personalized management is one of the three criteria that the
Bolton Committee suggests form part of an "economic" as opposed to
a "statistical" definition of the small firm:

> By "managed in a personalised way," we mean
> that the owners themselves actively participate
> in all aspects of the management of the business
> and there is no general devolution of the decision-
> making process. Thus, although they may have
> one or more intermediate layers, e.g. super-
> visors or foremen to interpret their decisions
> and transmit them to the employees, and al-
> though--in the larger small firms--they may
> devolve certain specialised functions, such as
> accounting or production, on to the more senior
> of their employees, the owners themselves
> still take all the principal decisions and exer-
> cise the principal management functions.[3]

The other two criteria in the committee's economic definition are,
first, that a small firm is one that has a relatively small share of
its market and therefore lacks power to influence its market environment to any degree, and, second, that a small firm is independent
and not part of any larger enterprise, thereby leaving the owner-
managers free from any outside controls over their decision-making
activities.

    In addition, however, to establishing criteria to distinguish
small firms from large firms, it is useful to make some distinction
between the small firm and what, in the relatively extensive American small business literature, is referred to as "little business"
(a distinction made by J. D. Phillips[4] and subsequently adopted by
E. D. Hollander[5]). Little business is characterized by the virtual
absence of paid employees and by direct participation of the proprietor in the physical work processes of the enterprise. Little business
includes, therefore, the self-employed craftsman or artisan, the

small shopkeeper with perhaps one or two assistants, "people who
have put themselves to work and such other members of their own
immediate family as do not demand pay for their services. If they
employ outsiders at all, it is on a very small scale, and the weekly
wage bill is a weekly worry. Their personal return is not on the investment they have made so much as on the labor they themselves
put in. It is wages rather than profits."[6] The principal factor distinguishing the small firm from the little business is that, whereas
little businesses are owner-operated, small firms are owner-
managed. In the small firm the work of the owner is concerned primarily with management or superintendence. Characteristically,
the owner himself will have to make decisions concerning production,
sales, finance, and administration without any specialist management
support or advice. In practice, of course, the dividing line between
little business and small firms is blurred as is the border between
the small firm and the larger organization in which ownership begins
to be divorced from control and management becomes progressively
institutionalized and professionalized.

THE NUMERICAL IMPORTANCE OF SMALL FIRMS

The answers to a number of questions can be clarified if both
the present and future importance of small firms within advanced industrialized economies can be realistically assessed. What, for example, is the potential payoff for the development of policies at government and industry level, or for the provision of facilities at the
level of the firm, which are designed specifically to help small companies to operate more effectively and more profitably? Is it worth
spending scarce resources in analyzing and understanding the particular problems of small firms if, by the turn of the century, world
trade will be dominated by 200 large multinational companies? As
we have seen it is not possible to describe small firms statistically
in terms of the economic definition proposed by the Bolton Committee,
nor is it possible to demonstrate from published statistics the numerical importance of little businesses and small firms as we have defined
them. Government statistics on small firms are usually classified by
numbers of employees or by sales turnover and, very infrequently,
by assets employed. Nevertheless some broad patterns of growth
and decline of small firms in different countries and in different economic sectors can be identified. For our purposes here the information presented will be limited primarily to that available for the
United States, which is well documented, and that available for the
United Kingdom, which, prior to the publication of the Bolton Committee Report in 1971, was extremely sketchy.

In the United States the total business population is on the increase, both in absolute terms and relative to the human population. Whereas in 1900 there were 22 business firms for every thousand people (the equivalent of 57 firms per thousand of the working population), by 1950 there were 26 business firms for every thousand people (or 67 per thousand of the working population).[7] Tables 4.1 and 4.2 illustrate some aspects of the structure of American business. Since World War II there has been growth in the number of companies, particularly in the retail trade and service sectors, and relative stability in the average size of company. There are wide variations in the structure of different industrial and commercial sectors and subsectors. In manufacturing, for example, the dominant share of employment is held by firms employing 250 or more people. In 1967 in the Blast Furnaces and Steel Mills subsector 99.5 percent of employees were in firms of 250 or more people compared with only 37 percent of those employed in sawmills and planing mills.[8] It has been estimated that in 1959 about 98 percent of firms in the United States employed less than 100 people and accounted for about 40 percent of all employment.[9] In 1967, 99.2 percent of U.S. companies employed less than 100 people and these companies accounted for 39.9 percent of all employment. In the postwar period in America "the large firms have grown larger, and the small firms more numerous,"[10] and this rise in the number of small firms has meant that small firms have kept a relatively unchanged share of total employment. Measured in this way, therefore, the degree of concentration in American industry has scarcely shifted since the war nor is it anticipated that it will shift markedly during the next decade. It would appear that in the United States postwar economic growth, a growing population, and rapid technological change have had two major effects on the structure of the business population. Advanced technology has led to growing economies of scale and larger business units, particularly in the manufacturing sector. At the same time expanding markets have led to increasing demands for highly specialized products and services thereby providing opportunities, particularly in the retail and service sectors, that small businesses are well placed to exploit.

Prior to the publication of the Bolton Committee Report there was no single source of information indicating patterns of growth and decline of small firms in different sectors of the British economy. Table 4.3 shows the small-firm sector as defined by the Bolton Committee. As can be seen the statistical definitions adopted for various industries differ considerably. In analyzing past trends in the small-firm sector, however, the committee concentrates primarily on manufacturing industry and on retail distribution. It is able to demonstrate, for example, that between 1924 and 1963 the numbers employed in small manufacturing establishments hardly changed, although, over the same period total employment in manufacturing industry increased by 55 percent. As a result the proportion of the total work force in small manufacturing establishments declined steadily throughout the whole period falling from 44 percent in 1924 to 31 percent in 1963.[11] While there had been a decline in the relative importance of small manufacturing establishments, therefore, in retail distribution the relative contribution of small retail establishments had remained substantially unchanged in the period from 1950 to 1966. The committee's overall conclusion is that "up to the middle 1960s the contribution of small firms to economic activity was declining in most industries with the possible exceptions of road transport and some of the miscellaneous service trades,"[12] a pattern which, they suggest, has probably continued since the middle 1960s into the 1970s.

TABLE 4.1

Size of U.S. Companies, 1963 and 1967

	Number of Companies (000's)		Average Number of Employees		Percent of Companies with Less Than 100 Employees	
	1963	1967	1963	1967	1963	1967
All industries	3,293	4,410	10.1	9.5	99.2	99.2
Manufacturing	274	267	67.8	80.1	93.5	93.0
Wholesale trade	236	233	9.9	11.4	99.1	98.9
Retail trade	1,679	1,683	5.1	5.8	99.8	99.7
Services	1,066	1,397	3.0	3.0	99.7	99.7
Transportation	8	15	12.7	9.9	98.7	99.1
Mineral industries	31	20	14.4	18.9	98.4	98.0
Construction industries	n.a.	796	n.a.	4.3	n.a.	99.5

Note: n.a. = not available.

Source: Enterprise Statistics 1967 (Washington, D.C.: U.S. Department of Commerce, January 1972).

TABLE 4.2

Distribution of U.S. Companies by Number of Employees and of
Employees by Size of Company, 1967

	Companies with Less Than 20 Employees		Companies with 20 to 249 Employees		Companies with 250 or More Employees	
	Percent of All Companies	Percent of All Employees	Percent of All Companies	Percent of All Employees	Percent of All Companies	Percent of All Employees
All industries	94.7	21.7	5.0	26.3	0.3	52.0
Manufacturing	71.0	4.5	26.3	19.8	2.7	75.7
Wholesale trade	88.0	40.7	11.8	46.1	0.3	13.2
Retail trade	96.3	39.4	3.6	25.8	0.1	34.8
Services	97.8	41.7	2.1	33.4	0.1	24.9
Sawmills and planing mills	81.9	17.4	17.4	45.6	0.7	36.9
Wood household furniture	71.4	6.4	25.1	34.2	3.6	59.4
Upholstered household furniture	58.3	7.5	38.6	50.5	3.1	42.0
Construction industries	96.2	38.9	3.7	41.7	0.1	19.3

Source: Enterprise Statistics 1967 (Washington, D.C.: U.S. Department of Commerce, January 1972).

TABLE 4.3

U.K. Small-Firm Sector as Defined by the Bolton Committee

Industry	Statistical Definition of Small Firms Adopted by the Committee	Small Firms as a Percent of All Firms in the Industry, 1963	Proportion of Total Employment in Small Firms, 1963	Average Employment per Small Firm, 1963
Manufacturing	200 employees or less	94	20	25
Retailing	turnover £50,000 p.a. or less	96	49	3
Wholesale trades	turnover £200,000 p.a. or less	77	25	7
Construction	25 employees or less	89	33	6
Mining/quarrying	25 employees or less	77	20	11
Motor trades	turnover £100,000 p.a. or less	87	32	3
Miscellaneous services	turnover £50,000 p.a. or less	90	82	4
Road transport	5 vehicles or less	85	36	4
Catering	all excluding multiples and brewery-managed public houses	96	75	3

Note: All figures relate to enterprises, but with the exception of Manufacturing relate only approximately to the year indicated.

Source: Small Firms--Report of the Committee of Inquiry on Small Firms (The Bolton Report) (London: HMSO, 1971), para. 1.9.

The most interesting conclusion from the committee's comparisons of the relative importance of the small firm sector in various
advanced industrial societies is that the greatest degree of industrial
concentration would appear to be in Britain. In manufacturing, for
example, only 31 percent of all employment in Britain in 1963 was in
small establishments, compared with 34 percent in Germany (where
the statistics excluded the Handwerker category), 39 percent in the
United States, 51 percent in France, and in Japan, in 1966, 54 percent. [13] Comparing the United States and British economies as a
whole the committee estimated that, in 1963, the small-firm sector
in the United States accounted for 34 percent of employment compared
with 29 percent in Britain. Nevertheless small firms in Britain still
comprise a large and important sector of the economy, a sector of at
least 1.25 million firms, employing 6 million people, or 25 percent
of the employed population, and contributing some 24 percent of the
net output of the private sector, the equivalent of nearly 20 percent
of the country's gross national product. [14]

It is clear, then, that whereas small companies will continue
to be of numerical importance, there will be considerable differences
in the contribution they make to different national economies and
within different industrial and business sectors. Such differences
are presumably related to different histories of industrialization,
differential growth rates in populations and markets, different rates
of technological innovation and diffusion, and different legal and political frameworks, as well as being related to cultural and social
values surrounding notions of "independence" and "entrepreneurship."
What is not clear is the extent to which the small firm in Britain will
continue to decline in numbers over the next few years and whether
the continuation of this decline will be of benefit to the British economy as a whole. American experience might well suggest that the
rate of new entries into the British business population is already
too low. Much will obviously depend on the impact of Britain's entry
into the Common Market and whether or not the anticipated economic
growth and access to larger markets will encourage an increase in
the rate of new births within the ranks of the small firm.

THE ECONOMIC IMPORTANCE OF SMALL FIRMS

Numerical measures of economic importance in terms of numbers of people employed or of capital resources utilized are, however, only one aspect of the economic function of the small-firm sector in an advanced industrial society. In particular small firms may
have an important role as economic innovators, there being much
evidence that many new goods and services, and improvements to

existing goods and services, begin their lives in small companies. The automobile, the jet engine, the hovercraft, the Polaroid camera, and the wireless are all examples of products that have been developed and manufactured initially by small firms. Small firms may be seen, then, as being vital to the continued advance of technology and to the creation of new goods and services.

Similarly, small firms may fill particular economic roles that cannot be adequately fitted by larger companies. One of the Bolton Committee's research reports classified firms in terms of the type of market in which they sold their output and suggested that there were three primary economic roles that small firms fitted. First, they could operate as satellites. In this category would be small firms that were heavily dependent on one large customer either because that customer absorbed a high proportion of the small firm's output or because the customer had designed a product or service and had then subcontracted its manufacture or supply to one or more small firms, a situation common, for example, in the motor industry and in the aircraft industry. Second, small firms could have an economic role as specialists. In this category would be small firms that carried out functions that large firms, seeking economies of scale based on long production runs, for example, found uneconomic to pursue. These firms would be those that fit into those interstices of the economy that arise either from patterns of growth in new industries or from lack of economic incentive for larger companies to close the gaps in their markets, gaps that small firms can exploit because of special advantages they have in being small.[15] Small firms in craft industries, such as firms manufacturing high-quality marble fittings for jewelry, would fill this category as would repair and maintenance firms in the building industry and many small retail outlets such as specialist bookshops. Third, small firms could be competitors or marketeers, competing in the same or similar markets as large firms: "Computer software companies, fashion merchandise manufacturers, restaurants, insurance brokers, travel agencies and garages, are all examples of businesses in which small firms market their services in more or less direct competition with large ones."[16] The distribution of small firms between these three roles of satellites, specialists, and competitors varies from industry to industry. In a sample of small manufacturing companies, for example, it was reported that 78 percent of the companies regarded themselves as competitors, 16 percent as satellites and 6 percent as specialists.[17]

A further measure of the economic importance of small firms vis-a-vis large ones is in their relative use of resources. Comparisons between the relative profitability of small and large companies are notoriously difficult to make. The unreliability of making any interfirm or interindustry comparisons on the basis of published accounts is well documented,[18] but the pitfalls are compounded in dealing with owner-managed businesses because of ambiguities in the treatment of the owner-manager's salary--how much of it is considered as salary and how much as a return on capital is quite arbitrary and subject to variable treatment depending on shifting tax considerations. Nevertheless the Bolton Committee made a brave effort to sift the available evidence in order to determine the relative efficiency of small and large firms in their respective use of resources. It found greater variability in profits among small firms but, in terms of efficiency, "all we can conclude is that our analysis so far provides no evidence for assuming that small firms are, in general, any less efficient than large, or vice versa. . . . Their output per person employed is on average lower than that of large companies, but this is in part explained by the labour-intensive nature of the trades in which small firms predominate, and by differences in the composition of the labour force. . . . It is also counterbalanced by a better return on capital employed."[19]

The Bolton Committee also explored the extent to which small firms contributed to invention, innovation, and technological progress. Two of the research reports it commissioned had a bearing on this question. The report on <u>Scientific and Engineering Manpower and Research in Small Firms</u> indicated that small firms employ a smaller proportion of qualified scientists, engineers, and technologists, relative to their share of total employment, than large firms, and that their expenditures per head on research and development were lower than large-firm expenditures.[20] The report itemized a number of industry differences in the employment of qualified scientists, engineers, and technologists. In the electronics industry, for example, small firms employed only 10 percent of the total number of employees in the industry but had 14 percent of the qualified staff. It was suggested that this situation arose as a result of the relatively low entry costs in the electronics industry, where the development and testing of electronic components could be successfully carried out in small firms since it did not necessarily require large or expensive facilities, whereas more generally the use of scientific and technological personnel would be linked to the capital-intensiveness of the industry. The report also pointed out the considerable reliance of small firms on outside laboratories and research associations for research and development work. The report on <u>The Role of Small Firms in Innovation in the United Kingdom since 1945</u> concluded that the contribution of firms employing less than 200 people to industrial innovation since 1945, as distinct from invention, had been less than their share of total employment or their share of net output, but while the small firms' share in output and employment

had been falling, their share of innovations had apparently been fairly steady or rising slightly over the period.[21] The innovations made
by small firms were concentrated mainly in a few industries, for example, in scientific instruments, electronics, textiles and textile
machinery, machine tools, timber and furniture, and construction,
whereas there were many industries where small firms made little
or no discernible contribution to innovation, either absolutely or
relatively. This was the case, for example, in aerospace, motor
vehicles, glass, steel, aluminum, and shipbuilding--broadly speak-
ing the more capital-intensive industries. The report further indicated that when industries were ranked in order of the share of
small enterprises in the number of innovations for each industry,
then this rank order largely corresponded with an industry ranking
of concentration based on the share of small enterprises in the net
output of each industry. Apparently, however, small firms produce
more innovations per pound (£) of research and development expenditure than their larger competitors and in this sense, therefore, the
report confirms the view that the innovative efficiency of small firms
may be greater than that of large firms.

In summing up the "role" of small firms in an advanced industrial economy the Bolton Committee pointed out that there is no single
function that can be uniquely assigned to small firms.

> Small firms perform a large number of very
> varied functions, the relative importance of
> which depends on the particular industry con-
> cerned. . . . We have distinguished eight im-
> portant economic functions performed by small
> firms, which comprise their special contribu-
> tion to the health of the economy. They are
> as follows:
> 1. The small firm provides a productive
>   outlet for the energies of that large
>   group of enterprising and independent
>   people who set great store by economic
>   independence and many of whom are
>   antipathetic or less suited to employ-
>   ment in a large organisation but who have
>   much to contribute to the vitality of the
>   economy.
> 2. In industries where the optimum size of
>   the production unit or the sales outlet is
>   small, often the most efficient form of
>   business organisation is a small firm.
>   For this reason many important trades
>   and industries consist mainly of small firms.

3. Many small firms act as specialist sup-
    pliers to large companies of parts, sub-
    assemblies or components, produced at
    lower cost than the large companies
    could achieve.

4. Small firms add greatly to the variety of
    products and services offered to the con-
    sumer because they can flourish in a lim-
    ited or specialised market which it would
    not be worthwhile or economic for a large
    firm to enter.

5. In an economy in which ever larger multi-
    product firms are emerging, small firms
    provide competition, both actual and poten-
    tial, and provide some check on monopoly
    profits, and on the inefficiency which
    monopoly breeds. In this way they con-
    tribute to the efficient working of the eco-
    nomic system as a whole.

6. Small firms, in spite of relatively low ex-
    penditure on research and development by
    the sector as a whole, are an important
    source of innovation in products, tech-
    niques and services.

7. The small firm sector is the traditional
    breeding ground for new industries--that
    is for innovation writ large.

8. Perhaps most important, small firms pro-
    vide the means of entry into business for
    new entrepreneurial talent and the seedbed
    from which new large companies will grow
    to challenge and stimulate the established
    leaders of industry. [22]

THE SURVIVAL OF THE SMALL FIRM

So what then is the future for small firms? Are they going to
be squeezed out by the increasing dominance of world trade by the
multinational companies? Are they going to decline in numbers as
a consequence of the spread of advanced technologies and the higher
entry costs that new firms will face in gaining a foothold in many industrial sectors? Examination of the available statistical information raises as many questions as it answers, but it does allow us to
conjecture on some of the stereotypes and myths that exist at the

present time about the nature of advanced industrial societies. These
are stereotypes and myths that are generated by concentration on data
from large organizations as the major source of information about
industrial societies. While such myths may contain partial truths
they tend to distort and oversimplify reality. In the context of the
current discussion two such myths can be highlighted. These are
the myth of the technological revolution and the myth of the 200
multinational companies.

The myth of the technological revolution is embodied in such
phrases as the ever-quickening rate of change, the automated society,
the white-heat of the technological revolution, which tend to overlook
the possibility that many technical innovations are highly selective in
their impact. There are still a large number of small firms in every
advanced industrial society whose methods of operation are closely
related to patterns that precede the industrial revolution. Their work
is still predominantly based on highly developed craft skills that have
been established since the time of the medieval guilds. Similarly
even the most cursory visiting of firms in Britain would reveal that
there are still a vast number of relatively large-scale enterprises
whose production methods have scarcely reached the stage of mechanization let alone anything approaching automation. And computers,
which have considerable potential for small firms, have made scarcely any impact as yet. Western industrialized societies are in danger
of succumbing to what might be called "the future-shock psychosis,"
a kind of mental paralysis in the face of change, a mental paralysis
brought about by a refusal to look at one's culture other than through
the frenetic antics of the news media. Futurologists, social theolo-
gians, technological forecasters, business strategists, and corporate
planners would do well to remember that the future will be much like
the present and not unlike the past:

> And the end of all our exploring
> Will be to arrive where we started
> And know the place for the first time.[23]

The myth of the 200 multinational companies takes on a variety
of forms, but the argument is generally along the lines that by a certain date (for example, the year 2000),[24] world trade will be dominated by 200 or so transnational enterprises, each of which has the
wealth and power of a nation-state. There is, of course, no doubt-
ing the growing power of the multinational companies and the threat
that they pose, particularly through their internal transactions and
their manipulation of transfer prices,[25] to the financial stability of
the countries where they trade. But while there may be a growing
concentration of physical assets within such firms, statistical

projections of the business population and its constituent parts, particularly for the United States--where, as we have seen, large firms have grown larger and small firms more numerous--would suggest that multinational companies will not come to dominate employment at all. Indeed, alongside a trend in some industries toward a greater concentration of capital assets within a few large organizations may well be a parallel trend toward dispersal of employment. Rising standards of living, and the consequent development of more specialized consumer-oriented markets, together with shorter working hours, are likely to attract more and more people into service industries and retail trade, sectors dominated by small firms, or into self-employment, or into the creation of little businesses of a handicraft kind both as a secondary source of income and as a leisure activity.

Statistical projections of the likely number of small firms in the future, together with economic logic, suggest that small business survival is inevitable and that the small-business sector of any advanced industrial economy will continue to be an important sector. What is clear from examining these two myths of our business culture is that we need to take less dogmatic views of the nature of advanced industrial societies and less simplistic views of the way in which they are developing. It seems more realistic to try to take a multidimensional perspective, a perspective that recognizes, for example, that at any one time different stages in the process of industrialization coexist side by side, industry by industry, both within and between small- and large-scale organizations.

NOTES

1. Small Firms--Report of the Committee of Inquiry on Small Firms (The Bolton Report) (London: H.M.S.O., 1971), para. 1.4.

2. Report of the Committee on the Training Problems of Small Firms, Central Training Council, 1968.

3. Small Firms, op. cit., para. 1.6.

4. J. D. Phillips, Little Business in the American Economy (Urbana: University of Illinois Press, 1958).

5. E. D. Hollander et al., The Future of Small Business (New York: Praeger, 1967).

6. Phillips, op. cit.

7. Kurt Mayer, "Business Enterprise: Traditional Symbol of Opportunity," American Journal of Sociology, June 1953, pp. 160-80.

8. See Hollander, op. cit., for 1947-62 data.

9. Gideon Rosenbluth, "The Trend in Concentration and its Implications for Small Business," Law and Contemporary Problems 24 (Winter 1959): 205.

10. Ibid.

11. Small Firms, op. cit., para. 5.6.

12. Ibid., para. 5.33.

13. Ibid., table 6.I, para. 6.2.

14. Ibid., para. 13, p. xix, and para. 8.2.

15. For further discussion, see E. T. Penrose, The Theory of the Growth of the Firm (London: Blackwell, 1959), chapter 10.

16. Small Firms, op. cit., para. 3.13.

17. Merrett Cyriax Associates, Dynamics of Small Firms, Committee of Inquiry on Small Firms, Research Report No. 12 (London: H.M.S.O., 1971).

18. See, for example, Published Accounts--your yardsticks of performance? (London: Centre for Interfirm Comparison, 1968).

19. Small Firms, op. cit., paras. 4.19 and 19.2.

20. J. G. Cox, Scientific and Engineering Manpower and Research in Small Firms, Committee of Inquiry on Small Firms, Research Report No. 2 (London: H.M.S.O., 1971).

21. C. Freeman, The Role of Small Firms in Innovation in the United Kingdom since 1945, Committee of Inquiry on Small Firms, Research Report No. 6 (London: H.M.S.O., 1971).

22. Small Firms, op. cit., paras. 8.3 and 19.5.

23. T. S. Eliot, Four Quartets (London: Faber and Faber, 1959).

24. See, for example, H. V. Perlmutter, "Super-giant Firms in the Future," Wharton Quarterly, Winter 1968. Perlmutter believes that by 1985 world industry will be dominated by 200 or 300 large international companies.

25. See, for example, M. Tugendhat, The Multinationals (London: Eyre and Spottiswoode, 1971).

5

SMALL COMPANIES IN
THE FURNITURE INDUSTRY

THE FURNITURE INDUSTRY IN BRITAIN

The British furniture industry has long been characterized by fragmentation in both manufacturing and retailing. The days are now past when a pound's worth of tools and a second pound in cash started a cabinetmaker on a career as an independent journeyman and double that amount converted him into an employer,[1] but nevertheless the economic barriers to entry are still relatively low and there is still a "constant ebb and flow of small firms in and out of the industry."[2] Throughout the 1950s and 1960s, however, there was rather more ebb than flow with the result that the industry has gradually moved in the postwar period toward greater concentration and larger-scale enterprises. In spite of this trend the industry remains comparatively fragmented, the average size of cabinetmaking company in 1970 being a company with 57 employees and the average size of upholstery company being one with 34 employees.[3] Similarly, 1965 estimates of the concentration ratio for domestic furniture manufacture suggested that about 8 percent of net output was produced by the three largest firms.[4]

The furniture industry presents a good example of an industrial structure that is, in terms of technological development, multidimensional. J. L. Oliver, in a book on the development and structure of the furniture industry, suggests that the period from 1801 to 1870 marked the closing years of the craft stage in furniture manufacture and was followed between 1870 and 1919 by the "dawn of the machine age; but in the furniture industry, the dawn was of machine-assisted craft. It was an age of slow transition."[5] Alongside some of the larger modern furniture companies with their mass-production processes there still exist numerous small craft-based enterprises, a

situation that is reflected in the fact that the demand for skilled labor
in the furniture industry is greater than in most other industries in
Britain. It is an industry that is labor-intensive rather than capital-
intensive with direct wages being as much as five times greater than
capital expenses in the cost of the final product. In 1965, for example,
the cost of capital in domestic furniture production was estimated at
about 3 percent of the total cost of the final product. [6] Over the ten-
year period from 1954 to 1964, pound, shilling, pence output per man
year in domestic furniture rose by around 17 percent or 1.5 percent
per annum, a figure that compares unfavorably with the average for
all manufacturing industries in Britain. [7] Perhaps even more important, however, is the fact that the furniture industry is an industry of
high material costs. Traditional materials, based on such natural
products as solid timber, animal glues, and fibers, have now largely
been superseded by various kinds of wood particle board and by
products of the science-based industries--plastics, lacquers, adhesives, and man-made fibers, for example. Nevertheless material
costs frequently represent around 50 percent of final sales value and
in some cases as much as 75 percent.

A variety of factors influence the demand for furniture, among
the most important of which are the rate of new housing starts and
completions, government monetary and fiscal policies, particularly
insofar as they affect credit sales, and long-term demographic factors such as birth and marriage rates. Because of its close links to
the building industry and its reliance on various forms of installment
credit to finance a large proportion of its sales, the furniture industry is very sensitive to the application of government economic regulators, particularly insofar as those regulators change the restrictions placed on hire purchase (installment) sales. Economists have
identified, therefore, an underlying cyclic trend in furniture sales
reflecting ups and downs in the economy associated with government
monetary and fiscal policy measures. They have also identified an
almost constant ratio between the value of retail sales of domestic
furniture and that of consumer expenditure, a phenomenon that has
occurred in spite of the rapid growth in demand for other consumer
durables, such as automobiles and electrical goods, which have a
much shorter replacement cycle than the products of the furniture
industry. [8] The industry, particularly the domestic furniture sector,
is also subject to sharp seasonal fluctuations in demand with peak
sales building up in the pre-Christmas period and, to a lesser extent,
around Easter. External economic and market factors are, therefore, important in determining aggregate demand and the demand for
furniture insofar as the individual company is concerned is consequently relatively inelastic, with slight reductions in price not leading
to any significant increases in sales nor slight increases in price
leading to significant decreases.

Fluctuations in the annual turnover of domestic furniture in
Britain, particularly since 1963, have been very marked, but over the
decade from 1960 to 1970 there was an average annual increase in
turnover in real terms of around 3 percent. At the same time the net
number of firms producing domestic furniture was declining, very
rapidly in the 1950s and then gradually leveling off during the 1960s.
Alongside the declining number of firms there has been some increased concentration of sales turnover in the larger companies.
Table 5.1 shows that in 1954, for example, 98 percent of furniture
firms had sales of under £500,000 per annum and that these firms
accounted for 63 percent of total sales whereas in 1969, 94 percent
of firms had sales turnovers of less than £500,000 per annum and
accounted for 45 percent of total sales. The problem with this kind
of comparison, however, is that it takes no account of the fact that a
furniture firm with an annual sales turnover of £500,000 in 1969 is a
very much smaller firm in terms of volume of business than was a
firm with a sales turnover of £500,000 in 1954. Consequently it is
perhaps more useful to try to assess the relative shares of small
firms in employment terms. Figures for a number of countries are
set out in Table 5.2. Looked at in this way it is clear that it is no
longer accurate in Britain toward the end of the 1960s to talk any
longer about the dramatic decline in the proportion of small firms in
the furniture industry. Indeed figures collected by the Furniture and
Timber Industry Training Board for 1969 and 1970, set out in Table
5.3, suggest that the trend toward larger establishments, as opposed
to larger enterprises, may have been halted if not reversed. In case
we are tempted to think that the continuing importance of the small
firm in the furniture industry is a particularly European phenomenon,
it is worth pointing out that an American commentator, reviewing the
household furniture industry in the United States in 1968, observed
that "in an age of mass production for mass consumption most of the
5,350 companies (90 percent employing less than 100 people) that
make up the industry are still insignificant in size, inbred in management, inefficient in production, and inherently opposed to technological change."[9] In spite of its fragmentation, therefore, there seems
no reason to believe that the British furniture industry is suffering
from any structural handicaps in competing with most European and
Scandinavian furniture industries other than the West German industry where, in 1968, only 35 percent of firms employed between 11 and
100 workers.[10] While there will probably continue to be a fairly
rapid turnover in the number of small firms in the British furniture
industry, it seems possible that the overall decline in absolute numbers of firms in the industry, so marked a feature of the postwar
period, may be halted during the 1970s.

TABLE 5.1

U.K. Furniture Firms with Sales Turnovers
of under £500,000 Per Annum

Year	Percent of Firms	Percent of Total Sales
1954	98	63
1959	97	58
1964	96	52
1969	94	45

Source: Furniture Development Council, Annual Statistical Reviews.

TABLE 5.2

Small Firms and the U.K. Furniture Industry

Country and Period		Percent of Firms Employing from 11 to 100 Workers		Increase or Decrease in Number of Firms During the Period
		At Beginning of Period	At End of Period	
Sweden	1958-67	96	95	Increase
France	1963-69	95	94	Increase
Italy	1966-68	92	91	Decrease
Austria	1959-68	78	78	Increase
Great Britain	1965-69	80	76	Decrease

Source: Union Europeenne de l'Ameublement, Statistical Series, published annually by the Furniture Development Council.

TABLE 5.3

U.K. Furniture Establishments, 1969 and 1970

	July 31, 1969	July 31, 1970
Percent of establishments employing under 100 employees	87.5	87.8
Percent of all employees in such establishments	40.2	41.0
Average size of establishment	52.6 employees	50.7 employees

Source: Furniture and Timber Industry Training Board, Manpower Returns.

FOUNDING AND DEVELOPMENT OF THE COMPANIES

During the course of the descriptive survey (see the Appendix for details about the survey), information was collected indicating the length of time that the 50 companies studied had been in existence, the relationship between the founder of each company and its present management, and the kind of work the founders had been engaged in before establishing their firms. None of the 50 companies had been founded before 1800, but 11 were in existence before 1900. Half of the companies had been founded since 1940. The oldest company in the survey was originally established in 1820 as a retail business and was still under the control of the descendants of the founder. The most recently established company was one set up in 1968, its managing director having previously been employed in the family upholstery business.

In 25 of the 50 companies the present managing director was a founder of the firm or a member of the first generation of the firm's management. In only 6 of the 50 companies was the present managing director unrelated to the founder of the firm; 5 out of these 6 companies had been in business in the nineteenth century. The backgrounds of the founders are classified in Table 5.4. As can be seen, at least 84 percent of the founders had been connected with the furniture or an allied trade prior to setting up the companies under study, mostly as skilled craftsmen or as owner-managers of earlier business ventures. The fact that over a third of the founders had previous business experience as owners underlines the finding from other research indicating that it is fairly common for an entrepreneur to own and operate a number of businesses during the course of his lifetime.[11]

TABLE 5.4

Backgrounds of the Founders
(n = 50)

Before Starting the Company the Founder of the Firm Was:	In the Furniture or an Allied Trade	In Some Other Trade
Running his own business	17	1
A skilled craftsman	20	1
In office or sales employment	3	1
A manager, supervisor, or foreman	2	--
Total	42	3
Miscellaneous or not known: 5		

Source: Compiled by the author.

A number of the companies studied had diversified and a number had completely changed their range of products since the date of their establishment. In some cases these changes were deliberate policy steps or the logical consequences of business expansion. Thus, for example, a company originally founded as a framemaking business had broadened its scope into the manufacture of three-piece suites. In other cases changes took place as a result of some chance occurrence or unforeseen opportunity. The company owned by Bob Rogers and John Harris had been set up ten years earlier as a partnership. Bob Rogers, a cabinetmaker by training, had previously been in partnership in the furniture trade and John Harris had run his father's cabinetmaking business for a number of years and had worked as a wood machinist. When they set up in business together it was with the intention of making top-grade reproduction furniture and of competing for special high-quality one-off (custom-built) jobs. But early in the life of the partnership a subcontract mail-order opportunity arose and, almost overnight, the firm switched to batch production of a range of chests of drawers and expanded rapidly to an annual sales turnover of £.25 million.

Just as grasping at unforeseen opportunities in some cases brought about major shifts in the nature of a company's products, so too it played a part in the original decision to set up in business. The founder of one company, for example, started up in business as a result of a government scheme training people how to make wicker baskets. The founder of another company started up on his own during the depression largely through force of circumstances. Married two months and unable to find employment, at his mother's request he made a wooden draining board and then, with £5 capital, started making draining boards for friends and neighbors. The company he founded with his patented draining board now manufactures a wide range of products--speaker cabinets, musical instrument cabinets, shop displays, laboratory furniture and fittings, and instrument cases.

In the furniture industry the founding of a firm would seem to be closely linked to occupational experience within the industry. Such occupational experience might be through apprenticeship as a skilled craftsman or through experience in the family firm. It would seem likely that a number of small firms in the industry will be one-generation firms, not surviving the death of their founders or being wound up within the founder's working life. Those small businesses that do survive, however, are likely to be passed on to the descendants of the founder. There is very little evidence among the companies studied of "outsiders" starting up small furniture firms. In a sense, therefore, many of these small firms are initially only marginally capitalist enterprises and need to be viewed primarily as extensions of particular occupational skills or of particular family traditions. Whereas there are clear patterns in the founding of these small firms, their subsequent development presents a much more haphazard picture. A few become highly profit-oriented ventures developing in a planned way. Others develop through market sensitivity and through their ability to adapt quickly to opportunities that present themselves. Some develop and decline in accordance with the skills and abilities of their founders or of subsequent generations of the founder's family and others never move beyond a subsistence level of operation, just sufficiently balancing the bad times against the good to keep afloat.

Barriers to entry into the furniture trade are low and patterns of development erratic with a stop-go kind of economic growth and considerable fluctuations in annual profitability. The first balance sheet for one of the companies in the study, for example, showed that in 1956, the company's first year of trading under new ownership, there was a gross loss of £28 and a net loss of £2,000 on a sales turnover of £12,000. The firm's total assets at that time amounted to £2,110, of which £940 was the value of the stock. Fixed assets were valued at £250, of which £50 was the value of the machinery, £105 the value of a Ford van, and £95 a somewhat dubious goodwill inherited from the bankrupt predecessor. By May 1968 the company was showing a gross profit of £19,500 (£12,800 net) on a sales turnover of £157,600 and its total assets were valued at nearly £70,000. The development of the company over these 13 years could be divided into four periods:

1. 1956-59: a period of initial struggle; the establishment of the new business as a financially viable concern;
2. 1959-61: a period of rapid growth in sales turnover following the purchase of new premises;
3. 1961-65: a period of consolidation with little increase in sales turnover;
4. 1965-68: a further period of rapid growth in sales turnover accompanied by additions to existing premises and purchase of further property.

The company operated on small profit margins, both in gross and net terms, but maintained a reasonable return on its total operating assets by means of a quick turnover of its goods, whether manufactured or factored, and by holding a relatively low level of raw materials stock and almost no stocks of finished goods. The company did not conform to some of the commonly accepted characteristics about the financial structure of small firms. In particular it did not have a high level of stocks and work-in-progress, it did not rely heavily on trade credit, and it had not made extensive use of bank borrowing and short-term capital. The company had been able to maintain a fairly rapid rate of growth and to build up adequate reserves without recourse to external finance.

PROFITABILITY, GROWTH, AND
FINANCIAL STRUCTURES

Wherever possible during the descriptive survey, audited financial information on each company's performance during the preceding five years was collected. Of the 50 companies, 45 provided some information on their profits relative to their sales turnover and to their assets. It should be emphasized that this information gave only a very crude guide to overall company financial performance. No attempt was made to carry out a detailed intercompany comparison exercise. In addition, fixed assets, for example, were taken at cost and no attempt was made to assess their current value. On the basis of this information companies were classified into one of four categories--high, medium, and low profitability, and unprofitable. High profitability meant, in broad terms, that a company had, each year over a period of up to five years, achieved a net trading profit before tax of 10 percent or more on sales turnover and 14 percent or more on its total fixed and current operating assets. Similarly, low profitability reflected a net trading profit before tax of less than 5 percent on sales turnover and less than 7 percent on total operating assets.

Even against what should be considered a very conservative standard of financial performance, only 4 of the 45 companies achieved a high profitability rating, 17 were rated medium, 20 low, and 4 unprofitable. The average profitability of the small companies in the survey was very low and had been becoming progressively worse over the five-year period under review. In 1964/65, for example, over 60 percent of the companies providing financial information for that year had a return on sales (net trading profit before tax as a percentage of sales turnover) of 5 percent or more, compared with 50 percent in 1965/66, 32 percent in 1966/67, about 40 percent in 1967/68, and only 25 percent in 1968/69. Indeed in 1968/69 almost one-third of the companies, nearly twice as many proportionately as in any of the other years, made no profits at all. Crude measures of the return on assets reflected a similar decline. The figures must be seen against a background of increasing turnover of domestic furniture at constant prices over the period but a sharp decline in the total number of producing companies.

The profitability of the companies was further analyzed in terms of size of firm, location, the length of time the firm had been in existence, and the relationship of the firm's present managing director to the founder of the company. The numbers being dealt with in subclassifications of this kind are small and the findings must be considered as indicators rather than conclusions. A number of points of interest emerged from this analysis. First, there was no evidence that size, as measured by number of employees or by sales turnover, was an important factor determining profitability among these companies. Second, there was no evidence that geographical region or a city, urban, or rural location were major determinants of profitability. Third, companies founded since 1950 tended to be slightly more profitable than those formed at an earlier date, with companies dating from the 1920s and 1930s having the poorest profit records over the period under review. Finally, there was some evidence to support the prevalent furniture industry stereotype of riches to rags in three generations, three of the four highly profitable companies being firms with first-generation management and all three companies with third-generation management having low profitability ratings.

As well as being classified in terms of profitability, the companies in the descriptive survey were divided into four growth categories--rapidly expanding companies, expanding companies, static companies, and contracting companies. A rapidly expanding company

was one with an annual increase in sales turnover of 20 percent or
more in at least two of the four years under review and an expanding
company was one with an annual increase on the same basis of from
7 percent to 20 percent in sales turnover. In this way companies
whose sales turnover increased in money terms only but not in real
terms would tend to be classified as static. The measure of growth,
like the measure of profitability, was a conservative one. Out of the
50 companies surveyed, 47 provided sufficient information for some
growth classification to be made. Three were classified as expanding rapidly, 20 as expanding, 21 as static, and 3 as contracting.

Of the three rapidly expanding companies one had a profitability
rating of high, one of medium, and one of low. Of the three contracting companies, two were rated unprofitable and one had a low profitability rating. None of the static companies had a high profitability
rating. The indication was, therefore, that whereas growth did not
necessarily result in profitability, contraction almost inevitably
meant loss or low profitability. Nevertheless, although static companies were more likely to have low than medium profitability ratings,
almost half the expanding companies had equally poor profit records.

Analysis of company growth by size and age of firm, by location,
and by management generation brought out a number of further points
of interest. There was, for example, no general evidence of any size
barriers to growth among these 47 companies. There were expanding companies in each employee size bracket and in each sales turnover category. Nor was there any evidence of major regional differences in company growth, although the small number of companies in
rural and semirural areas had a greater propensity to grow than
those in major cities or other urban areas. Of the three rapidly expanding companies, two had changed their location during the last
five years as had 7 of the 20 expanding companies, two of them twice.
The likelihood was, therefore, that about 40 percent of the expanding
small firms would change their location at least once every five
years. Finally, as might be expected, the older the company the
greater the likelihood of its being fairly static. Company growth was
more likely under first-generation management than at any subsequent time. Of the 23 companies that were expanding or expanding
rapidly, 17 were still being managed by their founders.

Wherever possible during the descriptive survey, information
was collected, initially from the managing director and then, if necessary, from Companies House London, on the performance of the
firm over the five-year period from 1964-65 to 1969. This information included the annual figures of sales, purchases, stock and work-
in-progress, wages, gross profit, net trading profit before tax,
fixed and current operating assets, and current liabilities. The
cooperation of the companies in this aspect of the survey was

encouraging and sufficient information was collected to allow some crude financial and cost indicators to be constructed. Some of the results are set out in Table 5.5. During the period under review there was very little change in the cost structures of the small companies that took part in the descriptive survey. Comparison with information collected by the Furniture Development Council on the cost structures of larger companies in the industry indicated that the smaller firms had, on average, higher material costs, higher direct labor costs, lower overhead costs, and lower net profits.

TABLE 5.5

Financial and Cost Structures

	Average	Median
Material costs as percent of sales turnover	48.4	47.9
Wage costs as percent of sales turnover	26.9	26.7
Overhead costs as percent of sales turnover	19.7	18.5
Net profit before tax as percent of sales turnover	3.6	1.8
Net profit before tax as percent of total assets	7.5	1.4
Stock turnover ratio	14.4	11.4
Current ratio	1.4	1.2
Added value	1.7	1.6

Source: Compiled by the author.

The survey made clear some of the dangers of applying conventional financial ratios to the audited accounts of small owner-managed firms. Thus, for example, 28 percent of the companies had current ratios of less than 1.0, which, at face value, would suggest difficulties in meeting short-term financial commitments. A further 55 percent of the firms, those with current ratios of 1.0 and over but less than 2.0, might be expected to have periodic difficulties, perhaps on a seasonal basis, in paying their bills. Only the remaining 18 percent of firms, those with current ratios of 2.0 and over, could be said, on a fairly conventional interpretation, to have strong liquidity positions. But in some cases it was apparent that the companies were in debt primarily to their owners, the current liabilities of companies including such items as directors' loan accounts and directors' bonuses owing, items that were unlikely to require payments in the foreseeable future. To determine what proportion of the companies in the survey were faced with inadequate short-term finance was, therefore, beyond the scope of the information collected. Similar difficulties arose in deciding whether the salaries of owner-managers of small firms ought not to be partially treated as profit.[12]

The characteristic picture that emerged from analysis of the profitability, growth, and financial structures of the small firms in the descriptive survey was of a company that, with little real growth in sales turnover from year to year, was making good-quality products that had relatively high material and direct labor costs. By keeping overheads and directors' remuneration to a minimum the company might just achieve a rate of return on sales and assets sufficient to guarantee survival. There are small companies in the British furniture industry that are highly profitable but for every company with a return on sales of more than 10 percent per annum there are probably three who are making no profits at all and who survive by selling or mortgaging their property or by gradually diminishing their assets and reserves. It was clear that the competitive pressures on the small furniture firm had been increasing over the five-year period under review and were likely to do so at an even faster rate throughout the 1970s.

Obviously there is no such thing as the "typical" furniture company. Nevertheless the following profile provides a caricature of the kind of small firm that took part in the descriptive survey: The furniture company is located in an urban area in the South-East of England and employs 45 staff. In 1970 it had an annual sales turnover of £150,000 and was founded in 1952 by its present managing director who had previously worked as a craftsman in the furniture trade. The company is owned and controlled by the managing director who is supported by a works manager, a sales manager, and an office administrator and accountant. The managing director's wife provides part-time secretarial assistance. The company's sales turnover is expanding slowly, but this mostly reflects increased prices for its relatively high-quality products. This gradual expansion is not bringing any increase in profitability, which remains low at 2 percent on sales turnover. It is unlikely that the company will survive the founder's grandson, but its most profitable days, generated by the initial energy of its founder and managing director, are already past.

PRODUCT AND MARKET DIFFERENTIATION

Most of the 50 companies in the descriptive survey concentrated their production on one particular group of products, as for example

upholstered furniture or office furniture. Only 14 companies were
sufficiently diverse to have more than a 10 percent interest in a secondary product group. Product specialization was a major feature
in the small firms studied. Diversification of products seemed to
take place as a result of awareness of the limitations that existed in
the markets for a company's major traditional products rather than
as a result of deliberate policies of expansion on a broad front.

Within the various product groups companies tended to differentiate their products even further by consciously aiming at particular quality sectors of the market. Thus, for example, a company
making dining-room furniture could see itself as dealing solely with
the "top" quality end of the market or, alternatively, as trying to
compete in the "mass" market with a lower-quality product. Surprisingly it was the smaller firms in the sample that tended to be
more diverse in their product range. Nor was there any evidence to
suggest that the smaller companies tended to aim at the higher-
quality markets, or that the larger companies were more likely to
produce a full range of products from high to low quality. Cabinet
furniture companies and upholstered furniture companies tended to
concentrate on one particular quality sector of the market, whereas
bedding companies generally offered a full range of mattresses and
divans from cheap to expensive. There was no doubt, however, that
generally the higher the quality of the market aimed at the higher the
profitability of the firm, the companies operating in the lower-quality
markets generally having much poorer profit records during the period under review. However, a number of those companies operating
on a low quality-low profitability basis were expanding in the hope
that they would quickly reach a scale of operations sufficient to allow
them to operate competitively in the mass market.

The importance of these findings is that they highlight the
growth versus specialization dilemma that many small companies
have to face. Some of the small firms studied were, often through
force of circumstance rather than conscious choice, pursuing policies that maximized the advantages of specialization. They concentrated their productive efforts on a limited range of products aimed
at a particular segment of the market often within a tightly prescribed
geographical area. In a few cases, given such market differentiation,
they had established monopoly or oligopoly positions. Where this
occurred it was usually based on the possession within the firm of a
high degree of craft skill as, for example, in the restoration or
renovation of antique furniture. It becomes theoretically possible,
therefore, to have a large number of small firms within an "industry" and yet very little direct competition, monopoly being a function
of market differentiation rather than of producer scale. In addition,
while the capital cost barriers to entry to the furniture industry are
very low, the skill development costs in the highly specialized

sectors can be very high--at the time of the study skilled woodcarvers, for example, were extremely scarce. It is this kind of situation that many skilled craftsmen seek to exploit by establishing their own businesses. And it is also this kind of situation that limits the growth of those businesses. For such a craft-based business, growth will frequently result in increasing competition since the geographical net for customers for high-quality "luxury" goods must be more widely spread. In addition many craftsmen who establish their own businesses seem to be craftsmen first and businessmen second. They may concentrate, therefore, on marketing a high quality product that bears witness to their own particular individual skill as craftsmen. Such a policy may circumscribe the expansion of the business to the limits imposed by the owner-manager's physical ability to exercise a direct quality-control function within his firm. The growth of small firms will clearly, therefore, be limited not only by economic factors but by the particular orientation that the owner-manager has toward his company. This question is discussed in greater detail in the chapter on the motivation and goals of the owner-manager.

MANAGEMENT PROBLEMS OF
SMALL FURNITURE FIRMS

During the descriptive survey each managing director was presented with a list of 13 management activities or functions and asked to say in which of the activities he thought his company was particularly strong and in which particularly weak. The 13 activities on the checklist were design, finance, purchasing, sales, accounts, stock control, personnel recruitment and selection, training, production, cost control, quality control, transport, and office administration. In addition the managing directors were given the opportunity to indicate any areas of company strength or weakness not included in the list presented.

The managing directors of the 50 small firms in the sample appeared to be more aware of their companies' strengths than of their companies' weaknesses, or they saw their strengths as lying in many areas and their weaknesses as being highly specific to a few areas only. On average each managing director rated over five areas as being areas of strength, compared with about two areas rated as areas of weakness. Of the 50 companies, 6 had, in the opinion of their managing directors, no weaknesses. Obviously there are limits to the extent to which company managing directors, who in small firms are the principal public relations spokesmen, will be willing to admit weaknesses to outsiders. Nevertheless, given the poor profit records of many of the firms in the sample, the apparent degree of complacency about company management activities was surprising.

The areas most frequently rated as being strong were production, which was rated as a strength by 60 percent of the managing directors, quality control (58 percent), purchasing (56 percent), cost control (46 percent), and design, finance, and office administration (all 44 percent). The areas most frequently rated as being weak were stock control and personnel recruitment and selection, both rated as weaknesses by 24 percent of the managing directors, and finance, sales, cost control, and training (all 18 percent). A number of managing directors, while recognizing specific weaknesses in their companies, thought that those weaknesses arose primarily through factors outside their control and that, consequently, there was no remedial action that they themselves could take to improve matters. The factors they considered to be outside their control were such general economic conditions as the nature of the trade or the state of the financial market or of the labor market. The following remarks were characteristic of this somewhat defeatist approach to common management problems:

> "Design is a weakness. We have no designer. We are entirely governed by the retailers."
> "Design is outside our control. People are always looking for something different. We are subject to fashion."
> "We have a liquid cash problem. It's outside our own control."
> "Finance is a weakness. People owe us more than they should but there's little that can be done."
> "Our weaknesses in finance and accounts are due to present market conditions."
> "Labor is the biggest problem. There are no rewards for craftsmanship any more. We can't compete for labor with the motor companies and we lose the boys we do train; they are moving out to new estates and not staying in the trade."

When asked about weaknesses in areas other than those covered by the presented checklist, a number of managing directors identified items specific to their own company's particular problems. Thus, for example, one managing director commented that his factory was not purpose-built and its facilities were inappropriate but

could not be economically changed because the building was subject
to a compulsory purchase order. Others identified weaknesses related to their own personal lives: "The biggest weakness is my
health. If I am feeling good the business buzzes. A company is as
strong as the person running it." Similarly, a number of managing
directors specified additional areas of strength. Four considered
their companies' personal service to their customers was a particularly strong feature and two spoke of their versatility and flexibility:
"We make the most of our opportunities as they come along and get
the business the big ones won't look at"; "Our versatility is a
strength. We can make up anything that is unusual." Others mentioned their traditions of craftsmanship, their pricing policies, or
their efficient conversion of wood. One company referred to its
management: "Teamwork is our strength--the management team.
We have weekly management meetings at which we all poke fingers
in one another's pies. We all have the ability to muck in with anything."

In the 12 companies that participated in the depth study (see the
Appendix for details of the depth study) a variety of management
problems were encountered, spanning every aspect of the functioning
of the firms. Some of the problems, such as problems of cash flow
or of financing expansion, were common to many of the firms in the
study and would probably be similar to the financial problems faced
by small companies in other industries. Other problems, such as
some transport and design problems, were specific to particular
companies and arose as a result of circumstances of location or
market peculiar to individual firms.

In terms of financial management, some owner-managers said
that they had to deal with the consequences of a lack of short-term
capital for carrying on the company's day-to-day business and the
consequences of lack of long-term capital for expansion. Kappa
Company, for example, had traditionally financed its growth out of
retained profits but high rates of personal and company taxation and
a lack of profitable business had made such a policy increasingly
difficult to operate. The money ploughed back would often be money
owing to directors and, in recent years, directors had often been
unable to draw their full monthly salaries since those salaries represented part of the working capital of the firm. Kappa was having to
look, therefore, at external sources of finance, something it was
reluctant to do since it felt that in some way this would limit its independence of operation. Many companies were also faced with
credit control problems, and those that dealt in terms of fixed-price
contracts were acutely aware of the way in which inflation was erod-
ing their profit margins.

The main sales problem faced by small furniture firms at the time of the research was that there was a shortage of demand largely stemming from restrictions on credit. This led, in the view of some manufacturers, to excessive cost competition, particularly in the lower-quality markets. Alpha Company, for example, which was in the bedding sector of the industry, felt particularly constrained by the structure of its markets and by the methods of retailing. Cheap beds, which make up the bulk of the market, offered the company a lower return on its capital than high-quality beds, often so low as to be unprofitable. Consequently, Alpha's owner-manager was trying to shift his output toward better-quality beds, a policy he found difficult to pursue because of strong cost competition and insufficient public awareness of differing quality factors. "I'd rather make a good-quality bed," he said, "and sell it at a reasonable price than sell a cheap bed--but it is the customer that counts. I've lost orders because of a shilling a bed." Alpha felt that bedding manufacturers, with the exception of a few large organizations who sold their own brand name beds, were completely at the mercy of the retailers. Delta Company, which manufactured woven furniture (basket chairs, ottomans, dressing stools, linen bins and boxes), also believed that relationships with retailers were a key issue. While the owner-manager agreed that many retailers put too much emphasis on price at the expense of quality, he also felt that there were many astute buyers who knew what the public wanted: "My experience is that your face has got to fit--somehow you've got to get on the right side of these chaps and then you have no problem."

Some of the companies studied were in the position where a large slice of their production went to one retailer. This was a situation of concern to some owner-managers who felt it placed them in a vulnerable position, but feelings of vulnerability could be offset by an awareness of the advantages of having a major outlet that was financially sound. The temptation of large repeat orders was difficult for a small firm to resist, especially in so seasonal an industry, and one company, for example, found the prompt weekly payments from his major customer significantly reduced his cash flow problems.

Seasonal factors obviously contributed to the production difficulties faced by the companies studied and to their difficulties in maintaining a stable, fully employed labor force. In the eyes of the owner-managers, however, production problems were seen as being relatively minor worries compared to those involved in sales and finance. Some of the production problems that existed were a result of unsuitable premises or aging plant and machinery. Others were related to the production planning complexities faced by firms that manufactured a diverse range of products. In Epsilon, for example, a cabinet and chairmaking company, production and distribution were in batches that were calculated monthly. At the start of each month Epsilon's owner-manager worked out a production schedule in order that all the units of any particular article that had been ordered could be manufactured at the same time. This greatly reduced production costs, less tooling-up being required, but could cause storage problems since one batch might be anything from 25 to 100 units. Similarly, distribution was in batches and all furniture for one area was stored for anything from a few days to a few weeks and then sent off as one van load. Not only, therefore, was there the problem of scheduling distribution so that the vans had maximum loads and minimum distances to travel, there was also the need to keep storage periods as short as possible. Lack of detailed information on costs, on profit margins, and on market requirements compounded production planning difficulties, decisions to increase the production of products that were not made to order often being taken on the basis of vague impressions about how the market was moving and about which products were most profitable.

In some respects the furniture industry is a fashion industry, especially in upholstery, where fabric tastes are constantly changing and where new ideas are introduced frequently. Every year most of the firms studied brought out new designs in time for the spring furniture show at London's Earls Court. Some used the services of designers commissioned for specific jobs and others employed their own design staff within the firm. Theta Company, for example, manufactured a wide range of upholstery, including three-piece suites, armchairs, shell-back chairs, and stools. Consequently there was a constant need in Theta for innovation in designs and fabrics and the owner-managers visited many trade fairs looking for ideas. They imported cloths and chair shells from abroad and commissioned many designs in Britain. After designs had been worked out, the next problem was to match them with a suitable cloth, there being little point in having an expensive design and a cheap cloth.

Yet it was not just firms at the fashion end of the trade that had design problems. Delta's owner-manager, for example, felt that radical rethinking in the designs of nursery furniture was required if the company wished to compete seriously. The company had not employed a designer and in the past had used the local College of Art to help them out, but the owner-manager felt that radical rethinking was now required in relation to the whole range of the company products. Sales, especially in nursery furniture, had been falling, largely because the range of Delta products was old fashioned, outdated, and something of a luxury good: "Modern mothers don't want draped wicker cribs--they want plastic carry-cots and push chairs." If Delta was going to compete with such companies as

Halex and Mothercare it would have to alter its products. This would mean a substantial change of image and a movement toward plastic processing. It was Delta's owner-manager's view that while a larger company had the advantages stemming from full-time employment of market researchers and designers, small firms like his were more flexible and could switch production quickly in order to keep in line with fashion changes.

NOTES

1. E. Aves, "The Furniture Trades," in Life and Labour of the People of London, Charles Booth, ed. (London: Macmillan, 1893).

2. The Economist Intelligence Unit, A Study of the Furniture Industry and Trade in the United Kingdom (London: EIU, 1958).

3. Furniture and Timber Industry Training Board, Report and Statement of Accounts for the year ended 31st March 1971, Appendix XV.

4. Furniture Trade and Consumer, A Consumer Council Study (London: H.M.S.O., 1965).

5. J. L. Oliver, The Development and Structure of the Furniture Industry (Oxford: Pergamon, 1966).

6. G. Chalkidis, "Obstacles in the road to higher productivity in the Furniture Industry," in An Economic Review for the Furniture Industry 1964-65 (Stevenage: Furniture Development Council, 1966).

7. See, for example, J. St. G. Jephcott, "The National Plan and the Furniture Industry," in An Economic Review for the Furniture Industry 1964-65, op. cit.

8. Ibid.

9. "A Review of the American Household Furniture Industry," in An Economic Review for the Furniture Industry, 1968-69 (Stevenage: Furniture Development Council, 1970).

10. Union Europeenne de l'Ameublement, Statistical series, published annually by the Furniture Development Council.

11. K. B. Mayer and S. Goldstein, The First Two Years: Problems of Small Firm Growth and Survival, Small Business Administration research series No. 2 (Washington, D.C.: Small Business Administration, 1961).

12. For further discussion on this and related problems, see Small Firms--Report of the Committee of Inquiry on Small Firms, chapter 4 (London: H.M.S.O., 1971).

6

FAMILY AND KINSHIP
IN THE SMALL FIRM

FAMILY OWNERSHIP AND CONTROL

One of the objectives of the descriptive survey was to provide information on the ownership and control of the small firms under study and, consequently, managing directors were asked who were the major shareholders of their company and to what extent these shareholders were involved in the running of the firm. In 43 out of the 50 companies, owner-managers and their wives held the majority of the shares. In 22 of these 43 companies the controlling interest was held by the managing-director or by the managing director and his wife, and in the others the shares were divided between two, three, or four families, all of whom were actively engaged in the management of the business but none of whom had an overall controlling interest. Two of the 50 companies were partnerships and one was run by a sole proprietor. In two of the remaining four companies the controlling interest was held by the mother of one of the managers, in one the shares were split equally between two families, only one of which was active in the management of the business, and in one the shareholding of the owner-managers and their families was not sufficiently large to give them control. Without exception, therefore, the companies were autonomous family firms in which there was virtually no divorce between ownership and control. Of 235 managers and supervisors employed, 99 (or 42 percent) had some ownership stake in the business. In addition about 64 percent of all shareholders in the 50 companies were active in some way in the running of the business, the wives of owner-managers often providing part-time secretarial help rather than being involved in a direct executive capacity within the firm.

Of the 229 managers interviewed in the course of the descriptive survey, 86 (37.6 percent) were shareholders in the companies where they worked. Of eight owner-managers who were not shareholders, one was a sole proprietor, six were partners in their business, and one was sole owner of a company that had no issued capital. Of the 229 managers, 45 percent were related in some way to some other person in the company where they worked. Table 6.1 indicates the extent of kinship ties within the company for each occupational group: the owner-managers, the nonshareholding managers, and the full-time supervisors and working foremen. As can be seen, 78 percent of owner managers were related to some other person in their companies, usually to other owner-managers, compared with 25 percent of the nonshareholding managers and 27 percent of the full-time supervisors and working foremen. Again, comparative data is not available. In many large firms the pattern is presumably reversed with less in-company kinship ties among the higher levels of management than among supervisory staff, the former being recruited from a wider geographical area than the latter.

TABLE 6.1

Kinship by Management Category

| Management Category | Managers with Relations Employed in the Company | |
	Number	Percent
Owner-managers (n = 94)	73	77.7
Nonshareholding managers (n = 87)	22	25.3
Full-time supervisors and working foremen (n = 48)	8	16.7
All managers (n = 229)	103	45.0

Source: Compiled by the author.

EMPLOYMENT OF THE OWNER-MANAGERS' RELATIVES

The 73 owner-managers who worked in the same companies as their relatives were employed in 39 out of the 50 companies in the descriptive survey. In 30 of these 39 companies (see Table 6.2) owner-managers worked alongside relatives in other managerial

TABLE 6.2

The Employment of Owner-Managers' Relatives

	Jewish Companies	Non-Jewish Companies	Total
Companies where owner-managers' relatives were only employed in managerial or supervisory positions	4	14	18
Companies where owner-managers' relatives were employed both in managerial or supervisory positions and in other positions	5	7	12
Companies where owner-managers' relatives were only employed in nonmanagerial/nonsupervisory positions	2	7	9
Companies where owner-managers' relatives were not employed	1	10	11
Total, above items	12	38	50
Companies with father and son working together	5	13	18
Companies with father and son-in-law working together	--	5	5
Companies with female relatives employed in secretarial or clerical work	7[a]	9[b]	16
Companies with brothers working together	4	3	7
Companies with cousins working together	--	5	5
Companies with brothers-in-law working together	--	7	7

[a]5 wives of owner-managers and 2 sisters
[b]7 wives of owner-managers, 1 sister, and 1 sister-in-law

Source: Compiled by the author.

or supervisory positions, and in 21 they worked with relatives in other positions in the company such as clerk, secretary, upholsterer, framemaker, or machinist. Table 6.2 introduces into the analysis a distinction between the Jewish and non-Jewish companies in the descriptive survey, it being likely that cultural factors and traditions will play some part in the extent of kinship ties in small firms. As Stephen Aris has pointed out, "The ethos that surrounds a family business can be extraordinarily powerful and seductive: the family is the firm and the firm is the family, the success of one reinforcing the power and glory of the other. And when that family happens to be Jewish, where family pride and tradition is particularly strong, the process is often doubly potent."[1] Almost one-quarter of the 50 companies in the descriptive survey were Jewish businesses, the furniture industry being one of those industries where Jewish immigrants from the Russo-Polish empire gained a foothold at the end of the nineteenth century, particularly in the ghettoes of London's East End and of industrial centers like Leeds and Glasgow. The figures in Table 6.2 are small and therefore not conclusive, but they do suggest that there is a greater tendency for family members to be employed within the small Jewish furniture firm than within the small non-Jewish furniture firm, and that the patterns in the employment of relatives (and, therefore, in what constitutes "family") are different, the Jewish firms being relatively stronger in terms of blood ties, that is in the employment of relatives from the family of procreation, and the non-Jewish firms being relatively stronger in terms of marriage ties, that is in the employment of relatives from the family of affiliation.

It is necessary to check, however, that these apparent differences in kinship employment are not merely factors stemming from differences in the ages of the firms under review. In fact 7 of the 12 Jewish companies were founder-managed and 5 were inheritor-managed firms compared with 18 founder-managed non-Jewish firms and 20 inheritor-managed non-Jewish firms. This would, therefore, tend to underline the different patterns described rather than to account for them in terms of some generational variable. It would possibly suggest, also, that small Jewish firms are likely to be seen as family enterprises from the outset, whereas non-Jewish companies are seen initially as individual founder-managed enterprises that later bring in family members primarily as a means of resolving problems of management succession. Thus of the 10 non-Jewish companies where owner-managers' relatives were not employed at the time of the descriptive survey, 7 were founder-managed businesses.

KINSH'P AND ORGANIZATION STRUCTURES
IN SMALL FIRMS

The organization structures of the 50 companies in the descriptive survey were very varied and in most cases reflected specific
developments in the firm or the relatively haphazard introduction of
sons or other relations into the business. Consequently it is dangerous to generalize about there being any particular patterns of organizational development in small companies. Nevertheless the companies
were divided into three major types and one minor type according to
the overt nature of their ownership, control, and management structures. These types were christened monocratic, oligarchic, patrician, and managerial.

Monocratic companies were those where the overall control of
company policy was in the hands of one man, the managing director
or sole proprietor, who was also the majority shareholder and who
was supported by a number of specialist managerial staff, none of
whom were shareholders in the company and none of whom were related by birth to him in any way. Of the 50 companies, 12 were owned
and managed by monocrats. They ranged in size from a company employing 29 persons to a company employing 73, the average size of
firm in this group having a staff of about 45 and the median companies
having staffs of 39 and 43, respectively. The specialist managers
most commonly employed in these companies were a works or production manager and a manager in charge of office administration and accounts. On average there were two specialist managers per company.

Oligarchic companies were those where the overall direction of
company policy was shared between two or more owner-managers,
each of whom, in addition to being concerned with general policy,
had some specialist functions to perform. These managers were not
necessarily related to one another but they were all shareholders or
partners in the firm. Of the 50 companies, 18 had an oligarchic
structure. They ranged in size from a company employing 29 persons to a company employing 65, the average size of firm having a
staff of about 41 and the median companies having staffs of 39 and 40,
respectively. In terms of size, therefore, these companies were
very similar to those run by the monocrats. Most oligarchic companies appeared to fall into one of two kinds. First there were the
"de facto" partnerships. Although only two of the companies were
partnerships in the legal sense, a further six were partnerships in
terms of their organization structure, some of them having maintained that form of organization while transferring from the status
of a legal partnership to that of a private limited liability company.
The second kind of oligarchic company was the "father and son" kind
where responsibilities were shared between the father and one or

more of his sons. There were eight such companies and in two of
them the fathers were only working part time, having passed over
most of the control of day-to-day matters to their sons. Of the remaining two oligarchic companies, one was run by four brothers
each with 25 percent of the issued share capital, and the other was
run by two brothers and their sister. Very few specialist managers
were employed in these companies since most functions were carried
out by the owner-managers themselves. Of these 18 companies, 7
employed works or production managers who were not shareholders
or partners and 2 employed a manager in charge of office administration and accounts.

Patrician companies were those where the overall control of
the company was in the hands of one man, the managing director,
supported by a number of specialist managerial staff, some or all of
whom were either shareholders in the company or were related to
the managing director in some way. The patrician company differed
from the monocratic one in that it employed more than one owner-
manager or more than one member of the managing director's family
in the business, and from the oligarchic company in that the other
owner-managers or family members did not share on equal terms
with the managing director in the general direction of company policy.
Of the 50 companies, 18 were classified as patrician. Although they
ranged in size from a company employing 28 persons to one employing 70, on average they were larger than the monocratic or oligarchic
companies, the average patrician firm having 53 staff, and the median companies employing 57 persons each. Partly because they
were mostly larger firms, these 18 companies employed a relatively
high proportion of specialist managers, about half of whom were
shareholders in their companies or relatives of the managing director.
For a number of companies the patrician form of organization structure may well be a transitional stage between a monocratic structure
and an oligarchic one of the father and son kind, with the possibility
of the company reverting to monocracy on the retirement of the father.

In the two managerial companies, although there were owner-
managers employed in the firm, effective executive control was in
the hands of a nonshareholding general manager. In one the owner
and managing director, although still employed part time in the business, was past retirement age and, having no sons or relations in
the company, had handed over control. The other company was run
by a general manager in conjunction with the son and son-in-law of
the 62-year-old chairman and managing director.

Examples of characteristic organization charts for each of the
four types of company structure identified are set out in Figure 6.1.
What becomes clear from the analysis of the organization of these
small companies is that to understand small company organization

FIGURE 6.1

Management Structures in Small Firms

MONOCRATIC

* Managing Director

Works Manager   Sales Manager   Office Administrator
                                          and Accountant

OLIGARCHIC

* Joint Managing Director   * Joint Managing Director

Works Manager

PATRICIAN

* Managing Director

Works Manager   * Sales Director   Company Secretary
                     (son-in-law)

MANAGERIAL

* Managing Director
(Part-time; retired)

General Manager

Production Manager   Sales Representative

---

*indicates shareholder

Source: Compiled by the author.

98

structure it is necessary to understand both the extent to which managers are shareholders in their companies and the family relationships that exist between them. Managerial structures in small firms often tend to be built around the available managers rather than managers recruited specifically to fill particular boxes on some organization chart. In addition the existence of close family relationships is seen in some firms as making it unecessary to differentiate precise areas of functional responsibility, the employed members of the family sharing equal controlling responsibilities and all having a finger in the major decision-making and problem-solving activities of the firm.

PROBLEMS OF THE SMALL FAMILY FIRM

The small firms studied were, by and large, not so family dominated as to adopt the slogan attributed to textile families in the North of France: "I have another child so I must acquire another mill."[2] Nevertheless some did share a number of common problems stemming from the family ties that existed within them, problems of providing for management succession either by bringing in younger family members or by attempting to attract able executives into firms where ultimate authority and control might never be relinquished by owning families, problems of personal relationships and family feuds being carried over into business relationships, problems arising from the employment of family members with limited business education, experience, and abilities, and problems arising from conflicts between the best interests of the business and the best interests of the family and from the intrusion of business affairs into family life.

In some cases owner-managers felt trapped in their family businesses. Sam Kerry, for example, was an owner-manager who felt that no other realistic employment alternatives were open to him. Sam, who was 41, and his brother Vic Kerry, aged 47, owned and managed a small modern upholstery business. At one time the two brothers had been union organizers, what they described as "union heavy boys--Vehement Vic and Solidarity Sam" in the days when the upholsterers' union was second only to the printers' in strength. Their own business, however, was a nonunion shop and their management methods were, they claimed, more democratic than when they had been "vicious" union shop chairmen. Vic Kerry's principal tasks in their business were the development of new designs and new production methods, buying fabrics, seeing sales representatives, supervising production work, and carrying out any needed machine maintenance. At the time of the survey he was most fully engaged in the production development work associated with new designs, which was, he felt, the most critical and important of his various tasks. His most pressing short-term problem was a transport problem. The growth of orders had outstripped the company's own vehicle capacity and contractors were not found to be very reliable. Vic Kerry recognized that the company would eventually have to purchase more vehicles itself but finance was not available to make this possible in the short term. Longer-term problems were foreseen as being mainly geared to the expansion of the company and the fulfillment of Vic Kerry's own considerable ambitions. Vic Kerry did not find any of his present activities or tasks difficult:

> I find certain aspects of the work unpleasant--
> particularly any office work, dealing with tele-
> phone queries, standing in for my brother on
> bonus and wage questions--but not difficult.
> Starting up a business is a matter of not knowing
> the obstacles; if you knew the obstacles you'd
> never start. General education is important,
> knowing what the public feel, knowing what they
> like and then making what they like; most people
> in the world are like me, not like Lord Boothby.

Brother Sam's principal tasks included liaison between customers and the company, occasional selling to buyers from large retailers, costings and prices, general supervision and mucking-in where required. He was also responsible for salaries, wages, and agents' commission, and for invoicing and accounts. Sam Kerry felt that he spent most of his time answering the telephone and that the most pressing short-term problem in his job was the lack of liquidity in the company's finances; this he felt was mainly because of the economic climate with its corresponding increase in bad debts and the greater extension of credit to customers. The most important long-term problem that Sam Kerry foresaw was a marketing problem: "The small retailers are going out of business and, if we are to keep our share of the market, we have to get in with the large stores. This means a greater financial requirement, both to give the kind of discounts needed and to employ more of our own representatives rather than agents. If we had the money we would like a top-notch sales director in the business." Sam Kerry did not find any aspects of his work difficult although he, like his brother, found no satisfaction in office work, other than seeing a good month's figures in the book.

> Coming in with a large order gives me sat-
> isfaction and so does the odd time when I do

a mechanical job like fixing a sewing machine. And
I enjoy a laugh. I enjoy going down to the cutting
shop and having a bawdy laugh--making people feel
they work with me and not for me. I enjoy the personal side. I think I would have made a good personnel officer in a large company. But I'm trapped
in this company now, and I work largely out of a
sense of moral duty.

Some of the difficulties and frustrations facing the nonshareholding manager in the small family firm are to be seen in the cases
of Mr. Landaeur and Mr. Mobley. Landaeur was company secretary,
but not a shareholder, in a long-established cabinet furniture business. At the time of the survey visit he was aged 53 and had been
with his employer for ten years, during the first two years of which
he had been office manager. His principal activities and tasks were
keeping financial and cost records dealing with sales correspondence,
preparing a monthly sales analysis, and handling all the general office
administration. He was also to some extent involved in estimation,
in interviewing customers, in liaison with the company's sales representatives, and in the control and supervision of the office staff.
Most of Landaeur's time was spent, he thought, on keeping the financial records straight. He felt that the greatest potential contribution
that he could make to the business would be the provision of cost figures but this was not being done at present since the managing director
did not see the need. Although he found nothing in the job itself very
difficult, Landaeur did mention two difficulties. The first was that
he found difficulty in controlling and supervising the office staff. The
second was that he found difficulty in getting policy decisions from
the directors:

There is a complete lack of policy decisions. Decisions are always particular, always have to suit
particular cases. Any ruling on discounts, for example, will be changed by the directors on a personal basis and often the new ruling won't be communicated to me. It is not a training problem.
Basically the company is production oriented and
there is an administration gap at director level.
I love figures, but the biggest satisfaction I get
from my work is that I feel I'm needed. We have
two practical directors who need the support of a
reasonable administration, but they don't use me.
I spend much of my time doing work that I feel
could be done just as well by someone who is not
paid so much as myself.

Mr. Mobley, at the time of the survey, was the 37-year-old general manager of a cabinet furniture business in which the 62-year-old founder, chairman, and managing director was only partly employed, the business being run by the general manager in conjunction with the chairman's son and son-in-law. Mobley had no shareholding in the business but had been promised a share of the annual profit, although no fixed percentage was set down in the agreement he had with the chairman. Mobley had previously worked for 20 years in a large company of shopfitters where he had worked his way up from apprentice joiner to works manager. At the time of the survey he had been with his present company for eight months. He described his principal activities and tasks as "progress chasing, making sure that everyone else is doing their job, installing systems into the factory and particularly into stores organization, and organizing development and prototype work." Mobley thought his most pressing short-term problem in his job was one of space, a problem that could largely be solved by changing production methods and plant layout to eliminate work-in-progress queues. His most important long-term problems were, he felt, problems of the quality of the supervision in the company and the quality of some of the labor employed. In particular he felt that some of the supervisors were not of the caliber that would be required and that they would not respond to training. Mobley felt that the main difficulty in his job was the difficulty of being a "professional" manager in a family firm: "I have a fairly free hand and things are moving in the right direction, but the only thing that matters ultimately is the profit overall. If the company doesn't make a profit, the son and son-in-law still have a job, but I haven't. So things have to be done my way. I have to be the dominant personality. The real problem is that you don't know where you stand with a family company. The others have a stake in the business but I have no long-term financial return."

However, it is not only the "professional" managers in small family firms who have difficult problems of adjustment to make. In some cases the pressure on the younger members of the family can be equally intense, even when they are crown princes. James Nevin, for example, was the 28-year-old production director of a cabinet furniture company and retail furnishers founded in 1860 by the grandfather of its present managing director. The managing director, who was aged 70, was in the process of gradually handing over control of the company to his nephew, James Nevin. James was the only relation of the managing director employed in the company, although many other relations were nonexecutive shareholders. There had been a past history of bitter family disputes over the policies to be pursued by the company and it was still one of the principal worries of the managing director that he had been unable to provide the members of the family with any return on their investments during the last few years preceding the survey visit. James Nevin's main activities and tasks, at the time of the survey visit, were buying, financial control, setting policies on retail and contract sales, looking at new markets and developing new projects, preparing reports and figures for board meetings, and general troubleshooting and problem-solving in the factory. The most difficult aspect of his job was, he thought, "convincing other members of the board that what I want to do is right, persuading others, who are older and differently motivated, to change." James Nevin listed three pressing short-term problems: (1) putting the retail side of the business on a viable basis, (2) increasing throughput in the works within existing limits of fixed overheads, and (3) planning for future new lines and new people. On a long-term basis

> my most important problem is to decide who is going to be on the board in three years' time. I shall be managing director and I have to build a team round me at the same time as running down the old team, fading them out. This is partly a problem of personal confidence. I am always questioning whether or not I am doing the right thing; it is important that I realize my own mistakes quickly and don't let them run on. One of the troubles with the company in the past was that, partly because of family divisions, directors would never admit that they had been wrong and so uneconomic projects would be persevered with almost to the point of total disaster. The thing that most annoys me is when people say "but we've always done it like that." The company has gradually and painfully realized that tradition in itself is not sufficient reason for doing anything.

NOTES

1. Stephen Aris, The Jews in Business (London: Jonathan Cape, 1970).

2. David Granick, The European Executive (London: Weidenfeld and Nicholson, 1962).

EDUCATIONAL AND OCCUPATIONAL HISTORIES OF OWNER-MANAGERS

EDUCATIONAL BACKGROUNDS

There have been a number of research studies in the United Kingdom that have set out to describe the educational backgrounds and career histories of industrial directors and managers. Some of these have been designed to find out who reaches the top and what kind of career patterns they follow, and some to find out whether changes in the educational system are reflected in a greater "professionalization" of management. Such studies have been almost exclusively of managers from large companies. Copeman's study, for example, was concerned only with the directors of public joint stock companies with assets at that time of £1 million or more.[1] Similarly, the Acton Society Trust Study included information on the educational backgrounds and career patterns of managers in a number of private manufacturing organizations employing 10,000 or more persons.[2] Clements' study looked at the career patterns of nearly 700 managers at all levels within what were predominantly public limited companies.[3] A study by Clark investigated the social and educational backgrounds and career patterns of a number of managers in public and private companies in the Manchester area.[4] Of the 36 private industrial firms taking part in this study, 12 employed less than 1,000 people, but the smallest firm included was one of 600 employees. International comparative studies also tend to deal solely with managers from large companies. One such study, sponsored by the European Institute of Business Administration (INSEAD), set out to answer the question, "Who are the chief executives who run the largest companies in Europe?"[5] All the companies in the sample were among the 500 largest in their respective countries. In spite of the careful qualifications of the researchers themselves, the large company bias of these studies tends to be ignored in the ensuing generalizations about "the characteristics of the modern manager."

The research on which this book is based provides a useful opportunity, therefore, to look at some of these generalizations about management and the manager in the light of the characteristics of small firms and their managers. This is particularly appropriate in the context of educational backgrounds and career histories, for in this area some readily comparable data from the large firm studies can be set alongside the research findings in the owner-manager study. One of the objectives of the descriptive survey was to describe the qualifications, experience, and past training of managers in small firms. During the course of the survey each manager was asked a number of questions designed to gain some understanding of his background and experience both within his present company and in the furniture industry generally. Questions on educational background covered secondary schooling, age on leaving school, examinations passed at school, full-time and part-time further education and qualifications obtained, and membership of professional bodies. Questions on work experience covered previous companies worked for, position and length of service, and details of the different jobs held in the manager's employing company and the amount of time spent in each job. The purpose of this chapter is to present an analysis of some of this information alongside similar information collected from studies of managers of large companies and to highlight the differences that exist between the two groups.

Table 7.1 summarizes some of the information available on the educational backgrounds of managers. It must be borne in mind that the research studies are spread over the period from 1955 to 1970 and that, consequently, a number of the variations, particularly in the proportion of managers who had received an elementary schooling only, will be affected by the 1944 Education Act. The most useful comparison is probably between the educational backgrounds of Clark's managers and those of the managers in small furniture firms.[6] A number of points emerge from such a comparison. First, 56 percent of the managers in the Clark study had attended grammar schools, compared with 24 percent of the managers in the small-firm descriptive survey. Second, twice as many, proportionately, of the small-firm managers had received an elementary education only, 34 percent compared with 17 percent of Clark's managers. Third, 22 percent of Clark's "top" managers had been educated privately as had 22 percent of the small-firm owner-managers. But 32 percent of the owner-managers had received elementary schooling only, compared with 12 percent of Clark's "top" managers. A further point of interest in Table 7.1 is the difference, in the furniture industry survey, between the educational backgrounds of owner-

TABLE 7.1

Educational Backgrounds of Managers
(in percent)

Research Study	Type of School Attended			
	Elementary	Secondary, Excluding Grammar	Grammar	Private
Large Firm Studies				
Copeman (1955)				
Directors	11	31		58
Acton Society Trust (1956)				
All managers	20	33	28	19
"Top" managers	7	60		33
Clark (1966)				
All managers	17	15	56	12
Managers (private industry)	18	15	55	13
"Top" managers (private industry)	12	18	48	22
Directors	11	15	48	26
Small Furniture Firms (1970)				
All managers	34	28	24	14
Owner-managers	32	22	23	22
Managers (non-shareholding)	26	31	32	10
Supervisors	54	33	10	2
Owner-managers-founders	42	32	13	13
Hereditary owner-managers	21	19	34	26

Source: Compiled by the author.

managers who founded their own firms or were first-generation management, and owner-managers who had joined an established family
business and were second- or third-generation management or were
more distantly related to the founder of the firm. Of the first generation owner-managers, 74 percent had received elementary or nonselective secondary schooling compared with 40 percent of the hereditary owner-managers; 13 percent had attended grammar schools,
compared with 34 percent of hereditary owner-managers; and 13 percent had been educated privately, compared with 26 percent of those
who had joined established family businesses. In addition a number
of the managers who had received grammar school or private education were the sons of owner-managers but they did not as yet have
any shareholding in the family business. The pattern is, then, a
familiar one. While those who have "come up the hard way" extol
the virtues of hard work and practical experience, they frequently
try to ensure that their sons receive a more formal and theoretical
education.

   As can be seen from Table 7.2, which shows the schooling of
managers by three age categories (under 40, 40-54, and 55 and over),
different patterns emerge from the various studies. Comparison
again between the Clark study and the small-firm study shows the extent to which managers in large companies are increasingly being
drawn from the grammar schools. Almost 36.6 percent of Clark's
managers aged 55 and over attended grammar schools, as did 53.7
percent of his managers in the 40-54 age group and 71.3 percent in
the under-40 age group. This change was primarily at the expense
of those who had received only an elementary or nonselective secondary education. Here the figures decline from 53.7 percent of the
managers aged 55 and over to 18.3 percent of those aged under 40.
The pattern of change in the educational backgrounds of owner-
managers and managers of small furniture companies is somewhat
different. Of these managers in the under-40 age group, 40.9 percent had attended grammar schools compared with 29.8 percent of
those in the 55 and over age group. At the same time almost a third
(31.8 percent) of the under-40 group had been educated privately
compared with about a tenth (10.5 percent) of the 55 and over group.
The figures for the 40-54 age group in the descriptive survey did not,
however, fit into any pattern, primarily, it is assumed, because of
the disruptive effect of the depression and World War II on the educational opportunities of a large number of those born in the 1920s.

   The most marked difference in further education undertaken by
managers in the large company studies and managers in small furniture firms is in the proportion of managers who had attended university. Of the managers in the Acton Society Trust study, 19 percent

TABLE 7.2

Schooling of Managers by Age
(in percent)

Age and Research Study	Type of School Attended			
	Elementary	Secondary, Excluding Grammar	Grammar	Private
Under 40				
Acton Society Trust				
All managers[a]	8.3	31.3	32.5	27.8
Clark				
All managers[b]	7.9	10.4	71.3	10.4
Small furniture firms				
Owner-managers				
and managers[c]	--	27.3	40.9	31.8
40-54				
Acton Society Trust				
All managers[a]	20.8	33.7	25.6	19.8
Clark				
All managers[b]	15.3	16.9	53.7	14.1
Small furniture firms				
Owner-managers				
and managers[c]	46.6	37.9	10.3	5.2
55 and over				
Acton Society Trust				
All managers[a]	33.8	30.6	26.7	8.9
Clark				
All managers[b]	34.3	19.4	36.6	9.7
Small furniture firms				
Owner-managers				
and managers[c]	45.6	14.0	29.8	10.5

[a]age in 1954.

[b]age at June 30, 1964.

[c]age at January 1, 1970.

Source: Compiled by the author.

were graduates as were 30 percent of the Acton Society's "top" managers. Of Copeman's directors, 36 percent had attended university and 7 percent had studied at the postgraduate level. An NEDC survey published in 1965 showed that 43 percent of entrants to management trainee positions in a sample of 102 "large" companies had obtained qualifications from a university or a college of advanced technology as had 42 percent of all new recruits or promotions to first management positions.[7] In the Clark study 35 percent of all the managers were graduates. Of the Clark managers who were aged over 54, 18 percent were graduates, compared with 31 percent of those in the 40-54 age group and 52 percent of those under the age of 40.

Among the 229 managers in the furniture industry survey there was only one graduate, a pharmacist who had sold his chemist's shop and joined the family chairframe business. It is interesting to note that the INSEAD study of European top executives found that Britain's chief executives were the least highly educated, 40 percent of them having been to university, compared with 55 percent of Netherlands chief executives, 78 percent of German and Italian chief executives, 85 percent of Belgian, and 89 percent of French chief executives who had received a university education.[8] However, 20 percent of the British chief executives who were not university graduates were chartered accountants.

Although there was only one graduate among the furniture survey managers, 20 percent of the owner-managers and 16 percent of the managers had attended a full-time course of further education since leaving school. No comparable figures on full-time further education are available from the large-company research studies. The Clark study does, however, contain information on the part-time further education of managers. Of Clark's private industry managers, 72 percent had at some time in their careers taken part in part-time further education courses compared with 59 percent of the owner-managers and 51 percent of the managers in the furniture industry survey. Table 7.3 breaks down the part-time further education of these three groups of managers according to the type of school attended. The general picture that emerges is that in most cases, irrespective of schooling, managers in large companies in the private sector had, at various stages of their careers, been more willing to undertake some form of part-time further education than managers in small companies in the furniture industry. Thus, for example, 85 percent of Clark's private industry managers who had received only elementary schooling had subsequently studied on a part-time basis, compared with 63 percent of furniture owner-managers and 48 percent of furniture managers.

TABLE 7.3

Part-Time Further Education of Managers by Schooling
(in percent)

| Percentage of Managers Who Had Received Part-Time Further Education | Type of School Attended | | | |
	Elementary	Secondary, Excluding Grammar	Grammar	Private
Clark--private industry managers	85.4	87.0	70.0	49.4
Small furniture firms Owner-managers	63.3	47.6	63.6	57.1
Managers	47.8	63.0	53.6	11.1

Source: Compiled by the author.

The most common subject areas for part-time study by owner-managers and managers in small furniture companies were craft, commercial, and general education courses. Only 8 percent of all the managers in the furniture survey had attended part-time courses in management subjects, and only 11 percent had received any kind of formal management or supervisory education, either on a full-time or a part-time basis. Even where managers had enrolled in part-time courses ostensibly leading to some kind of professional qualification, in most cases the qualification was never obtained. Those managers who were members of professional bodies (13 percent of the total) had not normally progressed to membership through any kind of educational qualification. This was clear when the "professional bodies" to which small furniture company managers belonged were analyzed. There were only three such bodies to which more than one manager among the 229 interviewed belonged, namely the Institute of Directors, the British Institute of Management, and the Society of Industrial Artists. Among the other organizations to which "professional membership" was claimed were the Liverymen of the City of London, the Incorporated British Institute of Certified Carpenters, the Institute of Machine Woodworking Technologists, the Liverymen of the Worshipful Company of Furniture Makers, and a number of accountancy associations. There were, however, no fully qualified chartered accountants among the managers interviewed.

Of all the managers in the Clark study, 21 percent had no qualifications whatsoever in the formal sense while a further 15.5

percent had what were described as only limited qualifications (for example, City and Guilds, Ordinary National Certificate [O.N.C.], Ordinary National Diploma [O.N.D.]). In the public sector only just over 5 percent of the managers had no formal qualifications compared with 24 percent of private industry managers. A study of managers in two large iron and steel companies indicated that in both companies more than half the managers had no formal educational qualifications at all, although in the case of younger managers, those born between 1919 and 1940, the proportion with no educational qualifications had dropped below half and in the case of one company was, for the group born between 1929 and 1940, as low as 10.5 percent.[9] What is clear from all the research studies is that the nature of the industry, the size of firm, and the ages of managers will to a large extent account for differences in managers' educational backgrounds and qualifications. Generalizations that do not take account of these three factors will be of limited value. This is underlined by the findings of a comparative study of the backgrounds and careers of managers from "large" companies in a number of different industries.[10] The chemical industry, for example, predominantly managed by university graduates, ex-grammar school boys drawn from the middle and upper working classes and trained for management by their employers, was seen as typifying the modern capital-intensive science-based industry. The textile industry, on the other hand, represented a more traditional and established pattern and was managed by older, less formally qualified, more experienced men, one-third of whom held neither a university degree nor any kind of formal qualification.

All the research studies of the educational backgrounds of large company managers have underlined the increasing emphasis on formal qualifications as a precondition for entry into management. One of the aims of the Acton Society Trust study, for example, was to find out to what extent opportunities to gain promotion from the shop floor were diminishing. Analysis of the backgrounds of the younger managers led to the conclusion that in the future managers would be better educated and have more formal educational qualifications, thereby reducing the proportion of managers rising from the bottom. Similarly, Clark's study indicated the growing preponderance of grammar-school-educated managers and of graduates among large company managers and led to the conclusion that, while managers were better educated than in the past, the opportunity for a man to leave school at an early age and by experience and loyalty obtain managerial status seemed to have declined. In terms of educational background and attainment, five main points of contrast emerge from the study of managers in small furniture firms. First, a comparatively high proportion of such small firm managers had received an elementary only or a nonselective secondary education. Second, nearly two-thirds

of the owner-managers and managers had not passed any kind of
formal examination while at school. Third, there were virtually no
graduates among the managers of these small companies. Fourth,
the involvement of small-firm managers in full-time or part-time
further education studies was less than that of managers in large
companies. Fifth, very few small-firm managers had, as a result
of their further education studies, any formal qualifications or had
received any formal management education.

The picture that emerges, therefore, is that, whereas managers
in both large and small companies are increasingly being drawn from
grammar and private schools, there is a widening gap between the two
groups in terms of educational attainment, both in terms of achievement at school and in terms of formal qualifications obtained through
the further education system. It is clear that managers in small furniture companies, while starting out with generally less advantageous
formal schooling, are not able to close the qualifications gap between
themselves and large-firm managers by intensive and effective use of
the further education system. Presumably, therefore, it will become
increasingly difficult for managers of small firms to move into positions within larger organizations, especially outside the industry or
industries where they have gained their practical experience.

There are some pointers here for those who are concerned with
management education and training in the context of the small firm.
One of the themes of this book, amplified in Chapter 11, is that the
content of management education and training programs for managers
of small companies needs to be different from the content of programs
aimed at large-firm managers. The present analysis underlines the
relatively low level of educational attainment and lack of formal management education among small company managers and draws attention to two needs. First, there is a need to ensure that the starting
point of any particular management education or training activity
aimed at small-firm managers is geared appropriately to their existing levels of understanding. Second, there is a need to ensure that
the methods of teaching adopted, or the learning opportunities offered,
recognize the difficulties that small-firm managers will undoubtedly
face if they are expected to return to "classroom" situations. Some
consequences of these requirements would seem to be that by and
large management education and training activities for small company
managers should be tailor-made to the requirements of well-defined
managerial groups, should emphasize learning by doing and by drawing on the experiences of the managers themselves, and should not
be mixed up with activities designed for the more formally qualified
professional managers of large companies. These are points that will
be amplified in Chapter 13 when we come to consider the education,
training, and development process in the small firm.

FIRST FULL-TIME OCCUPATIONS

Table 7.4 compares the first full-time occupations of managers from large companies in the private sector, as described by Clark, with those of owner-managers and managers from small furniture companies. As can be seen, a higher proportion of the small-firm managers started work as apprentices or in some manual occupation, 29 percent and 14 percent respectively for the furniture industry managers compared with 15 percent and 9 percent for private industry managers in the Clark study. In the Acton Society Trust study 21 percent of all the managers started work as craft apprentices or manual operatives. Of Copeman's directors' original occupations, 6 percent were in a skilled trade and 2 percent were in unskilled or semiskilled work.

TABLE 7.4

First Full-Time Occupations of Managers
(in percent)

First Full-Time Occupation	Research Study	
	Clark (1966) Managers (private industry)	Small Furniture Firms (1970) Owner-Managers and Managers
Manual	9	14
Apprenticeship	15	29
Clerical	26	21
Technician/draftsman	17	6
Laboratory assistant	16	1
Sales	5	9
Trainees	8	16
Managerial	2	4
Professional	2	1

Source: Compiled by the author.

One feature of all the studies is the relatively high proportion of managers who started their careers in clerical positions. Of the Acton Society Trust managers, 30 percent started in clerical work, as did over 25 percent of Clark's managers and over 20 percent of the owner-managers and managers in the descriptive survey. A rather smaller proportion (26 percent) of Copeman's directors held their first positions in clerical occupations but, nevertheless, Copeman does comment that the ex-clerk who proved so alert and became so indispensable that he was promoted right to the top, even though he did not at any time take professional qualifications, was a fairly common phenomenon. It would appear, however, that opportunities to go from office boy to board room were diminishing in a way similar to those for promotion from the factory floor. Just as only about one in eight of Clark's managers under the age of 40 had served an apprenticeship, compared with more than one in five of the managers over the age of 54, so only 19 percent of his under-40 managers had started out in clerical work compared with over 30 percent of those over 54 years. Clark concluded that many of the future managers would come from the ranks of laboratory assistant, technician, or draftsman and trainee, since over half of his managers in the under-40 age group were from these categories.

The occupations of technician, draftsman, and laboratory assistant are of relatively little importance in the context of small furniture companies since very few such firms employ these specialized categories of staff other than in furniture design. Nevertheless, 12 percent of owner-managers and managers under the age of 40 held first full-time occupations as technicians or draftsmen, compared with only 2 percent of such managers aged over 54 years. In other ways, too, the trends in the small furniture companies are similar to those of the large firms in Clark's study. Thus, for example, just under 50 percent of the owner-managers and managers aged 55 and over had started their careers as apprentices or in manual occupations, compared with just over 25 percent of owner-managers and managers in the under-40 age group. Similarly, 25 percent of the 55 and over age group started out in clerical work compared with 17 percent of those in the under-40 age group. It is clear that there is still ample opportunity in small furniture companies for the young man who starts out as an apprentice, or in manual or clerical work, and who has limited formal qualifications and no family connections in the company, to be promoted to a managerial position, but nevertheless, it appears likely that in the future such promotions will go increasingly to those who have started their careers in design, technical, or sales positions.

Perhaps one of the most surprising aspects of Table 7.4 is the large proportion of owner-managers and managers in the small-firm study who started out as trainees or in managerial positions, 20 percent of the total compared with 10 percent for private industry managers in the Clark study and 14 percent for managers in the Acton Society Trust study. The reason for this is, of course, the bringing-in to small furniture companies of "crown princes" and other relations

of the owners and grooming them for future control of the business.
The best comparison here is between the first occupations of these
small company owner-managers and the first occupations of Copeman's directors, over 50 percent of whom started their careers with
the advantage of having business connections in the family and 21 percent of whom received their first board appointment before they were
30 years of age, mostly in family businesses. Of Copeman's directors, 22 percent started their careers as trainees for executive posts.
Similarly, 22 percent of the owner-managers in the descriptive survey
started as trainees and 6 percent jumped straight in as managers.
Copeman pointed out that many businessmen had taken their sons into
the firm direct from school without requiring them to gain any particular professional qualifications, and that it had been common practice
for the son who was destined to control the business to do a thorough
apprenticeship in the various departments of the firm so that he might
become an experienced all-arounder. This is precisely the pattern
followed by many hereditary owner-managers in small furniture companies. What is so marked, however, in comparing the first occupations of Copeman's large company directors with those of the owner-
managers, is the proportion of Copeman's directors whose original
occupation was a professional one. Of Copeman's directors, 16 percent started out in the accountancy profession, 6 percent in law, and
7 percent in other professions. In addition, 25 percent held their
first jobs in science or engineering and 12 percent in administrative
or company secretarial work.

It would appear, therefore, that whereas in small companies
top managerial posts that are not filled on a hereditary basis go to
men who started on the shop floor, in the office, or on the road, in
large companies they go to those with a university education or professional qualifications. In addition one would guess that the sons of
Copeman's directors, should they receive a university education or
a professional qualification, would be prepared to take up a career
similar to that of their fathers, whereas those sons of small furniture
company owner-managers who have degrees or professional qualifications evidently do not take up careers in the family business. Nor,
in most cases, would they be encouraged to by their fathers. Even
family influence, therefore, to some extent militates against the introduction of more highly qualified managerial and professional staff
into small furniture companies.

INTERFIRM MOBILITY

The INSEAD study of European chief executives found that interfirm mobility appeared to be lowest in Great Britain and the Netherlands and highest in Germany. Forty-six percent of the British chief

executives and 40 percent of the Dutch had made their careers entirely in one company, whereas nine out of ten German chief executives had previously worked for at least one other company and 40 percent had changed companies three or more times. The comparative immobility of managers in large companies in Britain is confirmed by the other large-firm research studies. Of Copeman's directors for whom information on job changes was available, 43 percent had worked with one company only, as had 44 percent of the managers in the Acton Society Trust study, 33 percent in the Clements study,[11] and 34 percent in the Clark study. There was little evidence from any of these studies to suggest that interfirm mobility was increasing, although Clark did find that managers in the public sector appeared to be far more mobile than those in private industry, that graduate managers were more mobile than nongraduate managers, and that privately educated managers were the least mobile.

The study of managers in small furniture companies presents quite a different picture as can be seen from Table 7.5. Of the small-firm managers, 22 percent had worked for six or more companies during their careers, the comparable figures for the Clark study managers being 7 percent, and for Copeman's directors, 4 percent. Only 14 percent of the small-firm managers had never changed their companies, which is less than half as many immobile managers as in any of the large-firm studies. Analysis of the interfirm mobility of the small furniture managers by management category, by schooling, and by age throws up a number of additional points of interest. First, almost 25 percent of the owner-managers had never worked for any other company, whereas this was the case for only 7 percent of the nonshareholding managers and 6 percent of the supervisors. Second, the most mobile group of managers, in terms of number of companies worked for, were the nonshareholding managers, almost a third of whom had worked for six or more companies during their careers even though, on average, they were the youngest managerial group. Third, managers with elementary and nonselective secondary education were more mobile than managers who had attended grammar or private schools. Of the managers who had attended elementary or nonselective secondary schools, 9 percent had not changed their companies compared with 18 percent of those who had attended grammar schools and 26 percent of those who had been educated privately. Similarly, at the other end of the scale, 27 percent of the managers with elementary or nonselective secondary schooling had worked for six or more companies during their careers, compared with 20 percent of the grammar school managers and only 3 percent of the managers who had been privately educated. Fourth, there was little evidence to suggest that younger managers were significantly more mobile than older ones. Of the managers aged 40 and under, 20 percent had not changed their company and 20 percent had worked for six or more firms. Of the managers aged over 50, 11 percent had not changed companies during their careers and 22 percent had worked for six or more firms. Fifth, of those managers who had changed companies, 10 percent had spent an average of less than one year with their previous employers, 53 percent had spent from one to five years, and the remaining 37 percent had spent an average of five years or more with each previous employer. Finally, about 33 percent of the managers who had worked for more than one company had not previously been employed in the furniture industry, but about 50 percent had over five years' previous experience in the industry.

TABLE 7.5

Interfirm Mobility of Managers
(in percent)

	Research Study		
	Copeman (1955) Directors	Clark (1966) All Managers	Small Furniture Firms (1970) All Managers
One firm only	43	34	14
Two to five firms	53	59	65
Six firms or more	4	7	22

Source: Compiled by the author.

Clark advances two hypotheses about the relationship between educational background and interfirm mobility. The first is that a man with no formal educational qualifications will normally rely on his experience in order to do a managerial job, that this experience will be of a specialist nature and relevant to one particular firm, and that, consequently, he will stay put while the more qualified people move around. The second hypothesis is that men with no formal educational qualifications often enter industry very badly informed and so have to make several changes of company to gain promotion; these changes will usually be within the same industry so that experience gained in a particular firm can be carried forward to the benefit of the new employer. The evidence from small furniture companies seems to support the second of these two hypotheses. The

relatively high rates of intercompany mobility, particularly among
nonshareholding managers, can be seen as a compensation for lack
of formal educational or professional qualifications. Probably the
most important factor, however, in accounting for differences in
intercompany mobility between large-firm and small-firm managers
is the one of size of firm itself. Quite obviously the opportunities for
career development in a company with a managerial staff of, say,
five people, two of whom may be owners of the firm, are extremely
limited compared with the opportunities for internal career development in a company with a managerial staff of several hundred. Consequently even those who are coming into a small family business as
sons or relatives of the existing owners will frequently be encouraged
to work elsewhere for a while in order to gain some broader horizons
and wider experience than are available within the business. In spite,
therefore, of the hereditary influences at play in the selection of
managers in small furniture firms, such managers would appear to
be far less in-bred than the managers of large companies in Britain.

LENGTH OF SERVICE AND IN-COMPANY JOB CHANGES

Table 7.6 sets out the length of time that managers had spent
both with their present firms and in their present jobs. The differences in interfirm mobility between large and small company managers are partially reflected in this table. Thus, for example, 23
percent of the managers in the small furniture firm survey had been
with their companies for less than five years compared with 10 percent of Clark's private industry managers. In particular the table
reflects the mobility of the nonshareholding managers in the small
firms, 37 percent of whom had been with their present firms for less
than five years and only 18 percent of whom had been with their present firms for 20 years or more. There is no evidence, therefore,
from these figures that small firms necessarily have a more stable
managerial labor force or a lower managerial labor turnover than
large firms, in spite of the fact that a relatively high proportion of
small-firm managers have some stake in the ownership of their
companies.
    As one would expect, the lack of movement of large company
managers from firm to firm is compensated for by the movement
from job to job within their companies. Of Clark's private industry
managers, 46 percent had held their present jobs in their companies
for less than five years, which, since 10 percent had not completed
five years' service with their firms, means that just over 33 percent
of these private industry managers had changed their jobs in their
companies during the last five years. In the small furniture firm

TABLE 7.6

Length of Service of Managers
(in percent)

Research Study	Length of Service of Managers with Their Present Firms		
	Less Than 5 Years	5 Years but Less Than 20 Years	20 Years and Over
Clark (1966)			
Managers, private			
industry	10	50	40
"Top" managers	7	51	43
Directors	5	49	46
Small furniture firms (1970)			
All managers	23	44	33
Owner-managers	10	44	46
	Length of Service of Managers in Their Present Jobs		
Clark (1966)			
Managers, private			
industry	46	49	5
"Top" managers	39	63	8
Directors	35	54	11
Small furniture firms (1970)			
All managers	39	46	15
Owner-managers	21	53	26
Managers	57	38	5

Source: Compiled by the author.

study, on the other hand, although 39 percent of the managers had been in their present jobs for less than five years, 23 percent of the managers had not completed five years' service with their firms, which means that less than 20 percent of small-firm managers had changed jobs within their firms during the last five years. At the other end of the scale, 5 percent of Clark's private industry managers had been in their present jobs for 20 years or more compared with 15 percent of the managers in the descriptive survey, even

though 40 percent of Clark's managers had over 20 years' service
with their companies compared with 33 percent of the managers in
the small furniture firms. The general picture, then, is one of more
interfirm mobility among the small-firm managers and more in-
company interjob mobility among large-firm managers, with different patterns emerging for different managerial groups, the most
striking differences being between owner-managers and other managers in the small companies.

Clark concluded, on the basis of an analysis of managers'
length of service with their companies by the managers' ages, that
at some time in his 40s a manager's opportunities to move to another
firm declined very sharply, with the result that after this age he was
essentially immobile. Thus, for example, whereas 18 percent of
his managers in the under-40 age group had spent less than five years
with their present employers, in the 40-54 age group the percentage
with less than five years' service had dropped to 7 percent, and in
the 55 years and over age group to 2 percent. While the same pattern, of length of service with the present employer increasing according to the age of the manager, held true for the small furniture
firm managers it was not so marked that the older managers could
be described as immobile. Of the furniture managers over the age
of 50, 10 percent had spent less than five years with their present
companies compared with 16 percent of those in the 41-50 age group
and 43 percent of those aged 40 or less. Even among those managers
aged over 60, 9 percent had changed their jobs within the last five
years, probably from force of circumstances rather than from choice.

In the small furniture firms study there were marked differences between the owner-managers and the managers, both in the
number of years that they had been working with their present companies and in the pattern of their in-company job changes. Thus, for
example, 46 percent of the owner-managers had been with their companies for 20 years or more, compared with 18 percent of the managers. Second, 12 percent of the managers had less than one year's
service with their present employers, whereas only 1 percent of the
owner-managers had worked with their present companies for less
than a year. Third, in spite of their generally shorter length of
service, 62 percent of the managers had changed jobs in-company
since joining their present firms, compared with 54 percent of the
owner-managers. Fourth, the nonshareholding managers had
changed their jobs most frequently inside their companies. Of those
nonshareholding managers who had held more than one job in their
firm, 42 percent had changed jobs, on average, once every five
years, compared with 27 percent of the owner-managers. Finally,
over 25% of the owner-managers had been in their present positions
in their companies for 20 years or more. But over 25 percent of the

managers had been in their present positions for less than a year, whereas only 13 percent of owner-managers had so recently undertaken in-company job changes.

Indications from the Clark study are that large-company managers may change companies early in their careers but will then settle down within one company to progress by means of internal transfers and promotions. Therefore, management development in the large company, after initial recruitment and selection of managers at a relatively junior level or of management trainees, is concerned primarily with internal development of those managers within the organizational hierarchy. In the small companies, however, two separate problems would appear to exist. There is the continuing problem of recruitment, selection, and retention of nonshareholding managers in the business, and there is the problem of developing the next generation of executives primarily from within the families or personal contacts of the existing owner-managers.

CAREER PROFILES

"The profile of the average British managing director," emerging from the INSEAD study of the chief executives of Europe's biggest companies, "is that he is likely to be in his mid-fifties, and to have been born of an upper-class family. He probably went to a public school, and perhaps continued his education at Cambridge University. He would tend to marry the daughter of a professional family. His annual salary is approximately £15,000, he has held his present position for about seven years, and became managing director in his late forties."[12]

The "average" small furniture company owner-manager, as he emerges from this research, is likely to be in his early 50s and to have been born of a working-class family. He probably went to an elementary school and perhaps continued his education by attending evening classes. On completing a furniture craft apprenticeship he worked as a journeyman for a short time before being called up for war service. After the war he spent a few years with a furniture company on the bench before setting up in business on his own account. In 1970 he earned about £2,500 a year. The "average" nonshareholding manager in a small furniture company is, on the other hand, aged about 40 and earned £1,750 a year. After leaving grammar school at the age of 16 he continued his studies on a part-time basis by enrolling in a commercial course at the local college. In order to gain a wide range of experience he moved around a number of companies doing various clerical, office, and administrative jobs. He has been employed in his present firm for about six years,

and although he has no professional qualifications, he is now in charge
of all office administration and accounting matters.

Such caricatures, while they highlight in particular some of
the vivid differences between the educational and occupational backgrounds of managers in large and small companies, do not do justice
to the wide range of experience of managers and the variegated nature
of their career profiles. Clark concluded that there were apparently
no great changes in the career patterns of his large-company managers in spite of the changes in their educational backgrounds and
that, although society was producing a different type of manager in
terms of education and social background, industry seemed to be
molding these managers into a traditional career pattern. In the context of small furniture firms even hereditary owner-managers do not
necessarily follow a traditional career pattern. Mr. Arthur, for example, who is 65, left school at the age of 15 and joined his father's
firm as an apprentice cabinetmaker. After his apprenticeship he
worked in the firm as a journeyman, then on the sales side, eventually becoming a partner in the firm. Arthur then left the family
business and, for five years up until the outbreak of World War II,
managed his own company. During the war he was works manager
in a larger cabinet furniture company before setting up on his own
again in 1947.

Family disputes, unforeseen opportunities, force of circumstances, economic recession, and war are only some of the factors
that undermine any attempt to find common patterns among the career profiles of owner-managers and managers of small firms.
Mr. Bayley, for example, was an owner-manager who had "come up
the hard way." Leaving school as a 14-year old at the height of the
depression he worked for two years as an office junior with a company of dyers and cleaners. After war service he spent a few months
as a progress chaser with an engineering company before joining a
cabinetmaking company on the bench as "fitter up." Gradually over
a 20-year period Bayley moved within the company from his job on
the bench, via progress chasing, to full-time office administration.
He is now a director with responsibility for administration and production and has an 8 percent shareholding in the firm. Mr. Geeson,
on the other hand, with the exception of five-and-a-half years' war
service, has never worked for any organization other than the family
upholstery business where he and his cousin are now joint managing
directors. Born in 1911, Geeson left grammar school at the age of
16 with five credits in the Oxford Local Examination. He started in
the family firm by spending two years in the making shop to learn
framemaking, then spent six years on marking out timber, followed
by three years in general supervision of framemaking and two years
in sales. During his early days with the firm he spent three years

attending evening classes in woodworking. For the last 24 years
Geeson has been involved mainly in general sales management including direct representation. He has over 35 years' service with
the company and has been a director since 1937. In contrast Mr.
Harvey is a first generation owner-manager. Born in 1918 he left
elementary school at the age of 14 and pursued no further academic
studies. He has been running his own upholstery business for over
20 years, his job in the firm having gradually changed as the company expanded. Before setting up on his own, Harvey had completed
four years as an apprentice upholsterer, worked for a couple of years
as a pressing machine operator in a tailors, spent a period in the
army during which time he was trained as a motor fitter, and worked
for eight months with the "Pru" as a salesman.

Similar variations exist among the career profiles of the nonshareholding managers. Mr. Donald, for example, had no previous
experience of the furniture industry when he joined his present company, which makes divan headboards, as sales manager in 1967.
Aged 40, he left grammar school at the age of 15 and joined British
Rail where he worked for 12 years, ending up as a traffic controller.
Then, over a period of nine years, Donald had four different jobs--
sales clerk with a tile manufacturer, assistant branch superintendent
with a finance and credit service, sales and office manager with a
paper manufacturer, and office manager with a company making
thermometers. In contrast, Mr. Jerram had been connected with
the furniture industry for the whole of his working life. Born in 1928,
Jerram left elementary school at the age of 14 but continued his education for seven years on a part-time basis with evening classes at
the local technical college in cabinetmaking and woodworking. Prior
to joining his present employer he spent six years on the bench as a
cabinetmaker, three months as a progress chaser with a kitchen
furniture manufacturer, seven years as works manager of a cabinet
works in Ireland, and 18 months as site assistant manager for a laboratory furniture company. Jerram started with his present firm,
where he has been for a little over ten years, as a cabinetmaker. He
then spent four years as machine shop foreman before becoming works
manager in 1969.

Finally, Table 7.7 compares the ages of managers in some of
the large company studies with the ages of the managers in the small-
firm descriptive survey. One of the most striking aspects of the
comparison is the relatively high proportion of younger managers in
the small firms. Of the furniture company managers, 15 percent
were aged 30 years or less compared with 5 percent of the managers
in the Acton Society Trust study who were under the age of 30 and
3 percent of the managers in the Clark study. The difference in age
structure between small-firm and large-firm managers becomes

even more marked if a comparison is made between the owner-managers of small furniture companies, the Acton Society Trust "top" managers and Copeman's directors. Of the owner-managers, 35 percent were aged 40 or less. The proportion of large firm "top" managers under the age of 40 was 12 percent and of directors, 9 percent.

TABLE 7.7

Ages of Managers
(in percent)

Large Company Studies

| | | Acton Society Trust | | Clark | |
| | Copeman | All | "Top" | All | Managers, Private |
Age Groups	Directors	Managers	Managers	Managers	Industry
Under 30 }	9	5	} 12	3	3
30-39		21		29	32
40-49	30	37	43	32	31
50-59	31	29	35	28	26
60-69	23	} 8	10	8	8
70 and over	8				

Study of Small Furniture Companies

Age Groups	All Managers	Owner-Managers	Nonshareholding Managers	Supervisors
30 and under	15	14	21	8
31-40	20	20	23	15
41-50	20	18	21	21
51-60	31	30	26	42
61-69	13	16	9	15
70 and over	1	2	--	--

Source: Compiled by the author.

But as well as starting younger, small-firm managers tend to carry on working longer than is the case for some of the managers in the large-firm studies. Of all the small-firm managers, 14 percent were over the age of 60 compared with 8 percent of all the managers in both the Acton Society Trust and Clark studies who were 60 or over. On the other hand, 31 percent of Copeman's directors were 60 or over, compared with 10 percent of the Acton Society Trust's top managers and over 18 percent of the small-firm owner-managers. A more recent study than Copeman's, however, indicated that 5 percent of the chief executives of some of the largest companies in Great Britain were 65 and over, whereas 6 percent of the small-firm owner-managers in the furniture industry survey were still working on beyond normal retirement age. [13]

The fact that the small companies in the furniture industry survey were family firms obviously has a marked effect on the age structure of their managers. In small companies there are likely to be generational cycles that affect company age structure. This may, for example, along with the disruption arising from World War II, partially explain the relatively small proportion of owner-managers in the 41-50 age group. At one end of the scale sons coming into the business and assuming some managerial responsibilities at a relatively early age will mean a substantial number of young managers employed, whereas at the other end of the scale owners will be free to continue working into their 70s if they wish, or they may be obliged to do so by lack of adequate pension arrangements. The two extremes can be characterized by the following extracts from the furniture trade press:

> Mr. Peter William Chandler, the only son of Mr. and Mrs. P. H. Chandler, has been appointed a director of P. H. Chandler (Leyland) Ltd., Talbot Road, Leyland, Lancashire, chair frame manufacturers. The appointment coincides with Mr. Chandler's coming of age. [14]

> At the age of eighty, Mr. James Swann, a skilled upholsterer, has retired as governing director of the upholstery business of Swann Bros. (Leicester) Ltd., East Park Road, Leicester, which he founded some forty years ago. [15]

A number of points of difference emerge, therefore, from a comparison of the educational and occupational backgrounds and career profiles of large-company managers and managers in small

furniture firms. Managers in small firms achieve their managerial
status earlier in their careers and retain it longer, particularly if
they are, or become, shareholders in the company. Small-firm
managers are educationally less well qualified than large-firm managers. The gap in terms of educational attainment between small
and large-firm managers is further widened by the greater use made
by large-firm managers of opportunities provided by the further education system. On average younger managers in all sizes of companies are educationally better qualified than their elders. In small
firms, however, there are still opportunities to start at the bottom
and work up into a managerial position or to set up in business on
one's own account. Managers in small firms are less in-bred than
managers in large firms. The greater degree of interfirm mobility
among small-firm managers arises primarily from the lack of opportunity for in-company career development, and to some extent com-
pensates for lack of educational qualifications. There is less in-
company interjob mobility among small-firm managers. Previous
work experience is largely taken as a substitute for in-company training and development. The career profiles of small-firm managers
indicate a great diversity of experience, so much so as to make it
difficult to trace any consistent career development patterns.

It is clear, given such diversity of educational and occupational
background between large and small company managers and the very
different contexts within which they have to operate, that the management education and training needs of managers in small firms will be
quite different in content from those of large company managers.
Not only is it necessary to recognize the different education and
training needs of large and small company managers, but it is also
essential to develop appropriate education and training methods in
light of the different educational and occupational experiences of the
managers themselves. Within small companies this will require
some distinction at least between the development of nonshareholding
managers along more professional lines and the development of entrepreneurial skills in the owner-manager.

NOTES

1. George Copeman, Leaders of British Industry (London:
Gee and Co., 1955).
    2. Acton Society Trust, Management Succession (London, 1956).
    3. R. V. Clements, Managers--A Study of Their Careers in
Industry (London: Allen and Unwin, 1958).
    4. D. G. Clark, The Industrial Manager--His Background and
Career Pattern (London: Business Publications, 1966).

5. David Hall, H-Cl. de Bettignies, and G. Amado-Fischgrund, "The European Business Elite," European Business, October 1969.

6. Clark, op. cit.

7. National Economic Development Office, Management Recruitment and Development (London: H.M.S.O., 1965).

8. Hall et al., op. cit.

9. P. W. Musgrave, "The Educational Profiles of Management in Two British Iron and Steel Companies with some Comparisons, National and International," British Journal of Industrial Relations 4, no. 2 (July 1966).

10. T. M. Mosson and D. G. Clark, "Some Inter-Industry Comparisons of the Backgrounds and Careers of Managers," British Journal of Industrial Relations 6, no. 2 (July 1968).

11. Clements, op. cit.

12. David Hall and G. Amado-Fischgrund, "Chief Executives in Britain," European Business, January 1969. See also Hilda G. Brown, "Career Patterns of Foundry Managers," paper presented to the annual conference of The Institute of British Foundrymen, June 1970.

13. Hall et al., op. cit.

14. Cabinet Maker and Retail Furnisher, January 17, 1969.

15. Cabinet Maker and Retail Furnisher, January 16, 1970.

CHAPTER

8

THE TRAINING AND
DEVELOPMENT OF
THE OWNER-MANAGER

The managers interviewed during the descriptive survey were asked a number of questions about their training. These questions were designed to gain some understanding of the extent to which managers had been involved in training activities in the past, and to find out whether or not managers felt that training could help them with any problems and difficulties they faced in their work. Consequently managers were asked for details of training they had received since joining their companies and for information on training received in the company or external courses attended during the 12 months preceding the survey visit. They were also asked to describe any training they had received, prior to joining their present companies, that they felt was particularly relevant to their work. In addition, in order to probe managers' views of their training needs in relation to their jobs, questions were asked on the activities and tasks that made up those jobs, and on the frequency, difficulty, and criticality of those activities and tasks. Managers were also asked what they thought were their most pressing short- and long-term problems and what kind of training, if any, might help in handling those problems. This chapter describes some of the answers to these questions and considers their implications. It should be emphasized that much of the information collected from the managers was highly specific to their particular work situations at the time of the survey visit and was not the kind of information susceptible to general summary analysis. Where possible, therefore, the general picture presented by the statistical analysis has been rounded out by examples of the responsibilities and work problems of some of the managers interviewed.

IN-COMPANY AND EXTERNAL TRAINING

During the descriptive survey the first question that managers were asked on training matters was whether or not, since joining their companies, they had received any training either in the firm or externally. Just over 25 percent of the 229 managers had received some kind of in-company training with their employing firms and 45 percent had received training externally. A similar proportion, 45 percent, had not received any training of any kind since joining the firms that employed them at the time of the survey visit. Table 8.1 indicates the training involvement, since joining their employing firms, of the three groups of managers--the owner-managers, the nonshareholding managers, and the supervisors. A number of points emerge from this table. First, the owner-managers were the group most involved in in-company training. Of the owner-managers, 37 percent had received some kind of in-company training with their employing firms compared with 22 percent of the nonshareholding managers and 16 percent of the supervisors. Second, the owner-managers were also the group most involved in external training. Of the owner-managers, 51 percent had received external training since they joined their companies, compared with 44 percent of the nonshareholding managers and 33 percent of the supervisors. Third, the supervisors were the group with the highest proportion of managers who had not received any training with their employing firms, either in-company or by attendance at external courses. Of the supervisors, 61 percent had not received any such training, compared with 47 percent of the nonshareholding managers and 36 percent of the owner-managers.

As might be expected, previous experience in the industry was to some extent a substitute for training, whether internally or externally, by the employing company. Thus, for example, of the 101 managers who had over five years' previous experience in the industry before joining the companies in the survey, 4 percent had received some in-company training with their employing firms, just over 33 percent had been involved in some external training activity, and 63 percent had received no training. In contrast the corresponding figures for the 98 managers with less than five years' previous trade experience were for in-company training, 35 percent, for external training 45 percent, and for no training 39 percent. (The figures do not add up to 100 percent since a number of managers in each case had received both internal and external training. The 30 managers not included in this comparison were those who had never worked for any firm other than their employing company.)

TABLE 8.1

Training Involvement of Managers with
Their Employing Companies

Managers Who, Since Joining Their Employing Companies, Had Received	Management Category							
	Owner-Managers		Nonshareholding Managers		Supervisors		All Managers (n = 229)	
	No.	%	No.	%	No.	%	No.	%
Training in the firm only	12	13	8	9	3	6	23	10
Training externally only	25	27	27	31	11	23	63	28
Training both in the firm and externally	23	24	11	13	5	10	39	17
No training, either in the firm or externally	34	36	41	47	29	61	104	45

Source: Compiled by the author.

Surprisingly, a manager's length of service with his company
had no apparent bearing on his involvement in external training activities. Of the managers with less than five years' service with their
employing firms, 44 percent had received some kind of external training since joining their company, as had 44 percent of the managers
with from 5 to 20 years' service and 45 percent of the managers with
over 20 years' service. This would suggest that the involvement of
managers in external training programs was largely a development
of the five years preceding the survey visits, that is, the five-year
period from 1965. Since the Furniture and Timber Industry Training
Board was formally established in December 1965 it seems fair to
conclude that the availability of suitable external training facilities
and their use by small-firm managers have been direct consequences
of the activities of the board. This probability is underlined by the
fact that the likelihood of a manager's having received some kind of
in-company training with his employing firm did increase with his
length of service, this kind of in-company training very frequently

being of a traditional job-rotation kind that would have been in existence for many years prior to the advent of the Training Board.

Rotation training was in fact the most common kind of in-
company training received by owner-managers. This was a form of
job rotation involving periods of attachment to different parts of the
organization, usually on a relatively informal basis. It might be more
appropriately described as experience-gathering, the experience
gathered being related to the particular place in the organization to
which the attachment was made. In this respect it was different from
"understudy training," which involved attachment to one particular
person in order to pick up, again in a relatively informal way, the
basic components of that person's job. In a few cases, for example,
a son coming into the family business worked alongside his father as
a kind of understudy and in a few cases a nonshareholding manager,
in preparation for taking on new responsibilities, worked as "assistant
to" another manager. However, the most common kind of in-company
training received by both nonshareholding managers and supervisors
was an apprenticeship or a period of craft training "on-the-bench."
If those managers whose in-company training was of an exclusively
practical craft kind are excluded, together with the two managers
whose only in-company training was induction training, then only 37
(16 percent) of the 229 managers interviewed had received any kind of
in-company management or supervisory training since joining their
employing organizations. The large bulk of this in-company management and supervisory training was based on place or person attach-
ments. Other than such rotation or understudy training, four managers had attended in-company Training Within Industry courses, two
had been involved in management training schemes, and two had spent
a period in their companies working alongside consultants.

In addition to being asked about the training they had received
since joining their employing organizations, managers were requested
to itemize the training they had been involved in during the 12 months
immediately preceding the survey visit. Of the managers, 70 percent
had not received any kind of training during that 12-month period, 28
percent had been involved in some external training activity, and 4
percent had received some form of in-company training. There was
little difference between owner-managers and nonshareholding managers but supervisors had received relatively little training during
the year under review. Of the 229 managers interviewed, 64 had received training externally during the year preceding the visit to their
company. Thirteen of these managers had attended two external
training activities during the period and ten had attended three or
more such activities. Table 8.2 presents an analysis of managers'
external training activities both since joining their employing organizations and during the year preceding the survey visit (that is,

1969-70). Most of the external training activity involved attendance at seminars, courses, or conferences, usually of two or three days' duration and sometimes spread over the weekend. As might be expected there was a shift away from further education courses toward more involvement in short courses and seminars, evening class courses, for example, being a part of a manager's training early in his career. Nevertheless, many managers in the survey did apparently see it as important to keep themselves abreast of technical developments in the industry with the result that just over 25 percent of all the external training activity in the year preceding the survey visit was training related to craft and technical subjects.

TABLE 8.2

Managers' External Training Activities

External Training Activity	Percent of Total External Training Activities of Managers	
	Since Joining Their Employing Companies	During the Year Preceding the Survey Visit
Day release, block release, sandwich courses, evening classes, and correspondence courses		
Related to craft and technical subjects	12.9	1.2
Related to management subjects	5.9	2.4
Seminars, courses, and conferences		
Related to craft and technical subjects	17.8	25.9
Related to general management subjects	14.9	21.2
Related to specific management techniques	23.8	20.0
Related to specific management techniques applied particularly to the furniture trade	17.8	18.8
Overseas visits, study tours, and visits to other companies, etc.	6.9	10.6
Total	100.0	100.0

Source: Compiled by the author.

Further analysis of the involvement of managers in in-company
and external training activities revealed two other main points of
interest. First, there was a direct relationship between a manager's
training involvement and his age, the younger managers being more
likely to have received some kind of training, in spite of their shorter
occupational histories, than their older counterparts. The relationship between age and training involvement applied to both in-company
and to external training activities. Second, there was no clear relationship between profitability and the training that managers had received since joining their employing organizations, but there did
appear to be some relationship between company profitability ratings,
as described in Chapter 5, and management training activity in the
year preceding the survey visit. Thus, for example, none of the 13
managers in the four companies rated as unprofitable had received
any kind of training in that 12-month period, whereas half of the 26
managers in the four companies with high profitability ratings had
received training in the year preceding the survey visit. Whether
this arose because unprofitable companies could not afford to send
managers on training courses and other similar activities, or whether
those companies were unprofitable partly because their managements
had not been able to keep abreast of new techniques and developments,
it is not possible to say. Similarly a greater proportion of managers
in the more profitable and expanding companies had received some
form of in-company training in the preceding year than was the case
for the less profitable and more static firms. In addition there was
a fairly consistent relationship between the rate of company growth
and the involvement of managers in external courses during the year
in question, the expanding companies having a higher proportion of
managers involved in external training during the 12 months under
review. The expanding companies were, of course, far more likely
to have relatively young short-service managers in their employ and
these, as a group, were more involved in both in-company and external training activities in the year under review than their older
longer-serving colleagues.

TRAINING IN PREVIOUS EMPLOYMENT

The final question that managers were asked about their past
training was whether or not they had received any training, prior to
joining their employing organizations, that was particularly relevant
to their work at the time of the survey visit. Thirty of the 229 managers interviewed had never worked for any company other than their
employing organization. One of these 30, although he had never

worked for a commercial organization before and had no previous
experience in the furniture trade, had spent ten years in the army
and felt that the training he had received at Sandhurst (Military
Academy) was particularly relevant to his job. Of the remaining 199
managers, 62 felt they had received relevant training prior to joining
their employing firms. The past training most frequently mentioned
as particularly relevant was relatively informal in-company training
and experience-gathering. This was brought up by 17 of the 62 managers and included such responses as "trained through every department in father's firm," and "internal management training on communications and management methods." Next in frequency of response were apprenticeship and in-company craft or technical training. These were mentioned by 13 of the 62 managers. Eleven managers referred to specific management techniques courses they had
attended, covering such subjects as work measurement, production
management, human relations, and sales techniques, and six referred to general management education courses leading to certificates
or diplomas in business studies. A number of managers mentioned
the relevance of the secretarial, commercial, and accountancy training they had received prior to joining their employing organizations.
Others referred to the training they had received in the armed forces.
A large number of the 199 managers, while they felt they had not had
any specific relevant training with their previous employers, believed
that the experience they had gained in their past jobs was extremely
relevant to the work they were employed in at the time of the survey
and was the main factor that enabled them to handle that work competently.

  Economists have argued that under perfectly competitive conditions no firm would rationally pay any of the cost of completely
general training for their employees.[1] Such training increases the
employee's future productivity in all firms equally and is, therefore,
an investment that the employee is supposed to be willing to make
for himself. On the other hand, firms will have an incentive to meet
the costs of completely specific training for their employees for in
this situation the investment in training and the skills developed are
of no value to other companies. In practice, however, training is
frequently neither general nor specific but a mixture of both and so
employers have some interest in training investments that are predominantly general in character. The importance of the information
from our survey is that it throws some light on the question as to
whether or not investments in training are job-specific or are carried over from firm to firm as managers move from job to job. Here
we are only dealing with managers' perceptions of the spillover from
their previous training into their jobs at the time of the survey. What
is clear is that, in the firms studied, internal job changes and develop-

ment of managers within the firm were haphazard processes and that, while intercompany mobility might well be viewed as a form of training substitute, the possibility of previous experience and training being relevant to a new job situation was also a somewhat chancy affair. Although it was to some extent outside the scope of our enquiry, what we saw of the selection "methods" adopted by small firms in recruiting managers would confirm us in the view that any carryover of previous training into a new job would be more a matter of chance than of deliberate recruitment policy.

It is evident, therefore, that the development and training of owner-managers and of nonshareholding managers in small furniture firms follow different patterns. For owner-managers training and development is most commonly based on periods of attachment incompany to different parts of the organization or to different managers in the firm, usually on a very informal basis with no specific training objectives identified and no detailed written programs used. Where nonshareholding managers who have previous experience in the industry are recruited into the firm then that experience is largely taken by the new employer to be a sufficient substitute for any further training specific to the new job. Consequently many nonshareholding managers, both when brought into the firm from outside and when transferred or promoted within the firm, are expected to take over new jobs with a minimal amount of induction.

THE TRAINING FRAMEWORK

In the context of management training and development, our research was designed to identify the activities and tasks carried out by the managers of small firms, to indicate the frequency with which those activities and tasks were performed, to understand the degree of difficulty involved in their performance, and to assess their relevance to the successful attainment of the objectives of the business. Analysis of a manager's work along these three dimensions of frequency, difficulty, and criticality allows some useful ordering of training priorities and a basis for the sound identification of training and development requirements. Such an analysis makes it possible to distinguish between those administrative and entrepreneurial activities that are highly critical and frequent in the short-term and those that involve longer-term policy-making and planning. Similarly a task that is infrequent, yet critical, and that the individual manager finds some degree of difficulty in handling effectively, will provide a more appropriate focus for the attention of the training specialist than a more frequently carried out task that the manager finds comparatively easy to deal with and that is not so critical to the successful operation of the business. One of the limitations of many empirical studies of managers at work has been that they have identified only the frequency of particular activities and tasks and have implied that training priority is directly related to time spent. It is only relatively recently that critical incident techniques have been extended significantly to the analysis of managerial work.

What was being sought through the research design was, therefore, a method whereby managerial tasks could be set out on some simple scale indicating degrees of frequency, difficulty, and criticality and subsequently collected together in order of training priority or training need. While such a basis for analyzing training needs may represent a useful step forward it is, nevertheless, extremely crude in a number of respects. In particular it does not completely allow for the perspective of time. In the long term, for example, the greatest benefit may accrue to a small firm from a careful analysis of its stock levels and its stock turnover with a view to establishing some inventory control procedure. But in the short term the most immediate and critical factor may be to make sure that Joe, the supplier of a particular range of fabrics, dispatches them to the works in sufficient time to meet Monday's production requirements. A further difficulty arises from the fact that the assessment of difficulty is inevitably a subjective assessment. That is to say, a task that is equally critical and frequent for two owner-managers--say, the interviewing of job applicants--may be felt to be an extremely difficult task by one owner-manager and an extremely easy task by another. Degree of difficulty experienced in performing a particular task depends, therefore, on the skills, experience, and attitudes of the individual manager concerned. The methods of analysis used were designed, consequently, primarily to identify individual management training and development needs, to understand the problems that an owner-manager or manager faces at a particular time in a particular company, and to suggest ways in which specific task-related training can assist a manager in handling some of his problems. Any more general training programs will then be developed from problem areas that seem to present common difficulties to managers, and from the use of case-study material that proves helpful in discussing the nature of the work of owner-managers and managers and the general characteristics of their problem-solving activities. This analytical framework is set out diagrammatically in Figure 8.1.

With this training framework in mind the 229 managers interviewed during the descriptive survey were asked a number of questions designed to identify individual training needs. The principal questions asked were:

FIGURE 8.1

The Training Framework

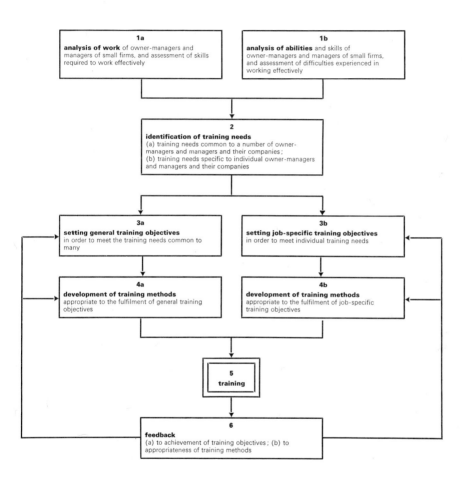

Source: Compiled by the author.

1. What are the principal activities and tasks that go to make up your job at the present time?
2. What activities or tasks take up most of your time at present?
3. Are there any activities or tasks in your job that you find difficult to handle? If so, what are they, and what kind of training, if any, do you think might help you in handling these difficult activities and tasks?
4. Which of the activities and tasks that you carry out contribute most to the success of your company?
5. What is the most pressing short-term problem that you face in your job at the present time, and what kind of training, if any, do you think might help you in handling short-term problems of this kind?
6. What is the most important long-term problem that you face in your work, and what kind of training, if any, do you think might help you in handling long-term problems of this kind?

The distribution of time among various activities and tasks was a major focus of the depth study and some of the results are described in Chapter 9 on the owner-manager and his work. The remainder of this chapter is primarily concerned with describing some of the management training and development needs that emerged from the descriptive survey.

MANAGERS' DIFFICULTIES AND PROBLEMS

Of the 229 managers interviewed, 68, or just under 30 percent, said that there were activities or tasks in their jobs that they found difficult to handle. Of the 94 owner-managers, 37 (or 39 percent) spoke of difficult aspects to their jobs, compared with 26 of the non-shareholding managers (30 percent) and 5 of the 48 supervisors (10 percent). Some of the 68 managers who were aware of difficulties in their jobs thought that the difficulties were unavoidable and could not be overcome by training. Difficulties arose, for example, with aging: "I find labor problems difficult to handle and this is largely because of the changes that have taken place since the war. But I am 68 now and I doubt if you could change my approach." Some managers' training requirements were highly specific to their difficulties, as, for example, with the owner-manager who spent a third of his time in export sales visits abroad and who thought this was the most critical and difficult aspect of his work at that particular stage in the company's development. He saw his training requirement quite clearly as being one of languages, primarily French, German, and Italian. Other managers, while not finding any of their present work activities or tasks difficult, felt that training could help them to understand the totality of the company's problems rather than those that arose solely within the sphere of their own responsibilities. Thus, for example, a nonshareholding manager said, "I have no difficulties on the financial side but training in marketing and production would help me to realize the rest of the problems of the business." A number of managers had their own personal fads: "The most difficult aspects of my work arise from the vagueness of the instructions I receive from the managing director; internal communications in the firm are very poor and what we all need is some kind of group dynamics training." Some managers' difficulties arose because the size and limited resources of their companies meant that they had to undertake tasks for which they felt they had insufficient aptitude or skill: "My most difficult task is designing; I would prefer to employ a designer and perhaps we shall eventually be able to do this on a part-time basis." Other managers found that difficulties arose through lack of experience and felt that, given time, they would sort themselves out: "My most difficult task is planning work through the factory but I don't know that training can help: You get plenty of training through practice and learn as you go along." A number of other managers also expressed some scepticism about the value of training, training being associated in their minds primarily with external courses and not with activities relevant and particular to their jobs in their companies: "One of my principal tasks is production scheduling. This is the most difficult aspect of my work. We do so many lines that it makes it difficult to keep ahead. I doubt if training is the answer. Any knowledge is helpful but our system is peculiar and involves very complex shuffling."

The activities and tasks that managers found difficult in their jobs were classified against a number of broad functional headings. The number of managers expressing some degree of difficulty in handling tasks within this general classification was as follows:

		Managers
1.	Personal difficulties	16
2.	Internal organizational and political difficulties	11
3.	Paperwork, figurework, and routine administration	8
4.	Sales and marketing (including customer relations)	6
5.	Continual interruptions and lack of time	5
	Product costing and estimating	5
	Technical difficulties and keeping-up-to-date with technical information	5

		Managers
6.	Designing	4
	Production Scheduling	4
7.	Financial management and accounts	3
8.	Other items	3

A few managers said that they found more than one of their tasks difficult to handle and one manager said that "the whole bloody lot is difficult; trade is bad and that makes it more hectic because you are constantly worrying about orders coming in and about staff being on short-time; you keep unproductive staff to the minimum and consequently your own efforts have to be thinly spread and you never have time to do anything properly." The general area in which the largest number of managers found some particular difficulty in their jobs was the area of personnel management. This arises partly, of course, because all of the managers had some responsibilities within this area, whereas not all of them had design, sales, or finance responsibilities. The difficult tasks described that were classified as "personnel difficulties" included the recruitment, allocation, and retention of labor, difficulties with bonus schemes and payment systems, and with management-employee relations, "finding out the abilities, aptitudes, motivation of each man and trying to work with them," and "trying to keep the workers happy in what is a seasonal trade." The tasks that were classified as "internal organizational and political difficulties" included "interesting the directors in changes," "getting decisions at director level," "the difficulty of being a professional manager in a family firm," "a sense of responsibility toward family shareholders because preference share dividends are owing for the last nine years," "internal company politics," "relying on other people," "not interfering in departmental management and making a conscious effort to allow managers to make mistakes," and "delegation." The three "other items" were "stock control," "company law," and "getting information on current performance early enough to take action on it."

A similar classification as that used to analyze managers' difficulties was used to summarize their description of their short-term problems. The number of managers describing short-term problems within this general classification was as follows:

		Managers
1.	Sales and marketing (particularly lack of orders)	39
2.	Personnel management	33
3.	Production scheduling and control	29

	Managers
4. Finance and accounts (particularly credit control)	26
5. Internal organizational and political problems	14
6. Purchasing and stock control	13
7. Design and development	12
8. Paperwork, figurework, and routine administration	10
9. Continual interruptions and lack of time	9
10. Product costing, estimating, and cost control	8
Quality control	8
Production methods and layout	8
11. Transport	6
12. Technical difficulties and keeping up-to-date with technical information	5
13. Age, retirement, and health problems	3
14. Training	2
Planning for the future	2
15. Managers with no perceived short-term problems	26

As can be seen, 17 percent of the managers felt that their most pressing short-term problem was a sales or marketing problem, 14 percent that it was a personnel problem, 13 percent that it was a problem concerning production scheduling and control, and 11 percent that it was a financial problem. Of the managers, 26 (or 11 percent), said that they had no pressing short-term problems.

The owner-managers, when asked about the most pressing short-term problem in their jobs, tended to talk about the most pressing problem that their company was facing at the time of the survey visit. There was complete identification between their companies and themselves. Consequently many of the short-term problems highlighted, particularly those in the areas of sales and finance, where acute problems arose from lack of orders and from shortage of cash, were problems faced by the companies. A number of examples of short-term problems are set out below:

1. Sales and marketing

"Shortage of orders, which is general in the upholstery trade at the present time, is the most pressing problem. It means short-time working and this makes labor problems very difficult and creates despondency among the workers."

"We are not able to find sufficient orders to keep us going. In addition the money is not coming in and we are having to give extended credit. The H.P. (Hire Purchase) houses (companies which arrange finance for installment sales) are working on our money. I don't see how training can help sell more furniture or help get the money in quicker."

"Sales is the main problem at the moment. We are small and mostly mail order so in the past we haven't kept up with the retail side. Now we are trying to get in with the big retail groups. I need information, training if you like, on premium-selling techniques --the use of coupons, discounts, special offers, etc."

2. Personnel

"Our most urgent problem is one of staff shortages arising through illness. These cannot be readily absorbed and it has meant that over the last four months I have had to spend my time filling in the gaps."

"Young people today are not interested in apprenticeships in this trade. Boys locally are very taken up with electronics and we get nobody through the Youth Employment Officer. There is nothing we can do about it."

3. Production scheduling and control

"The most pressing problem in my job is the lack of flow in the work. We are always having to deal with one-off (custom-built) items. Continual modifications mean constant jumping around from one order to another. We very rarely get orders for 50 or more of anything. It's all individual pieces. I don't know if training can help. What it wants is one person overall to say how each order is to go through the different departments."

4. Finance and accounts

"My most pressing problem? Getting money in and making sure that people we supply don't go bust overnight. We have more bad debts than ever before. Quite nice people are going bust."

"We have a momentary financial crisis. A gentlemanly business cannot concentrate too forcefully on getting in money."

"Lack of liquid capital is the most pressing problem at the moment. A considerable proportion of our turnover is in export work and this means a very elongated cash flow. I don't know what the answer is. We have tried the theoretical ways--ECGD [Export Credit Guarantee Department], bills of exchange--but these have only been a hindrance, so we are back to a system of open account. We are trying to be more selective in our choice of customers. Could training help? Well the company is quite strong financially but something on internal cash control and cash flow problems might be a help."

5. <u>Internal organizational problems</u>

"There is more work to do than the two of us can cope with. The pressing question is whether we should employ someone on the administrative side and, if so, how we should use him. Training ought to be able to help us to decide on the appropriate staffing for a company with our sales turnover, and on the appropriate volume and allocation of work within the firm."

"We need young blood in the company in order to expand, someone to take over responsibility from me. Training can obviously help but first we need to find someone suitable."

"The most urgent problem I face is getting my son to be able to take over completey from me, letting me go into semiretirement. At present I am passing work over gradually to him and am available for consultation. But how do you transfer 32 years' experience?"

As with the answers to the question on short-term problems there was considerable identification with the long-term problems of the company. A number of managers identified more than one important long-term problem facing them or their company and a number saw the long-term problems as being a continuation over time of the short-term problems, particularly in the areas of shortage of orders and shortage of suitable labor. Twice as many managers saw themselves having no important long-term problems as believed they had no pressing short-term problems. Of the managers, 52 (or 23 percent) said that there were no important long-term problems facing them in their work: "We can only plan two to three weeks ahead at the most," "We can't even think of tomorrow." The nature of the long-term problems described were classified as follows:

		Managers
1.	Sales and marketing	33
2.	Company growth and survival	27
3.	Internal organizational development	26
4.	Personnel Management	23
5.	Finance and accounts	18
6.	Production methods and layout	17
7.	Design and development	13
8.	Production scheduling and control	10
9.	Product costing, estimating, and cost control	7
10.	Paperwork, figurework, and routine administration	6
11.	Quality control	5

	Managers
12. Age, retirement, and health problems	4
13. Salary and personal security	3
14. Transport	2
15. Managers who felt they had no long-term problems	52

Thus 14 percent of the managers felt that their most important long-term problem was a sales or marketing problem, 12 percent that it was a problem connected with the growth and survival of their company, 11 percent that it was a problem involving internal development and change within their firm, and 10 percent that it was a personnel problem.

In many ways the classification of the managers' problems into different areas is a somewhat arbitrary one. Many of the problems described covered interrelated areas and were not seen by the managers themselves as being problems in one particular functional area (for example, "sales" problems) but rather as problems concerning the development of the business as a whole. In a number of examples set out below, therefore, the important long-term problems described are broader than the headings under which they are classified might suggest.

1. Sales and marketing

"The grouping of local education authorities into a consortium purchasing in bulk may cut us out of our traditional market. Exploring alternative markets is the most important long-term problem we face."

"We have to decide which direction we want to move in, how much we should concentrate on contract work and how much on retail sales, how much work we should buy in and how much we should make ourselves."

"We have to avoid putting all our eggs in one basket. There is a danger that we will become too tied to large multiple retailers who want a guaranteed production."

"From January 1971 four new metric sizes will become standard for beds. The most important problem I have is to decide whether to go over wholly to the four new sizes or to keep my options open for a very popular size, the three-feet divan. Unfortunately the company is not strong enough or big enough to dictate to the retail trade. If training could assist me in selling ideas to the retailers that would be a great help."

2. Company growth and survival

"Over the next five to ten years small upholsterers like ourselves will be squeezed out and we will go with them."

"We can't see the future; there is no room for expansion, no incentive to grow further. We would have to move to a factory four times as big as this one and all we would get is four times as much headache. We are in-between size for the type of furniture we are making but we have been in these lines all our lives and couldn't change now. If a compulsory purchase order comes along we would sell up, but it could be another ten years before that happens."

"Our present rate of expansion means that eventually we are going to need new premises and will move into one large factory. This in turn will highlight problems of product mix. Training can help with all problems of this kind. Outside experts may not know all the answers but there is great value in hearing an external point of view and in discussing one's problem with other people. This industry is far too insular."

3. Internal organizational development

"The most important long-term problem we face is making up our mind where we are going. So far we have drifted with the stream. We have to decide how big we want to be, how we are to finance any growth, and who is to manage the business in the future. We have to develop a better quality management and supervision."

"A lot of our factory supervisors are coming up to retirement and we have a problem of replacing them. In addition the present managing director will be phasing out over the next five years or more but no plans have been laid to train a successor."

"My main problem is that I have to run the business on my own. I don't have anyone sufficiently experienced to sit with, talk with, and decide how to improve the business. As yet my son hasn't got sufficient experience. If the opportunity arose to sell the business as a going concern I would sell up and take on a smaller business with less headaches."

4. Personnel Management

"Shortage of skilled labor, particularly of Windsor chairmakers, is our most important long-term problem. We already have great difficulty in finding and keeping young 15-year-olds as learners. The wages in the industry do not compare with those in engineering and we no longer seem able to recruit through the families of our present employees."

"We are going to be hard pushed to find somebody to replace the upholsterers we have now. They are mostly old men. It is obviously vital to us to train up replacements but it is very difficult to attract young persons into the trade."

5. Managers who felt they had no long-term problems

"We don't work on a long-term basis. We are mainly concerned with keeping things ticking over on a short-term basis, working two months ahead at most but normally only two to three weeks ahead."

"It is very difficult, in fact almost impossible, to plan long term; our production is not big enough to plan long term. But our lack of mechanization means that we can switch quicker; we can make up special jobs and odd items that the big boys wouldn't touch."

A number of points emerge from managers' descriptions of the difficulties in their jobs and of their short- and long-term problems which throw some light on their attitudes toward training as well as indicating some of their specific needs. Some of the attitudes are fairly familiar. The idea, for example, that training is for other people, particularly apprentices and others under the age of 21, and nothing to do with "me" is fairly common. So too is the notion that administrative or entrepreneurial skill can only be acquired through long years of experience and cannot be learned other than through a process of attrition and trial and error within the company. The association in the minds of many managers of "training" with "courses" has already been commented on. Complementary to this viewpoint is the idea that training is primarily about "theory" rather than about "practice." Although many managers were able to describe the problems they faced in their work, few felt that training was in any way relevant to helping toward solutions of those problems. In general there was little awareness of the relevance of training in improving organizational performance and in a number of cases, unfortunately, a feeling that training was not relevant had been reinforced by attendance at courses whose content had apparently not been appropriate to the requirements of small furniture companies. Three other points emerge from managers' descriptions of their difficulties and problems, points that are rather more general in character. First, many managers of small companies appear to resent interference but want help. This was particularly apparent in their attitude toward the government (the interviews mostly took place before the 1970 General Election, at which the Conservatives under Edward Heath replaced Labour under Harold Wilson). On the one hand many of the owner-managers complained bitterly of government "interference." On the other hand, even though some were aware of the work of the Bolton Committee of Inquiry on Small Firms, many complained that "no one is interested in small firms." Ability to help small companies depends to some extent on their willingness to provide the kind of information that will indicate what forms of assistance are most needed. Second, many owner-managers felt that their problems were a result of factors outside their control, the state of the market for their product, the state of the labor market or credit restrictions, for example, and that there was nothing they could do to mitigate the effects of such external factors on the performance of their companies. At the same time, although these

factors were felt to be outside the control of the company, a number
of managers seemed to believe that they were in a unique situation,
that somehow the effects of these external influences acted quite differently on their firm, and that their competitors did not face the
same difficulties. Third, owner-managers in particular described
their work problems in terms primarily of the problems facing their
companies either in the short or long term. In addition, in many
cases the problems they described were problems relating to different aspects of their business rather than to specific problems in one
functional area only; they were "business management" problems
rather than "design" or "production" or "sales" problems. In contrast, however, many of the training courses offered to small business managers are structured in terms of functional specialisms
that reflect the specialized interests of the trainer rather than the
requirements of the owner-manager.

TRAINING AND DEVELOPMENT NEEDS

As we have seen, many of the training needs identified by the
descriptive survey were highly specific to the work situations and
problems of particular managers in their companies at the time of
the survey visits. Such training needs can probably only adequately
be met by advisory and consultancy services that are closely in touch
with the growth and development of the individual companies and
their managers. A number of more general training needs did
emerge, however. These are described below in order of priority
based on managers' perception of their areas of difficulty and their
short- and long-term problems.

1. Sales and marketing
About half of the companies in the survey had remained
relatively static in terms of annual sales value over the last four or
five years. Lack of orders was a major problem for a number of
firms at the time of the survey, but in some cases was seen as being
a matter outside the control of the management of the firm. There
is undoubtedly a need for developing among the managers of small
firms a greater awareness of the advantages and disadvantages of
product diversification, and of the practical problems to be overcome
in exploring alternative markets and in changing a company's product
mix. Such training must develop an understanding of the workings
of the price mechanism in a competitive market, an understanding
of the distinctive features of the different markets for quality products, consideration of the advantages and disadvantages of working
through independent retail outlets and of dependence on a few large

customers, and details of approaches to offsetting the effects of
seasonal peaks and troughs in product demand.

    2. Personnel management

      About a quarter of the managing directors felt that their
companies were weak in the areas of personnel recruitment and selection, although a number believed this was entirely due to the state
of the labor market and difficulties of attracting young persons into
their firms. In addition a number of managers felt that the greatest
difficulties in their own jobs were "personnel" difficulties. There is
a need for training designed to help owner-managers to overcome
the problems involved in developing a self-motivated labor force--
problems primarily of work organization, payment systems, and
employee relations. Understanding of the operation of labor markets
would be an important component part of any training program, together with an introduction to recruitment and selection techniques.

    3. Internal organizational development

      Small companies face two major problems that have been
grouped under this heading. The first is to provide for continuity of
management, either through the family of the owner-manager or
through the introduction of "professional" managers into the firm.
This in itself raises a number of personal and "political" difficulties
that have to be overcome, together with the training difficulties involved in the identification and transfer of managerial skill. The
second major problem, which is primarily a problem faced by the
expanding small firm, is to recognize in what ways the company's
organization and management system must adapt and change with
different phases in the company's growth. This problem relates in
particular to the responsibilities and development of the owner-
manager of the business and the way in which he uses his own time
and such managerial assistance as he has available.

    4. Finance and accounts

      The profit records of the 50 companies that took part in the
survey were, in general, extremely poor. About a third of the managing directors had no assistance in their companies on financial
matters and consequently had to rely solely on their own experience
and, in some cases, very limited knowledge in handling the financial
side of their business. There is a clear need for training, designed
specifically in the context of the small firm, in the interpretation
of financial data and the use of financial information in the control
and development of a small company's business. This is particularly
necessary in order to assist the owner-manager to deal effectively
with his cash flow and credit control problems. Too much of the
financial advice aimed at small companies is designed primarily to
inform them about the capital market and too little is designed to
inform them about the use and control of credit, about lend-lease

arrangements and other methods of interbusiness financing. There
is a clear need, too, for developing in small firm owner-managers a
greater understanding of the necessity for tax planning, particularly
in the context of handling management succession problems.

A number of other areas of training need were identified by the
descriptive survey. There is a need for training in simple systems
of production scheduling, product costing and estimating, and stock
control. It is important that the systems and procedures that are the
subject of such training should be closely tailored to the needs of
small companies and should involve the minimum of paperwork. A
further area of training need is the area of production methods and
layout. In view of the number of companies involved in changes in
their location in any one year, training in economic production
methods and layout might usefully be linked to examination of the
general sire requirements of small firms and the problems to be
overcome in moving from one site to another. Finally there is, in
the furniture industry if not for small firms generally, a need for
greater emphasis on design, and on design and development problems,
in the training of owner-managers and managers.

In addition to looking at the content of the management training
requirements highlighted by the survey, an attempt was also made to
quantify, on the basis of the information collected, the training needs
of the three groups of managers--the owner-managers, the nonshareholding managers, and the supervisors. This was done by using the
information collected on the ages of managers, retirements and
labor turnover, job transfers and promotions, and their experience
of difficulties in their work, to build up very crude training targets,
the targets being expressed in terms of the percentage of managers
in each group that "should" be receiving some kind of training in any
one year. These targets were based on a number of assumptions,
notably that, first, there would be relatively little change from one
year to the next in the total number of managers required in the industry; second, that any manager taking on new responsibilities,
whether coming from outside the company or from within it, would
require some form of training; and third, that all managers need to
keep up to date with changes and developments that affect their own
managerial skill or the effectiveness of their company and that this
should involve, for each manager, at least one period of training,
however short, every five years. On the basis of these assumptions
it was calculated that the training target for owner-managers of
small furniture firms should be a 33 percent involvement in some
kind of training in any one year. Similarly 50 percent of nonshareholding managers and 32 percent of supervisors should be receiving
training in any one year. If all managers were grouped together the

annual training target would be a 43 percent involvement in management training activity. Only 14 of the 50 companies in the descriptive
survey had a management training involvement of 43 percent or more
during the 12 months preceding the survey visit to their firms. Taking all managers together, about 30 percent had taken part in some
kind of training activity, often of a very rudimentary nature, during
the year under review. It was apparent, therefore, that the numbers
undergoing management training in any one year could be increased by
over a third before the training needs of the managers could be adequately met. At the same time, however, as encouraging an increase
in the "quantity" of management training involvement it is important
to ensure that the training available--whether through courses, advisory and consultancy services, or other mediums--should be suitable in content to the particular requirements of small companies,
a matter to which we will give further consideration in Chapter 13.

Finally, as part of the descriptive survey each of the 50 companies studied was given a management training index based on the
number of their managerial and supervisory staff that had been involved in some kind of training activity during the 12 months prior to
the date of the survey visit. Of the 50 companies, 4 had a 100 percent record on this index, all of their managers and supervisors having been involved in some form of training during that 12-month
period; 20 companies had a nil management training involvement over
the same period. The median companies had percentage involvements
of their managerial and supervisory staff of 17.7 percent and 20 percent respectively.

NOTE

1. D. Lees and B. Chiplin, "The Economics of Industrial
Training," Lloyds Bank Review, April 1970, pp. 29-41.

9

THE OWNER-MANAGER
AND HIS WORK

MANAGERIAL WORK IN THE SMALL FIRM

One of the objectives of the descriptive survey was to provide
information on the extent of delegation of managerial tasks within
the small firm in order to examine to what degree the small-firm
owner-manager's work called for specialist managerial skills. During the survey, managing directors were asked about the structure
and organization of their firms, and details were collected of the
employment of staff in different occupational categories. The main
difficulty that has to be faced in analyzing data of this kind is that,
in the context of small companies, definitions of management in terms
of "levels" of responsibility or hierarchical supervisory systems
must be viewed with some scepticism. The managing director in a
small firm may be both chief executive and first-line supervisor,
responsible for planning the introduction of new designs and for inspecting the quality of finished work. Consequently the classification
of managers adopted during the course of the descriptive survey attempted to indicate, for each manager, three aspects of his position
in the company: first, whether or not he was an owner of the firm,
either as a shareholder, a partner, or as sole proprietor; second,
whether his responsibilities were general or specialist in character,
generalists being those whose work covered more than one management function and whose jobs were not designated by functional titles,
and specialists being those whose work was concentrated mainly in
one functional area and whose jobs were designated by such functional
titles as company secretary, works director, sales manager, etc.;
third, whether he was considered by the managing director to be a
manager or a supervisor, the latter generally having such designa-
tions as foreman or working foreman. In this way the 235 managers

and supervisors employed in the 50 companies in the survey were
split into the eight categories indicated in Table 9.1. As can be seen,
29 percent of the 235 managers and supervisors were classified as
generalists and 49 percent as specialists. If the categories of full-
time supervisors and working foremen are excluded then 37 percent
of the managers are generalists (68 out of 186) and 62 percent are
specialists (115 out of 186). On the same basis 35 percent of the
owner-managers were specialists compared with 92 percent of the
nonshareholding managers. Specialist managers were generally
younger than the managers in other categories, young men under the
age of 31 being found fairly often in specialist managerial positions,
whether or not they were owners of the business. While no comparative data are readily available from other studies it is clear that in
the small firm ownership generally has a major impact on the degree
of work specialization at a managerial level. Further discussion of
the organization patterns in small firms is included in Chapter 12.

TABLE 9.1

Managerial Specialization in the Small Firm
(n = 235)

Classification	Number Employed	Percent of 235
Owner-manager/generalist	61	26
Owner-manager/specialist	35	15
Owner-manager/full-time supervisor	2	1
Owner-manager/working foreman	1	--
Generalist manager	7	3
Specialist manager	80	34
Full-time supervisor	20	9
Working foreman	29	12
Generalists, 1 and 5	68	29
Specialists, 2 and 6	115	49

Notes: Category 1 includes one managing director/odd job man;
categories 5 and 6 include directors who are not shareholders; category 8 covers supervisors, foremen, or chargehands who spent 50
percent or more of their time in supervisory duties but less than
100 percent.

Source: Compiled by the author.

The management activity most often carried out by the managing directors of the small firms in the descriptive survey, without any assistance from other managers in the company, was finance. In 30 percent of the companies the managing director kept complete control of all financial matters and in 18 percent of the companies he was the only manager involved in purchasing, cost control, or office administration. Production and quality control were the two activities where most managerial support and assistance were available to the managing director.

A continuous observation study with sample activity recordings was carried out on the owner-managers of seven companies for a total of 25 days or just over 214 hours of working time. During this study 2,146 separate work episodes were identified and each was timed to the nearest minute. The information recorded about each episode included the management function with which the episode was concerned, the place where the episode occurred, the other person or persons involved in the episode, and whether or not the episode was initiated by the owner-manager. Telephone calls were analyzed separately and "non-work" activities ignored except insofar as they were the result of accompanying work-related activities.

The number of hours worked per day by the managing directors of these seven small owner-managed firms ranged from 6-1/4 hours to 11-1/2 hours, the average being 8 hours 34 minutes. The view that small-firm owner-managers are human dynamos working very long hours could not be applied to the group studied, nor could the half-time-Britain stereotype of absentee managers spending half their working day on the local golf course. Of the two managing directors who worked the longest hours, one was the managing director of the most profitable company among those examined in the depth study and one was the managing director of one of the least profitable firms in the group.

The average number of daily work episodes with which each managing director was involved was 86, within a range from 60 to 117. The average length of the 2,146 episodes noted was six minutes. On average, therefore, the managing directors of these small companies worked at tasks of relatively short duration or, more usually, at tasks that were frequently interrupted by visitors or by telephone calls. Lines of communication in small firms are very short and it is usually easy for people both inside and outside the firm to make personal contact with the man at the top. The range of episode lengths was from four minutes to ten minutes. Two types of managing director, or two management styles, emerged from the analysis of the number and length of episodes in the small-firm managerial working day. First, there was the cool, well-organized owner-manager who was on top of his job and who was protected by an assistant or by a secretary from too many trivial interruptions. Second, there was the harassed, oppressed man who tried to keep in close touch with everything that was happening and who spent his time reacting to events and to people. In the first category was Zeta's managing director who had a number of other senior people in the company, thereby allowing him to concentrate on his chosen tasks. In the second category was Delta's managing director, who was trying to be managing director of a group of companies for two or three days a week and run one of the companies in the group for the remainder of the time. This meant that he was constantly running around and his life was a series of unsolicited interruptions. There was no obvious relationship between management style and company financial performance, although the "cool" managing directors seemed to work in marginally more profitable firms. If any relationship of this kind did exist it would probably operate through an intervening factor such as ability. It may merely have been that the more profitable companies could afford to employ people in "filter" positions.

WORK FUNCTIONS AND ACTIVITIES
OF OWNER-MANAGERS

There is no universally agreed system for allocating episodes to functions and each attempt in the literature uses its own. The allocation and the classification used in this research were also arbitrary but they were applied consistently from firm to firm and this is probably the most important factor. A classification of 15 functions was chosen.[1] The percentage distribution of the working time of the small-firm managing directors studied is indicated in Figure 9.1. The most striking feature of this analysis is the large number of different aspects of the operation of their businesses with which the managing directors concerned themselves. They were interested in almost every aspect of the running of their businesses from the buying in of raw materials to the collection of outstanding debts from customers. It is this wide range of activities that has led some observers to the conclusion that the small-business owner-manager is likely to be "an amateur in all, or most, of the managerial activities he undertakes."[2]

As can be seen from Figure 9.1, the function that took up the largest proportion of the managing directors' time was sales, which accounted for 20 percent of total time spent. Managing directors were spending time securing new customers and chasing old customers for repeat orders, a situation that reflected both the competition facing the companies studied and the work interests of their managing

FIGURE 9.1

Distribution of Managerial Time by Functions
(in percent)

Function	Percent
Production	14
Sales	20
Marketing	4
Purchasing	9
Accounts/Finance	10
Personnel	6
Drawing/Design	2
Transport/Delivery	2
Costing/Estimating	1.1
Quality Control	1
Routine Clerical/Administration	12
Work Organization	3
General Management	8
Personal	4
Other	4

Source: Furniture and Timber Industry Board, Research Reports.

directors. The second most important function in terms of time spent was production. If the frequent comments made by managing directors about the need for technical expertise in their jobs had been taken at face value, one would have expected that they would spend more time on production than on any other function. In only two companies, however, did production take up more time than sales. In one this was the direct result of the market stability provided by a long-term contract with a government department, and in the other was the consequence of there being no production manager, a situation that the managing director was seeking to rectify. In most of the other companies managing directors had clearly identified sales as a more pressing problem and had delegated much of the day-to-day decisions on production matters to factory or works managers. In some cases the relatively simple technology of the production process allowed them to do this with complete confidence. To these managing directors, production tasks mostly involved chatting to works managers and checking that everything was running smoothly.

Another interesting feature of Figure 9.1 is the 12 percent of managing directors' time spent on routine clerical work and administration. Some of this, for example reading the mail, may have been unavoidable, but there was no doubt that the managing directors studied spent many hours acting as highly paid clerks. Most of them, however, never considered costing the time they spent on routine clerical work or seriously pursued the possibility of delegating such tasks. Their most common complaint remained, "There aren't enough hours in the day for me." The problem is further highlighted by analysis of the pattern of distribution of episodes between management functions (see Figure 9.2). As can be seen, routine clerical work and administration accounted for 27 percent of episodes, indicating the frequency and disruptive nature of such tasks.

The distribution of time and episodes by activities is set out in Table 9.2. Over half of the total working time of the managing directors was spent in face-to-face conversation, that is in the activity of talking and listening, and none of the other activities took up significant proportions of managerial time. Owner-managers receive information, give instructions, listen to complaints and advise on solutions, meet representatives and customers, and discuss terms of purchase or sale. They appear to be people who like to sort out problems on a face-to-face basis, who like to make on-the-spot decisions in consultation with the other persons affected, and who prefer to work with a minimum of formal or written communications. Telephone activity, a further form of direct communications, took up an additional 7 percent of the time of the managing directors. Telephone episodes were, however, relatively frequent, indicating that calls were generally of fairly short duration and likely, therefore, to have

FIGURE 9.2

Distribution of Work Episodes by Functions
(in percent)

Production	13
Sales	15
Marketing	0
Purchasing	7
Accounts/Finance	12
Personnel	5
Drawing/Design	3
Transport/Delivery	4
Costing/Estimating	1
Quality Control	2
Routine Clerical/Administration	27
Work Organization	3
General Management	5
Personal	3
Other	1

Source: Furniture and Timber Industry Board, Research Reports.

a disruptive effect that was disproportionate to the time they actually took. Other studies have shown that managers tend to overestimate quite dramatically the amount of time they spend on the telephone.[3] Such overestimates may arise because the telephone is a major and frequent source of interruption to the manager's work.

TABLE 9.2

Distribution of Owner-Managers' Time
and Work Episodes by Activities

Activity	Percent of Time	Percent of Episodes
Reading	7	9
Writing/dictation	11	13
Telephoning	7	16
Talking/listening	51	46
Traveling	12	2
Calculating	5	4
Observing	2	9
Miscellaneous	5	1

Source: Furniture and Timber Industry Training Board, Research Reports.

The managing directors studied spent, on average 55 percent of their working time in their own offices and a further 17 percent elsewhere in the company. An average of 12 percent of time was spent in traveling, mostly on sales trips, and a further 16 percent in activities away from the company's premises.

COMMUNICATION PATTERNS

Table 9.3 indicates the distribution of the working time and the work episodes of the managing directors according to the persons with whom interaction was taking place. On average just over a third of their working time was spent alone but this average conceals some significant differences. At one extreme, for example, was a managing director who spent 64 percent of his time alone, much of this time being taken up in traveling on sales visits. At the other extreme was a managing director who was alone for only 11 percent

of his working time. This managing director had very precise ideas
about the nature of his work role, which he saw as being a coordinator
of others' activities by means of face-to-face communications. Contact between managing directors and company staff took place more
frequently than contact with outsiders and was more episodic in character. The most frequent external contacts were with customers,
though again there were significant variations between companies,
the range of time spent in contact with customers being from 3 percent to 21 percent.

TABLE 9.3

Distribution of Owner-Managers' Time and Work
Episodes by Interpersonal Contacts

Interpersonal Contact	Percent of Time	Percent of Episodes
Customer	9	6
Suppliers	4	5
Managers	9	12
Supervisors	7	9
Office employees	7	15
Works employees	7	9
Researcher[a]	6	4
Others[b]	15	7
Alone[a]	36	33

[a]Where there was some discussion between the researcher and
the manager an interpersonal contact was recorded. At other times,
when only the researcher was present as an observer, the managing
director was considered to be "alone."
    [b]"Others" included participants in a marketing conference, in-
surance agents, journalists, policemen, relatives, friends, bank
managers, travel agents, tax officers, job applicants, etc.

    Source: Furniture and Timber Industry Training Board, Re-
search Reports.

    The extent to which small-firm owner-managers controlled
their own work pace and work procedures, as opposed to being controlled by the demands made on them by their staff or their customers,
was thought to be an important subject for research. Table 9.4 shows
the extent to which the time and the work episodes of the managing

directors studied were self-initiated and indicates the sources of other initiated work activities. As can be seen, 75 percent of the working time of the owner-managers in the depth study was spent on tasks that were self-initiated. In spite, therefore, of the episodic nature of much of their work and the fact that they are involved in a wide variety of management functions, it would seem clear that small-firm owner-managers are able to exercise a significant degree of control over their work activities. The managing directors studied were, by and large, not people who spent their working lives merely responding to the requests and demands of others but were, rather, people in command of their jobs who were frequently the motivating and mobilizing force within their firms. There was no other group of people who initiated the managing directors' activities to any significant degree. A similar pattern emerged in terms of work episodes, although the self-initiated episodes were slightly longer on average than the other-initiated episodes, many of the other-initiated episodes being in the form of short interruptions from managers, supervisors, or employees, and most particularly from office staff, or in the form of short incoming telephone calls.

TABLE 9.4

Distribution of Owner-Managers' Time and Work
Episodes by Initiation of Activity

Initiator of Activity	Percent of Time	Percent of Episodes
Self	75	68
Customers	5	4
Suppliers	3	2
Managers	4	5
Supervisors	4	5
Office employees	1	6
Works employees	3	4
Researcher	2	2
Others	3	4

Source: Furniture and Timber Industry Training Board, Research Reports.

Although the average figure for self-initiated time was 75 percent, this was within a range from 48 percent to 93 percent. The "controlled" managing director, whose self-initiated activity represented only 48 percent of his time, was a time-served cabinetmaker who had inherited his business from his father. He knew furniture manufacturing methods intimately and was very close to his works

employees who frequently brought their difficulties directly to him.
As a result he often gave the impression of being harassed. The
background, personality, and management style of the "controlling"
managing director who initiated 93 percent of his work time was very
different. He was an ex-civil servant with a law degree and no previous knowledge of the furniture trade when he bought his company
ten years ago. He left production in the hands of his works manager,
preferring to spend his time on well-planned sales trips. He was
well-organized, on top of his work, raised problems with people before they raised them with him, and, in general, had his fingers on
the pulse of his business. This difference between the controlled
managing director and the controlling managing director is highlighted
by the nature of their customer contacts. Of the controlling managing
director's time, 13 percent was spent with customers, yet customers
initiated only 1 percent of his time. In contrast, all 21 percent of the
time that the controlled managing director spent with customers was
initiated by the customers and none of it by the managing director
himself. Similarly, 15 percent of the controlling managing director's contact time was with other managers in his firm but only 2.5
percent of this time was initiated by the other managers. In contrast
the controlled managing director was constantly being chased by his
supervisors, all 12 percent of his contact time with supervisors being other-initiated.

Of the managing directors' working time, 7 percent was spent
on the telephone, the range for individual managing directors being
from 3 percent to 14 percent. Of all working-time episodes, 16 percent were telephone episodes, the range being from 9 percent to 23
percent. The majority of the calls, 62 percent of the total, were outgoing calls. The managing directors of two firms made many more
outgoing calls than they received incoming calls and this primarily
reflected the fact that incoming calls were frequently dealt with by
secretaries. The managing director of another of the firms, however,
operated the switchboard personally and, therefore, every caller
reached him direct.

WORK PROFILES OF OWNER-MANAGERS
AND STYLES OF MANAGEMENT

What then, were the main characteristics of the ways in which
each managing director performed his job and in what ways were their
work patterns similar? The following brief sketches of the ways in
which 10 of the 12 small firms in the depth study were managed illustrate the variety of approaches of owner-managers to their work
and the diversity of management styles used by the managing directors

of these companies. (Four of these 10 profiles, those for the Epsilon, Theta, Iota, and Kappa companies, are not based on continuous observation studies but are compiled from interviews with the firms' owner-managers.) The management style of an owner-manager may evolve from conscious perception on his part of the nature of his role in the firm, or may evolve unconsciously as appropriate behavior for the particular work situation in which he finds himself. In either case the background, experience, and personality of each owner-manager will partly determine the management style he perceives as appropriate or unconsciously adopts. What is clear from the 10 profiles that follow is that similar job situations can give rise to very different management styles and that, given the lack of any apparent relationship between management styles and small firm profitability, it would be foolish to suggest that any one kind of management style was better, in economic terms, than another.

Alpha Company: The Aloof Leader

Alpha's owner-manager covered a large number of functions during his working hours but did not involve himself too deeply in any of these functions. He dealt directly only with those matters that he felt could not be properly handled by anyone else in the firm, all other tasks being passed down the line to his employees. He interfered with the work of his subordinates very little, only checking on them occasionally. A great deal of Alpha's time was spent talking to other people, mostly in his own office or away from the firm. Relatively little of his time was spent in direct contact with shop-floor employees, since Alpha tended to keep to formal channels and usually communicated with the shop floor through his works supervisor. Most of Alpha's work activities were self-initiated and he was in full control of his work pattern. He used the telephone frequently, but calls were invariably very short with the result that he did not spend much time on the telephone.

Alpha's managing director had everyone's duties and responsibilities clearly defined, including his own, and left people to get on with their jobs. He had regular discussions with his principal employees about their work and about the problems they faced. He was very clear minded, always able to give unambiguous, precise, and well-organized information with little prompting. Sometimes he would take a brief walk around the factory for a general inspection, watching what people were doing and having a brief word with some of them, but he seemed aloof from his employees and admitted that he had difficulty in communicating with them. This did not greatly bother him since he felt he did not need to communicate directly with the shop floor and, in any case, did not want to undermine the authority of his supervisors. Only once during the study did Alpha's managing director compliment any of his staff on their work. His staff appeared very obedient and, with the exception of the sales manager, never questioned anything he said.

Beta Company: The Friendly Manager

The owner-manager of Beta worked long hours, starting around 9:00 a.m. each morning but working in the evenings, visiting customers, and taking work home on weekends. His life revolved round his work. His pattern of work was an extremely fragmented one since he was constantly being interrupted by employees, visitors, and incoming telephone calls. The result was that he rarely had an opportunity to concentrate exclusively on any one problem. Most of Beta's time was spent on production, sales, and personnel functions. This was largely a reflection of the one-off nature of the company's products. Each job had to be individually planned and costed, involved liaison with the client and constant checking to iron out production problems. Beta's managing director spent much of his time in face-to-face communications. He took personal responsibility for all aspects of the company's operations and was in touch with his employees, customers, and suppliers, gathering information and giving instructions. His most important internal contacts were customers. Only half of Beta's work activities were self-initiated and for the balance of his time Beta was responding to the demands and requests of others, especially of foremen and customers. He was not, therefore, fully in control of his work pattern.

Beta's owner-manager was familiar with all the jobs in the organization and with all the contracts being worked on at any time. He continually inquired after progress, both of individual contracts and of the people performing the work. He knew each of his employees by their first names and was also friendly with many of his customers and suppliers. He communicated easily with everyone and was familiar with their personal and family circumstances. Beta did not operate in terms of formal communications within an established hierarchy nor did he stick to prescribed lines of authority. Delegation of managerial and supervisory responsibilities within the firm was minimal and the owner-manager was the dominant influence in the firm, decision-making on even relatively minor matters being referred to him.

Gamma Company: The Do-it-Yourself Manager

A 9.5-hour day was the average for Gamma's owner-manager,
broken by a few sandwiches in his office around lunchtime. His normal work pattern was that he would settle down in his office on his own
to carry out some relatively routine bonus calculations or costings
and would then be constantly interrupted by telephone calls, visitors,
or employees. If someone else was also working in the office, as
for example his part-time clerk, then Gamma's owner-manager
would keep up an almost constant flow of conversation with them no
matter what he was doing, much of the conversation being general
chat unrelated to work. From time to time he went on to the shop
floor to help with production problems or to make a brief inspection.
Most of his time was spent dealing with immediate short-term problems, usually problems of sales or production. He saw all visitors
personally, took most telephone calls direct, and was easily accessible to his foremen and employees. He also did a certain amount of
letter writing and typing himself. Most of his work activities were
self-initiated.

Gamma's managing director was aware of and involved in almost everything that happened within the firm. He attended to a very
wide range of tasks from preparing Board of Trade returns to repair-
ing the company vending machine. He was a combination of export
sales director, works supervisor, and office manager. He spent
most of his time on small problems in the office and the factory.
When problems arose Gamma went straight to his employees or they
came straight to him, neither of them necessarily working through
the foremen. When Gamma's owner-manager did not have something
of an immediate nature with which to concern himself he looked
around until he found such a problem. He always managed to bring
an air of urgency to items on which he was working and often handled
several at once. For example, on one occasion when he was on the
telephone he was also calculating some figures on an adding machine
and talking to one of his employees. He tended to dominate in his
relationships with others in the company, yet was easy to approach
and had good relations with his employees. He drove himself hard
and produced an air of tension and momentum in the daily operation
of the firm.

Delta Company: The Office Manager

Delta's managing director normally worked between 7.50 and
9.50 hours each day, starting around 8:30 a.m. and working until
about 5:30 p.m. Lunch usually took about 1.25 hours and the

managing director always went out for lunch and, especially if visiting the main Delta group offices, he went out with his colleagues and
discussed company business. Delta's owner-manager also worked
on Saturday mornings and for about two hours on a Sunday and said
that he did an hour's work "fairly frequently" in the evenings. He did
not spend a great deal of time away from the company, although he
was planning to take a trip to Denmark partly for business and partly
for pleasure; he intended to visit a trade fair and look around some
shops for design ideas. Delta's normal work pattern was that, except for an occasional visit to the factory floor, he spent most of his
day in his office working on accounts, sales, or purchasing tasks,
doing small routine jobs, making and receiving telephone calls, and
talking to colleagues, employees, and visitors. But this time was
broken up by many interruptions, most of which did not last very
long. Delta's owner-manager tended not to become too involved in
problems of an immediate nature and dealt with those things that he
felt most demanded his attention. Other tasks were delegated. He
spent more than half of his working day in verbal contact with other
people and made extensive use of the telephone. Within the company
his most frequent contacts were with his colleagues and his clerical
and secretarial staff. Externally they were with customers and suppliers. Most of the activities of Delta's managing director were self-
initiated.

The owner-manager of Delta was very much a businessman
rather than a furniture manufacturer. He scarcely concerned himself with the furniture production process but bothered more about
organizing sales, about accounts and cash flow, and about the purchasing of supplies. He was psychologically distant from his works
and office employees, treated them well, could communicate effectively with them on work matters, but never really managed, or even
tried, to get close to them. He did not discuss any nonbusiness
questions with them. He usually worked through foremen and leading
hands and talked very little to shop-floor workers. Yet he also
talked little to the foremen or leading hands and more or less left
them to get on with their jobs. Delta's rather distant style of working may have been a result of his lack of experience at a lower level
in the furniture industry. He had never worked as a salesman or a
craftsman in the industry, neither was he born into it, being 47 years
old when he first became employed in a furniture business. The
style of Delta's managing director may also be a result of the uniformity of the production process within his company. The process
rarely varied and could be left in the hands of supervisory staff. It
is probable, therefore, that Delta's management style stems from a
mixture of his background, particularly his army experience, his
lack of detailed technical knowledge of furniture production methods,

the uniformity of the production process within the firm, and his assessment of the critical problems facing the company. There was no doubt, however, that the composite style that emerged was well suited to the circumstances in which Delta's owner manager and the Delta company were operating; it was a situation-relevant style.

Epsilon Company: The Organization Man

Epsilon's owner-manager estimated that he spent 1.5 to 2 days each week visiting universities, schools, and hospitals looking for contract work, though he would also visit some of his larger retail customers. When he was working in his office he generally arrived between 9:00 a.m. and 9:15 a.m. and spent about three-quarters of an hour reading the mail and noting its contents. At about 10:00 the works manager and the office manager would come to see him to discuss any problems that had arisen and Epsilon would give out any instructions he had for them. Normally this involved discussing the orders that had come in the mail and deciding when the goods would be manufactured and delivered. They also discussed such matters as requests for estimates, the cost of supplies, and bonus problems, any final decisions on such problems being made by the managing director. This meeting was important because it meant that, except for a few telephone calls from customers and for interruptions from any important visitors who might arrive, Epsilon's owner manager was more or less left alone during the rest of the day to get on with his work. The morning meeting was open-ended and usually lasted about an hour.

Epsilon always went home for lunch, leaving his office just before 1:00 p.m. in order to catch the one o'clock news and returning between 2:15 p.m. and 2:30 p.m. The rest of his working day, to around 5:30 p.m. when he went home, was spent in a variety of tasks. Many of these were of a "routine" nature, talking on the telephone to customers and suppliers, checking orders, dictating to his secretary/typist, signing letters, and walking around the factory on a general inspection. By and large, Epsilon's owner-manager was left comparatively alone during this time and this gave him an opportunity to concentrate on longer-term tasks. These included studying cost sheets, filling in monthly statistical returns for government departments, looking at designs for new products, planning monthly production and delivery schedules, and generally thinking about the problems facing the company. He also did some accountancy and financial work such as checking bank statements, sending out demands for payment of outstanding accounts, looking after problems of cash-flow, and costing contracts. Occasionally Epsilon did a few hours' work at home in the evening. Epsilon's director was, then, very well organized, his daily meeting with the works manager and the office manager being typical of his style. He was very much of the "old school" of businessman--important, aloof from his staff, fairly difficult to approach, and rarely going down onto the factory floor. He was not immediately familiar with what happened further down the organization, not knowing, for example, precisely how many workers were employed at any one time. He gave a considerable degree of autonomy to his two immediate subordinates.

Zeta Company: The Father Figure

On average, the managing director of Zeta worked approximately ten hours every day. He began at 8:30 a.m. and usually remained after 6:00 p.m. He sometimes took work home with him, but most of his evening and weekend work consisted of attending trade functions and meetings of the local Rotary Association. Contact with external bodies was clearly regarded by Zeta as one of the most important aspects of his work. When he was at the factory the managing director usually went for lunch to the coffee lounge of the art gallery, a ten-minute walk from company premises, and talked business with the sales manager, his son-in-law. On a Monday he lunched at his Rotary Association. Each morning Zeta's managing director had a ten-minute walk around his factory before going into his own office. He greeted supervisors and works employees, not stopping unless someone communicated a problem to him. The tour was a check on the level of activity in the factory, since Zeta liked to see that everyone was busy. He made two or three other trips around the factory in the course of the day. These were usually much longer and Zeta would stop and ask employees and supervisors about the progress of their work. He felt such trips were important for keeping everyone on their toes. After his morning tour the managing director would open all the company mail and then hand out relevant correspondence to the other managers, talking to each of them about priorities. If any of the others were not available he would often leave them a note detailing his instructions. All export mail was handled by Zeta himself. Unusual items in the mail had to be investigated, either in the factory, the stores, the showroom, or with one of the staff, and, consequently, during his mail-reading exercise, Zeta would pop out of his office to seek information from various people. He felt that by personally reading all incoming mail he could keep in close touch with what was happening in the firm: "I see any irate letters that arrive. No-one can hide them from me." In the evening the managing director usually stayed after 5:30 p.m. so that

he could dictate letters, this being the only time of the day that he
was free from interruption. In addition employees on external tours
of work telephoned every evening after the cheap telephone rate began to give any news and to collect messages.

Zeta's owner-manager spent many of his working hours away
from his company. Twice a month he went to visit the two other
companies in his group, each trip taking one or two days. He frequently went to see items he wanted to buy and also made a point of
visiting his more important customers from time to time. He was a
member of the Confederation of British Industry and often attended
their meetings, and he was a Justice of the Peace. The company
was also an active member of its trade association and participated
in shows and exhibitions. The managing director, his son, and his
son-in-law attended the annual general meetings and prize-givings of
various sporting associations. Zeta manufactured sports goods and
many trophies had been donated by the firm. The managing director
felt that attending such meetings kept him in touch with sporting developments and also got him known to sports club officials, which was
good for business.

Zeta's owner-manager had a style of management that was both
authoritarian and paternalistic. He was very open with employees
and criticized mistakes directly and often but without animosity. He
knew how to do all the jobs in the factory and was respected and
obeyed immediately. No one disagreed with him. Zeta did not always work directly through managers or supervisors. During his
trips through the factory he chastised employees for untidiness, poor
housekeeping, and for wasting electricity. He mentioned that often
no one informed him when problems arose and he did not learn of
them until he saw for himself on one of these trips. Perhaps this
was an inevitable result of his particular style of management. Much
of his work was just keeping in touch with what was happening in the
firm and showing his presence to his staff and the company's presence to its customers and the external business community. Zeta
was shrewd and always alive to opportunities for saving or earning
money. The business was one of the most successful studied but
this was obviously due in part to its dominance in its particular
market.

Eta Company: The Gentleman Manager

The managing director of Eta worked about seven hours a day,
normally starting work between 8:15 and 8:30 a.m. and finishing between 4:30 and 4:45 p.m. He had from 1.5 to 2 hours at home for
lunch. His normal pattern was to spend his time in his own office

carrying out various tasks that were subject to almost constant interruption from telephone calls, visitors, and employees, sometimes
even the interruptions being interrupted by further interruptions. In
addition Eta occasionally went out into the yard or factory and sometimes went down-town but was rarely away from his office for very
long at one time. On one of the days of the study many employees,
including the owner-manager's assistant, were away from company
premises all day working on a rush contract involving on-site fittings.
This took the strain of immediacy away from the managing director.
Only a very few people came in to see him and he spent the day working on costings at his own leisurely pace and reading the mail. Apparently this happened quite frequently. The continuous observation
study revealed a number of further aspects of Eta's method of working. His time was spread fairly evenly over the various functions,
though he did very little sales work. The bulk of his work time was
spent in verbal communication with others and about one-third of the
time was spent on his own. Far the greater part of Eta's work time
was initiated by himself.

Eta's owner-manager had the style of a contented man. He
was not the pushing type and did not go around his company constantly
checking on people and progress. He mostly left people to get on
with their jobs while he got on with his, though he did like to keep in
touch with everything that was happening in the company. He knew
all his employees personally and was interested in their welfare,
always being available to talk to them and not appearing distant in his
attitude. Most of the company's production work was left to the general foreman who assessed and allocated jobs and, in addition, a
foreman in each department kept a close watch on progress. Eta's
owner-manager was very cost conscious and admitted that he always
used the cheapest envelopes and the cheapest office materials. He
tried hard to keep down the number of "nonproductive" personnel and
was very pleased with an arrangement whereby his assistant managed
to split his time between office work and production work. The hours
worked by Eta's owner-manager were much shorter than those of the
other owner-managers studied, though this may have been because
the Eta study was carried out during a very sunny June and Eta liked
to spend time on his cabin cruiser. Another indication of his more
relaxed relationship to his company was the fact that he had recently
returned from a holiday and intended to have another when the works
closed for two weeks in July. Most of the other managing directors
studied took annual holidays only when their works were closed.
Eta's relaxed style was undoubtedly a product of two further factors.
First, he was a man of independent means not totally reliant on his
business as a source of income and, second, the company had a long-
standing government contract that provided the bread and butter of
its annual sales.

Theta Company: The Troubleshooters

Theta was managed by two brothers, the firm's joint managing directors, one of whom primarily looked after the sales side of the business and the other the production side. The joint managing directors worked together very much as a team and each knew everything that was going on. Every time there was a telephone call or a discussion involving one of them, the other, if he was in the office, joined in. It was a very fluid system but it must be doubtful whether it would have worked successfully had they not been brothers and had they not got on very well together. Although the office and the factory had an official lunch break, both managing directors continued working or chatting while eating a few sandwiches and drinking cups of coffee from the vending machine. The general manager of the factory usually joined them. The production director, who was involved with the day-to-day running of the business, spent nearly all his time in the factory and only left the premises occasionally. The sales director, on the other hand, spent much of his time outside the factory with representatives and customers, although he too was closely involved in the factory's day-to-day affairs. The period of the research coincided with preparations for the annual furniture exhibition in London and the sales director attended a London photographer's studio on two occasions arranging for catalog photographs to be taken. The two directors also held a "preview and discussion" of the new products with their sales representatives and agents who came to the factory from all over the country. This was so that salesmen could see the new models before the exhibition and put any suggestions they might have to the company. Many of the comments made were critical, although positive, and several suggestions were put forward for changes in fabrics or in design. When this happened Theta's joint managing directors quickly costed the proposed alterations and worked out how much it would add to the retail cost. Then they either accepted or rejected the suggestion or agreed to think it over and take note of the criticism.

Most of the time of Theta's production director was spent, however, in dealing with problems of a much more immediate nature, usually in production, costing, or purchasing, although he was also aware of problems in accounts, routine administration, and sales. He saw most visitors personally, took most telephone calls, and was easily accessible to his foremen and all his employees on an "open-door/don't knock" basis. He was involved in much that happened in the company and each morning, for example, he opened all the mail. He spent a lot of time in discussion with other people and made extensive use of the telephone. His work pattern was a hectic one since his job involved dealing with many problems at once, most of which were of an immediate nature. Long-term planning, and thinking about the future of the company, were activities that could only take place after working hours.

The management style of the Theta brothers was very much one of trying to keep in touch by direct personal contact with everything that was going on in the firm. They personally attended to a wide range of tasks and theirs was a style that consisted of long hours of work, an open-door policy to all staff, and frequent visits to the factory floor to chat to employees or, in the case of the sales director, visits to customers. It was a style based on extensive technical knowledge of the company's products. Both managing directors were familiar with all the jobs in the organization and with all the contracts being worked on at any one time. They were continually enquiring after progress, both of the jobs themselves and of the people doing the jobs. They knew most of their employees by their first names, communicated easily with them, and were familiar with their personal and family circumstances. Neither managing director stuck closely to any prescribed lines of authority or division of responsibility but each was willing to chat to any employee and to listen and take part in all conversations within earshot, although they might be trying to do something else at the same time. They talked to each other constantly, were the prime motivators in the company and completely dominated it, everything flowing from them or to them. Both were capable of handling several work items at the same time--for example, writing, talking, and making telephone calls--and they managed to bring an air of urgency to whatever they were doing. They were both dominant in their relationships with other people, yet were easy to approach. They obviously drove themselves hard.

Iota Company: The Salesman Manager

Iota's managing director had overall responsibility for two factories but did not manage them on a day-to-day basis since he also acted as the company's sales director. Iota described his average weekly work pattern as consisting of one-and-a-half days a week selling, one day a week chasing money, one day a week discussing factory and general administration problems, half a day a week on new product design and future company developments, and the rest of the time in talking to representatives, dealing with customer complaints, handling cash-flow problems, and general troubleshooting. Although he did not run either factory on a day-to-day basis, Iota's owner-manager was still involved with daily production problems and would be called on to participate whenever he was available. Iota found that he was working from 9:00 a.m. to 8:00 p.m. and, not liking the arrangement very much, tried to reorganize his hours so that he worked from 8:00 a.m. to 6:00 p.m. But this did not work since he frequently got caught up in late meetings with the sales office manager and the production manager. The sales office manager also tried to rearrange his hours on a similar basis. Although he was more successful than the managing director, he found the new arrange ment unsatisfactory because during the day he was always being interrupted, whereas if he worked a little extra at night rather than in the morning he had more chance of some peace and quiet. Because of the amount of time he spent outside the firm, Iota's owner-manager was closely in touch with market trends and knew the problems of the retailers and when best to visit customers with a view to generating sales. In addition every three months or so he tried to spend one or two days with each of his sales representatives since, as well as keeping him in touch with market trends, this helped to boost their confidence. When Iota was not away, his office tended to become busy with a constant flow of people coming to see him--foremen, drivers, secretaries, and the production and sales office managers --so busy indeed that at one point when on the telephone Iota locked his office door so that he could have some peace. (Whether this situation was the cause or effect of his frequent marketing trips was hard to say!)

When in his office Iota's managing director spent much of his time in discussion with his management colleagues, discussions on the production of new models, on product prices, new designs, unpaid accounts, personnel difficulties, the balance of the product range, in fact every aspect of the running of the company. When the managing director was not around, however, the company continued functioning with either the sales office manager or the production manager taking over. The roles of each manager were, therefore, far more flexible than their official job titles indicated.

Iota's attempted management style was to give everyone a job to do and then let them get on with it while he concentrated primarily on sales and customer relations and spent as much time as possible away from the factory. He was a marketing man and did not have a great deal of technical knowledge related to furniture production methods. In this he was different from the many managing directors in the furniture industry who are trained and experienced production men, a fact that Iota felt was a reason why so many small firm managers were unable to make a success of their companies: "It's no use turning out beautiful furniture if it costs too much or if it doesn't sell."

Kappa Company: The Coordinating Manager

Kappa was run by a managing director and three other direc-
tors--a sales director, a production director, and a design director.
The production director was the managing director's son and the other
two directors were sons of the chairman of the company who was no
longer managerially active in the firm. Kappa's managing director
described his job as one of overall control of the company. He had
learned many aspects of company management when business was, he
thought, "much simpler." In addition he had picked up information
over the years on such matters as purchase tax, import deposits, and
investment grants at the times when they had been introduced and so
was able to handle them effectively and understand where they fitted
into the overall pattern of company operations. Nevertheless, he still
felt that he was involved in many things he was not competent to handle. For example, he looked after insurance and, since the company
could obtain rebates on fire insurance for improvements in sprinkler
systems and mechanical and electrical fire-warning devices, it was
part of his job to keep abreast of technical improvements in such
systems and devices.

Shortly before the study of Kappa took place weekly management
meetings had been introduced in the firm. Before these meetings
were initiated much information had had to be relayed several times,
people sometimes being forgotten, thereby causing chaos and decisions being taken with little discussion. At the weekly meetings
everything could be discussed fully and decisions were recorded; this
had proved of benefit particularly when one management member was
missing. Similar meetings had also been tried at lower levels in the
organization but they had failed. Kappa's managing director suggested
two reasons for this failure: first, the meetings could not take place
inside working hours because machines had to be manned and supervisors were reluctant to stay late and, second, many people found it
difficult to take criticism. The managing director was now hoping to
achieve the same objectives by having a weekly chat with each foreman.

The tasks of Kappa's production director included routine sales
and production work, deliveries, complaints, production schedules,
and correspondence. He felt that he was doing many things that were
properly the responsibility of other departments, especially the sales
department, but because things were generally so hectic he was never
free to sort out these organizational problems. The sales director
saw as his main tasks control of sales representatives, liaison with
the design team, formulation of sales policy, compilation of pattern
books and mailing lists, direct customer contact, handling of exhibitions, and routine sales administration. The sales director felt that
it was only fairly recently that his job had been shaping up as he would

wish. Previously the company was run, he said, like a one-man
business with the managing director deciding which orders the company could accept and which would be rejected. The design director
of Kappa had responsibilities in the area of production methods, including prefabrication, in costings, in assessing productivity, and in
materials control. He felt that a work study department was needed
to look for ways of improving production methods but until this was
possible he would be left with this task. But he saw its value in design terms: "Design is not just a pretty picture. It means working
out how the product will be put together."

Kappa's managing director played the role of seer in Kappa.
He was by far the oldest and most experienced of the management
team and was able to guide the other directors in running their departments. At the same time he tried not to interfere too much with their
work. He was directly in charge of the financial aspects of running
the company and represented the company to the financial world of
banks, insurance companies, and accountants. The managing director ran Kappa very loosely, mostly leaving everyone to get on with
their jobs and encouraging them to interact with each other. He felt
that a small family firm had a number of management strengths it
could capitalize on. First, it was less well-prepared and had less
expert knowledge and less processed information than a large company: "We work on hunch, which really is a jumbled mass of information." As a consequence it had fewer fixed approaches to problems.
Second, it was more versatile; all the managers knew about all the
jobs to be done and there were no rigid organizational barriers.
Third, communications were easier: "In large companies people are
insulated from each other." The managing director hoped that Kappa
would continue to run in a similarly open manner after he retired.
His perception of the management style of the firm was not always
shared by others, however. Some of the managers in Kappa felt that
the managing director was often unreasonable in his expectations and
in his demands of the time within which jobs should be completed.
The managing director said that he aimed for perfection and came
down heavily on mistakes and that this was the only way to manage
the business successfully: "When I retire I hope whoever takes over
will have this attitude of mind."

                    THE "TYPICAL" OWNER-MANAGER

It is abundantly clear from the profiles of the owner-managers
in the depth study that there is no such thing as the typical owner-
manager. All that can be traced are a few common threads. In general, for example, these owner-managers were energetic men who

pushed their companies along and saw their main tasks as jogging everyone into action and occasionally checking that things were going as planned. Many of them had a close knowledge of what happened on the factory floor in their firms and were able to keep in contact with all developments in the company. They tended to be authoritarian and to work at a fast pace, but this was not altogether surprising since they were usually the primary source of authority in the company. Two patterns of attitude toward employees were present among the owner-managers studied. One group of owner-managers was aloof, noncommunicative with the shop floor, leaving everyone to get on with their work, and preferring to manage their firms through prescribed channels of authority and clearly defined responsibilities. The other group were closer to their employees, knew them all individually, talked to them about their work whenever the opportunity arose, and did not attempt to manage through intermediaries such as supervisors. This group of employee-involved owner-managers tended to be men with experience of working on the factory floor, either in their own businesses or with other furniture manufacturing companies; they knew the technical aspects of the jobs being done and were familiar with the problems that could arise. The first group, in contrast, were more concerned with managing their businesses than with helping to make furniture. They tended to work in companies where the production process was a relatively simple one, with few variations on major product themes and less one-off (custom-built) contracts, and where the most pressing problems were problems of sales or cash flow. The patterns of attitude adopted, therefore, which find expression in characteristic management styles, were determined both by the previous occupational experiences of the owner-managers and by the nature of the production processes within their firms.

Apart from a detailed look at a number of owner-managers at work, the depth study included the collection of some information about the general life-styles of the owner-managers--their family circumstances, leisure activities, and political beliefs. Again no one pattern emerged but there were a number of common threads on the basis of which the following caricature of the owner-manager was constructed:

> The owner-manager lives in a large detached house
> in the West End of town. He has two children, the
> elder a girl of 21 recently married to an architect
> and the younger a boy of 17 who attends boarding
> school in the Midlands. Father does not expect, or
> want, his son to enter the family business but hopes
> that he will study law at a good university.

The owner-manager drives a Ford Corsair 2000E which is nominally owned by the company and paid for by the firm. He admits that this is a considerable benefit on top of his taxable earnings, though he has never costed it accurately. He thinks the car suitably reflects his social position and, furthermore, it is useful for transporting employees or materials to jobs.

At present running his firm takes up most of the owner-manager's time. He spends all day at the factory and usually brings some work home with him in the evening. Because of this he has very little time for hobbies or outside interests. He is a member of a local golf club, enjoys the game very much but can only manage to play on weekends. He also likes to listen to classical music.

The owner-manager works hard and is deeply committed to his company. He has a dominating, confident personality and his actions are carried out with a great deal of aggressiveness and urgency. He works at a fast pace and rarely stops, even for lunch, which he takes in his own small office. He makes it his business to know about everything that is happening in his company. He is friendly with his employees, has many personal friends among his customers and suppliers, is easy to get along with, and has a down-to-earth manner. He is generous toward his staff but expects something in return and when this is not forthcoming is quick to complain.

The owner-manager enjoys his work very much. He likes being the boss, particularly the freedom and independence that it gives him, and admits he would find it difficult to work for someone else. What does he enjoy about it? "The general feel that the whole unit is moving properly." This includes seeing the right figures at the end of the month, getting a good order, especially when he does not expect it, seeing a new design come out right, and developing young craftsmen. The things that give him least satisfaction are the things outside his control as, for example, supplies that do not arrive on time.

The business has given the successful owner-manager rewards in several areas. He is comfortable financially and secure to an extent he might never have achieved in working for someone else. Much of the money the business has made over the years has been ploughed back, thereby increasing its worth as a going concern and its value to the owner-manager. This strengthens his feeling of security. The owner-manager also enjoys the freedom his job gives him; he feels he has personal control over his own life and can organize his working day as he chooses. He prefers to accept the rigorous demands of his job than the demands of a boss. A further reward for the owner-manager is the social position that is accorded to him as a well-respected businessman, leading a firm with a good reputation for top-quality work. This gives him access to a cross-section of the community. In addition he likes the feeling that his company is progressing soundly and he enjoys participating in its growth and development and in the growth and development of the people who work for him.

The owner-manager is very aware of the loneliness of men at the top of business concerns and feels that this is a difficult problem for him. He believes he has compensated in various ways, in particular by meeting other businessmen and by discussing his business affairs with his wife. It is unlikely, however, that the loneliness of the top position would make him sell his business and, in the past, he has always refused offers that have been made. Even if he did sell the business he would probably try to do something else independently since he could not readily work for someone else nor would he enjoy an early retirement even if it were financially possible.

Politically the owner-manager is a Conservative and votes accordingly. Yet he is not doctrinaire about his beliefs and claims that on many issues he is a "bit of a Socialist." He is attracted by Conservative emphasis on economic freedom and lower rates of personal and company taxation. He feels that trade unions in many industries are irresponsible although he, personally, gets on very

well with the local trade union official and never
tries to discourage men from joining the union. He
does not play an active part in party politics, "I'm
too busy looking after my business," and does not
give donations to the Conservative party. The owner-
manager is a regular church-goer and member.

The owner-manager dislikes civil service methods and constantly expresses strong disapproval of
what he sees as the excessive bureaucracy of government departments and government-sponsored
agencies. He also resents the power of the City
Corporation who recently placed a compulsory purchase order on his old factory in order to build a
ring-road. After a long argument he was eventually
forced to purchase and convert a new factory. He
feels he was not given adequate compensation for
the forced sale.

This caricature is, then, made up of some of the common
threads in the life-styles and modes of thought of the owner-managers
taking part in the depth study. It is not a model followed closely by
all, or indeed any, of the owner-managers studied. In particular it
is worth reemphasizing here that the firms studied were among the
more successful in the industry and that this was reflected, for example, in terms of the financial rewards of the owner-managers participating in the depth study project. This becomes clear if we compare their salaries with those of the managers who took part in the
descriptive survey.

Of the 224 managers providing information on earnings in the
course of the descriptive survey* 62.4 percent were earning, in the
spring of 1970, salaries of less than £2,000 a year and 88.2 percent
were earning less than £3,000 a year. Four of the managers were on
salaries of £5,000 per annum or more. The salary range with the
highest proportion of managers (33.6 percent) was the range from
£1,500 per annum to £1,999 per annum and the range with the second
highest proportion (28.8 percent of managers) was the range up to
£1,500 per annum. Some perspective can be fained if it is borne in
mind that in 1970 the recently qualified graduate entering industry
could expect to earn around £1,400 to £1,500 per annum and the
average wages of manual workers were around £25 per week.

---

*229 managers were interviewed but three were not prepared to
disclose their earnings (in the author's view because of embarrassmen
at their <u>lowness</u>), and two drew only fees from their companies and
had no fixed salaries.

In 1970 the owner-managers in the depth study project earned, on average, around £4,000 per annum. Of the owner-managers for whom salary information was available from the descriptive survey, 11 percent earned less than £1,500 a year, 41 percent earned less than £2,000 a year, and 79 percent earned less than £3,000 a year; the comparable figures for nonshareholding managers were 29 percent, 69 percent, and 96 percent. One of those owner-managers earning less than £1,500 per annum was a 60-year-old managing director who had cut his salary because of current financial difficulties faced by his firm. Such evidence suggested that it would not be unusual in times of financial difficulty for the owners of small companies to have lower annual incomes than many of the staff they employed. In only very few of the companies did directors draw fees on top of their basic salaries and only very rarely did they receive any dividends on their shareholdings.

Size of firm had no significant effect on the salaries of the managers, but there were considerable variations between managers in different geographical regions of the country. In the North of England, for example, 42.6 percent of the 56 managers earned less than £1,500 per annum compared with 17.6 percent of the 68 managers in London and the South East. This would suggest that the labor markets for small-firm managers are very local markets and that interregional mobility would be very small. Although there were few formalized profit-sharing plans in operation in the 50 companies that took part in the descriptive survey, company profitability did appear to have some impact on managers' salaries. Thus, for example, none of the 13 managers employed in the four companies rated as unprofitable in the descriptive survey earned more than £2,500 per annum, whereas twice as many of the managers earning £3,000 per annum or over were employed in companies rated high or medium in profitability than were employed in companies with low profitability ratings.

NOTES

1. Examples of the episodes allocated to each of these 15 functions were as follows:

Production--discussions with works managers, foremen, employees, etc., on production scheduling, progress, repairs, methods, problems and breakdowns, inspection of work; measuring and assessing jobs on location; physical work performance.

Sales--visiting customers; making and receiving customer telephone calls; discussions with sales managers and assistants; writing/dictating letters to customers; reading customers' letters (complaints, enquiries); checking performance of salesmen, discussions on discounts, advertising literature, exports, and exhibitions; sorting out problems of customer orders.

Marketing--attending a marketing conference; discussion with public relations personnel.

Purchasing--telephone calls to/from suppliers; discussions with suppliers and their agents; letters to/from suppliers; checking goods with a view to buying; discussions with managers, foremen, etc., on supplies needed; examining suppliers' literature.

Accounts/finance--discussions with clerical staff, assistants, cashiers, etc., on budgets, tax, preparation of accounts, unpaid bills, pensions, and insurance; checking ledgers; making up checks; reading financial figures; telephoning and writing to customers for payment of accounts.

Personnel--discussions with works managers, supervisors, and foremen on vacancies, labor shortage, training, progress of new employees, safety, interpretation of agreements; discussions with shop stewards; discussions with employees on time-keeping, absenteeism, or discipline; interviewing; bonus calculations; visiting training centers; discussions with group training officers.

Drawing/design--discussions with designers; studying drawings; designing; making alterations.

Transport/delivery--discussions with works supervisors, foremen, drivers on priorities, routes, etc.; discussions with and telephone calls to/from customers about delivery; studying time-tables; telephone calls to transport contractors.

Costing/estimating--costing and estimating from drawings or finished articles.

Quality control/inspection--discussions with works supervisors, foremen, or employees on quality; tours of general inspection; inspecting incoming supplies.

Routine clerical/administration--reading mail; tidying desk; searching through files; discussions with clerks, secretaries, and assistants on clerical matters; typing; searching for employees.

Work organization--reading and writing in personal diaries; organizing personal work schedule.

General management--all discussions with the researcher; discussions with management and foremen on wider topics like general company policy and authority in the company.

Personal--telephone calls to/from relatives (usually wife) and friends; fixing a radio; attending a funeral; writing personal letters; shopping.

Other--discussion on a missing camera; chairing a Confederation of British Industry (C.B.I.) meeting; attending a local business meeting; discussions on broken refrigerators, machinery noise, and sharing an exhibition stand.

2. T. Lupton, "Small New Firms and Their Significance," New Society, December 21, 1967.

3. J. Deeks, "Job-Specific Management Training: an experimental approach," Industrial and Commercial Training 4, no. 4 (April 1972).

PART

III

**FURTHER
CONSIDERATIONS**

10

THE MOTIVATION AND GOALS OF THE OWNER-MANAGER

In Part I the entrepreneur of economic theory and the entrepreneur of psychological theory were described. Both these theories incorporate views of the forces that motivate the entrepreneur. Some economic theories see the entrepreneur as primarily motivated by financial self-interest expressed through striving for goals of profit maximization. In some psychological theories the entrepreneur is seen as being primarily motivated by a high need for achievement, and financial success becomes an expression of the concreteness of his achievement.

In Part II various points of research data that would appear to be at odds with these theories of entrepreneurial motivation were detailed. In Chapter 5, for example, we noticed that small business ventures were sometimes started up as a result of adverse economic circumstances that closed off alternative employment opportunities. We noticed that many of the small firms in our sample were only marginally capitalist enterprises and might be more appropriately viewed as extensions of the particular occupational skills of their owner-managers or as the continuation of family traditions. Similarly, some of the small companies in our sample changed their product range in response to some chance occurrence or unforeseen opportunity that was not subjected to any careful economic analysis. Other companies pursued policies that maximized the advantages of specialization, as much out of preference for a particular product range as out of economic self-interest. We noticed that craftsmen who establish their own businesses may continue to be craftsmen first and businessmen second and that, consequently, the growth of small firms may be limited both by economic circumstances and by the particular orientation that the owner-manager has toward his company and his work.

In this chapter, therefore, we reexamine some of the prevailing stereotypes about the motivation and goals of the entrepreneur in the light of the available research data on the attitudes, expectations, and work behavior of small-firm owner-managers. We then attempt to find some more suitable model for describing the motivation and goals of the owner-manager.

ENTREPRENEURIAL STEREOTYPES

There would appear to be two distinct stereotypes about the nature of small business and the motivation of the small businessman, the "classical economic" and the "literary medieval." The "classical economic" view sees the small businessman as the archetypal capitalist entrepreneur. The entrepreneur is risk-taking, profit-maximizing economic man, independent, competitive, materialistic, and single-minded in his pursuit of wealth. Economists may argue about methods of profit maximization and means of growth. They may question whether or not the entrepreneur has sufficient information available to him to adopt a marginal cost method rather than a cost-plus method for pricing his products. They may discuss the barriers that the entrepreneur faces in expanding his business and the advantages and disadvantages firms face at various stages of development. But that the entrepreneur is concerned to maximize his profits, and eager and willing to expand the scale of his operations, is taken for granted. Assumptions about means may be questioned but assumptions about ends are sacrosanct.

There are numerous examples of this classical economic stereotype guiding academic thinking and public policy. It is a stereotype that pervades the Report of the Committee of Inquiry on Small Firms where, as we saw in Chapter 4, the small firm is seen as providing a productive outlet for the energies of "that large group of enterprising and independent people who set great store by economic independence."[1] It is a stereotype beloved of politicians defending the private enterprise system: "The hon. Member . . . who suggested the setting up of a State holding company to help small businesses cannot know the ethic and motivation of men who run small businesses. They are entrepreneurs, aggressively and robustly independent, who are just as likely to thumb their noses at a Conservative Government as at a Government of any other complexion-- and long live that attitude."[2] J. K. Galbraith suggests that until recent times this stereotype of the capitalist entrepreneur persisted within big business where "senior officials of the mature corporation were inclined to assume the public mantle of the entrepreneur. They pictured themselves as self-reliant men, individualistic, with a trace of justifiable arrogance, fiercely competitive and with a desire to live dangerously."[3] In Britain arguments about whether or not the professional salaried manager is sufficiently concerned with profit maximization stem from the growing divorce between business ownership and managerial control after the passing of the Joint Stock and Limited Liability Acts in the nineteenth century. Indeed some people believed that the 1873-96 depression arose because the managing of affairs by salaried managers, rather than by "highly interested and finely skilled" owners, had taken the inspiration from commercial life.[4] Subsequently the question as to whether or not the professional manager would seek to maximize profits rather than, for example, to maximize growth or to maximize his own security, has generally been discussed against a model that assumes that the owner-manager's or the entrepreneur's decisions would be largely determined by a desire for profit maximization: "There are no conclusive findings on how the goals of investor-controlled firms might differ from the goals of those controlled by professional managers. But a long list of commentators, from Adolph Berle and Gardiner Means and Robert A. Gordon in the early 1940s to John Kenneth Galbraith in 1968, would argue that investor-controlled firms seek to maximise such system goals as profits whereas those dominated by professional managers seek to maximise growth and security."[5]

In the "literary medieval" stereotype the small businessman is the archetypal conservative. He is master craftsman rather than entrepreneur, the upholder of traditional values and beliefs, skeptical of progress, proud of the quality of his work and of the personal loyalties within his firm, a focal point of stability and order in a rapidly changing environment. This is the world conjured up by John Betjeman in "Summoned by Bells":

>   Most of all
>   I think my father loved me when we went
>   In early-morning pipe-smoke on the tram
>   Down to the Angel, visiting the Works.
>   "Fourth generation--yes, this is the boy."
>   . . . .
>   Why now
>   When, staying in a quiet country house,
>   I see an onyx ashtray of the firm,
>   Or in my bedroom, find the figured wood
>   Of my smooth-sliding dressing-table drawers
>   Has got a look about it of the Works,
>   Does my mind flinch so?

Partly it is guilt;
"Following in Father's footsteps" was the theme
Of all my early childhood. With what pride
He introduced me to old gentlemen,
Pin-striped commercial travellers of the firm
And tall proprietors of Bond Street shops.

. . . .

Partly my guilt is letting down the men--
William our coachman who, turned chauffeur, still
Longed for his mare and feared the motor-car
Which he would hiss at, polishing its sides;
Bradshaw and Pettit of the lathe and plane;
Fieldhouse and Lovely, and the old and bent
With wire framed spectacles and aproned knees;
The young apprentices old custom called,
Indentures done, to passing-out parade
Down a long alley formed among the men
Beating on bits of metal. How they all
Trusted that I would fill my father's place!
"The Guv'nor's looking for you, Master John. . . ."
"Well now, my boy, I want your solemn word
To carry on the firm when I am gone:
Fourth generation, John--they'll look to you.
They're artist-craftsmen to their fingertips. . . .
Go on creating beauty! "[6]

Oliver records that "the family firm of G. Betjeman and Sons Ltd.
was founded in (Upper) Ashby St, Clerkenwell, E.C.1., and in 1870
made a short migration, typical of the industry at that time, to 36-44
Pentonville Rd, N.1., only half a mile away. Like many moderate-
sized establishments, it survived by specialization. It produced
French bibelots, that is, small cabinet pieces such as cigar cabinets
and presentation cabinets."[7] At that time it was common in the
Hoxton and Islington areas of London for furniture businesses to be
set up as domestic workshops. As they grew the manufacturing
processes would invade the whole house and garden and then neigh-
boring houses. Here, then, in the small family firm, tightly knit into
a local community, was a source of a different strain of small business qualities. The small business "has been a great motive force
among our people. It stimulates expression of the fundamental virtues of thrift, industry, intelligence, schooling, home ties, and
family pride--in short, those fireside virtues which have counted for
so much in developing our strength and character."[8]
    The literary medieval stereotype also has its dangers, as a
postwar Board of Trade Working Party in Britain pointed out:

We do not regard it as inevitable that bad conditions
should be associated with small firms, although it
is clear that their ability to provide amenities is
limited by their lack of financial resources. So far
as we can see there will always be a place for some
small firms for specialised work, for repairs and
for meeting purely local needs. We think, however,
that the survival of a large number of small firms,
particularly those which have tried to produce furniture in competition with the factory, is much more
open to question. There is a tendency in some quar-
ters to sentimentalise about small firms and to
represent them all as being craftsmen producing
the finest furniture. In fact, a relatively small
proportion of them are in this category and far too
many of them are producing shoddy furniture under
shocking conditions.[9]

While the classical economic and the literary medieval stereotypes
of the small businessman would appear to be irreconcilable, they do,
nevertheless, provide a useful background for understanding and
interpreting research findings on the attitudes, expectations, and
motivations of small-firm owner-managers. It is to some of these
findings that we now turn.

ATTITUDES AND MOTIVATIONS
OF SMALL-FIRM OWNERS

One of the research reports commissioned by the Bolton Committee was a study of the attitudes and motivations of the owners of
small firms.[10] The study, carried out by C. W. Golby and G. Johns
in 1970, set out to investigate the attitudes of owner-managers to
their jobs, the problems that they encountered in running their businesses, and their opinions as to the role of small firms in the economy. It was hoped that by analyzing the overt attitudes of owner-
managers some information would be forthcoming on their underlying
motivations. Information was obtained from 14 nondirective group
discussions in which a total of 69 owner-managers took part, 59 of
them being from companies employing less than 50 staff.[11] In these
discussions a researcher introduced a subject or problem area in
broad terms and then tried to encourage free and spontaneous discussion by members of the group and to make sure that any points
that might yield useful hypotheses were properly amplified. Such a
method would seem to be peculiarly suited to the collection of

sanctioned cultural stereotypes and opinions that are acceptable to owner-managers as a group. While, therefore, the researchers claim that their role is to interpret such attitudinal data in order to detect differences between surface attitudes and underlying motivations, their report is largely given over to reflecting some common opinions and prejudices of owner-managers and contains little useful evaluative or perceptive insights by the researchers themselves. Nevertheless, treated purely as a description of group attitudes and opinions, the study is useful in filling out the details of the articulated self-perception of owner-managers.

Golby and John's owner-managers see themselves as "keeping alive the virtues of hard work, individual initiative, self-reliance, craggy independence and a sense of personal responsibility in a world where uninvolved clock-watching from nine to five in a huge, impersonal organisation had become the accepted norm." They value their roles as owner-managers because of the opportunities provided for expressing their independence and individuality, because they can develop their own ideas and gain the satisfaction of personally supervising the implementation of those ideas, because of the challenge and sense of achievement in running their own businesses, and because of the financial rewards. Only one respondent criticized the efficiency of small companies, the general consensus being that the small firm has a vital role to fill in the economy, providing, as the owner-managers see it, a personal service, speed and adaptability, specialization, a source of innovation, craftsmanship, value for money, and a guarantee of consumer choice. Government is perceived as biased against small business and discriminates unfavorably through the tax system, through its statistical enquiries, through restrictions and regulations governing such items as driving hours, vehicle inspection requirements, and the statutory provisions concerning the employment of those aged under 16. Almost all the owner-managers who took part in the discussions were opposed to any suggestion of direct assistance or advice, either from government or from other outside advisory services, and most were neither interested in nor aware of outside services available. Nevertheless, they appeared to be unanimously in favor of the protection afforded by retail price maintenance legislation: "Here respondents argued along lines diametrically opposed to those usually adopted during the rest of the enquiry. In almost all other areas, there was criticism of government restrictions, opposition to government intervention and in general that familiar demand to 'set the people free.' When their own interests were seen as directly threatened, however, the small businessman, like other members of the community, can apparently see government protection as his right."

The owner-managers' accounts of their problems read like an illustrated casebook of small businessman's hypochondria.   Everything is seen to be wrong with the social and economic climate created by the policies of successive governments. Financial problems arise from government credit squeezes, from the constant price rises of basic commodities, from the slowness of incoming payments. Large firms are a problem. They are seen as inefficient, especially where their accounting procedures are computerized, as ruthless, as monopolizers of skilled labor, as poachers of staff from small firms, as providing severe cost competition for the small producers, and as undercutting the small retailer and wholesalers by buying in bulk. "What made matters worse," said one owner-manager, "was the way in which large firms exploited their advantages!" Labor problems are another major focus for the owner-managers' concern and the causes of such problems are seen to be primarily political. The tax system is believed to operate as a disincentive, especially to overtime working; "socialism," the welfare state, and "grandmotherly legislation" have destroyed the will to work; an increasingly irresponsible, inefficient and powerful labor force is being aided by "university men" in the government to dictate the terms of their employment. The Babbitt-like cliches flow thick and fast. One is reminded of the syndrome expressed in the following letter allegedly from a small businessman: "In reply to your request to send a cheque, I wish to inform you that the present condition of my bank account makes it almost impossible. My shattered financial condition is due to federal laws, state laws, county laws, brother-in-laws, sister-in-laws and outlaws."

Golby and Johns suggest that the underlying motivation of the owner-managers they met can best be summarized as "the need to attain and preserve independence" and that this need sums up a wide range of personal gratifications provided by being one's own boss. In this respect, therefore, owner-managers pay lip-service to some aspects of the classical economic stereotype of the individualistic independent entrepreneur. However, Golby and Johns' owner-managers, alongside their professed avowal of the virtues of independence within a private enterprise system, exhibit a number of very conservative tendencies. We have already described their wish to have the protection of retail price maintenance reestablished. The owner-managers studied also had conservative attitudes toward obtaining credit, risk-taking, and economic growth. Only one owner-manager, for example, appeared to be willing to seek finance from any source other than the local bank manager. Many were afraid that other sources of credit would have unwelcome financial strings attached and that borrowing money inevitably resulted in loss of independence. Among the owner-managers in our own study there

were some who never financed capital expenditures other than out of
retained profits or their own personal equity in the business, an approach that was sometimes reinforced by moral scruples about the
sin of usury. Owner-managers' claims, therefore, that a willingness
to take risks and to back hunches are a central feature of small business management are frequently belied by their own conservative
behavior. Their attitudes toward growth and their behavior in terms
of seeking or avoiding growth reveal a similar inconsistency. Golby
and Johns found that the attitudes of their owner-managers toward
growth and expansion were highly ambivalent:

> Many of these owners of small businesses appeared
> to be torn on the one hand by the desire to remain
> small and so retain their independence and its con-
> comitant personal satisfactions and, on the other
> hand, by the need, as businessmen, to conform to
> the idea of growth--almost as a moral imperative.
> In the majority of cases, the need for preserving
> the more personal satisfaction of independence won
> out and there was a clear preference to maintain
> the business at its existing level of activity--and to
> pay only lip-service to growth and expansion.

The attitudes of owner-managers, then, frequently do not express the reality of their behavior. It is in this sense that we can
describe the attitudes as cultural stereotypes, a mixture of the independence associated with our classical economic entrepreneur and
the conservatism of our literary medieval model. Such attitudes are
important, both as reinforcement for the owner-manager of his own
self-image and self-esteem and as justification for his economic
function. But they tell us little about the motivations that lie behind
his business behavior.   Thus a business philosophy that stresses,
for example, the advantages of independence may exist side by side
with a business reality of total dependence. A number of writers
have suggested that the independence of many small businessmen is
largely an illusion; particularly for the self-employed owner-operators
of little businesses:

> The very names used in reference to the self-
> employed suggest a degree of economic well-
> being which does not correspond with the facts.
> The term independent is a good example of this:
> Independent proprietor, independent contractor,
> independent businessman--the only thing these
> men are independent of is an employer. In every

> other respect, their competitors, customers, the
> wholesaler, banker, landlord, etc. dictate to the
> small businessman much as would an employer.
> They do so somewhat less directly perhaps. But
> by limiting the amount of business he does, by
> influencing the prices he charges, by determining
> the margin of profit he shall retain for himself,
> or by granting or withholding credit, they make
> him quite as dependent economically as is the
> person who works for others. [12]

Phillips suggests that another indication of the illusory character of
the independence of many small businesses is the appearance of many
new firms when alternative employment opportunities are bad. [13] He
cites the German experience in the 1926-36 period when, alongside
widespread unemployment, there appeared a large increase in the
number of business enterprises. Thousands of workers were forced
into self-employment, chiefly in the form of one-man shops, "independence" being the only alternative to unemployment. More recently
in Britain redundancies following the nationalization of General Electric Company (GEC) plants after the GEC takeover of Associated
Electrical Industries (AEI) led to the mushrooming of new firms in
the Stafford-Stone area. [14]

   Given, then, the possibility that independence may be more of
a dream than a reality for the small businessman, given too their
hypochondria about their business problems, and given the fact, as
we saw in Chapter 9, of limited and variable financial rewards, one
wonders why owner-managers bother. Perhaps they would all sub-
scribe to the view that "starting up a business is a matter of not
knowing the obstacles; if you knew the obstacles you'd never start. "[15]
One can understand the pressures pushing sons and relatives of
owner-managers into family businesses, but what are the expectations and motivations of owner-managers who found their own companies?

EXPECTATIONS AND MOTIVATIONS OF FOUNDERS

   An American study by Mayer and Goldstein, published in 1961,
throws much light on the question. [16] This was an investigation over
a two-year period of 81 newly established owner-operated retail and
service enterprises in the Providence (Rhode Island) Metropolitan
Area. It covered a variety of different kinds of little business, the
major concentrations being in restaurants, gas stations, and grocery
stores. These 81 businesses were operated by 93 owners, assisted

by 84 full- or part-time workers, 46 of whom were paid employees
and 38 unpaid helpers. None of the businesses were operated from
the owner's home, but many of them relied to some extent on unpaid
family assistance. Only eight of the firms had more than one paid
employee.

Mayer and Goldstein set out primarily to find out what problems
these little businesses faced during the first two years of their existence and what characteristics differentiated those businesses that
survived from those that closed down within the two-year period. At
the same time the researchers collected data on the occupational and
educational backgrounds of those who started up these businesses,
probed their reasons for going into business, and examined the resources available to them. They asked such questions as: what
prompted people to set up a new business enterprise; what factors
determined their timing, their choice of business and their choice of
location; what were the capital resources and what were the credit
arrangements; what were the major decisions facing the going concern and the major factors determining the development of the business; and, if the enterprise was discontinued, what were the circumstances, what were the reasons, and what happened to the owners.

The average initial capital investment of the 81 firms amounted
to just under $5,000 (1958) and about half of the businesses had initial
investments of under $3,000. Most owners had only very hazy no-
tions about the amounts of cash, stock, and credit required to maintain operations until the business could carry itself, and most committed all their liquid resources at the beginning of the venture. This
left them without reserves on which to draw when unexpected obstacles
or emergencies arose. In addition, most of the owners did not separate their business and personal finances. They would, for example,
dip into the cash register whenever they needed personal spending
money. Nevertheless, many owners exercised great restraint with
regard to cash withdrawals, some of them drawing less than $500 a
year in salary and expenses. At the end of the two years only three
of the enterprises were classified as profitable by the researchers.
The authors concluded that, even if all five firms classified as poten-
tially profitable should eventually enter the profitable category, the
really successful businesses would still represent no more than 10
percent of the total sample.

The most striking fact revealed by Mayer and Goldstein's
analysis of the reasons why these little businesses were set up is the
small number of owner-operators who set out deliberately to seek
maximum money rewards. Only 6 of the 81 openings conformed to our
classical economic stereotype of the capitalist entrepreneur attempting to isolate the most profitable opportunities by careful calculation
of costs, sales volume, location, competition, and, above all,

comparison of financial returns to be expected from self-employment as compared to potential income from paid employment. In many cases Mayer and Goldstein's owner-operators did not consciously know why they went into business. Often they had no clear goals in mind, having little if any appreciation of the business world in general. The researchers' questions on reasons for going into business tended to be answered in terms of cultural stereotypes, like "to be independent" or "to make money," but it was apparent to the authors of the study that these cliches were rationalizations rather than basic motives. In fact about one-quarter of the 81 new business ventures were prompted by a desperate need for providing some income because the prospective owner had either already lost his job or was in imminent danger of becoming unemployed. For most of these 92 owner-operators, then, the running of their business was seen as self-employment in the sense of an alternative to job-holding. They viewed their businesses simply as a source of livelihood, a job as well as an investment, rather than as a rationally organized profit-oriented venture.

Most of Mayer and Goldstein's owner-operators had very little formal education directly relevant to their business careers. Previous business experience rather than formal schooling provided the most significant training for business ownership, it being fairly common for an owner-operator to own and run several different businesses during the course of his lifetime. Whereas experience as an employee in a given line of business did not ensure success as a business owner in the same line, previous experience as an owner was important, particularly so if in the same line of business. Of the 93 owner-operators in the study, 37 had previously owned their own businesses and 13 of these had owned more than one firm. Nevertheless, 50 out of the 93 were lacking in both business experience and formal education.

The little businesses in the Mayer and Goldstein study were established predominantly by persons with manual occupational backgrounds. Of the 93 owner-operators, 64 had at some time been employed in manual work and 36 of these had done nothing but manual work right up until the time they opened their own business. And it was to manual work that these owner-operators tended to return when their business ventures proved unsuccessful. Small business ownership was, then, one of the few middle-income occupations attainable by manual workers since they were usually excluded, by their educational limitations, from any executive or professional career. The Mayer and Goldstein research underlined, therefore, the findings of earlier work in the United States that showed that small-business ownership was one of the last potential avenues of upward social mobility for the manual worker, and that the creed of the "self-made

man" had become by and large a working-class preoccupation.[17]
But while small-business ownership appeared as one of the main
avenues of social mobility open to manual workers, it was a precarious route and seldom assured the permanent achievement of the
higher social status psychologically associated with it. As Chinoy
pointed out in his study of automobile workers, small-business ownership may provide ever-open possibilities for economic achievement of the higher social status psychologically associated with it.
As Chinoy pointed out in his study of automobile workers, small-
business ownership may provide ever-open possibilities for economic
achievement and independence, but for those new entrants with limited capital resources only the riskier fields of enterprise, where
typically business mortality is high and profits are low, are open.[18]
Nevertheless, in both Britain and the United States, the idea of
starting up one's own business apparently continues to have appeal
for the industrial worker even though relatively few ever attempt to
turn their dreams into reality. Most affluent workers' aspirations
for self-employment appear to be held "with no great expectation
that they would one day be fulfilled."[19] Indeed it would seem that
affluent workers may be more clear-sighted about the barriers and
difficulties confronting the aspiring entrepreneur than many of those
who do take the step into self-employment.[20]

     Given some of the reasons for their establishment, it is not
surprising to find that 13 of Mayer and Goldstein's 81 little businesses did not survive six months, an additional 15 closed during
the second half of their first year, and a further 12 during their
second year of business operation. Scarcely half, then, of the original 81 businesses survived for two years. Of the 40 businesses
that closed down, 32 failed financially, in the sense that they were
closed because the owner-operator did not feel that the business was
providing him with an adequate monetary return, and 8 were closed
for nonfinancial reasons. In most instances failure could be traced
by the researchers to a combination of errors in several major areas
of decision-making: faulty location, disregard of competition, inadequate capital resources, overindebtedness, inept merchandising
policies, careless credit arrangements, organizational errors.
Such factors were sometimes compounded by deficiencies in the
owner himself: lack of technical know-how, personality defects,
lack of sufficient perseverance, irrationality. Similarly, the survival of any given firm could not usually be attributed to a single
factor but was the result of a combination of factors. The survivors
appeared to be characterized by a higher degree of rationality, more
realistic expectations, greater managerial competence, and more
suitable personality characteristics than the failures. Motivation,
in Mayer and Goldstein's view, was a major factor in explaining

success, but motivation for success was coupled in each instance with adequate resources, special training or previous business experience, and a generally rational approach to business conduct. Those owner-operators with higher education tended to be more circumspect and rational in establishing their business enterprises. In addition stamina and determination to ride out difficulties were crucial factors in survival, as was the willingness of several owner-operators to work very hard and not to confine themselves to supervisory operations. In particular those owner-operators in the older age groups tended to be more persistent and to struggle on much longer before being willing to admit failure. One of the reasons for this greater persistence of older owner-operators may have been that there were less alternative employment opportunities available for those in the older age groups. Mayer and Goldstein concluded that, if there was any formula for success in setting up a little business, the ingredients consisted largely of the ability to evaluate objectively, to plan carefully, and to be prepared emotionally to persist long enough to overcome temporary setbacks until the business reached its full potential.

In a number of respects, therefore, the pattern that emerges from the Mayer and Goldstein study and from our own study of small furniture firms in Britain is a surprisingly coherent one. We have seen, in Part II, for example, that the profit records of small owner-managed furniture firms are, in general, extremely poor and that many owner-managers relied on their own experience and limited knowledge in handling the financial side of their business. There is no reason to suspect that small British furniture firms are unusual in these respects. Indeed a survey carried out in 1971 of small painting and decorating firms employing from 8 to 24 persons concluded that such firms have very little conception of what is meant by return on capital or the meaning of profitability.[21] We have seen, too, that salaries received by many owner-managers were not high and that in times of financial difficulties for their companies some owner-managers would receive lower incomes than many of the people they employed. It seems clear, therefore, that the relatively poor profit records of the small furniture firms studied is a reflection not only of lack of financial know-how among some owner-managers but also a reflection of their limited financial expectations and motivations. Many owner-managers, particularly those who were founders of their firms, expected a financial return from their business comparable or marginally greater than the income that they would receive as employees. Indeed many of them spoke of their salaries as "wages"; their expectations might well be satisfied provided they could earn more than the average weekly wages of a skilled upholsterer or cabinetmaker. The owner-operators of little businesses and the owner-managers of small firms have, it would

appear, a number of common characteristics, most notably a relatively low standard of formal education, a predominantly manual occupational experience, close-knit family ties within their businesses,
and limited expectations of financial rewards. They are concerned
initially with problems of survival rather than with problems of
growth and, once established, are more likely to seek to stabilize
their business operations at a level that gives them an acceptable
standard of living rather than to seek out opportunities for expansion.

The assumption that the small-firm owner-manager is motivated
by classical economic ideas of the competitive, risk-taking entrepreneur setting out to maximize profits is undermined, not only by the
fact that many feel free to pursue, through the operation of their
firms, what are, in economic terms, essentially nonrational objectives. This is reflected, for example, in decisions taken to curtail
the growth of the firm in order that the owner-manager or his family
should not lose effective control, or in decisions to set the satisfaction of a particular customer or a long-serving employee above any
prospects of financial gain. It is an approach that may be particularly prevalent in small firms where the manufacturing processes
involve a high degree of craft skill, as, for example, in reproduction
furniture and in antique restoration, and where the owner-manager
is himself a skilled craftsman concerned primarily with quality, with
reputation, and with creating an article that has his own personal
hallmark on it. In such companies the motivation of the owner-
manager is more in keeping with that of the master craftsman of our
literary medieval stereotype than with that of the capitalist entrepreneur of the classical economists. As well as limiting output in
order to be able personally to supervise the manufacture of each individual piece, a number of owner-managers in such firms find the
greatest satisfaction in working on their bench practicing their craft.
It is to the nature of the satisfaction that owner-managers find in
their work that we now turn.

WORK SATISFACTION AND THE OWNER-MANAGER

During the course of the descriptive survey, owner-managers
and managers were asked, first, what part of their work gave them
the greatest personal satisfaction and why, and second, what part of
their work gave them the least personal satisfaction and why. In
some cases answers tended to be in terms of a number of satisfying
factors. One owner-manager said, for example, that "as a businessman my greatest satisfaction is in the profit we make; as a tradesman
it's seeing a nice job going out of the works." In order not to lose
sight of the variety of satisfactions expressed by owner-managers by

subsuming each answer under some too generalized set of headings, Table 10.1 sets out in some detail a classification of the terms in which owner-manager founders and owner-manager inheritors expressed satisfaction and dissatisfaction with their work, together with examples of the kind of responses coded under each subheading. This immediately makes apparent both the difficulty of summarizing answers to questions on work satisfactions and dissatisfactions and the problems of interpreting such a varied set of responses.

A number of points emerge from Table 10.1. First there is the higher proportion of satisfaction responses and the greater stress that owner-managers place on the positive aspects of their personal work situation than on the negative aspects, a not unusual phenomenon in work satisfaction studies. A number of owner-managers said that there were no aspects of their work that they disliked. Second, there are a number of apparent differences between the satisfactions expressed by owner-manager founders and owner-manager inheritors. (The 44 owner-managers classified as "founders" include all owner-managers working in founder-managed businesses, that is, they are the first generation of management in the firm. The 50 "inheritors" include owner-managers working in businesses that are being run by the second or subsequent generations of the founder's family or in businesses that no longer have any family connections with the original founder.) Owner-manager founders are more likely to express personal work satisfactions in terms of productive performance, design and product innovation, craftsmanship and product quality, and a sense of achievement than owner-manager inheritors who, in contrast, place greater emphasis on stability, on sales performance, on personal relationships within and outside the firm, and on organizational aspects. Third, the table underlines the observation made in Chapter 8 that owner-managers tend to identify closely with their companies. Many owner-managers, asked about their own personal work satisfaction, express satisfying or dissatisfying aspects of their company's financial, productive, sales, staff, or administrative performance.

To what extent, however, can expressions of work satisfaction throw light on the motivation and goals of owner-managers? Theories of motivation attempt to explain, to give reasons for, individual behavior or behavior patterns. Peters has pointed out that there are a variety of possible levels of explanation of behavior and that, consequently, attempts by psychologists to find some all-inclusive theory of human motivation are bedded in conceptual confusion.[22] We would suggest that corresponding to the variety of satisfactions found in their work by owner-managers are a variety of orientations to work and a variety of goals pursued through work. We have seen that owner-manager founders may start up in business for different

TABLE 10.1

Work Satisfactions and Dissatisfactions of Owner-Manager Founders and Inheritors
(Founders, n = 44; Inheritors, n = 50)

Classification and examples--satisfaction and dissatisfaction expressed in terms of:	Numbers Expressing					
	Satisfaction			Dissatisfaction		
	F*	I	T	F	I	T
Financial aspects						
1. Financial performance: "running the business profitably"; "seeing the right figures at the end of the month";----"someone catching me for £500, going skimpt with my money"	6	7	13	1	2	3
2. Financial stability: "knowing the future of the place is assured";----"lack of finance"; "worry involved if the thing goes down"	--	2	2	--	2	2
3. Personal financial rewards: "receiving my salary cheque";----"don't get my wages when cash is short"	1	--	1	1	1	2
Total	7	9	16	2	5	7
Production aspects						
1. Productive performance: "to see a good productive week"; "seeing the stuff going out the door"; ----"bad production figures"	5	2	7	1	2	3
2. Stability of production process: "when things are running smoothly"; "keeping full-time working going in what is a seasonal trade";----"bottlenecks in production"	1	4	5	2	2	4
3. Design, and product innovation: "getting out a new design"; "beating problems of design"; "designing"	7	4	11	--	--	--
4. Craftsmanship and product quality: "trying to keep up our quality standards";----"bad workmanship"	6	1	7	4	1	5
5. Innovation and development in production methods: "evolving different and new methods";----"tradition--we've always done it like that"	3	--	3	--	1	1
6. Physical work performance: "my heart is still in the works--I like making things"; "working in the mill"; "doing half an hour's turning"	3	6	9	--	--	--
Total	15	17	42	7	6	13
Sales aspects						
1. Sales performance: "winning a contract"; "selling"; "taking a good order";----"customer promises that don't materialize"	3	9	12	3	3	6
2. Customer satisfaction: "producing the work to the pleasure of the customer";----"dealing with customer complaints"	2	2	4	5	3	8
Total	5	11	16	8	6	14
Personnel aspects						
1. Staff performance: "finding that jobs are not done properly"; "having to haul staff over the coals for skimped work"; "lack of sense of responsibility and urgency by some of the staff"	--	--	--	10	7	17
2. Staff development and welfare: "developing young craftsmen";----"seeing young apprentices on boring repetitious work"	1	2	3	1	2	3

Classification and examples--satisfaction and dissatisfaction expressed in terms of:	Numbers Expressing					
	Satisfaction			Dissatisfaction		
	F	I	T	F	I	T
3. Personal relationships in the firm: "working with a partner I like"; "a happy and satisfied staff pleased to work for me";----"serious differences of opinion at top level"	2	8	10	1	1	2
4. Personal relationships outside the firm: "knowing I have the confidence of customers"	1	3	4	--	--	--
Total	4	13	27	12	10	22
Organizational aspects						
1. Administrative performance: "to see the results of efficient management; I'm not interested in furniture as an object and have no artistic appreciation of furniture"; "organizing something that comes out right in every way"	2	5	7	4	2	6
2. Dealing with paperwork and government returns: "keeping the books in a nice order";---- "correspondence"; "being chairbound"; "filling in forms"	--	3	3	4	7	11
3. Interruptions/wasted time: "constant telephone interruptions"; "time wasted travelling"	--	--	--	2	1	3
Total	2	8	10	10	10	20
Psychological aspects						
1. Independence: "being my own boss"; "the hours--more freedom and leisure time"	1	2	3	--	--	--
2. Sense of achievement: "I like all of it. I built it up from nothing. It's a personal triumph, a personal achievement"----"frustration; the business is running me instead of me the business"	9	4	13	--	1	1
3. Variety of work: "variety--in touch with every level of life"	2	1	3	--	--	--
4. The business "game" itself: " a bit of a fight, a bit of a battle--I personally enjoy the challenge of it"; "I prefer the trouble--you tend to let things slide when you are doing alright"	3	3	6	--	--	--
Total	15	10	25	--	1	1
Total responses	58	68	126	39	38	77
Percent of responses expressing satisfaction and dissatisfaction in terms of:						
Financial aspects	12.1	13.2	12.7	5.1	13.2	9.1
Production aspects	43.1	25.0	33.3	17.9	15.8	16.9
Sales aspects	8.6	16.2	12.7	20.5	15.8	18.2
Personnel aspects	6.9	19.1	13.5	13.5	26.3	28.6
Organizational aspects	3.4	11.8	7.9	25.6	26.3	26.0
Psychological aspects	25.9	14.7	19.8	--	2.6	1.3

*F = Founders; I = Inheritors; T = Total.

Source: Compiled by the author.

reasons, some of them economic, some of them a response to cultural stereotypes, some of them to satisfy individual psychological needs, some of them to pursue particular occupational careers. Similarly, owner-managers may persist in their own businesses for reasons that are quite different from the reasons bringing new entrants to the small business community. The motivation to found a small company and the motivation to continue to work in one may be quite different, though each will be circumscribed by the alternative work opportunities that exist. Analysis of expressions of work satisfaction can give some indication, then, of this second set of owner-manager motivations, that is of motivations to continue in their present work. Here we must recognize that the notion of motivation implies some conscious choice and the opportunity to express preferences between alternative courses of action, whereas in reality the alternatives, as we have seen, may be between "independence" and unemployment.

A number of orientations to work can be seen in Table 10.1. A proportion of responses indicate a performance orientation to work, a concern with the financial results of the business, with weekly production or sales figures, with staff output and productivity, with the efficiency of administrative systems. Some owner-managers have a conservative orientation to work, being primarily concerned with stability, some have a craft and handwork orientation, being concerned with product quality or with themselves working in craft jobs within their firms, and some have an innovative and creative orientation, being concerned with new designs or new methods. Other owner-managers may be said to have a predominantly social or communal orientation to their work. They stress the satisfaction of customer service or of personal relationships in the work community. There is little sign, however, of the kinds of work orientation generally ascribed to the employed. There is little evidence here, for example, to suggest that many owner-managers have an instrumental orientation toward their work, an orientation where "work is regarded as a means of acquiring the income necessary to support a valued way of life of which work itself is not an integral part."[23] Only one owner-manager stressed the satisfaction of personal financial rewards and one other suggested that catching the 5:16 train on Friday night was the highlight of his week. There is little evidence of a bureaucratic orientation to work among owner-managers, nor would such an orientation be appropriate to the economic and organizational circumstances in which they find themselves, but there is some evidence, as we have seen, of those aspects of a solidaristic work orientation that emphasize high ego-involvement in work and where "the social relationships and shared activities of work are found emotionally rewarding."[24]

ORGANIZATIONAL GOALS AND THE SMALL FIRM

To what extent is it possible, however, to classify the goals pursued by small firms in order to provide some basis for understanding the behavior of owner-managers as well as their attitudes and expressed work satisfactions? There have been a number of attempts to classify organizational goals, particularly, as we have seen in Chapter 1, in economic analysis. Sociologists have tried to underline the complexity of the organizational goals problem by placing economic goals in their wider social and cultural contexts. Perrow, for example, distinguishes types or levels of goals in relation to the perspectives that different interest groups have vis-a-vis an organization. [25] Thus

> for society, the justification of a steel company's existence may be to produce needed goods; for customers, the goal of a firm may be to produce certain kinds of steel and deliver them on time; for the investors, the aim may be to pay out large dividends; for top executives, the purpose may be to run a stable, secure organisation where life is fairly predictable and not too stressful; for a division manager the goal may be to make the best damn steel around . . . this means that organisational goals are not only multiple but may be conflicting, and that they can be pursued all at once or in sequence.

In the small firm these different perspectives may have to be reconciled by the owner-manager himself rather than through the interaction of conflicting interest groups. The owner-manager may, for example, be pursuing through his business enterprise particular familial or societal goals and the generation and maintenance of particular cultural values. He may also, as investor, be concerned with an acceptable level of economic return, a return that may be defined in terms of personal financial expectations or in terms of profit satisfaction criteria that are related to other goals such as stability or growth. In addition, as we have seen, the owner-manager may have what Perrow calls product or product-characteristic goals and be concerned with design, quality, and craftsmanship. The major problem in the analysis of organizational goals hinges, however, not so much on the question of describing the multiplicity of goals that organizations can be observed pursuing, as on the question of teasing out, in any particular situation, which goals are means and which goals are ends. If a small company, for example, is observed placing great emphasis on product quality and craftsmanship, is this because the owner-manager sees these as goals in themselves or as means to other ends such as profit or customer satisfaction or stability? The strength of the economist's point of view is that, for many organizations, notions of profit maximization or profit satisfaction appear to be global end-goals under which most other goals can be theoretically subsumed as means-goals. The weakness of the economist's point of view is that little account is taken in such a perspective of the strength of social, familial, and cultural factors. A sociological perspective on organizations tends to emphasize, therefore, the definition of end-goals in terms of social needs and a psychological perspective tends to emphasize end-goals in relation to the idiosyncratic motivations of those leaders or decision-makers who occupy positions of power or influence. In such perspectives profit is relegated to a means-goal, a measure of efficiency or effectiveness or a condition of survival rather than an end in itself. The paradox of the sociological and psychological perspectives rests in the fact that capitalist societies have tended to bolster profit as an end-goal for organizations by ideologies and philosophies--the Protestant Ethic, Utilitarianism, Social Darwinism--that in themselves become important cultural factors and possible influences upon individual motivation. The problem becomes one, therefore, not merely of seeing profit as a means-goal but of seeing it as only one among a number of measures of organizational performance. Just as it is patently absurd to believe that a highly authoritarian industrial organization or trade union can, in a wider context, be a valuable component part of a democratic system, so too it is patently absurd to believe that an organization can justifiably and exclusively pursue profit as a means to social ends, independently of social means consequences. Once one accepts the notion that commercial and industrial organizations have social responsibilities, a whole series of consequences follow, both for the organization's relationship with its customers and shareholders and for its internal processes.

There is, of course, a vast difference between assertion of the goals that organizations should pursue and identification of the goals that they do pursue. In practice the test, in analyzing whether or not noneconomic goals are important to organizations, must be whether or not such goals will be pursued at the expense of profits, given the assumption that sufficient information and room for maneuver is available to make such a choice for the organization a possibility. In studying small firms, it is clear that just as a rational economic model cannot adequately explain the entry of new businesses, neither can it adequately account for the practice of small business management. Certainly there are small businesses that pursue economic

goals alone, that attempt to maximize profits insofar as they can, or
to maximize growth, or to maximize sales income, or to maximize
the economic rewards of specialization or craftsmanship, businesses
that are set up with the straightforward aim: "to succeed or get out."
But it is equally clear that many small businesses do pursue other
goals and pursue them at the expense of profits. Some pursue profit
satisfaction goals as an alternative to profit maximization goals
rather than as the best possible approximation of a profit maximization policy. Some pursue specialization and craftsmanship as ends
in themselves. Some fear growth and its consequences, feel reluctant to trust "outsiders" with the performance of tasks traditionally
carried out by the owner himself, reluctant to lose effective control
of the day-to-day operations of their firm, reluctant to shut themselves off from close personal contacts with their employees, reluctant to inject external capital into a business that has hitherto been
a reflection of their own personal efforts and sacrifices. Personal
and family loyalties may take precedence over economic concerns.
Indeed the spillover of business into family life and vice versa may
make it impossible for the small-firm owner-manager to divorce his
business behavior from his social behavior. Initially, it seems,
many small businesses are likely to pursue survival goals and, once
established at what their owners consider to be a stable and secure
level of operation, then to pursue conservation goals.

SUMMARY

Neither the classical economic stereotype of the entrepreneur
nor the literary medieval view of the owner-manager as artist-
craftsman provide adequate explanations of the motivation and goals
of small businessmen. Attitudinal studies have tended to underline
the pervasiveness of such stereotypes rather than to provide insights
that will account for the behavior of owner-managers in different
economic and cultural contexts. In particular the much-valued independence of the small businessman in many cases proves illusory.

A model of entrepreneurial behavior that takes account of the
expectations that owner-managers have in respect to their business
ventures, and that accommodates the possible modification of initial
expectations in the light of owner-managers' experiences of the economic realities of small business management, is likely to prove
more useful as a basis for analysis and prediction than the simplistic
models of entrepreneurial motivation commonly adopted by economists
and psychologists. Such a model must handle the possibility that a
wide variety of goals may be pursued by small enterprises, that some
goals may be highly specific to individual owner-managers, and that

the goals pursued will change over time both in conjunction with the development of the business and in relation to the socioeconomic circumstances of its owners.

Research studies suggest that perhaps as few as one in ten owner-managers conform to the classical economic model of entrepreneurial behavior. The motivations and organizational goals of the remainder are extremely diverse. Just as some large company executives may be concerned with the social responsibilities of business, with questions of environmental pollution, the quality of life, and with the organization's obligations to customers and employees as well as to shareholders,[26] so too some owner-operators and owner-managers of small firms. Indeed in the small firm there would in many cases never have been any question that the firm might have a solely economic function even if, in the early days of the business, social responsibility was not thought to stretch much beyond the owner's family and friends. It is perhaps ironic that it is the professional manager who has increasingly sought to justify his business behavior by appeals to the economic icons of profitability and efficiency and to the values enshrined in the Protestant Ethic. If in future the big-business executive and the entrepreneur are to remain blood relations,[27] it may not be so much in their enslavement to the notion of profit maximization as in a joint sense of their social responsibilities.

NOTES

1. Small Firms--Report of the Committee of Inquiry on Small Firms (The Bolton Report) (London: H.M.S.O., 1971), para. 19.5

2. Hansard, vol. 838 no. 132, 1038, June 12, 1972.

3. J. K. Galbraith, The New Industrial State (London: Hamish Hamilton, 1967).

4. P. Gregg, A Social and Economic History of Britain: 1760-1965 (London: Harrap, 1965).

5. C. Perrow, Organisational Analysis (London: Tavistock, 1970). The writings referred to are: A. A. Berle and G. C. Means, The Modern Corporation and Private Property (New York: Macmillan, 1932); R. A. Gordon, Business Leadership in the Large Corporation (Berkeley: University of California Press, 1961) (first published in 1945); and Galbraith, op. cit.

6. J. Betjeman, Summoned by Bells (London: John Murray, 1960).

7. J. L. Oliver, The Development and Structure of the Furniture Industry (Oxford: Pergamon Press, 1966).

8. Senate Small Business Committee, quoted in J. H. Bunzel, The American Small Businessman (New York: Knopf, 1962).

9. Furniture, Board of Trade Working Party Report (London: H.M.S.O., 1946).

10. C. W. Golby and G. Johns, Attitude and Motivation, Committee of Inquiry on Small Firms, Research Report No. 7.

11. The researchers give no indication in their report of how these groups of owner-managers were selected. Discussion groups were held in the period April to June 1970, that is immediately preceding a General Election in which the Conservative party in Britain was returned to power. At such a time, we suggest, cultural stereotypes surrounding individualism and the virtues of private enterprise are likely to be especially noticeable in the attitudes of small businessmen.

12. F. Safier, "Small Business Wants Old-Age Security," Senate Small Business Committee Print No. 17, pp. 7-8 (1943), quoted in J. D. Phillips, Little Business in the American Economy (Urbana: University of Illinois Press, 1958).

13. Phillips, op. cit.

14. See article by R. Jones, "The entrepreneur: a lone wolf or an imitator?" The Times, May 8, 1972.

15. See Chapter 6.

16. K. B. Mayer and S. Goldstein, The First Two Years: Problems of Small Firm Growth and Survival, Small Business Research Series No. 2 (Washington, D.C.: Small Business Administration, 1961).

17. S. M. Lipset and R. Bendix, "Social Mobility and Occupational Career Patterns," American Journal of Sociology, January and March 1952, pp. 366-74 and 494-504.

18. E. Chinoy, Automobile Workers and the American Dream (New York: Doubleday, 1955).

19. J. H. Goldthorpe, D. Lockwood, F. Bechhofer, and J. Platt, The Affluent Worker: Industrial Attitudes and Behaviour (Cambridge: University Press, 1970).

20. Ibid., pp. 131-35.

21. Sponsored by I.C.I. Paints Division on behalf of the National Federation of Master Painters and Decorators and reported in the Financial Times, June 11, 1971.

22. R. S. Peters, The Concept of Motivation (London: Routledge and Kegan Paul, 1958). Peters distinguishes between "his reason" explanations, "the reason" explanations, causal explanations, and end-state explanations.

23. Goldthorpe et al., op. cit.

24. Ibid.

25. Perrow, op. cit.

26. Barbara E. Shenfield, Company Boards: Their Responsibilities to Shareholders, Employees and their Community (London: Political and Economic Planning, 1971).

27. See R. Caves, American Industry--Structure, Conduct, Performance (Englewood Cliffs, N.J.: Prentice-Hall, 1964).

11

THE MANAGERIAL
PROCESS IN THE
SMALL FIRM

It is clear from the research findings described and analyzed in Part II that small firms have a number of distinctive characteristics that have a bearing on the way they are managed, characteristics such as instability in the markets they serve, the existence of close family and kinship ties within them, the educational and occupational experiences of their owners and managers, and their patterns of management training and development. This chapter describes some of the ways in which the management process in the small firm differs from the management process in the large company and looks at some of the implications of these differences for an improved understanding of the abilities and skills required in successful management of a small enterprise.

PREDICTIVE AND ADAPTIVE
MANAGEMENT PROCESSES

In the large firm the management process has been seen historically as being primarily a predictive process. Traditionally the skills and techniques taught in management courses have been those associated with planning and control, for example, critical path analysis methods, PERT (Program Evaluation Review Technique), budgetary and cost control systems. The assumption behind such courses has been that the management process is primarily concerned with planning and controlling activities within a predictable environment and, consequently, management education and training have been geared largely to this view of the management process as a predictive process. Management in the large firm is believed to be primarily concerned with the clarification of long-term objectives, the formulation of appropriate policies and strategies to meet such objectives,

and the feedback of information to indicate successful or unsuccessful
achievement of the goals established.

It is evident, however, that small firms are more concerned
with short-term rather than with long-term objectives, with short-
term rather than long-term results, and with tactical issues rather
than with strategic goals. Day-to-day activities take precedence
over long-term planning and long-term investment in capital or manpower is viewed as secondary to the achievement of short-term goals.
The following extract from the report on one of the pilot projects that
preceded our depth studies of owner-managers indicates this characteristic short-term perspective of many owner-managers and illustrates how the management activity pattern in the small firm can differ from the popular concept of the executive at work.

> The pace of action was fast, certainly fast enough
> to make accurate durational recording difficult, a
> task made more complex by the simultaneity and
> interspersion of many of the activities. The
> Managing Director, Mr. Boshier, was mobile
> within the firm, some 26 percent of his time be-
> ing spent away from his office--in the showroom,
> in the various workshops and in the transport
> yard. He worked long hours, arriving between
> 8:00 a.m. and 9:00 a.m. and leaving between 6:00
> p.m. and 7:00 p.m., ate lunch in his office and
> sometimes transacted business while doing so.
> He was rarely alone. In the odd moments when
> nothing was happening he was usually in the com-
> pany of his two order clerks. On average he was
> involved in a telephone call, a contact with one of
> the clerks or one of his principal subordinates or
> one of his customers, every two and a half min-
> utes. It was clear that Mr. Boshier had the per-
> sonal qualities appropriate to such a role--charm,
> quick wittedness, a good memory, bargaining
> skill and the capacity to remain unruffled by the
> many demands made for his attention.
>   It would be wrong, however, to give the im-
> pression that Mr. Boshier simply performed well
> in a situation that had got out of hand, or that he
> was passively at the receiving end of information
> and requests from others. An analysis of a batch
> of telephone calls indicated, for example, that 37
> percent of them were outgoing calls initiated by
> the managing director, and an examination of

face-to-face contacts with staff and customers
showed that over 70 percent of such contacts were
initiated by Mr. Boshier. The observer's impression was that Mr. Boshier worked in the way he
did because he chose to and because he thought it
likely to produce the desired results, as indeed it
had done in the past. At no time was the managing director observed to attempt any task requiring uninterrupted concentration. The only task of
this nature that he referred to was costing, something he did mainly at home. Otherwise, work
which he did at home took the form of jotting down
reminders for the following day.

There was a conspicuous absence of written
communications, there being no internal written
communications during the week of the study and
only one outgoing letter, the gist of which the
managing director explained to one of the clerks
and left her to compose something appropriate
for him to check. Mr. Boshier seldom left the
factory and office premises during the working
day. He did not exercise any formal representative functions within his local community and
mentioned that he had no time to attend meetings
of trade bodies and associations. Nevertheless he
was undoubtedly well informed about market conditions and happenings in the trade. He had a
network of personal contacts within the trade
whom he could, and did, telephone for information and assistance. Similarly much of Mr.
Boshier's "social" conversation with visitors,
particularly with suppliers' representatives,
took the form of trade gossip and was an important source of "grape-vine" information. Virtually all Mr. Boshier's communications were by
telephone or face-to-face and all his trade information was gleaned on an informal basis.

To sum up, Mr. Boshier's work was characterized by the short duration of his activities, by
a preponderance of day-to-day business with little
apparent evidence of planning more than three
months ahead at the most, by constant attention
to detail, rather than concern with general issues
of policy, and by lack of formal written communications. He appeared to be well informed and
highly effective.

The tendency in the management literature, insofar as it considers small-firm management from an empirical standpoint, has been to accept that certainly small firms do behave in this apparently hand-to-mouth, day-to-day manner--that is precisely their deficiency. It is assumed that it should not be so, that if only small firms would adopt some of the planning and control systems of the larger companies then all would be well. But the evidence does not support this assumption that what the small firm needs is an injection of predictive management techniques. Mr. Boshier, for example, was managing what, in terms of his expectations and motivation, was a successful business, a business that he had founded in 1956 with an initial capital of around £2,000 and which, at the time of the study, had a total net worth of nearly £70,000. He is not, however, the exception that proves the rule.

The author of a study on cash planning in small manufacturing companies in the United States started out with precisely the predictive management process assumptions that we have characterized.[1] He believed that many small independent business owners allowed themselves to be pushed into hasty, ad hoc decisions as a result of a lack of forward planning. He believed, too, that this kind of ad hoc decision-making was likely to prove particularly disastrous if there were no forward plans in a company to meet demands for cash and that, consequently, a lack of formal financial planning might well be a significant reason for small business failures. He set up his research, therefore, to test four hypotheses: (1) that most small manufacturing firms did not prepare formal cash projections; (2) that most small manufacturing firms thought that they did sufficient cash planning; (3) that the financial health of small manufacturing firms was directly related to the amount of formal cash planning that was done; and (4) that there was some minimum amount of cash planning required of all small manufacturing firms. In the Los Angeles area, 28 were studied, most of them light engineering firms. The smallest company had 6 employees, the largest 158, and the median company 66 employees. Information was collected by questionnaire and interview with the chief executive of each company and subsequently by questionnaires directed to the company's auditors, the company's bank, and to Dun and Bradstreet for a credit rating. Of the companies in the study, 71.4 percent did not prepare or use written forecasts of cash requirements. Almost all the company presidents, however, felt that they were pretty well aware of their future cash needs. They said that they gave almost continuous thought to making sales, collecting outstanding debts, and to meeting their bills. It was their belief that they were able to do sufficient cash planning for the future in their heads, or with the aid of some occasional notations on the back of an envelope. The research discovered no cause-and-effect

relationship between the existence of written cash plans and successful financial results, the companies that did not prepare cash-flow
statements being no less successful than those using cash budgets.
There was no evidence to confirm the idea that there must be some
prescribed minimum amount of formal cash budgeting. The company
chief executives believed that "mental awareness of cash requirements" was sufficient and the bankers and accountants in general
agreed.

We would argue, then, that the concentration of owner-managers
on relatively short-term issues and on day-to-day details, rather
than being a sign of some deficiency in their managerial process, is
a necessary part of that process. Concentration on short-term tactical goals, and the ability to pursue such goals without reference to
precisely stated long-term or strategic objectives, can contribute,
therefore, to the survival of the small firm. In other words, owner-
managers are not misplacing their energies. They rightly see that
the concentration of those energies on immediate survival is an important means of ensuring survival in the long-term, next year being
"365 tomorrows." There is a danger, however, that we interpret
the position as one in which no planning or policy-making activities
either take place or are necessary in the small firm. The research
findings indicate that owner-managers of small companies can often
operate quite successfully without any formal written plans. But
lack of formal written plans does not necessarily mean that the
owner-manager does not have a clear idea of what he is trying to
achieve and the progress that he is making. In addition, although
there may be little observable evidence of policy-making and planning
activities being carried out by the owner-manager, such activities
may well evolve from the day-to-day detail. The management process
in the small firm may not be a readily visible process, having an
abstract rather than a concrete form, but may, nevertheless, be a
process that is well suited to the economic conditions within which
most small firms operate.

Predictive management processes, as we have described them,
may be suitable for large companies that have some possibility of
influencing the markets within which they sell their products or services. Predictive management processes are essentially concerned
with strategic behavior, that is with attempts to shape events and to
control change. Many small firms, however, do not operate in market
conditions, either in terms of the scale of their operations or the
degree of specialization of their products, that allow them to influence
their trading environment to any significant extent. Even when they
do operate in monopoly or oligopoly conditions they may not only lack
the motivation to exploit the situation but the market advantages that
they have may exist, paradoxically, simply because they are not

exploited. Most small firms concentrate their efforts, then, not on attempting to predict and control their environment, but on adapting as rapidly as possible to the changing demands of that environment. The management process in the small firm is primarily an adaptive process, concerned with adjusting a limited amount of resources in order to gain some immediate and short-term advantage. Adaptive management processes are essentially concerned with tactical rather than strategic behavior, that is, with attempts to mitigate the consequences of events and to exploit the opportunities presented by change.

THE ADMINISTRATOR AND THE ENTREPRENEUR

More light is thrown on the differences between predictive and adaptive management processes if we attempt to distinguish between the work and work attitudes of the administrator in a large organization and those of the man who runs his own business. The historical development of management theory followed closely the growing scale of industrial and commercial organizations and the consequent divorce between those who owned an enterprise and those who controlled its activities. But in the small firm, as we have seen in Chapter 6, ownership and control may frequently be vested in one man, the owner-manager, or in a small family or kinship group who actively participate in the management of the enterprise's affairs. These people are entrepreneurs rather than managers or administrators. The term entrepreneur, that is, a person in effective control of a commercial undertaking, underlines the adaptive nature of managerial processes in the small firm. It has connotations of enterprise, opportunism, individuality, and flair in contrast to the connotations of the terms manager and administrator, which are associated with notions of organization, planning, professionalism, and the predictive management processes. This is not merely some semantic quibble. What we are suggesting on the basis of our research findings is that the small-firm owner-manager or entrepreneur has both a different function from the large-firm manager or administrator and a different structure of attitudes or beliefs about the nature of the management process.

As we have seen in Part II, small firms have a number of organizational characteristics that influence the character of their management process. Relationships are often informal, there being no precise definitions of rights and obligations, duties and responsibilities. Appointment and promotion are frequently made on the basis of birth or personal friendship rather than on the basis of educational or technical qualifications. Organization structures, insofar as they exist, are likely to develop around the interests and abilities of owner-managers employed in the firm, the organization being characteristically structured in a loose organic way. Large companies, in contrast, are likely to operate with more clearly defined formal relationships between their managers, with a greater divorce of the planners from the doers, and with the use of technical competence and expertise as the basis of appointment and promotion, large company organizations being characteristically structured in a formal mechanistic way. (This is, of course, a caricature of large-scale organization. For further discussion see Chapter 12.) But as well as these structural differences, which partly arise simply as a consequence of scale, there are important psychological differences between the organizational role of the entrepreneur and the organizational role of the administrator or manager independently of size of firm, differences that rest in the psychological consequences of ownership.

There appear to have been no studies that have set out to compare the orientations and attitudes toward work of owner-managers or entrepreneurs with employed-managers or administrators. The crucial difference, we suggest, between the entrepreneur and the administrator rests in ownership and from this stem differences in attitudes toward work, authority and responsibility, and the function and purpose of the enterprise itself. What, then, are the consequences of ownership? First, the owner-manager's commitment to the business is obviously different to that of the professional salary-earning manager or administrator. The owner-manager is emotionally and financially committed to his company in a way that, with full employment and the development of the idea of a management profession, is becoming less and less common among salaried administrators. Second, ownership has a number of consequences in terms of the methods adopted in managing the business and in terms of the kinds of power and authority relationships that exist within the company. The entrepreneur, for example, believes he exercises authority as of right; his authority stems from his ownership of the assets of the company and his freedom, if he so wishes, to sell up his business. It is a personal authority vested in him and his family. The manager, on the other hand, derives authority solely from the office he holds. He is, consequently, concerned to justify that authority on the grounds of his own professional and technical expertise or by soliciting the consensus of shareholders or of employees. Any personal authority the manager may build up will rest on successful performance throughout the company or in his particular area of responsibility, whereas the authority of the entrepreneur is in no way diminished by a debit on the profit and loss account. In addition the entrepreneur is accountable only to himself and, as we have seen in Chapter 10, feels free to pursue noneconomic goals without rationalizing his motives in economic terms. This may take several forms. It may be reflected in decisions to curtail the growth of the firm in order that the owner or his family should not lose effective control, or in decisions to set the satisfaction of a particular customer or a long-serving employee above considerations of profit maximization.

As well, however, as looking at the psychological and organizational consequences of legal ownership rights it is worth considering the consequences of what have been described as "felt" ownership rights. In answering the question "When do we 'feel' we own-- whether we do in the eyes of the law or not," it has been suggested that there are two conditions under which a person may come to feel that he owns his work.[2] One of these is that a person is left alone; this is the common law of custom and practice and of squatters' rights. The other condition, more relevant to our argument here, is that a person makes decisions about his work. When someone identifies with his work, makes a kind of personal psychological investment in it, then he will feel rights of ownership: "Where we make a decision, there do we 'put ourselves into that which we do' and so feel an identification and a sense of ownership. Here a sense of ownership springs straight from a sense of control. Locke expressed something of the same sentiment when he said that 'property' should be considered as 'that with which a man hath mixed his labour.' . . . Psychologically, 'property' can be seen as that which is an extension of the self. That with which we have identified is 'ours.'"[3] If we take this idea that "we feel we own when we feel we control" and look at it in relation to the legal and felt ownership rights of the entrepreneur and the administrator, we find it gives us a number of new insights into the nature of the different psychological contracts that exist in large- and small-scale enterprises. We have already noted in Chapter 8 that the small-firm owner-manager, when talking about his work problems, tends to talk about the problems facing his company and to identify completely with his firm, l'enterprise c'est moi. The owner-manager's psychological contract is, therefore, clear in that he exercises both legal and felt ownership rights within his firm. The situation of the chief executive or the top management group in the large firm is, in spite of the lack of legal ownership rights, very similar to that of the small-firm owner-manager. The divorce between legal ownership and management control in the large firm means that senior executives very readily take on felt ownership rights. They are generally free of interference from the legal owners, the shareholders. Their felt ownership is based not only on their controlling position as decision-makers but also on the fact that to all intents and purposes they are left alone by the legal owners, allowed their own little scene "to monarchise, be fear'd, and kill with looks."[4] While they may claim, therefore, that their managerial prerogatives derive from rights vested in them as agents of the owners, their behavior is underpinned psychologically by these felt ownership rights.

But it is more interesting perhaps to speculate on the psychological contracts of the middle-level manager or administrator in the large organization and of the nonshareholding nonfamily manager in the small firm. The administrator or professional middle manager in the large organization can claim no legal ownership rights, neither is he sufficiently in control of decisions about his work nor sufficiently left alone by his seniors in the hierarchy to develop felt ownership rights. It becomes necessary for him, therefore, to buttress his position from outside the organization, and this he does through membership of specialist professional management organizations. (On the basis of these speculations, therefore, we would hypothesize that the activist members of professional associations will be those whose occupational positions provide limited opportunities for the development of a sense of ownership within their work organizations). We can now, perhaps, begin to understand the peculiar frustrations of the nonshareholding manager in the small family firm, frustrations that we illustrated in Chapter 6 with the cases of Mr. Landaeur and Mr. Mobley. The nonshareholding manager in the small firm often has none of the psychological security provided by legal or felt ownership or by membership of the owning family or of some extra-organizational professional group. As we saw in Chapter 7, only 13 percent of the 229 managers interviewed during our descriptive survey were members of professional bodies and in only a very few cases was their membership consequent upon the holding of some educational qualification. There seem to be a number of reactions on the part of nonshareholding managers in small family businesses to their psychological disfranchisement. One reaction is obviously expressed in the relatively high rate of interfirm mobility among nonshareholding managers. We can now view this mobility, not only as a necessary compensation for lack of formal educational or professional qualifications, but also as a reaction to a lack of felt or legal ownership rights. Another reaction, which was that of Mr. Mobley, is to strive for dominance within the family firm by displaying abilities and skills that the firm will come to find indispensable and thereby displacing the owners from their power-holding and decision-controlling positions: "Things have to be done my way. I have to be the dominant personality." We believe a more common reaction, however, to psychological disfranchisement is a kind of overcompensating normative identification. In a number of cases we observed nonshareholding managers who seemed to be more ardent advocates of the traditional values enshrined in the family firm, more dedicated to the need for profitability, more vociferous advocates of the virtues of private enterprise, of hard work, and of loyalty to the firm than the owner-managers who employed them. This is a phenomenon that, in a quite unscientific way, we have also observed in large organizations where it is frequently the middle managers and administrators who pay the greatest lip-service to the values of the Protestant Ethic and who trot out simple cliches like "the purpose of business is to make a profit." Finally, that time-honored way out for the disfranchised manager in the small firm takes on a new meaning --marriage to the boss' daughter becomes both a legal and a psychological contract!

THE ENTREPRENEURIAL PHILOSOPHY

How, then, can we describe the values of the entrepreneur or owner-manager, and in what ways does the entrepreneurial philosophy, that fragmented set of beliefs, stereotypes, myths, and attitudes that reinforces the owner-manager's sense of the value of his work, differ from the work philosophy of the administrator or the professional manager in a large organization? We suggest that the entrepreneurial philosophy that lies behind essential parts of the small-firm management process has five principal characteristics.

First, the entrepreneurial philosophy is dominated by the owner-manager's awareness that the success of his company is the primary arbiter of his own personal wealth and standard of living. We have seen, for example, that in times of company financial difficulty owner-managers have of necessity reduced the salaries they receive from their businesses to levels below the payments made to many of their employees. One of the consequences of this close link between the success of the firm and the financial rewards of the owner-manager will be a difference in attitude toward risk-taking. It is obvious that the attitude toward risk-taking of an owner-manager investing and managing his own capital is likely to be very different from the attitude of an executive who is investing and managing finance on behalf of a somewhat nebulous body of shareholders. One of the signs of an owner-manager's transition from an entrepreneurial to a managerial orientation toward his business would be, then, his ability to treat the finance in the company as if it were not his own, a change that may well be linked in practice with the introduction into the business for the first time of finance from commercial rather than from personal or family sources.

Second, and conversely, the economic and social aspirations of the entrepreneur have an important effect on the margin of profit or rate of growth that he wishes his firm to achieve. These aspirations will, in turn, vary according to the stage that the entrepreneur has reached in his life cycle: "In one small company I came across, profit was evaluated on the basis of how much the owner needed to support his wife, send two children away to school, have four weeks holiday in Spain each year, support mother and auntie, and replace most of the plant every seven years."[5] The management process in the small firm is highly personalized and frequently reflects the motivations, preferences, prejudices, and attitudes of the entrepreneur. The purpose of the enterprise changes in accordance with shifts in the expectations and values held by the entrepreneur. Similarly the work that the owner-manager does within his firm expands and contracts, partly in response to the adaptive necessities of operating in an unpredictable and uncontrollable economic environment, and partly in response to the personality and needs of the owner-manager himself. The management process in the small firm, therefore, cannot be viewed in isolation from the skills, experience, personality, and values system of the firm's owner-manager.

Third, the entrepreneurial philosophy is a unitary philosophy in that it treats the running of a business as a single process rather than as a conglomeration of separate specialist activities, each of which has its own highly developed expertise. Consequently, the traditional organizational problems of the large-firm manager or administrator--problems of accountability, delegation of authority and responsibility, coordination and control of the work of subordinates--do not exist, as problems, for the entrepreneur. Fourth, and as a corollary to this unitary approach to the management process, the entrepreneurial philosophy is not concerned with professional, administrative, or managerial skills, knowledge or expertise as ends in themselves, but solely as means for the achievement of the personal goals of the entrepreneur. The consequence of this orientation toward professional expertise should be a very critical and pragmatic approach toward management tools and techniques. In practice, while the entrepreneur may be scathing about the value of the contribution that anyone not trained through the hard school of experience can make to the development of his business, he may, nevertheless, be impressed in spite of himself by the formally educated professional manager and his display of managerial technology. Many small-business owner-managers are unduly defensive about what they perceive as their own "lack of sophistication" as managers and as a result are particularly vulnerable to those mendicant charlatans of the management consultancy fraternity who peddle quack remedies as panaceas for all organizational ills.

Fifth, the entrepreneurial philosophy is one that sees no breakdown between the values of the work place and the values of society as a whole. Success at work, however the entrepreneur chooses to define it, necessarily underpins the social prestige of the owner-

manager, and the authority and role that he has in the community are
partly reflections of his authority and role within his firm. Similarly
the entrepreneur's sense of social responsibility is worked out within
the company, in, for example, his relations with his employees, as
well as in the community.

ADMINISTRATIVE AND ENTREPRENEURIAL SKILLS

We turn now from discussion of the differences in orientation
toward work of small-firm owner-managers and of large-firm administrators to consideration of the nature of the skills they require
to carry out their managerial functions appropriately. If we accept
the distinction between predictive and adaptive management processes, then it follows that, given the market environment within
which most small firms operate, the small company will require a
different mix of managerial skills from the large company. Consequently, "successful" owner-managers, as measured in terms of
traditional economic criteria, will be distinguished from "unsuccessful" owner-managers more by their ability to make appropriate
adaptations to market, technical, economic, and personnel changes,
than by their appreciation of general management "principles" or
by their use of sophisticated planning and control systems.

The administrator in the large firm is primarily concerned
with those skills relevant to predictive management processes, that
is with skills of prediction and control, whereas the owner-manager
of a small firm needs primarily to develop skills relevant to adaptive
management processes, skills that enable him to exploit the advantages he has in being small. The administrator strives to exercise
predictive, prognostic, and strategic skills and, through the use of
such skills, to shape events and to control change; these management
skills are administrative skills. The entrepreneur is striving to
exercise adaptive, diagnostic, and tactical skills and, through the
use of such skills, to mitigate the consequences of events and to
exploit change; these management skills are entrepreneurial skills.
Some definitions will help to clarify this distinction between administrative and entrepreneurial skills. Prognosis, for example, is the
forecast of the course of a disease and therefore an essential ingre-
dient of preventative medicine, whereas diagnosis, the identification
of a disease by means of the patient's symptoms, occurs at a later
stage when only prescriptive medicine is involved. In decision-
making terms the administrator in a large company, through his

prognostic skills, can shape events, whereas for the entrepreneur
in the small firm less alternatives are available and so he must use
diagnostic skills that allow him to mitigate the consequences of
events. Similarly strategy is the art of so moving or disposing
troops or ships as to impose upon the enemy the place and time and
conditions for fighting preferred by oneself, that is, the control of
conditions under which battle will take place, or, in terms of an
enterprise, the attempted control of the environment within which
business activity operates. Tactics, on the other hand, the art of
disposing military or naval forces especially in actual contact with
the enemy, is concerned with the exploitation of advantages on the
field of battle itself; it does not preclude planning but is, nevertheless, mobile, dynamic, and opportunist in character.

The management process as we are defining it, therefore, incorporates both an administrative element and an entrepreneurial
element. In the large firm the emphasis is likely to be primarily
on the administrative element of the management process and in the
small firm primarily on the entrepreneurial element. But while we
have made a distinction between the owner-manager or the entrepreneur and the employee-manager or administrator, a distinction that
largely arises from the consequences of differences in the size of
enterprises, this is not to say that the small-firm management process requires only entrepreneurial skills and the large-firm management process requires only administrative skills. One of the problems posed by the owner-manager's job is that he has to fill a role
that requires both entrepreneurial and administrative skills. Similarly, just as the small-firm owner-manager requires administrative
skills, particularly if his company is expanding, so too the manager
in the large company, especially at the top executive level, may require entrepreneurial skills. The two sets of skills are not mutually
exclusive but complementary, both within a company and, in many
cases, within one particular job. It is the emphasis that is necessarily different when considering the demands of large and small
firms for these two kinds of management skill, necessarily different
because of differences in the market environment, in the scale of
operations, in the degree of specialization, and in the professionalization of management of the small and the large firm. It is obviously
not possible, for example, for the owner-manager of a small business to assimilate, in depth, knowledge about all the techniques applicable to the wide spectrum of management activities that we have
observed he handles. It is not possible for him to have a detailed
understanding of sophisticated systems and techniques of financial
analysis, marketing, production planning and cost control, or of new
developments in work study or personnel management, even though
there will be occasions on which such in depth knowledge would be

helpful to him. The large firm, in contrast, can afford to employ
managers who have a highly developed and highly specialized knowledge of particular management techniques. The small firm, with its
more limited managerial resources, must either look outside the
company for specialist knowledge or must attempt to develop less
sophisticated techniques internally.

Our observation studies of the work activities of a number of
small-firm owner-managers indicate that, in identifying and analyzing
administrative and entrepreneurial skills, attention has to be given
both to periods of relatively routine work and to those problem-
solving and decision-making activities more normally associated
with the managerial process. It is close involvement in the day-to-
day routine that provides the owner-manager with the ready store of
information that he needs to handle the many contingencies that arise.
Much of the success of a small firm in the early stages of its development is a result of the ability and capacity of the owner-manager
to carry in his head knowledge of the detailed operation of all aspects
of his business and to remain in effective control of each activity.
Even where the small firm employs specialist managers, the owner-
manager often remains in touch on a day-to-day basis with, for example, the progress of individual customers' orders through the
works and with details of incoming orders and supplies. It is necessary, therefore, to consider the skills being used both in the day-to-
day control of the firm and in problem-solving or decision-making
tasks. A number of other factors, however, also have an important
bearing on the way in which the small-firm owner-manager tackles
his work. Physical fitness and energy have a part to play--"If I am
feeling good, the business buzzes"--as do psychological and sociological factors, the owner-manager's approach to his work being a
partial reflection of his personality, intelligence, knowledge, and
abilities, and of his social, educational, and occupational experiences.
In addition many owner-managers can pattern their work activities
on the basis of their own personal preferences. They have some
choice as to which aspects of the running of their company they will
attend to personally, this being one of the freedoms, as we saw in
Chapter 10, that may have attracted them toward setting up their own
businesses. Analysis of the abilities and skills required for successful small-firm management has to take account, therefore, of the
fact that not all of the owner-manager's work activities stem from the
requirements of the job. The owner-manager's work activities will
reflect, in part, the probability that the owner-manager has structured his job, and the consequent organization of his business, in
such a way that the abilities and skills he possesses and enjoys using
will be fully utilized. Consequently the physiological and psychological characteristics and the personal preferences of owner-managers

are a powerful force in determining how work is organized in the small firm and how any management structure emerges and develops.

THE DEVELOPMENT OF A MANAGERIAL
SKILLS TAXONOMY

In order to identify more precisely the specific nature of the managerial skills that the owner-manager requires for successful performance of his job, it is necessary to indicate the principal activities that the owner-manager is engaged in during the course of his work and, then, to examine the extent to which the performance of those activities calls for particular mixes of entrepreneurial and administrative skills. In considering the results of this approach two points should be kept in mind. First, the process of analysis is one that attempts to reduce highly complex and highly divergent real-life situations to a number of relatively simple points upon which practical management training and development policies for small-firm owner-managers can be built. Second, the successful performance of any particular activity does not necessarily involve either entrepreneurial skills or administrative skills but may involve both kinds of skill to a greater or lesser extent. The appropriate skill requirements will depend on such factors as the nature of the activities to be performed, previous organizational experience of such activities, the degree of innovation involved, the time-scale for results, and external market and economic pressures. It is because such factors as these are so variable that it is relevant here to underline the complexities of the real-life situation.

Five management processes that owner-managers are involved in are organizing, coordinating, communicating, negotiating, and troubleshooting. The owner-manager has to organize both his own work and that of his subordinates, but it is the organization of his own time that is most crucial. He needs to explore the possibilities of delegating tasks to any other managers or members of his staff. He has to maintain control over the activities of his organization, to be the puppetmaster rather than the puppet. As well as organizing other people's work, the owner-manager has to coordinate their activities. He is the point at which any conflicts of interest will be reconciled. In the small firm it is often only the owner-manager who can effectively fulfill this coordinating role since he is frequently the only person in the firm who knows the whole picture and the desired pattern of the company's development. In addition, direct face-to-face communications are an important aspect of the owner-manager's work. He has to make himself understood by others and to give them confidence both in their own abilities and in his. The owner-manager has to communicate with his staff, to listen to their problems, and to encourage them to bring difficulties to him wherever necessary. To his customers and suppliers the owner-manager is the embodiment of the company and confidence in him is confidence in his business. The owner-manager is also involved in negotiations, primarily with customers and suppliers. Successful negotiating involves a complex of knowledge and abilities. It involves personal traits of objectivity, persuasiveness, and understanding of other people's motives and attitudes, and it involves information on the subject being discussed and judgment on when the best possible bargain has been reached. Finally, the owner-manager is often required to troubleshoot contingencies that arise and to do so immediately. He is similarly required to cope with a variety of pressing problems amid the possibility of frequent interruptions from the telephone or from unexpected visitors. An ability to think quickly, to communicate answers and instructions without becoming flustered, and a willingness to tolerate the frustration of any planned activities are essential in such situations of potential stress.

Implicit in these five processes are some executive administrative skills, the skills of organizing and coordinating, and some executive entrepreneurial skills, the skills of negotiating and troubleshooting. It is clear, however, that the small-firm owner-manager requires, as well as executive skills, two kinds of policy-making skills. He requires some administrative policy-making skills, principally strategic planning and decision-making skills. Such skills involve the ability to clarify and define longer-term company objectives, to set realistic and measurable performance targets, and to evolve general policies and particular procedures to ensure that objectives and targets are being met. The elements of administrative policy-making skills are prediction and mechanistic control. The small-firm owner-manager also requires entrepreneurial policy-making skills, principally tactical planning and problem-solving skills. These involve the ability to respond quickly to unforeseen contingencies and prepare alternative short-term plans, to identify problems requiring immediate action and to initiate any necessary changes, and the ability to handle crises without losing sight of the longer-term interests of the business. The elements of entrepreneurial policy-making skills are adaptation and organic control. Such skills have frequently to be exercised in a context in which the requisite information for satisfactory performance is not available and cannot be quickly collected. They are high-risk skills.

There are a number of managerial skills that would seem, however, to be necessary at both the policy level and at the executive level, and important both for the work of the owner-manager or entrepreneur and for the work of the employee-manager or administrator. Three core managerial skills have been identified, the linked skills of decision-making, of problem-solving, and of information-processing. Three core managerial skills have been identified, the linked skills of decision-making, of problem-solving, and of information-processing. First, the main distinction between the small-firm owner-manager and the large-company administrator in terms of their respective decision-making activities is that the owner-manager is concerned more with particular decisions for particular situations than with making general decisions that will cover a variety of nonspecific situations. The owner-manager's policies evolve more from the custom and practice of tried and tested decisions in particular situations than from any attempt to identify and standardize particular principles, guidelines, and procedures. Access to detailed information about specific situations is a necessary prerequisite for successful ad hoc nonseriable decision-making (that is, decision-making where there are no precedents to act as guidelines) of this kind. Second, the notion of problem-solving involves a number of distinct stages including problem recognition, the consideration of alternative courses of action, judgment and decision-making activity, and feedback and evaluation. In the large company various control mechanisms are built into the system to try to predict the course of events or to provide early warning of deviations from the desired pattern. The problem-solving activities of the administrator are, therefore, primarily aimed at shaping events and his characteristic skills are skills of prognosis. The context within which the owner-manager operates, however, is one where less control can be exercised over the business environment and where the time scale of operations is often such that fewer alternative courses of action are open. The problem-solving activities of the entrepreneur in the small firm are, consequently, primarily aimed at mitigating the consequences of events and his characteristic skills are skills of diagnosis rather than skills of prognosis. Finally, because of the size of the information load that he has to carry, the owner-manager clearly requires information-processing skills. The small-firm owner-manager tries to assimilate information on production, sales, finance and accounts, purchasing, personnel matters, design, transport, costing, quality control--on the whole range of management functions. The capacity of the owner-manager to hold together the requisite information load, and his ability to organize and assimilate information, to judge its importance and to use it productively, are crucial factors in successful small-firm management. The information-processing skills that the owner-manager requires have both an administrative and an entrepreneurial element to them. The owner-manager as administrator is required to ensure that any formal information processing

procedures are tailor-made to provide the up-to-date control data
currently required or likely to be required in the foreseeable future.
But the generation of information about different aspects of company
performance is not enough, there being no significant correlation
between the volume of information generated and the speed or appropriateness of any consequent decisions. The owner-manager as entrepreneur is required to judge what information is necessary and relevant. He is required to use information as a basis for setting and
reviewing short- and long-term objectives, as a basis for identifying
problems and formulating solutions, and as a basis for evaluating
decisions. In order that he can acquire this entrepreneurial skill,
and in order that he can control the information system within his
firm rather than be controlled by it, it is necessary for the owner-
manager to develop the highly personal framework that allows him to
evaluate new pieces of information as they become available.

It is clear, then, that the small-firm owner-manager as well
as requiring entrepreneurial and administrative skills requires those
skills at both the policy-making and the executive levels. In large
companies managers are not generally called upon to exhibit skills
in both policy-making and policy-execution. It is frequently "top"
management who are expected to formulate company policy and
"middle" management who are expected to see that company policy
is implemented. In small firms, where the management team is
unlikely to consist of more than three or four people and may only
consist of the owner-manager himself, the owner-manager is required both to make policy and to translate policy into executive action, in some cases working as first-line supervisor and in some
cases working as an operative. There is no distinction in the small
firm between the planner and the doer, between the "elite" and the
"unwashed peasantry."[6]

SUMMARY

Table 11.1 summarizes the distinction made between the administrator and the entrepreneur, between some of the characteristics of large and small enterprises, and between the nature of entrepreneurial and administrative skills. Figure 11.1 summarizes the
managerial skills taxonomy that emerges from our analysis and indicates the range of entrepreneurial and administrative skills required by the owner-manager at both the policy and executive levels.
A variety of factors will determine the managerial skill requirements
of a particular company. These will include the market environment
within which the business operates and the extent to which success
within that environment requires risk-taking and innovation by the

TABLE 11.1

Small- and Large-Firm Management Processes: Summary

ORGANIZATIONAL CHARACTERISTICS

Small firm
- informal relationships
- no divorce between the planners and the doers
- appointment and promotion often on basis of birth or personal friendship
- everyone prepared to muck-in as required
- open system of communications

Large firm
- formal relationships
- divorce of planning from doing
- technical qualifications as basis of appointment and promotion
- precise definition of rights and obligations, duties and responsibilities
- structured communications system

AUTHORITY AND PHILOSOPHY

The entrepreneur or owner-manager

Source of authority
- tradition (ownership)
- personal

Basis of philosophy
- no diffusion between ownership and control
- no conflict between personal and company objectives
- no distinction between person and role
- integration of work and social values
- not subservient to economic goals

The administrator or employee-manager
- expertise
- office

- control without ownership
- conflict between individual and organizational goals
- very clear distinction between the individual and the office he fills
- values of the workplace divorced from both individual and social values
- economic "performance" as ultimate criterion

NATURE OF CHARACTERISTIC SKILLS

Entrepreneurial
- adaptive
- diagnostic
- exploitation of change; opportunism
- tactical facility
- pragmatic use of techniques as aid to problem solving
- social skills applied on a personal basis
- consequence-mitigating decision-making

Administrative
- predictive
- prognostic
- control of change
- strategic facility
- coordination and control of specialists
- manipulative skills applied largely on an impersonal basis
- event-shaping decision-making

Source: Compiled by the author.

227

FIGURE 11.1

Managerial Skills Taxonomy

Principal Entrepreneurial
Skills (adaptive and organic)

Principal Administrative
Skills (predictive and mechanistic)

Policy Level

1. Innovation
2. Risk-taking*
3. Tactical planning*

1. Objective setting
2. Policy formulation
3. Strategic planning

Common Core

of Skills

1. Decision-making*
2. Problem-solving*
3. Information
   processing*

Executive Level

1. Negotiating*
2. Troubleshooting*
3. Interpersonal
   communications*

1. Organizing*
2. Coordinating*
3. Formal communications
4. Monitoring
5. Stabilizing

*Main activities of small-firm owner-managers.

Source: Compiled by the author.

firm. They will include technology, the scale of operations, the degree of specialization possible within the organization, and the availability of financial resources. Companies are likely to require, therefore, different mixes of administrative and entrepreneurial skills. In addition they are likely to employ owner-managers and managers who, as a result of their educational and occupational backgrounds, bring to their jobs a variety of skills and abilities, some more and some less relevant to the context of the firm's requirements. It is important, consequently, while trying to identify any common managerial skills that may exist, to recognize the uniqueness of each individual situation within which those skills are to be used.

NOTES

1. J. C. Schabacker, Cash Planning in Small Manufacturing Companies, Small Business Administration Research Series No. 1 (Washington, D.C.: Small Business Administration, 1960).

2. The framework for this paragraph is derived from R. Holmes, The Ownership of Work: A Psychological Approach (London: London School of Economics and Political Science, Department of Social Psychology, November 1966).

3. Ibid.

4. Richard II, Act II, Scene III, lines 164-65.

5. N. Stait, "Management-by-Objectives and the Small Company," Enterprise 1, no. 4 (1971).

6. See P. F. Drucker, The Practice of Management (New York: Harper, 1954).

12

THE OWNER-MANAGER
AND ORGANIZATION
THEORY

THE OWNER-MANAGER AND
ORGANIZATION STRUCTURE

In Chapter 11 we observed that small firms are characteristically structured in a loose organic way and that small-firm organization structures, insofar as they exist, tend to be built around people. It is clear, therefore, that in the context of the owner-manager's work the traditional bureaucratic idea that the job exists independently of the individual jobholder has severe limitations. This notion, which is central to Weber's ideal-type construct of bureaucracy[1] and underpins most of the writing of the "classical" or "scientific" management school, continues to be a basic precept underlying many current management practices, particularly in the area of personnel recruitment, selection, and appraisal:

> A manager is really a person who fills the role or
> takes up the position of manager. It is important
> to distinguish between the person and the role.
> The role requires the person to carry out certain
> tasks. To enable the person to carry out these
> tasks, the role empowers him with authority.
> He is then authorised to carry out these tasks by
> virtue of his office. That the authority is con-
> fined to his position is seen by the fact that the
> person cannot use it in his club, or in the street,
> as he can in his firm.[2]

There have, of course, been attacks on the bureaucratic and mechanistic aspects of job descriptions, job specifications, and organization charts. These attacks have tended to focus either on the inappropriateness of job demarcations to the needs of the organization, particularly in changing conditions, or on the inappropriateness of the allocation of tasks to the psychological needs of the jobholder. The outcome has often been, however, some redefinition of jobs and tasks into organizationally or psychologically more satisfactory wholes, with an unwillingness to cater for complexity and variability in the man-job relationship.

Consideration of the work of owner-managers calls into question the relevance of the basic premise on which most job analysis rests, the premise that there is, or there should be, a clearly defined job that has limits of discretion and responsibility dictated by the needs of the organization. In the small firm the job of the owner-manager must constantly be adapting to a changing situation. It is a fluid and fluctuating role rather than a role that can be adequately analyzed, defined, and specified on a once-for-all basis. The job must be thought of in terms of an open adaptive system able to adjust to financial, technical, and market demands. But even this is not enough. Not only must there be some concept of the job that allows for adaptation to the external environment but also a concept that allows for the contraction and expansion of the job in response to the social and psychological needs of the jobholder. This, as we shall see in Chapter 13, receives some point in relation to management education, training, and development processes in the small firm. There is generally no extensive management ladder in the small firm and insufficient levels of management to allow for career development on the basis of promotion. Consequently, management development must be thought of in terms of the expansion of the individual's job. The impetus for such expansion will come not only from the shifting demands of the external environment but also from the jobholder's demand for personal growth. The jobholder must expand his job with him rather than progress to another post in the firm, and, if he is to expand his job, he must inevitably expand the business too.

The evidence in Part II has suggested that those activities in which owner-managers are most involved are not necessarily all demands of the job but rather a reflection of the way in which a particular owner-manager has structured his job, or even his whole business in order that the abilities he displays at work are those he possesses and about which he is enthusiastic. Some owner-managers who have knowledge of accountancy and finance prefer to do their own accounting. Others, not in possession of such knowledge, prefer to leave the task completely in the hands of accountants, either internal or external. This is not surprising. Most people prefer doing those things that they do best. The owner-manager often has the opportunity to choose what he does and makes the most of that opportunity. Our argument has been, then, that the job of the small-firm owner-

manager expands and contracts with the man filling it, and that this
expansion or contraction is partly conditioned by the adaptive needs
of the management situation in which he operates, and is partly dependent on the personality and needs of the individual himself. If
this is so, then the man is a more appropriate unit for analysis than
the job. This approach to analyzing the work of the small-firm
owner-manager allows room for examination of the apparent mystique,
intuition, or flair often associated with the successful running of a
small firm. There is no reason to believe that such factors are any
less susceptible to analysis, providing appropriate tools can be developed, than the knack of the skilled craftsman.

The way in which small-firm organization structures are influenced by the skills, abilities, and personalities of their owners
can be illustrated by describing one of the companies that took part
in the pilot projects that preceded the depth study part of the research
program. The company, Contrafurn Limited, was formed in the
autumn of 1962 as a result of a casual meeting between two friends,
John Langton and Robert Reid. The progress of the business in the
crucial first two years was very satisfactory with John Langton,
whose previous experience included work with a furniture manufacturing company, concentrating primarily on the production side of
the business and Robert Reid on the sales side. Then, however,
there was a major disagreement between the two directors, the final
upshot of which was that Reid left the company during the spring of
1966, Langton agreeing to buy Reid's shares in the business and the
company undertaking the liability of a £5,000 payment to Reid in
compensation for loss of office. This left Langton at the age of 28 in
fully effective control of the company's operations both as majority
shareholder and managing director.

At the time when the company was first visited, in May 1969,
five people were employed in managerial or supervisory positions,
of whom four--the managing director, the sales manager, the works
manager, and the supervisor of the metalwork shop--were aged
under 35. The fifth person, the supervisor of the upholstery shop,
was in his late fifties. The pilot observation study revealed that 35
percent of Langton's time was spent in activities classified as office
administration and accounts, and a further 19 percent on purchasing,
sales, and transport, the second most time-consuming set of functions. Many of the tasks under both these headings were tasks concerned with fairly routine details. But checking on the flow of money
into and out of the business was, for example, an aspect of his work
which Langton particularly enjoyed, primarily because he felt it was
"his" money. He recognized, however, that he was spending too
much of his time in detailed procedural and administrative matters
and that, consequently, he was not able to spend the time he would

have liked, and which would become increasingly necessary, on plans for setting up a new manufacturing unit. Similarly, many of the owner-manager's tasks associated with purchasing, sales, and transport were concerned with answering specific queries about individual orders and their progress through the works or dealing with queries on the purchase of relatively small quantities of raw materials or upholstery.

Contrafurn, it appeared, had reached an interesting stage in its development insofar as the work of its owner-manager was concerned. It is arguable that much of the success of a small firm in its early stages of development is a result of the ability and capacity of the owner-manager to carry in his head knowledge of the detailed operation of all aspects of his business and to remain in fairly effective control of each function. Even where the company has reached the stage of employing both a sales manager and a works manager, the owner-manager may still be in touch on a day-to-day basis with the progress of individual customers' orders through the works and with details of incoming orders and supplies. This can raise a number of problems. One, for example, is that the owner-manager, because he knows as much if not more than his individual managers about the work of their departments, cannot restrain himself from managing those departments when the opportunity arises. Thus, he will, on his periodic trips around the factory answer operatives' queries on quality standards and give instructions to them on which batches of work should be given preference. Many small-firm owner-managers who have built up their firms from scratch have done, and can do, all the jobs in the business from setting up and operating the machinery to going out on the road and drumming up sales. The temptation to "show that you know" is extremely great, but can make the task of the manager in the middle a very difficult one. If decisions on detail are being taken by the owner-manager of a small firm, even though a number of other managers are employed ostensibly to handle such details, then fairly obviously a difficult position is created for those other managers. To use the conventional terminology of the classical organization theorists, ill-defined responsibilities are being delegated without any authority attached to them.

Possibly some of the difficulties that Contrafurn had experienced in the past in finding suitable works managers may have arisen from the unwillingness of Langton to wholly pass over responsibility for day-to-day decisions on production matters. The failure of a number of works managers to fulfill the standards required by the job simply reinforced a vicious circle by demonstrating the dangers involved if the owner-manager did not take a personal interest in day-to-day detail. It is easy to say, however, that the owner-manager should, once his company has developed to a particular size, concern himself more with long-term marketing policy, the design and development of new lines, the possibilities of using new materials in existing product ranges, and the location and building of a new plant, and that he should not interfere in the day-to-day detail. But it is not easy to break what may be the habits of a lifetime, habits that in the past have proved to be extremely effective in building up a business, and habits that have led to a pattern of work the owner-manager enjoys.

But not only are there psychological adjustments to be made by owner-managers of growing organizations. There also has to be some additional questioning of the perspective that associates the growth of the business as necessarily implying greater degrees of formalization and proceduralization. Given such differences in skills and attitudes as those we have described between the administrator and the entrepreneur, then particular difficulties will arise as a firm expands. Developing the owner-manager of a small but expanding business from an entrepreneurial orientation toward an administrative one may involve a complete reappraisal of his business philosophy and attitudes during the transitional stages. A more appropriate alternative may be, however, to find ways of utilizing entrepreneurial skills within the structure of large-scale organizations.

SYSTEMS THEORIES AND THE SMALL FIRM

The problems large-scale organizations face in adapting to changes in their market environment or to innovations in their production systems and technology have been a major focus for organizational studies over recent years, as has concern with problems of organizational growth and development. As a firm expands it may well lose the flexibility and innovative capacity on which its earlier success depended. The formalization of communication channels, the need for a greater degree of interdepartmental consultation and liaison, the institutionalization of organizational subsystems pursuing their own independent goals and objectives, may all work in opposition to successful innovation and change. Consequently some organization theorists have been concerned, assuming a growing rate of market and technological innovation as a given factor in the business environment, to find organization structures, or at least to establish design criteria for organization structures, that can facilitate rather than inhibit innovation. In some cases these attempts culminate in advocacy of new designs that simply rearrange structural components. Thus, for example, a matrix organization may be seen as a method of establishing "a flexible and adaptable system of resources and procedures to achieve a series of project objectives"[3] and, therefore, a system of organization that embodies new relationships appropriate to handling changing conditions. In practice, however, such an organization simply replaces one structural dimension, usually a functional dimension, with two structural dimensions, a functional dimension and a project dimension, whereas what is really under question is the very efficacy of structural approaches per se. Organizational development practitioners, in contrast, have concentrated on the processes by which organizations change and have probed methods enabling openness to change to become part and parcel of an organization's climate. They have tended to move away from stable structural theories and talk, for example, about "adhocracies" or "adaptive, problem-solving, temporary systems."[4] Organizational development is firmly rooted in open systems theories and these theories provide some useful theoretical perspectives for understanding small-firm management processes.

Open systems theories in organizational studies stem from analogies with biological and ecological systems where there is a continuous interaction between organisms and their environment and where adjustment or change in one organism or one subsystem sets off a chain reaction that has consequences for the other organisms or subsystems that make up the total system under review: "From the physical point of view, the characteristic state of the living organism is that of an open system. A system is closed if no material enters or leaves it; it is open if there is import and export and, therefore, change of the components. Living systems are open systems, maintaining themselves in exchange of materials with environment, and in continuous building up and breaking down of their components."[5] To view the organization in the light of open systems theories, then, is to see it as being

> in constant interaction with its environment, taking
> in raw materials, people, energy, and information,
> and transforming or converting these into products
> and services that are exported into the environ-
> ment. . . . the organization exists in a dynamic
> environment that consists of other systems, some
> larger, some smaller than the organization. The
> environment places demands upon and constrains
> the organization in various ways. The total func-
> tioning of the organization cannot be understood,
> therefore, without explicit consideration of these
> environmental demands and constraints.[6]

Open systems theories, therefore, describe organisms and organizations in terms of the dynamics of the import, conversion, export, and renewal processes they utilize in order to keep them in some form of

steady state relative to their environments.[7] Consequently the concerns of the systems theory approaches to the study of organizations
are not so much with characteristics such as size, shape, function,
or structure, but more with problems of the relationships and interdependence between subsystems, problems of exchange and interaction between systems and their environment, and problems of environmental control. In particular, systems theory approaches raise
definitional problems in sorting out just where one system or subsystem begins and another ends; the control of the boundaries between
one system or subsystem and another becomes a focal point for study
as does the degree of turbulence in the environment within which the
system exists.[8]

A number of so-called open systems approaches to organizational behavior are not, however, open systems at all in the adaptive,
reactive sense explicit in biological systems. Rather they are systems that are seeking to predict and control the organization's environment and, therefore, have a built-in tendency toward closure.
This tendency toward predictive, proactive systems, while it may be
an essential component of any viable theory of human organizations,
is not a necessary part of a biological organism. The weakness of
many systems theories in organization studies is that they do not
recognize this inherent contradiction, as we see it, between open
systems theories and the notion of environmental control. The sociotechnical systems approach, for example, recognizing the interdependence between the technical system of work organization and the
social system in an organization, recognizing that a number of organizational choices are possible and that it is possible to treat technology as a limiting rather than a determining factor in organizational
design, seeks to jointly optimize the technical and social systems
against some generally unexplicit economic criteria.[9] Such an approach can be attacked, not only on the grounds that it tends to gloss
over the possibility of conflict about the goals of an organization, but
also on the grounds that its theoretical underpinnings are inadequate.
It is an attempt to find, through appeal to open systems theory concepts, one best or most appropriate set of organizational design
choices, that is, some new kind of fixed structure designed to take
account of the social and psychological aspects of work organizations
as well as the technical requirements concomitant upon the organization's need to fulfill particular task objectives. But such an approach
does not meet the problems posed by three factors: first, that organizations may be trying, at any one time, to satisfy a multiplicity
of goals; second, that goals, and the relative importance of goals,
shift over time; and, third, that the external environment may be
changing in such a way as to make the new structural form immediately obsolete. It is no surprise, therefore, to find that the application

of the sociotechnical systems approach in particular companies tends, for all the talk about open systems and management processes, to revolve around organizational changes of a structural kind. We are not suggesting that no differentiation of tasks is required in an organization. What we would argue, however, is that, in the context of a small firm and in the context of a large firm operating in an unstable environment, the structural differentiation of tasks between people is of only peripheral interest and that it may well be that the vaguer the differentiation the better. If one is really going to apply open systems theories to the study of organizations it is necessary to curtail any structural components, such as precise task allocation, that encourage psychological predispositions toward closure, order, unambiguity, and the establishment of territorial boundaries. The notion of the anarchic firm may be rather difficult to sustain but it has been suggested that the innovating entrepreneur has to pursue tactics similar to those of the guerrilla leader if he is to successfully bring about change: "Carlson's battle to establish xerography, Land's entrepreneuring of polaroid photography, Sarnoff's championing of color television, all display variants of the embattled 'loner' who becomes an adversary of the system (of a firm or of an entire industry) in order to innovate."[10]

The confusion in applying open systems theories to purposive organizations arises in part, therefore, from the difficulty in organizational analysis of distinguishing process from structure, and both process and structure from goals, and in part from a psychological predication toward control. Our analysis suggests, however, that the small firm is unlikely to be able to influence its environment to a degree sufficient to warrant the pursuit of processes of environmental control. It is here that some of the confusion in systems theories of organization can be clarified because it is here that the distinction between large and small firms may be crucial, particularly the distinction between adaptive and predictive management processes that we described in Chapter 11. It is important to realize that the processes of "adapting to and shaping the external environment" are very different processes and not part and parcel of one overall "problem of adaptability."[11] In our terminology, therefore, an adaptive system is not one that "tends to achieve environmental constancy by bringing the external world under control,"[12] thereby maintaining predictability for the operations of the organization, but rather a system that seeks "internal modification of its own organizational structures to meet the needs of a changing world."[13] The dominant tendency in the small firm, to paraphrase Katz and Kahn, will be to modify internal structures to accord with external changes rather than to seek control over the environment;[14] the small organization will thus best proceed on the principle that it is easier to

adjust to the world than it is to make the world adjust. In this sense
it becomes clear that open systems theories, with their emphasis on
organic-adaptive functions, provide a closer analogy to the operations
of small companies than they do to the operations of large firms. It
is in such a system that the ability of an organization to respond appropriately to new information from its environment will be a crucial
test of its chances of survival.

THE OWNER-MANAGER AS INFORMATION PROCESSOR

We have already commented on the tendency of owner-managers
to be involved in the day-to-day details of their businesses and to have
a finger in every pie. We now turn to look at some of the advantages
and disadvantages of such involvement and to suggest some theoretical
grounds for encouraging rather than discouraging owner-managers in
their concern for detail. To provide a focus for discussion we first
describe some of the activities of the owner-manager studied in the
third of our pilot projects.

Dylan was a successful and profitable firm of timber importers
and merchants employing nine people. In 1958, its first year of
trading, it had a gross profit of £1,400 on a sales turnover of £68,000.
In the year ending March 31, 1968 the company's sales turnover was
£263,000 with a gross profit of £41,000. The growth of the company
over this ten-year period had been financed almost entirely by retained profits and by the personal capital of the owner-manager,
Brian Dylan. At the time of the study Dylan was aged 49 and had
over 30 years' experience in the timber trade. Almost 90 percent
of Dylan's time during the study was spent in face-to-face contacts
or on the telephone. The arrival of the morning mail, together with
incoming telephone calls, triggered off Dylan's initial activities for
the day. Some of the sequences would be quite short. Thus, the
day's instructions to the cashier revolved primarily around any matters arising from the incoming mail. Other sequences were spread
out over a longer period. On one morning, for example, an inquiry
to Dylan for prices for a variety of products came in the mail. From
9:04 a.m. to 9:20 a.m. Dylan was in his office pricing some of the
items on this inquiry. Where the goods were those supplied by the
company in its normal course of trading, prices were quoted from
memory or after brief consultation with Roger Hassell, the office
manager. Adjustments were then made to the prices according to
the quantity specified on the inquiry, the aim being to present an
attractive mixture of prices rather than a list of lowest possible fig-
ures--thus, a highly competitive price might be quoted for certain

materials that were expected to form the bulk of any forthcoming
order and rather less competitive rates for other items. At 9:20 a.m.
Dylan checked the credit rating of the inquiring company by referring
to Dun and Bradstreet. He then looked up the telephone number of a
Formica supplier and telephoned, intending to obtain quotes for some
of the items on the inquiry that were not covered by Dylan in its normal trading operations. The contact he wished to speak to was not
available so he left details of the dimensions required. By the middle
of the afternoon this supplier had not telephoned back as requested,
so Dylan rang again at 4:20 p.m. and located his contact. After some
discussion on the dimensions required and the prices it was left that
the supplier would telephone back with detailed costings for the items
required. This was a fairly typical sequence of work for Dylan as far
as could be judged. Apart from procedural discussions early in the
morning with the sales director and the office manager there appeared
to be little logic to his working day, things being done as the need
arose or as it occurred to Dylan to do them. However, a very different sequence of events, although triggered off in much the same
unplanned casual way, occurred on another day of the observation
study. This sequence, which revolved primarily around a marketing
question, lasted for over four and a half hours. Just before 11:00
a.m. a representative of a London agency arrived unannounced to
see Dylan. He had brought with him some samples of a vinyl veneer
being manufactured by a new process, a veneer for which his agency
had obtained sole distribution rights. The agent, Bob Jones, was
well known to Dylan. The two companies had worked together for
some years past and Jones made a point of dropping in to see Dylan
whenever he was in the area. This time he had come in to discuss
the distribution network for products using the vinyl veneer, since
his agency was interested in appointing two authorized distributors
to handle the marketing and sales of the product in Wales and in the
South West of England. The discussion between Dylan and Jones
continued throughout the remainder of the morning and over lunch
and it was not until almost 3:30 p.m. that Jones finally left. Not by
any means all of this time was involved in questions concerning the
marketing of vinyl-veneered boards. Other topics discussed included,
for example, the availability of Malaysian timbers and the quantity
and prices of future shipments from various plywood mills. But 80
percent of the time was spent in going over the various pros and cons
for Dylan acting as distributors for vinyl-veneered products. It is
not possible to recount the whole of this discussion, but some of the
salient points are set out below. It should be emphasized that the
actual discussion jumped around from point to point whereas this
summary sets the points out in a systematic way.

1. <u>Manufacturing process</u>: the production technique was outlined by Jones; Dylan was anxious to find out who the manufacturer was but this was not something Jones wished to disclose. Dylan raised the question of the supply of chipboard and plywood for the manufacturer but this was not followed up.

2. <u>Technical properties of the veneer</u>: Dylan asked a number of questions about the weather and fire resistance of the vinyl veneer and about the bonding used; these were answered by Jones and various simple tests were carried out on some of the samples brought--these included trying to scratch the veneer off with a coin, burning it with a match, scuffing rubber-soled shoes on it, and stamping on it.

3. <u>Design features</u>: the range of imitation woods available was described and some of the samples considered; Dylan thought the knotty pine did not look at all natural and suggested an alternative design feature; apparently, however, the design had been fixed and photographic processes already completed.

4. <u>Distributorship</u>: Dylan asked who the other distributor would be assuming he accepted one of the two distributorships; Jones pointed out that the limitation to two would only operate if sufficient sales were forthcoming through those two companies, and went on to describe which other companies in the area had been approached.

5. <u>Quantity and costs</u>: the volume of stock to be bought by distributors was discussed together with the contractual procedures and methods of payment; the possibility of a retrospective discount system was raised.

6. <u>Competitive products</u>: Dylan pointed out that another company was producing a similar product at what appeared to be the considerably cheaper price of 8.5 pence (compared to 1 shilling); this apparently came as something of a surprise to Jones who tried to find out more about the other product; Dylan pointed out, however, that the price he had heard was only hearsay and he was not too sure of the facts.

The outcome of the meeting was that Dylan agreed to accept one of two distributorships for Wales and the South West and to send out details to his customers as soon as he had received a swatch of samples from the agent. After the agent had left the observer asked Dylan why he had taken on this distributorship and why he had decided to accept the opportunities presented by vinyl-veneered products. A number of reasons were given. First, Dylan had a good reputation for launching new products and had handled such opportunities successfully in the past. Second, the price of the product was competitive in spite of the interest of another producer in the same field; in any case, alternative vinyl-veneer products might not become available to Dylan and, if they did, he would not be under any contractual obligation to supply only the products marketed through Jones' agency; by accepting the distributorship now Dylan was, therefore, ensuring his own supply of a competitive product and retaining his freedom of maneuver should the need arise. Third, in Dylan's judgment, the market conditions were right for such a product; money was tight and at such times it was very useful to have a cheap board on stock. Fourth, the company had the necessary cash available for the initial outlay on stock. Finally, future development in the use of board products seemed likely to require a substitute for the "v" board which had been very popular for a number of years; changes in adhesives would probably lead to the gradual obsolescence of "v" boards and the new vinyl-veneer products might well provide a most suitable substitute.

The process of information-processing and decision-making involved in this sequence of behavior is highly rational, a process of which any marketing economist might be proud. It is not thought of in terms of assessing potential demand and reviewing the substitution possibilities of competitive products but, nevertheless, that is what is happening in an informal way. The kind of information sought from Jones, the agent, is a necessary preliminary to making judgments about how well the vinyl-veneer products fitted in to the company's immediate requirements. Later in the afternoon Dylan realized that he had forgotten to ask Jones a small technical point. This concerned whether or not the vinyl board could be turned over the edge, which would be a requirement for a particular customer he had in mind.

This sequence of behavior, triggered off by an unforeseen call from an agent, was highly concentrated and contrasts vividly with the somewhat haphazard and dispersed activities in much of Brian Dylan's work. Of Dylan's activities during the observation period, 47 percent were classified as self-initiated, 49 percent as other-initiated, and 4 percent as procedural--procedural activities being such things as weekly sales meetings. Thus for almost half of his time Dylan was responding to external events--to the ringing of the telephone or the arrival of salesmen or agents without any prior appointment. This does not mean that events are necessarily in control rather than the owner-manager. What it does mean is that the owner-manager, if he chooses to work in this way, has only a limited control over his own time. Since he has no control over the timing of external events, and only a limited control over the duration of the sequence of activities that will be triggered off by such other-initiated events, then inevitably any attempt to plan and control those activities that are self-initiated will be severely disrupted. By definition it is a characteristic of other-directed activities that they require immediate attention. One of the effects of allowing work to be dominated by such activities is a tendency to become wholly

dependent on others in deciding on how time shall be spent. Thus, if
the telephone does not constantly keep ringing, or people are not constantly bringing in queries and asking for information, the manager
feels at a loss to know what to do with himself. This is not to say,
however, that entrepreneurial jobs are not best handled in this responsive troubleshooting fashion. In the work of the owner-manager
of a small firm, room needs to be made for responding quickly to
events that were not foreseen and for grasping the opportunities that
may be triggered off by, for example, an incoming telephone call from
a prospective customer.

The Dylan case illustrates the importance of personal contacts
to the small-firm owner-manager, the importance of being responsive
to new information from the environment, the importance of having a
perceptual set or cognitive style that allows ready assimilation and
evaluation of that new information, and the central point that information processing has in problem-solving and decision-making activities.
The owner-manager's information-processing role is one that picks
up cues from the external environment and links external information
to the internal processes of the firm. Successful performance in the
role of information processor is, we suggest, based on detailed knowledge of the day-to-day activities of the firm because it is that knowledge that sensitizes the owner-manager to important cues from the
environment. We would speculate, therefore, that the more successful owner-managers are those with a more open cognitive style--
everything is grist to their mill and they are willing to cull ideas from
all sources. [15] This open cognitive style will tend to reflect a radical
rather than a conservative personality, an entrepreneurial rather than
an administrative attitude of mind.

PLANNING AND THE SMALL FIRM:
A TACTICAL STRATEGY

The Dylan case also illustrates the lack of forward planning that
is often evident in small companies. As we have seen in Part II,
small-firm owner-managers are more aware of short-term than
long-term problems and in many cases do not think more than a few
months ahead. Such plans as did exist in the companies studied in
depth tended to be couched in terms of immediate needs to expand
sales in order to solve problems stemming from unused productive
capacity and low profitability. Some companies had longer-term
aspirations, usually of growth, but these rarely included objectives
or targets to be reached over a specified period of time. While
longer-term planning may generally be unnecessary in small firms,
there is evidence to suggest that it is an important element in dealing

successfully with management succession problems. An American
study of 108 small manufacturing companies, all but three of which
were approaching or had just passed a transfer of top management
responsibility, concluded that "when the fifty one cases of completed
succession are examined, the results show that lack of planning does
appear to be followed by lower profitability."[16] The problem of
planning for management succession is one that is considered in more
detail in Chapter 13.

    Owner-managers of small firms, unsupported by any high de-
gree of managerial specialization or differentiation, are constantly
involved in making decisions on a variety of matters, some of them
relatively trivial, some of them crucial to the success of their enterprises. Their ability in such decision-making rests in part on their
detailed knowledge of the management processes within their firms
and on their proximity to sources of information, both external
sources informing them of details of their market environment and
internal sources informing them of the readiness of their firm to
move in new directions. Internally, for example, owner-managers
may need to be familiar with the length of time each production operation takes in order that they can draft appropriate production schedules, estimate times for orders to be completed, check on progress,
and identify potential bottlenecks; they will also probably be involved
in the purchase and maintenance of machinery and in the purchase,
supply, and utilization of raw materials. Externally, owner-
managers may be involved in direct contacts with customers and
suppliers and in building up a network of personal contacts that can
be tapped for information about market trends, prices, new products
and materials, and the behavior of competitors. This information
may provide the background knowledge they require in order to make
their own decisions on such items as the design, price, and range of
their products. There comes a point at which openness to information, quite apart from the difficulties it imposes on the owner-
manager in terms of mental capacity, will preclude any detailed
planning of a long-term kind. In other words, in the context of such
an adaptive managerial process, planning, other than of a vague
aspirational kind, becomes not only unnecessary but impossible.

    Contingencies, crises, uncertainties, and risks may face the
entrepreneur. He is not necessarily controlled by his environment
or completely at the mercy of extraneous events but he will, nevertheless, frequently feel that he is running very fast in order to stay
in the same place and that he all too easily loses sight of any policy
objectives he may have as he grapples with his day-to-day difficulties.
It is not very helpful to such a person to tell him that his short-term
plans should be closely related to some clear set of long-term objectives, that his tactical behavior in the day-to-day situation should

be subordinated to a defined long–term strategy. Such a prescriptive approach ignores the complexities of the real–life situation, ignores the deficiencies in the information available for decision–making, and ignores too the owner–manager's personal engrossment in his work. What we need to recognize, in trying to understand the rationale of the owner–manager's behavior, is that the pursuit of a series of short–term tactical goals may in itself prove a viable strategy for managing a small firm successfully.

In attempting to classify goal–seeking behaviors, Schutzenberger starts with a very simple example:

> Let us suppose a man is on the top of a hill and that he wishes to get to a house in the valley; let us assume that the "goal" is his arrival there in the shortest possible time. Between him and the house are many causes of delay: boulders, marshes, escarpments, and so on. Travelling in a bee–line is out of the question. Let us consider his possible modes of behaviour.
>
> An exhaustive, and final, solution of the problem would be given by taking a map of the district, dividing it into small areas, finding the time taken to cross each area individually, joining the areas into all possible chains between the top of the hill and the house, and then finding which chain gives the smallest total time for the journey. The path so selected is absolutely the best and has been selected by what I shall call the "strategy" of the problem. . . . Usually, of course, the traveller would not use so elaborate a method. A common method would be to make the selection in stages. He would first select a point about a hundred feet down to which he could get rapidly; then, arrived there, he would select another point a hundred feet lower still to which a rapid descent was possible, and so on till he reached the house. This method I shall call a simple tactic, as contrasted with the previous strategy. The tactic differs from the former in that the tactic does not take into account the whole of the situation, but proceeds according to a criterion of optimality that is applied locally, stage by stage.[17]

Schutzenberger goes on to demonstrate that in some cases the optimal strategy simply consists of attempting to do one's best on a purely local basis, that is, the tactics become the strategy. Two factors, he suggests, will have a bearing on the viability of such a tactical strategy. First, there is the "span of foresight": "If the man coming down the hill plans each next move according to the details of the next hundred feet he will do better than if he were to plan only over the next ten feet. The spans of foresight are here a hundred feet and ten feet respectively. Should the span of foresight be equal to the distance from the goal, then obviously the tactic and the strategy become identical." Secondly, there is the behavior's "flexibility": "Suppose the span of foresight is '100 feet below'; once the man has covered half this distance he may discover that his provisional goal was not the best, and that he should now take a different path for a different goal, again at one unit of foresight ahead. Clearly, in the strategy of the traveller with complete foresight the concept of flexibility plays no part, and neither does it at the other extreme. . . . It is in the intermediate degrees that the concept becomes important."

The owner-manager is operating in an unpredictable environment that restricts his span of foresight and that demands a constant flexibility in the face of changing external circumstances, a flexibility that has to cope both with changes in the best courses of action to meet specified goals and with changes in the goals themselves. For the owner-manager, therefore, a tactical strategy is likely to be optimal in many of the situations that he has to deal with. Given the need for managerial behavior that is sensitive to the environmental conditions of the firm, given the need for situation-conditioned decision-making rather than for the application of general policies to particular events, it should not be a matter of surprise to find that small-firm owner-managers tend to manage their companies by the seat of their pants. It should not be a matter of surprise that the business policies of small firms are rarely made explicit and that they can only with difficulty be separated out from company practice and procedure and from the flow of daily operating problems. It is clear, of course, that the owner-manager "often doesn't know what is in the seat of his pants,"[18] and that he makes little effort to evaluate what his company's tactical strategies or operating rules of thumb are and whether or not they are valid in his current situation. But it is also clear that the answer to the question, "What makes a small firm tick <u>successfully</u>?" is more likely to be found in analyzing the heuristics that evidently make the small firm tick <u>at all</u> than in concentrating on the absence of those features of large-scale enterprises that are assumed to be significant components of business success.

THE OWNER-MANAGER AND LEARNING SYSTEMS

The owner-manager is, then, characteristically operating in a situation of environmental uncertainty with limited possibilities for controlling market or technological changes that impinge on his company. He brings to this situation a particular set of goals and expectations that themselves change as he grows older or as he adjusts his aspirations to economic realities. The interaction over time between the owner-manager's goals and the pressures of the environment leads to the development of a set of experiences that the owner-manager, albeit unconsciously, translates into rules-of-thumb to guide him in the day-to-day activities of managing his company. The extent to which these rules of thumb become fixed lodestars of his management behavior will depend primarily on two sets of factors. First, where there is a limited degree of turbulence in the firm's operational environment, where the environment throws up few situations that cannot be interpreted through the owner-manager's existing perceptual set, then particular tactical rules of thumb will tend to become guiding strategic principles. Second, where through aspects of his personality, cognitive style, or particular past experiences, or through the natural processes of aging, there has developed in the owner-manager an established and patterned way of doing things that is unresponsive to external environmental factors, then there too will appeals be made, on the basis perhaps of superior experience or wisdom, to simple all-embracing management principles. The theoretical model that best accommodates these two sets of factors is a learning systems model.

Learning systems models approach learning in terms of the interaction between the learner and a learning environment. The learner brings to the learning situation a particular individualized set of factors--a hodgepodge of prejudices, experiences, expectations, assumptions--that will partly determine his willingness to admit and assimilate that information that is a necessary input to the learning process. At the same time, factors in the learning environment itself will have some impact on his readiness to learn--the perceived expertise, trustworthiness and credibility of the source of information, the way information is communicated, the extent to which it is couched in terms that can be related to specific difficulties, problems or experiences of the learner, the nature of group influences, the physical environment. Optimizing a learning system, therefore, becomes a process of finding the best match between learner and learning environment. Since individual personality factors, other than in clinical situations, will generally be taken as uncontrollable variables, this optimization process will involve trying to design learning situations or learning environments that closely match the needs, expectations, and present knowledge of the learner. Since these factors are constantly changing and developing, learning systems, in terms of the dynamics of the interaction between the learner and learning environment, can be seen to have a number of parallels with the open adaptive biological systems that we have described earlier in this chapter.

We can view the small firm as a learning system of an open adaptive kind. The close relationship in the small firm between the motivation and skills of the owner-manager and the performance of the company makes the learning and development of the owner-manager crucial to the development of the firm in the face of new or changing environmental conditions. In looking at the owner-manager, therefore, we are suggesting that he and his firm have to be responsive to changing situations and requirements and have to form part of a system able to bring about its own transformation, that is part of a learning system. Schon suggests that one aspect of such a learning system is that it provides for feedback from the environment, whereas agencies that have no such built-in feedback tend simply to optimize the use of their existing resources, becoming agency-centered rather than client-centered, producer-oriented rather than consumer-oriented: "most agencies systematically avoid follow-up --that is, avoid discovering what happens to their clients after service has been provided. As a consequence the system is cut off and protected from the opportunity of learning."[19] We have already commented on the need for owner-managers to keep in touch with the day-to-day details of their business operations. In addition, however, to being a necessary aspect of tactical decision-making, concern with grass-roots information is important for the owner-manager as a means of feedback and of learning. Cutting himself off from such information is likely, for the owner-manager operating in an unstable environment, to lead toward stagnation. But it is necessary to recognize at the same time the psychological forces that will push owner-managers toward formalization. Systematization is one method of imposing some order on an apparently chaotic, uncertain, and ambiguous real-world situation. Owner-managers will feel the need to simplify the complex, to provide buffers between themselves and the contingencies of daily events, to distance themselves psychologically from the importunities and inconveniences consequent upon openness to new information and a readiness to accept "the warlike and disruptive character of change."[20] The small firm, like any social system, will have a built-in tendency toward what Schon describes as "dynamic conservatism." The function of crisis in the small firm, therefore, may be that crisis raises sufficient energy within the firm to overcome the forces of dynamic conservatism and to move the system to the threshold of change. The small firm, and the position of the owner-manager within it, provide a microcosm of the stress between two sets of elements in any open adaptive system that takes account of the goals and motivations of the actors within it, namely the environmental need for change and the psychological need for stability: "A learning system, then, must be one in which dynamic conservatism operates at such a level and in such a way as to permit change of state without intolerable threat to the essential functions the system fulfils for the self. Our systems need to maintain their identity, and their ability to support the self-identity of those who belong to them, but they must at the same time be capable of frequently transforming themselves."[21]

The psychological contract between an individual and his work, the sense of personal and social identity that his work gives him, will influence, therefore, his degree of tolerance of the ambiguities inherent in working within an open adaptive system. As we saw in Chapter 11, the small-firm owner-manager has a very strong psychological contract with his work, a contract that embodies both legal and felt ownership rights. His psychological contract is not threatened by change. The disfranchised, however, are likely to feel particularly insecure in the face of change, as will those who face disfranchisement through displacement by the entry of a younger generation into the business. If the system is to cope with change, however, it needs to spread more widely the kind of psychological security that the owner-manager feels. If we widen the context to incorporate large organizations, then it is clear that organizational development programs alone will not be sufficient to manage the problems stemming from innovation. Such programs attempt to create self-renewing organizations by opening up organizational processes to inspection, by developing a freer system of interpersonal communications, and by examining the methods by which information from the environment is fed into and utilized by the organization. Loosening up organizational processes in order to make the system more sensitive to its environment will need to be supported by steps to create a wider sharing of power, a greater degree of effective participation in the decision-making activities of the enterprise, and secure psychological contracts for the employed as well as the employers. It is no accident that some of the most successful organization development programs have been those that have been prepared to challenge the values inherent in existing organizational power structures and to develop forms of industrial democracy as the necessary preconditions for stimulating innovation and learning.[22] Paradoxically, a willingness to innovate, to experiment, to change, may be a product of a high degree of psychological security, rooted either in a particularly strong sense of self-identity and self-esteem or in a very secure psychological contract between the individual and the organization.

A learning systems model of the firm provides a perspective
that clarifies, therefore, some of the problems that organizations
face in coming to terms with their environments. It also allows some
recognition of the stresses between behavioral theories of the firm
and systems theories and suggests that both sets of theories have a
contribution to make in understanding the management processes of
the small firm. The owner-manager, as we have seen, is concerned
with relating his firm to its environment and with working out, through
the development of his business, his own personal goals and objectives.
One of the strengths of the successful owner-manager may be his
ability to sense the tactical needs of a situation rather than to pursue
some strategy based on clearly thought-out principles, an ability to
interpret situations in the light of previous experience without closing
the mind to those important cues from the environment that indicate
the essential differences of the new situation as it is:

> No theory drawn from past experience may be taken
> as literally applicable to this situation, nor will a
> theory based on the experience of this situation prove
> literally applicable to the next situation. But theo-
> ories drawn from other situations may provide per-
> spectives or "projective models" for this situation,
> which help to shape it and permit action within it.
> However, this process of existential theory-building
> must grow out of the experience of the here-and-
> now of this situation, must be nourished by and tested
> against it. It cannot be the basis for a "general
> theory," drawn from this situation, which will prove
> literally applicable to "other situations like this."
> It will need to be tested against the experience of the
> next situation, and the next situation may well turn
> out to be different. [23]

SUMMARY

Since organization structures in small firms tend to develop
around people, the "man-in-job" becomes an important focus for
understanding organizational behavior. When small firms grow it is
necessary to find some way of preserving the entrepreneurial skills
and orientation of the owner-manager within the framework of the
larger organization.

Small firms operate as adaptive open systems to a greater extent than do large firms. Such a basis for their operations is necessary because of the general inability of small firms to influence and
control their environment to any significant extent. If the small firm

is viewed as an open adaptive system then the central role of the owner-manager as processor and interpreter of information from the environment is highlighted. As a consequence the owner-manager has to organize his time in such a way as to enable him to respond quickly to unexpected opportunities that arise. His concern with some day-to-day detail is a necessary prerequisite for environmental responsiveness and speedy decision-making.

The owner-manager works in a situation that gives him a limited span of foresight and that demands flexibility in the face of changing external circumstances. The most viable strategy for dealing with such a situation will often be a tactical strategy. Understanding the rules-of-thumb used by owner-managers is, therefore, necessary for understanding what makes small businesses successful and for indicating where training and development needs may lie.

A learning systems model of the small firm is able to relate the goals, aspirations, and expectations of the owner-manager to the open adaptive organizational processes necessary to handle environmental instability and change. Such a model can accommodate the stress that may exist between the psychological needs of owner-managers and the environmental demands placed upon them.

These theoretical perspectives indicate that efforts to develop small businesses must be based on adequate knowledge of the motivation and goals of small businessmen, on the ways in which they manage their companies, and on the environments within which these businesses operate. In Chapter 13, therefore, we consider the education, training, and development processes appropriate in the light of these theoretical perspectives. Our premise will be that it is best to build on the strengths of owner-managers and that, consequently, attention must be paid to the informal learning processes that already exist in the small firm.

NOTES

1. See H. H. Gerth and C. Wright Mills, From Max Weber: Essays in Sociology (London: Routledge and Kegan Paul, 1970).

2. D. King, Training Within the Organisation (London: Tavistock, 1968).

3. J. F. Mee, "Matrix Organisation," Business Horizons 7, no. 2 (Summer 1964).

4. W. G. Bennis, "Beyond Bureaucracy," Trans-Action 2, no. 3 (July-August 1965); see also W. G. Bennis, Changing Organizations (New York: McGraw-Hill, 1966).

5. L. von Bertalanffy, "The Theory of Open Systems in Physics and Biology," in Systems Thinking, ed. F. E. Emery (Harmondsworth: Penguin Books, 1969).

6. E. H. Schein, Organizational Psychology, 2d ed. (Englewood Cliffs, N.J.: Prentice-Hall, 1970).

7. There are a number of philosophical problems in analogies between organisms and organizations that are similar to those posed by Social Darwinist analogies between evolutionary processes in nature and the processes of social change. This kind of analogy has become very popular in recent years and is implicit in the works of Robert Ardrey (African Genesis, The Territorial Imperative, The Social Contract) and of Desmond Morris (The Naked Ape, The Human Zoo). The perspective that is missing from all such analogies is that of human choice, the perspective embodied in the views, expectations, and purposive behavior of the actors in the system.

8. The work of the "Tavistock School" has been particularly concerned with boundary problems and with establishing degrees of environmental turbulence; see, for example, F. E. Emery and E. L. Trist, "The Causal Texture of Organisational Environments," Human Relations 18 (1965); and E. J. Miller and A. K. Rice, Systems of Organisation (London: Tavistock, 1967).

9. See, for example, P. Hill, Towards a New Philosophy of Management (London: Gower Press, 1971).

10. D. A. Schon, Beyond the Stable State (London: Temple Smith, 1971).

11. A confusion introduced by Bennis in Changing Organizations, op. cit.

12. D. Katz and R. L. Kahn, The Social Psychology of Organizations (New York: John Wiley, 1966).

13. Ibid.

14. Ibid.

15. Compare the conclusions that (a) "innovative organisations are aware of their interdependence with the technological task environment and exploit a diversity of external organisations while sluggish organisations are less aware of their interdependence and rely heavily on their internal creativity and on a limited number of external organisations"; (b) "initiation and search in innovative organisations take place in boundary units which have a diversity of contacts with both internal units and external organisations while initiation and search in sluggish organisations occur in units which have less contacts with other internal units and external organisations"; (c) "highly innovative organisations exhibit a lower degree of structure than sluggish organisations do." R. E. Miller, Innovation, Organisation and Environment (Quebec: Institute of Research, University of Sherbrooke, 1971).

16. D. B. Trow, "Executive Succession in Small Companies," Administrative Science Quarterly 6 (1961-62).

17. M. P. Schutzenberger, "A tentative classification of goal-seeking behaviours," in Emery, Systems Thinking, op. cit.

18. C. R. Christensen, Management Succession in Small and Growing Enterprises (Boston: Harvard University Graduate School of Business Administration, 1953).

19. Schon, op. cit.

20. Ibid.

21. Ibid.

22. Compare the notion that a democratic environment and its open systems of enquiry are necessary for coping with change: Bennis, Changing Organizations, op. cit.

23. Schon, op. cit.

13

EDUCATION, TRAINING, AND DEVELOPMENT PROCESSES AND THE SMALL FIRM

As we saw in Chapter 7, studies of the educational backgrounds of large-company managers have underlined the increasing emphasis on formal qualifications as a precondition for entry to management positions. In the large firm the opportunities for a man to leave school at an early age and by experience and loyalty obtain managerial status have declined. Our data on the educational and occupational backgrounds of owner-managers and managers in small firms indicated a number of points of contrast. A high proportion of the managers we interviewed had obtained no formal qualifications either at school or subsequently and there were virtually no graduates among them. They were less involved in full-time or part-time studies than managers of large companies. Whereas, therefore, managers in both large and small firms were increasingly being drawn from grammar and private schools, there was a widening gap between the two groups in terms of educational attainment, both in respect of achievements at school and in respect of formal qualifications obtained through the further education system. Owner-managers and managers in small furniture firms, while starting out with generally less advantageous formal schooling, were not able to close the qualifications gap between themselves and large-firm managers by intensive and effective use of the further education system.

We suggested, therefore, that it will become increasingly difficult for managers of small firms to move into positions within large organizations, especially outside the industries where they have gained their practical experience. In addition, the training that small-company owner-managers and managers receive within their firms becomes crucially important both in terms of their own personal development and in terms of preventing the waste of valuable economic resources in the small-business sector. However, as we saw in Chapter 8, the training and development received by the small-firm managers studied was of a piecemeal and haphazard kind. Previous experience in the industry was often seen as a substitute for training, whether internally or externally. Of the three most common kinds of in-company training received by owner-managers, two were informal job rotation and understudy training, more appropriately described as experience gathering, and the third was an apprenticeship or period of craft training "on-the-bench." Very few of the owner-managers and managers studied had received any kind of formal in-company management training or development, and almost half had not received any kind of training, either internally or externally, since joining their employing firms. Many of them, while they had not had any specific relevant training with their previous employers, felt that the experience they had gained in their past jobs was extremely relevant to their present work and was the main factor that enabled them to handle that work competently. Other studies of small firms confirm that, in general, small-company owner-managers and managers have relatively low levels of educational attainment and have usually received no form of managerial or supervisory education or training. Founder owner-managers in particular tend to lay great stress on the importance of their trade experience in setting up and running their firms, forgetting that "experience as an employee in a business is not business experience."[1]

This chapter, therefore, in the light of our data on the education and training received by small-firm owner-managers and managers, looks first at educational processes in the small firm. It then goes on to define some of the appropriate content of management training and development programs geared to the needs of small companies and to suggest a means of defining appropriate training methods. Finally it considers some alternative ways of meeting the management training and development needs of small firms and considers some of the functions that can be filled most usefully by training agencies.

EDUCATION, TRAINING, AND DEVELOPMENT PROCESSES AND THE OWNER-MANAGER

A number of the findings of Part II and considerations of earlier chapters in Part III have an important bearing on the way in which education, training, and development processes in small firms need to be viewed. We have seen, for example, that the job of the small-firm owner-manager is constantly adapting to a changing situation. It is a fluid and fluctuating role rather than a role that can be adequately analyzed, defined, and specified on a once-for-all basis.

We have described the owner-manager's job as part of an open adaptive system continuously adjusting to financial, technical, and market demands. At the same time as the owner-manager's job adapts to the needs of a changing external environment, we have also suggested that it expands or contracts in response to the social and psychological needs of the owner-manager himself. A consequence of these perspectives is to see that the management development process in the small firm is linked inexorably both with the development and motivation of the individual manager and with the development of the business in response to external factors. In other words we have to consider both the internal and external dynamics of the owner-manager's situation and the interaction between these two sets of factors.

In addition, since the owner-manager, unlike the professional manager or administrator, is emotionally and financially committed to his company, he tends to see the training and development process as being highly specific to his immediate and short-term needs, rather than as part of a process of fitting him for some future undefined job. However, his immediate and short-term needs are constantly changing and at different stages in the development of his business the small-firm owner-manager requires different mixes of entrepreneurial and administrative skills. As a firm expands, therefore, the development process is likely to involve the owner-manager in a transition from an entrepreneurial toward an administrative orientation. This transitional period can be used, not only for reappraisal by the owner-manager of his business goals and objectives, but also to explore ways of utilizing the owner-manager's entrepreneurial skills within the structure of the larger-scale organization.

It is necessary, when considering the training and development of small-firm owner-managers and managers, to distinguish between owner-operators of little businesses and owner-managers of small firms, between those managers who are shareholders in their business and nonshareholding managers, and between inheritor owner-managers and founder owner-managers. All these groups are likely to have relatively low levels of educational attainment and little formal management education or training. Consequently, as we pointed out in Chapter 7, the starting point for management training or development activities aimed at any one of these groups needs to be geared appropriately to their existing level of understanding and to take account of their different educational and occupational experiences.

We suggest that probably as few as 10 percent of small-firm owner-managers and managers are able to translate general management principles and adapt them to the specific requirements of their own organizations or their own jobs. These are the 10 percent that are best able to help themselves and least need the stimulus of external assistance, yet they may also be the 10 percent that most of the external services reach. It is, however, with the remaining 90 percent that the greatest potential impact for development lies. For this large majority the training and development process, if it is to be effective, needs to be highly specific to the industry, firm, and job of the individual manager and designed to increase his competence in his current work situation.

As well as being related to the educational levels and occupational experiences of different groups of small-firm owner-managers and managers, training and development programs must also be relevant to the organizational context within which such managers operate. In small firms, the man and the job frequently develop together, there being little opportunity after initial training for the development of managers through job transfers or job rotation. Distinctions between job description and man description break down in the small firm where organization structures, insofar as they exist, are likely to be developed around the interests and abilities of the available managers rather than managers recruited to fill highly prescribed and well-defined functions within the firm. In the small firm posts are often molded to people rather than people to posts. In a number of respects the training and development process of small-firm owner-managers bears some resemblance to the process at the very top of large companies, particularly in the way in which succession problems are handled. The findings of an American study underline some of the similarities that exist.[2] The authors set out to learn more about the factors affecting advancement to top management positions and to shed light on how progress toward senior executive status was influenced by factors such as management development activities, organization policies, supervisory practices, and personal characteristics. To analyze what took place when decisions on management succession were being made, they interviewed a number of individuals who had been promoted and those who had made the promotion decisions, their subjects being primarily top people from relatively large and successful companies that took an active interest in management development. Two of their observations are of particular relevance to our argument. First, the development and succession of top managers is, they suggest, more than an extension of the same process that operates in the middle management ranks: "In a sense, the situation with respect to selection and placement of top-level executives reverts to the small business context. That is, at the top, the group of individuals is once again relatively small and has highly personal relations, and its members interact as they would in a small company. The individuals generally know each other rather well, or at least some members of the decision-making group can speak about a candidate from close personal contact or direct observation." Informal procedures therefore supplant formal ones. Second, they point out that the distinctions between job description and man description break down at the upper management levels of large organizations and suggest that the man-in-job emerges as a single concept, just as we have suggested that it is difficult and probably unnecessary in the small company to distinguish between the owner-manager and the office or functions he carries out: "I am my job." Several of the companies in the American study made organizational changes to mold a position to the available person just in the way that we have observed small family firms structuring their organizations to accommodate the talents and skills of new family members joining the company. This practice of structuring management organizations around people was considered by the American firms, not as mere improvisation to meet contingencies, but as a desirable practice. Along with it went a greater tolerance of individuality in the higher echelons of management, a willingness to allow the top-level manager a high degree of autonomy and freedom to develop his own personalized management style, and a rejection of conformity-inducing notions of there being one best way of performing a management job.

It appears, then, that just as in the small firm the education, training, and development of the son of the owner will be different from that of the nonshareholding or nonfamily manager, so too in the large firm the selection of the manager for a top executive position will be carried out against different criteria than those used for the promotion and development of a manager within the middle ranks of management. But if we accept the notion that in the future entrepreneurial innovation will become the very heart and core of management,[3] then the requirements of top managerial posts may well be quite different from the requirements of middle management positions and the content of training and development programs will vary accordingly. What the large organization may well require at the top, therefore, are the entrepreneurial skills and orientation of the successful owner-manager whereas within the middle ranks of large companies managers will continue to be concerned primarily with administration, with administrative skills, and with stabilizing, monitoring, and facilitating activities.[4] Unfortunately, of course, "the qualities that lead to the promotion of the salaried employee are radically different from those which would make him a successful, independent businessman,"[5] and most management training and development programs in large organizations start out at one level below that of the top executives. Whereas, therefore, there is undoubtedly a need to develop a more professional kind of management among nonshareholding managers in the small firm and among middle

managers in the large firm, both owner-managers and large-firm top
executives need to develop those entrepreneurial skills associated
with the successful conduct of a business. Just as many small firms
are short of administrative know-how and have problems in attracting and retaining professional managers, so many large companies
are short of entrepreneurial and innovative skills and have no systematic method for developing such skills in present or potential top
executives. Understanding the nature of entrepreneurial skill and
entrepreneurial innovation, and learning more about the design of
flexible work structures that allow the individual to develop his abilities and skills more fully are likely to prove relevant to executive
development in large firms as well as to the management training
and development process in the small firm.

A further important aspect in the education, training, and development process is the attitudes of managers toward training and
their motivation to learn. With many small-firm owner-managers
and managers, both attitudinal and motivational barriers have to be
broken down before any learning process is likely to prove effective.
We saw in Chapter 8, for example, that training is frequently seen
as for other people, particularly for apprentices and young persons.
It is associated with courses and with theory rather than practice.
It is a common belief among small-firm owner-managers and managers that managerial or entrepreneurial skills can only be acquired
through long years of experience, through a process of attrition, and
through trial-and-error learning within the firm. Consequently, although many such managers are able to describe the problems they
face in their work, few feel that training can help toward finding
relevant solutions to those problems and there is little awareness of
the value of training in improving company performance. Trainers
and management development specialists, for their part, need to
understand the processes by which owner-managers and managers
at present acquire their skills in small companies and need to build
on those processes rather than to construct elaborate formal training and development artifacts that bear no relation to those processes
and may, in practice, stifle all learning activity.

There are a number of respects in which the education, training, and development process appropriate for owner-managers and
managers of small firms is similar to the process appropriate for
older workers generally. The majority of the owner-managers and
managers participating in our study were over the age of 40. Such
managers, having little practice or experience in formal learning
situations, often lack confidence in their ability to learn and find
difficulty in assimilating skills that are mental and perceptual in
character. They find it increasingly difficult to retain information
and to translate it into purposeful action, and they find that the

problems of working under stress and of making decisions under severe time pressures become more acute as they grow older. In addition the motivation to learn tends to decline with increasing age. For many small-firm owner-managers and managers, therefore, an education, training, and development process that involves doing or discovering, that is an active participative process, is likely to prove a more effective learning medium than one involving reading, listening, or watching.

Any learning system has two major components. The first is made up of the features that the would-be learner brings into the system with him. These include his environment, experiences, set of expectations, previous learning history, existing knowledge, skills and abilities, and various personality characteristics, the most important of which are probably cognitive style, motivation, and intelligence. The second set of components is made up of features that question and challenge in some way the would-be learner's composite world picture, requiring him to restructure his thinking in order to accommodate new information or a different viewpoint. Traditionally this part of the system is identified with the role of the teacher and with various kinds of information input. Although the teacher's role may take a variety of forms--instructor, information provider, consultant, adviser, catalyst, coach--it is not a necessary part of a learning system that there should be a teacher at all. This should not, however, lead to reliance on the belief that managers will learn by experience. All the evidence suggests that managers do not learn by experience unless that experience is subjected to some form of scrutiny and analysis. Nevertheless, one of the aims of any educational process, given the scarcity of teaching resources, is to maximize the situations in which learning takes place without teaching and minimize the situations in which teaching takes place without learning. In the context of small-firm owner-managers and managers it is necessary, therefore, to identify education, training, and development processes that are closely related to the experience, expectations, and needs of the learner, in other words processes that incorporate an individualized environment-based learning system.

DEFINING TRAINING AND DEVELOPMENT CONTENT

At various points in Part II we touched on aspects relevant to the training and development needs of the owner-managers and managers participating in our research program. In Chapter 5 we described the perceptions that owner-managers had of the functional strengths and weaknesses of their firms and identified some of the management problems of small furniture firms. In Chapter 8 we set out the framework we were using to identify training needs and described in some detail the difficulties and problems managers faced in their work and the training and development needs identified by our descriptive survey. In Chapter 9 we described the time spent by the owner-managers in our depth study on various management functions and activities. In this section we try to draw together some of these findings, together with the managerial skills taxonomy developed in Chapter 11, in order to suggest a structure for defining the training and development content appropriate to some of the different groups of small-firm owner-managers and managers.

If, as we have suggested, concentration on short-term goals is crucial to the survival of the small business, then training and development programs must contribute to tactical success in specific situations as much as to the clarification and achievement of longer-term strategic objectives. Many of the training needs identified in the course of the research program have been highly specific to the work difficulties and work problems faced by particular managers within their companies at particular points in time, and the greatest need that emerges is the need for the development of job-specific training programs for individual owner-managers and managers of small firms. Training in effective adaptation to change is likely to be of more value to the small firm, therefore, than training in predictive management techniques that involve long-term control of change. Crises, for example, in the sense of unforeseen contingencies requiring immediate action or attention, are the rule rather than the exception in the small firm and need to be catered for accordingly. In making a distinction between adaptive organic entrepreneurial skills and predictive mechanistic administrative skills we have attempted to indicate the kinds of focus that might be appropriate in helping owner-managers handle crisis situations. Nevertheless further research is still needed to identify more precisely the heuristic skills, rules of thumb, and tactics adopted by effective owner-managers or entrepreneurs in handling crisis situations.

We also need, in the small-firm context, to take an overall view of managerial work that accommodates the possibility of peaks and troughs in managerial activity. We have seen in Part II that owner-managers may spend time busying themselves with bits and pieces of day-to-day detail and that the most frequent observable activities carried out by managers may be those of a relatively routine kind, perhaps concerned with the administrative aspects of their work. In a manager's work there may be relatively little activity of a managerial kind, and these periods may be punctuated by short bursts of decision-making or problem-solving activity. On the one hand there is the danger, therefore, of building up training programs to cover tasks and functions that arise frequently in the course of a manager's work but are neither difficult to carry out nor critical to company success. On the other hand there is the danger of assuming that only activities and tasks that involve decision-making and problem-solving at the policy level can be either difficult or critical, and that the routine day-to-day operations can to all intents and purposes be ignored in the training and development context. Consequently it is necessary to consider both the executive-level skills being used in the day-to-day running of the business and the skills required for policy-making and to realize that the information assimilated by the owner-manager on a day-to-day basis may be a crucial component of his success in problem-solving and decision-making on policy matters. In addition it is necessary, in trying to define the appropriate training and development content for any given group of owner-managers or managers in small firms, to avoid confusion between skills and techniques. Techniques are the tools of management. Skill arises in the use to which those tools are put. The sophistication of the management techniques required by a business will depend on such factors as the kinds of market it serves, the nature of its technology, the scale of its operations--factors that will also influence the mix of entrepreneurial and administrative skills that the business requires. Once some distinction of this kind between entrepreneurial skills, administrative skills, and operational techniques of business management has been made, it becomes possible to construct a model for analyzing the various degrees of sophistication and specialization in skills and techniques required by managers in different companies or by different managerial groups. An outline of such a model is given in Figure 13.1. In practice there will naturally be a constant interplay between administrative skills, entrepreneurial skills, and operational techniques, the development of any one in response to changed environmental conditions influencing the requirement for the others, in much the same way as developments in production technology may change the requirement for operator skills.

Figure 13.2 illustrates a framework for identifying the managerial skills most in need of development among the three managerial groups of owner-manager founders, owner-manager inheritors, and nonshareholding managers. Thus the content of any training and development program geared to the major skills needs of owner-manager founders will be such as to develop skills in tactical planning, objective setting, policy formulation, decision-making, and problem-solving. For owner-manager inheritors the major needs will be met by programs that develop innovative and risk-taking skills, and skill in interpersonal communications, as well as decision-making and problem-solving skills. For the nonshareholding manager, training and development content must be geared initially toward developing the entrepreneurial skills of tactical planning, troubleshooting,

FIGURE 13.1

Structure for Defining Training and Development Content

	Variable Degrees of Sophistication/Specialization				
	1	2	3	4	5
Managerial skills and techniques	from high		————		to low
Entrepreneurial skills					
1. Innovation		*			
2. Risk-taking, etc.	*				
Administrative skills					
1. Objective setting				*	
2. Policy formulation, etc.			*		
Common managerial skills					
1. Decision-making	*				
2. Problem-solving, etc.	*				
Techniques					
1. Sales and marketing			*		
2. Personnel management, etc.		*			

*Example: Model can be used to indicate either company requirement in total or individual job requirements.

Procedure for defining individual training and development content:

Stage 1: Use of model to indicate skills and techniques appropriate to individuals and their jobs.

Stage 2: Assessment of present performance--dimensions of frequency, difficulty, and criticality.

Stage 3: Identification of training and development needs or of other appropriate action required.

Source: Compiled by the author.

FIGURE 13.2

Managerial Skills: Job Relevance and Training Need by Managerial Group

(***** = High; * = Low)

| | Managerial Group | | | | | |
| Managerial Skills Classification | Owner-Manager Founders | | Owner-Manager Inheritors | | Nonshareholding Managers | |
	Job Relevance	Training Need	Job Relevance	Training Need	Job Relevance	Training Need
Entrepreneurial skills						
1. Innovation	*****	****	*****	*****	*	**
2. Risk-taking	*****	****	*****	*****	*	*
3. Tactical planning	*****	*****	****	****	****	*****
4. Negotiating	*****	*	****	**	**	*
5. Troubleshooting	*****	**	***	**	*****	*****
6. Interpersonal communications	*****	****	*****	*****	*****	*****
Administrative skills						
1. Objective setting	***	*****	***	***	**	***
2. Policy formulation	***	*****	***	***	*	*
3. Strategic planning	**	****	**	***	*	*
4. Organizing	*****	***	****	*	*****	*****
5. Coordinating	*****	*	****	*	**	*
6. Formal communications	*	*	**	*	**	**
7. Monitoring	*	*	**	*	*****	*****
8. Stabilizing	*	*	***	*	*****	****
Common managerial skills						
1. Decision-making	*****	*****	*****	*****	**	***
2. Problem-solving	*****	*****	*****	*****	****	*****
3. Information-processing	*****	***	****	****	***	*****

Source: Compiled by the author.

and interpersonal communications, the administrative skills of organizing and monitoring, and the common managerial skills of problem-solving and information-processing. Figure 13.3 illustrates a framework for identifying the managerial techniques that are most relevant to the jobs of the three managerial groups and for identifying where the major training needs lie in terms of knowledge and understanding of the relevant techniques and management functions. Thus the content of any training and development program geared to the major knowledge needs of both founder and inheritor owner-managers will initially be such as to develop understanding of the techniques and knowledge of the management functions involved in sales and marketing, personnel management, internal organizational development, finance and accounts, product costing and estimating, and cost control. For the nonshareholding manager the major needs will be met by providing training and development in the application of stock control techniques and in techniques appropriate to successful sales and marketing, to production scheduling and control, and to effective cost control. For all managerial groups it will be possible, using the framework provided by these two figures as a model, to define the training and development content of any specific program in such a way as to incorporate both an understanding of relevant managerial techniques and an opportunity to develop appropriate entrepreneurial, administrative and managerial skills.

Figures 13.2 and 13.3 attempt to use the kind of model set out in Figure 13.1 to describe in summary form the relevance of different managerial skills and techniques and the existence of training needs in these skills and techniques for three small-firm managerial groups--owner-manager founders, owner-manager inheritors, and nonshareholding managers. As we have tried to make clear earlier, training and development needs are highly person- and job-specific and cannot be readily compartmentalized into little boxes without grave distortion to the reality of each individual work situation. In many ways, for example, the classification of the difficulties and problems faced by owner-managers and managers into different management categories, with the implication that general training needs exist within such management categories, is both arbitrary and misleading. As we have seen, many of the problems described by owner-managers and managers are not viewed by the managers as being problems in one particular functional area but rather as problems concerning the development of the business as a whole. Owner-managers in particular are likely to identify completely with their companies and to talk about their own work problems and the problems facing their company as one and the same thing. In presenting Figures 13.2 and 13.3 we do so, therefore, in the knowledge of the distortion they represent but in the hope that they might provide a

FIGURE 13.3

Managerial Techniques: Job Relevance and Training Need by Managerial Group

(***** = High; * = Low)

| | Managerial Group | | | | | |
| Managerial Techniques Classification | Owner-Manager Founders | | Owner-Manager Inheritors | | Nonshareholding Managers | |
	Job Relevance	Training Need	Job Relevance	Training Need	Job Relevance	Training Need
1. Sales and marketing	****	*****	****	*****	****	****
2. Personnel management	*****	*****	*****	*****	***	***
3. Internal organizational development including management succession	****	*****	***	*****	*	*
4. Finance and accounts including credit control	*****	*****	*****	*****	***	***
5. Production scheduling and control	*	**	*	**	*****	****
6. Product costing and estimating	***	****	***	****	**	***
7. Cost control	***	****	***	****	*****	****
8. Stock control	**	***	**	***	****	*****
9. Quality control	**	*	**	**	**	***
10. Office administration	***	****	***	**	***	**
11. Production methods and layout	*	*	*	**	***	***
12. Design and development	***	***	**	****	*	*
13. Purchasing	****	*	***	**	*	*
14. Distribution	***	**	***	*	**	*

Source: Compiled by the author.

useful structure for training and development practitioners, a structure that will assist them in defining the training and development
content of any program geared to a particular group of small-firm
owner-managers and managers. The utility of the model can only
be tested out by its practical application. The allocation of high
to low indicators of job relevance and training need is based on the
data summarized in Part II and on the more theoretical considerations implicit in the managerial skills taxonomy set out in Chapter 11.

DESIGNING AND UTILIZING APPROPRIATE
TRAINING METHODS

Having outlined some of the training needs of small-firm owner-
managers and managers, and suggested an approach to defining appropriate training and development content more precisely, it is
necessary to consider the various training methods available and to
indicate those which would appear to be most appropriate both in
terms of the characteristics of the managers concerned and in terms
of the skills and techniques that are to be learned. In this section,
therefore, we consider a framework for use in the selection of suitable training methods for any program geared to a particular group
of owner-managers and managers. The framework is designed in
the light of earlier discussion on education, training, and development processes and the owner-manager.

Figure 13.4 illustrates a structure for assessing the suitability
of various methods in the training of different kinds of small-firm
manager. By and large individualized and small-group training
methods are suggested as being the most appropriate for the owner-
managers and managers of small firms, with programmed learning
methods also having a role to play. Job-specific training methods
(coaching, consultancy, experience-exchange groups, special tailor-
made workshops, problem clinics) are recommended as being more
appropriate in the training and development of small-firm owner-
managers and managers than the teaching of general management
principles by more formal training methods. Figures 13.5, 13.6,
and 13.7 illustrate a structure for assessing the suitability of different training methods according to the skill and knowledge content of
the training program, Figure 13.5 dealing with the entrepreneurial
skills identified, Figure 13.6 with administrative skills, and Figure
13.7 with common managerial skills and managerial techniques.
These figures together with Figures 13.2, 13.3, and 13.4 can be used
to identify likely training priorities and needs of different small-firm
managerial groups and to identify the most appropriate training methods to be adopted in meeting those needs. An example is set out in
Figure 13.8.

FIGURE 13.4

Suitability of Training and Development Methods to Various Managerial Groups
(***** = Highly suitable; * = Not very suitable)

Classification of Training and Development Methods	Managerial Group					
	Owner-Manager Founders		Owner-Manager Inheritors		Nonshareholding Managers	
	Over 35	Under 35	Over 35	Under 35	Over 35	Under 35
I Individualized						
1. Action research	***	****	***	****	***	****
2. Coaching	*****	*****	*****	*****	*****	*****
3. Consultancy and advisory services	*****	*****	*****	*****	*****	*****
4. Counseling	*****	***	*****	***	***	**
5. Intercompany exchange	***	*****	***	*****	**	****
6. Planned experience	*	*	**	*****	***	*****
7. Project work	*	**	*	***	***	*****
8. Self-appraisal and self-development aids	*****	*****	*****	*****	****	****
II Small Group						
1. Brainstorming	***	*****	***	*****	**	***
2. Business games and exercises	****	*****	****	*****	****	*****
3. Case studies	***	****	***	****	****	*****
4. Experience-exchange groups	*****	****	*****	****	****	***
5. Job-specific workshops	***	*****	***	*****	****	*****
6. Problem clinics	*****	****	*****	***	***	***
7. Role playing	**	***	**	***	**	****
8. Sensitivity and T-group training	**	***	**	***	**	***
III General						
1. Correspondence courses	*	*	*	*	*	**
2. Films	*	*	*	*	*	*
3. Information services	***	***	***	***	**	**
4. Lecture courses	*	**	*	**	**	***
5. Programmed learning	*****	****	*****	****	*****	****
6. Publications	*	**	*	**	**	***
7. Seminars	**	***	**	***	***	***
8. Training packages and kits	**	***	**	***	**	***

Source: Compiled by the author.

FIGURE 13.5

Suitability of Methods to Entrepreneurial Skills Training
(***** = Highly suitable; * = Not very suitable)

Classification of Training and Development Methods	Entrepreneurial Skills					
	Innovation	Risk-Taking	Tactical Planning	Negotiating	Trouble-Shooting	Interpersonal Communications
I Individualized						
1. Action research	**	*	**	***	**	*****
2. Coaching	**	***	*****	****	**	***
3. Consultancy and advisory services	***	***	*****	***	**	***
4. Counseling	**	*	*	*	*	*****
5. Intercompany exchange	*****	****	*	*	*	**
6. Planned experience	*	****	****	****	*****	***
7. Project work	*****	***	***	*	*	**
8. Self-appraisal and self-development aids	**	*	***	*	*	*
II Small Group						
1. Brainstorming	*****	***	*	*	**	*
2. Business games and exercises	****	*****	****	***	***	***
3. Case studies	**	*	**	***	**	**
4. Experience-exchange groups	***	*	*	*	*	**
5. Job-specific workshops	**	***	***	***	**	**
6. Problem clinics	*	*	**	*	***	**
7. Role playing	*	*	*	*****	****	***
8. Sensitivity and T-group training	*	*	*	***	***	****
III General						
1. Correspondence courses	*	*	*	*	*	*
2. Films	*	*	*	*	*	**
3. Information services	**	*	*	*	*	*
4. Lecture courses	*	*	**	*	*	**
5. Programmed learning	*	*	*	*	*	*
6. Publications	**	*	**	*	*	**
7. Seminars	*	*	**	**	**	**
8. Training packages and kits	*	*	**	*	*	*

Source: Compiled by the author.

FIGURE 13.6

Suitability of Methods to Administrative Skills Training
(***** = Highly suitable; * = Not very suitable)

Classification of Training and Development Methods	Administrative Skills							
	Objective Setting	Policy Formulation	Strategic Planning	Organizing	Coordinating	Formal Communication	Monitoring	Stabilizing
I Individualized								
1. Action research	*	**	*	**	*	*	*	*
2. Coaching	*****	*****	*****	*****	*****	***	*	*
3. Consultancy and advisory services	*****	*****	*****	*****	*****	*****	*****	*****
4. Counseling	***	*****	*****	**	*	**	*	*
5. Intercompany exchange	**	***	**	***	*	*	***	*
6. Planned experience	*	*	*	*	*****	***	***	*****
7. Project work	*****	*****	*****	*	*	*	*	*
8. Self-appraisal and self-development aids	****	****	****	***	**	**	****	**
II Small Group								
1. Brainstorming	***	***	**	*	*	*	*	*
2. Business games and exercises	****	****	****	****	***	***	***	***
3. Case studies	***	***	***	**	**	**	**	**
4. Experience-exchange groups	*****	*****	****	***	**	***	***	**
5. Job-specific workshops	****	*****	****	***	**	***	***	**
6. Problem clinics	*	*****	*	*	*	*	*	*
7. Role playing	*	*	*	**	**	**	**	**
8. Sensitivity and T-group training	*	*	*	**	***	**	**	****
III General								
1. Correspondence courses	*	*	*	*	*	*	*	*
2. Films	*	*	*	*	*	*	*	*
3. Information services	*	*	*	*	*	*	*	*
4. Lecture courses	**	**	**	**	**	***	**	**
5. Programmed learning	*	*	*	*	*	*	*	*
6. Publications	*	*	*	*	*	*	*	*
7. Seminars	**	**	**	**	**	***	**	**
8. Training packages and kits	***	***	***	*	*	*	*	*

Source: Compiled by the author.

FIGURE 13.7

Suitability of Methods to Common Managerial Skills and
Managerial Techniques Training
(***** = Highly suitable; * = Not very suitable)

Classification of Training and Development Methods	Common Managerial Skills			Managerial Techniques
	Decision-Making	Problem-Solving	Information-Processing	
I Individualized				
1. Action research	*	****	****	**
2. Coaching	****	****	****	*****
3. Consultancy and advisory services	****	****	*****	*****
4. Counseling	*	***	*	***
5. Intercompany exchange	***	***	*****	***
6. Planned experience	*****	*****	****	***
7. Project work	*	*****	****	***
8. Self-appraisal and self-development aids	*	***	***	***
II Small Group				
1. Brainstorming	*	***	*	*
2. Business games and exercises	*****	*****	*****	*****
3. Case studies	****	****	****	****
4. Experience-exchange groups	*	*	***	*
5. Job-specific workshops	*****	*****	*****	***
6. Problem clinics	*	**	***	*
7. Role playing	**	***	**	*
8. Sensitivity and T-group training	*	**	***	*
III General				
1. Correspondence courses	*	*	*	****
2. Films	*	*	*	**
3. Information services	*	*	**	**
4. Lecture courses	**	**	**	***
5. Programmed learning	*	*	****	*****
6. Publications	*	*	*	***
7. Seminars	**	**	**	****
8. Training packages and kits	**	**	**	****

Source: Compiled by the author.

270

FIGURE 13.8

Matching Training Needs to Training Methods: An Example
Owner-Manager Founder, aged 45

Major Skill Training Needs	Most Suitable Training Methods
Tactical planning	1. Coaching 2. Consultancy and advisory services
Objective setting	1. Coaching 2. Consultancy and advisory services
Policy formulation	1. Coaching 2. Consultancy and advisory services 3. Counseling 4. Experience-exchange groups 5. Problem clinics
Decision-making and Problem solving	1. Coaching 2. Consultancy and advisory services 3. Business games and exercises
Major Technique Training Needs Sales and marketing Personnel management Internal organizational development Finance and accounts	1. Coaching 2. Consultancy and advisory services 3. Programmed learning

Source: Compiled by the author.

There is of course no one best training method for dealing with any particular training need. The actual selection of methods to be used will depend, in practice, on a detailed analysis of the characteristic skills, abilities, and training needs of the manager or managers for whom the training is designed and a precise specification of the proposed training content. Again the purpose of recommending a framework is to provide an analytical model that can usefully be adapted to the practical realities of a variety of different situations rather than to propose a straightjacketed new training gospel. The frameworks suggested, therefore, should be seen as rules of thumb and not as rules, as guidelines not as instructions.

It will be seen, in studying these figures, that they reflect the emphasis that we have laid on the need to develop individual job-specific training programs geared to the development of those skills we believe necessary for successful small-firm management. They also reflect the necessity, in the small-firm context, of finding training methods that minimize the demands made on the working time of owner-managers. External training courses of more than one or two days duration, for example, raise particular difficulties for managers from small companies. The involvement of managers in day-to-day operations and the limited amount of slack in the managerial system in small companies can make the absence of a key person for any length of time a major inconvenience. The content of many external courses ostensibly designed for small-firm managers is often inappropriate. We suggest that general management education courses, for example, many of which are geared to the development of predictive management skills and which are often extremely time-consuming, have a very limited application to small firms. Similarly, many training courses in operational management techniques are often oversophisticated for the needs of small-firm owner-managers and managers and must be slanted much more toward small companies if they are to fulfill a useful purpose. Nevertheless such courses, if designed with the needs of small-firm managers in mind and if used to supplement individually tailored training and development programs, can have a contribution to make.

In Figures 13.4 and 13.6 we suggest that some small-group training methods, notably problem clinics and experience-exchange groups, are particularly appropriate for helping older owner-managers to develop skills in policy formulation. In the United States, problem clinics have been developed under the auspices of the Small Business Administration agency. In such clinics a small group of owner-managers, under the guidance of a leader, come together to discuss their current problems. In Switzerland the Swiss Research Institute of Small Business in St. Gallen, partly as a consequence of its consultancy activities with small companies, organizes a system of experience-exchange, or Ex-Ex, groups for small-business managers.[6] Ex-Ex groups provide a kind of collective consultancy in the form of organized exchanges of experiences that is not dissimilar from the American problem clinic idea. The groups comprise eight to twelve small-business owners and managers from the same industry or trade who usually meet six times a year.

These meetings last for a whole working day and are given over primarily to discussion of management problems. Subjects are decided upon in advance in consultation between the members of the group and the institute, leaving sufficient flexibility to deal with problems that arise unexpectedly. During the session the institute member leading the group generally gives an introduction to each new subject, in order to inform the participants and to secure some common ground for the subsequent discussion. The debate aims at a frank exchange of information, knowledge, and experience so that it turns out to be of mutual benefit to all participants. Toward the end of the session the leader sums up the results that are subsequently recorded in a written report for all members of the group, and only for them. For very specialized subjects external experts are invited. The Ex-Ex activities are not restricted to roundtable meetings but include visits to member firms, to other companies and to trade exhibitions, and the development of contacts with other similar groups.

The success of Ex-Ex groups depends upon a number of factors. In particular, all participants have to be totally frank and outspoken. It is not appropriate to allow some members of a group to keep their so-called business secrets to themselves while the others contribute confidential information about their firms. Such an atmosphere of trust among the members of the group can only be realized when they are not immediate competitors. Members of the Swiss Ex-Ex groups are, therefore, mostly recruited from different regions or areas but their types of business have to be comparable in order to guarantee a common base for discussion and problem-solving. The Swiss experience also indicates that this kind of management development activity for small business owner-managers provides much more than merely an exchange of ideas and information. It also creates mutual incentives to take some positive action. A kind of psychological mechanism works toward the introduction of concrete measures in their firms by members of the Ex-Ex groups. As soon as there are two or three dynamic people within a group they infect the others to become more active. No Swiss entrepreneur, apparently, likes confessing or showing that he is indolent and inflexible. In this way the profit of the Ex-Ex activities seems often to be higher for average than for elite participants but, nevertheless, the elite participants are in most cases generous enough to pass on their knowledge and know-how. Ex-Ex groups, therefore, are one training and development method that builds on the experience of the participating managers and guides them toward self-development situations. Where some other small group methods, such as case studies, business games, and problem-solving and decision-making exercises, form part of a training program for owner-managers, it

is essential that they are appropriate and relevant to the small-firm
context and that, if possible, they simulate the pace, stress, and
memory requirements of the owner-manager's work.

Another useful method in the training and development of small-
firm owner-managers and managers is the job-specific training workshop, incorporating, as such a workshop does, elements of coaching
and project work as well as more formal tuition. In a well-designed
workshop, in-company and external training are complementary as
are individualized and group training methods. Such a workshop may,
for example, be built around an initial survey designed to identify
the specific training and development needs of selected managers in
a small number of companies in terms of entrepreneurial or administrative skills and/or in terms of managerial techniques. A short
seminar may then be run to provide instruction generally relevant
to the needs of all the managers selected and individual tuition in
areas where the needs are more specialized. This may be followed
up by a project carried out by each manager in his company under
the guidance of, and with direct coaching assistance from, a tutor
or consultant. Additional seminars may be arranged as part of the
program leading to the implementation of improvement plans by the
manager within his company. A number of points need to be kept in
mind in designing job-specific training workshops of this kind. First,
such workshops involve a very considerable investment of time and
effort, both by the managers themselves and by training staff, tutors,
or consultants. Second, the training material used must be relevant
to the managers taking part and should ideally draw upon the work
experiences and problems of the participants. Third, the design
stage and the initial survey are crucial; it is at that point that some
attempt will be made to measure the work behavior or work performance of managers or to collect information on the particular problems they face in their companies. Fourth, at any one time only a
relatively small number of managers can be effectively involved in
such an exercise; this raises the costs significantly as does the emphasis on in-company coaching and on maintaining a continuing relationship between the owner-manager and the workshop tutor.

Individualized training methods are also time-consuming and
require the maximum cooperation and participation from owner-
managers and managers. They necessitate direct contact with the
manager in his work situation since this is a prerequisite for identifying individual training needs and developing job-specific training
programs. Some consultancy and advisory services have the necessary access. They can provide a diagnosis of the manager's problems and suggest new frameworks for considering appropriate solutions. In this context their function is that of a catalyst. Similarly,
participation in action research studies can prove a form of develop-

ment for the owner-manager. As we have seen in our depth studies, the presence of an outside observer frequently provides a sounding board for the owner-manager's ideas and gives him some objective feedback against which to test his judgment. Such studies also provide a vehicle for building on the informal learning processes that already exist within a company and for relating job-specific training and development programs to the individual capacities and abilities of owner-managers and managers. Self-development and self-appraisal techniques involve finding suitable ways of prompting the small-firm owner-manager to recognize his own training needs and to take appropriate action.

Since many owner-managers and managers are over the age of 40, the methods appropriate in their training and development will be similar to those methods that have been tried and tested with older workers generally. [7] Learning needs to be related to some practical end use, needs to develop from participative activities rather than from the memorizing of taught material, and needs to maximize opportunities for "finding out for oneself." Group training methods need to be based on cooperation rather than competition. Simulations and training exercises need to be designed in such a way as to enable learning to be directly related to practice. The older learner needs to be allowed to proceed at his own pace, to structure his own program within certain defined limits, to build on his own knowledge and experience, and to be involved in a process of discovery, understanding, and practical consolidation.

What is required, then, in terms of training and development methods for the owner-managers and managers of small firms, are methods that satisfy a number of criteria associated with independent environment-based learning systems. In the context of any specific training and development need of small-firm owner-managers and managers, therefore, a number of questions can be asked to help assess the likely suitability of alternative training and development methods. For example, does the method encourage independent learning while maintaining the motivational advantages of those communal and social elements inherent in most learning systems? Is it a necessary part of the training and development method that the participant is actively involved of his own volition? Does the method draw on the work experience and work environment of the participant manager and effectively allow the manager to develop an understanding of that experience and environment? Does the method help the manager to become a more self-organized learner and allow him freedom to develop his own perception of where his training and development needs lie? The importance of designing and utilizing appropriate methods in the training and development of small-firm owner-managers and managers cannot be overstressed. The methods

adopted will determine the attitudes of participant managers to the
learning process, will influence their ability to adapt what they learn
to new situations, and will affect their willingness to cooperate with
others in training and development programs. Nevertheless, although
experimentation with different training methods is to be encouraged,
the content of the learning system (in the sense of the message rather
than the medium) is equally important. Where knowledge and skill
requirements can be precisely stated then the major test of the appropriateness of any particular training method is its effectiveness
in imparting the requisite training content.

MEETING TRAINING AND DEVELOPMENT NEEDS

So far we have been concerned with the identification of the
training and development needs of small-firm owner-managers and
managers, the specification of relevant training and development
content, and the appropriateness of various training methods to meet
the needs identified. Our assumption has been that needs can best be
met by changing the knowledge, skills, and abilities of present owner-
managers and managers. Now we take a wider perspective in looking
at ways of meeting the future managerial skill requirements of small
firms. We examine alternative methods of increasing the availability
of managerial skills and techniques to the small firm and consider
some means of developing more effective approaches to the management problems of small firms.

For small firms the solving of management succession problems is crucial to the continued survival of the organization. Whether
the next generation of management are members of the present
owner-managers' families or whether they are nonfamily "outsiders,"
difficulties will arise in ensuring that they have the necessary skills
and knowledge to successfully take over the management of the firm.
In either case planning for management succession is an essential
prerequisite for the successful transfer of management. For the
family firm such planning has to be in the context of steps taken to
transfer the assets of the business and adequate arrangement for
meeting tax and estate duty liabilities. Small firms face a number
of unique difficulties in dealing with their management succession
problems. Typically small firms only occasionally have any need
to fill executive positions and so there is nobody in the firm with any
great experience of management recruitment. The usual approach,
therefore, is to rely on inquiries among friends and relations, or
to ask the auditor or the solicitor for suggestions. The whole process
of handling management succession problems in small firms is extremely haphazard. In many of the small companies studied by

Christensen, for example, failure to think ahead about succession problems had resulted in liquidation or forced sale of a business, in a period of unsatisfactory operations when an unseasoned manager assumed control, or in hurried selection of a new manager under time pressures that prevented selection of the man best fitted for the job. [8] Christensen suggests that there are a number of warning signals of pending management succession problems. These include situations where the owner-manager makes all the major decisions himself and his department heads are only assistants in charge of the routine business of the day; situations where a management group has grown old together; situations where a company is unwilling to make use of any external help; and situations where there is a stock-pile of unresolved problems in the business.

Christensen recognizes that there are a number of factors that limit the capacity a small firm has for developing managers. These include the small size of the management group, the domination of the firm by one man, lack of adequate financial resources, and methods of operating geared primarily to keeping the company alive in the face of strong competitive pressures. Small family firms also have to contend with some of the factors that we have outlined in Chapter 6. These include the desire to preserve family leadership with its consequent dangers of inbreeding and loss of new ideas, the lack of sufficient inducements to attract able professional managers into firms whose control is family-dominated, the stresses brought into such businesses as a consequence of family feuds and disputes, and the difficulties that crown princes may have in gaining acceptance from existing managers within the business. Christensen observed a number of approaches among those small firms that were most successful in handling their management development problems. He suggests that successful executive development in the small company involves using day-to-day problems and activities as a means of developing managers to assume more responsible positions. In this process the role and motivation of the owner-manager is crucial. The owner-manager's "heavy involvement in the detail of day-to-day operations, his concentration on immediate tactics rather than on longer-run strategy, his ability to do rather than to teach, and his essentially optimistic philosophy that things will turn out all right do much to explain his lack of success in working out provision for management succession."[9] Successful approaches to the problem, therefore, were observed when it was clear that the owner-manager was able to sense the teaching opportunities inherent in the day-to-day problems and situations that confronted his management group, when he recognized that the development of his organization was de-pendent upon some change in his own pattern of work and in his idio-syncratic methods of running the company, and when he appreciated that management development was an important responsibility that demanded time and effort, raised problems, and cost money. Those small businesses that have successfully provided for continuity of management have, Christensen suggests, three common attributes: (1) a willingness to look ahead and make advance preparations for the period of crisis; (2) the presence of some counsel or advice, independent of the immediate management group, which can arouse interest in the problems and make sure that it receives continuing attention; and (3) a willingness on the part of the owner-manager to change the pattern of his day-to-day working relationships in order to increase the participation of other members of his organization and to develop strong candidates for his own position, even though this may make him, or seem to make him, less indispensable to the business.

As well as developing their own managerial talent internally, it seems likely that there should increasingly be scope for the employment of graduate managers in small companies and particularly for business school graduates. But there is a wide communications gap to be bridged.[10] Most small firms have no notion of how to establish contact with potential managers of graduate caliber, of what they could expect from them, and of how they could utilize professional management skills within their firms. Nor, in fairness, have many of the universities and business schools attempted to acquaint themselves with the opportunities that exist within small firms or with the different nature of the managerial problems of small companies compared with those of large organizations. In addition, as we have seen, small firms frequently do not have the financial resources to attract the caliber of "outsider" they need. Their managerial resources may be centered in one man, the owner-manager, or dispersed among a small and aging managerial group. When the management succession crisis comes it often brings with it a crisis in financial ownership and the external advice and counsel that is needed to deal with such a crisis is not readily available or is sought too late to be of any benefit. Small-firm owner-managers need to be made aware of the difficulties that will arise if they do not take adequate steps at the right time to ensure a smooth handover of management and ownership. Outside counsel and assistance, provided through part-time board directors, through Ex-Ex groups or problem clinics, through opportunities for detailed discussions with friends and business associates, or through the professional advice of the owner-manager's accountant, solicitor, or bank manager, or from other sources, are probably necessary if succession plans are to be successfully formulated and carried through. The owner-manager himself has to be encouraged to give other members of the managerial group within his firm the opportunity to take on increased responsibilities in order to strengthen the group from which his successor may be chosen. This necessitates a willingness on the owner-manager's part to change the pattern of his daily work and to take direct responsibility for the development of his subordinates, using day-to-day problems and activities as a means of training them to assume greater responsibilities. Whether a particular owner-manager is suited to playing the role of coach and developer to his subordinate managers will depend largely on his personality characteristics. If he is not able to develop the necessary skills then they can, perhaps, be provided by someone from outside the company.

There are a number of other areas where the small firm has to seek direct external advice and help rather than try to develop skills among existing owner-managers and managers. This is most obviously the case in respect to professional advice from the bank manager, accountant, or solicitor. Here there is a need to inform owner-managers of the kinds of service available from such professional advisers and to acquaint the professions with the particular problems and needs of small businessmen. By themselves many small firms cannot afford to employ directly the specialist management services they require. In addition their requirement for such services will frequently be of a piecemeal and occasional kind and not of such a kind as to justify permanent employment of a specialist manager. Similarly, such firms may feel they cannot afford to buy-in commercial consultants on a continuing basis in order to help them deal with their problems. Attention needs to be given, therefore, to the development of group management services for small companies, such group services possibly to be set up along lines similar to those of successful British group training schemes. (In the United Kingdom, group training schemes, encouraged by the Industrial Training Boards, are generally formed when a number of small firms, normally within reasonable geographical distance from each other and belonging to the same or similar trades, decide to join together to provide themselves with training services they might otherwise not be able to afford. A central feature of such schemes is generally the appointment of a qualified training officer to develop training for all member firms within the group.) The principles on which a group management service might operate would be somewhat different from those of conventional consultancy services, although the content of some of the services provided might well be similar. In particular the specialist manager employed by a group of small firms could carry out specific pieces of work in each of the companies in his group and have some executive responsibilities within each firm. The development of group management services would not only create a pool of professional managers who were familiar with the day-to-day problems of running a small firm, thereby perhaps providing a solution to the succession difficulties of a number of small companies, but would also provide career opportunities for those business graduates, experienced managers, and consultants who would be more happily employed in general management in a small firm than in a highly specialized position in a large corporation. Just as the principle embodied in the group training schemes could usefully be extended to common management services, so the role of the training adviser or group training officer could usefully be extended in a number of directions. A number of such specialist staff have skills in other fields, such as work-study or personnel management, which could be applied in the small-firm context; they could, for example, assist owner-managers in the selection of new staff, in the design and introduction of new payment systems, or in some simple planning to meet future manpower needs.

If the management training and development needs of small firms are to be more adequately met in the future then, in addition to developing more effective individual and group training methods for small-firm owner-managers and managers, it will also be necessary in Britain to develop the resources and skills of advisers and consultants who may be called upon to assist small companies either directly in-company or through participation in external training activities. Management studies departments in educational institutions might usefully design and run job-specific management training workshops for selected small firms in their locality, incorporating the areas of need identified by research. Similarly, consultancy organizations need to familiarize themselves with the special problems involved in the training and development of small-firm owner-managers and managers and to develop better methods of meeting the needs that exist.

THE ROLE OF TRAINING AGENCIES

While there has recently been increasing interest in the small-firm sector in a number of European countries, notably in Britain, other European countries, particularly Scandinavian countries, have lengthy experience in attempting to encourage the development of their small business sectors and in trying to stimulate training programs for owner-managers and managers of small firms. In Denmark, for example, the government-aided but self-governing Technological Institute in Copenhagen has been involved in training programs for small-industry owners since 1906.[11] During its early years the main purpose of the Institute's training and service activities was to raise technological standards in small enterprises. Increased demand for special courses in management techniques led,

however, to the establishment in the 1920s of a Management Division
to develop training in management economics for small-firm owners.
In 1942 a one-year part-time management training course was started
for small-business owners and skilled workers who had a journeyman's certificate. The program covered general business economics
subjects such as bookkeeping, the analysis of accounts, costs, and
prices, and business law, and at the end of the course students could
take an examination for a Master's Certificate. In 1956 the Institute
established a regional management service for handicraft and small
industry structured around ten district consultants, each coordinating
the activities of from 10 to 15 instructors. These instructors were
small-business owners who, after training, were able with the help
of specially prepared manuals to give short evening courses for their
colleagues in the local district. The Institute found that one of the
advantages of using small-business owners as instructors was that
communication during the course between instructors and participants
was not limited by the usual distance between pupil and teacher; the
instructor, being a local business owner himself, could talk in
language which the participants were familiar with and understood.
Since 1967 the Institute, together with the Jutland Technological Institute founded in 1943, has also been involved in training and consultancy projects for small industry in sparsely industrialized areas.
The purpose of any project is to assist small-industry owners within
a local area to improve the industrial environment in the area, and
to investigate possibilities for cooperation between the participating
enterprises. This is achieved through general business analyses of
the participating enterprises, through group training for the owners
and managers in the functions of management, and through discussion activities in which labor organizations, local credit institutions,
and local government representatives also participate. In many
cases companies have found opportunities for cooperation on such
matters as marketing, product development, in-plant training, and
distribution.

The Norwegian Government Institute of Technology, set up in
1917 under the auspices of the Norwegian Ministry of Education, has
three primary objectives: (1) to increase the proficiency of skilled
workers, foremen, vocational teachers, and managers in subjects
of importance to their occupations and to keep them informed of new
developments, thereby increasing the technical and managerial proficiency of Norwegian industry as a whole; (2) to provide a consultancy
and advisory service primarily for small-and medium-sized firms in
the manufacturing, handicrafts, and construction industries, thereby
helping such firms to increase their efficiency through practical
advice; and (3) to carry on applied research and testing that is co-
ordinated and supports the educational and consulting efforts of the

Institute.[12] The Institute's Business Administration Section, established in 1958, runs a variety of courses primarily aimed at increasing the level of knowledge in business subjects of managers in small- and medium-sized manufacturing and handicraft enterprises, together with consultancy operations mainly geared to the introduction of standardized cost accounting systems and the carrying out of inter-firm cost comparisons. The Institute also has nine district offices that were set up to provide a management consultancy and educational service on a regional basis. The activities of these offices include running special sessions on a group basis to create contacts between firms and to enable managers to help one another in solving problems. The experience of the Norwegian Institute suggested that the number of firms reached by these methods, given the capacity and financial resources of the agency, was too small and that what was required to widen the impact of the institute were methods of teaching owner-managers to learn on their own account. The Institute has found a number of ways of promoting this kind of self-learning. These include management conferences where owner-managers from 10 to 12 firms in a neighborhood come together for three or four days to discuss, with the help of an analysis of their firms prepared by members of the Institute, problems faced by their companies. They also include the preparation of common training programs for all the firms in a defined geographical area, and the performance of consultancy tasks for a group of firms at the same time.

Agencies vary from country to country. In Austria the Regional Economic Chambers, which have a statutory basis dating back to 1850 and are financed by levies on member firms, provide focal points for small-company management development. In Ireland the Irish Management Institute set up a small-industries program in 1968. The Institute's Small Business Division works closely with regional technical and vocational colleges of the educational system. In Sweden the Employers' Confederation has developed a business analysis package for small businessmen under the title "Look After Your Firm." The package is intended as working material for direct use in small companies by entrepreneurs and is designed to give them simple measures for reviewing the efficiency and profitability of their firms. In the United Kingdom the Industrial Training Boards are the training agency that has had the greatest single impact on management training and development practices in small firms. Boards have been active in promoting group training associations, thereby giving many small companies access to professional training staff for the first time and bringing them the financial benefits of the application of modern training methods, and have developed and implemented a variety of methods of providing relevant and realistic training assistance to small companies, particularly in the context of their management problems.

All these agencies face a number of common problems in dealing with small companies, and the evolution of agency activities over the years reflects their attempts to come to grips with these problems. A number of agencies started out by offering short introductory management courses for small firms, often on marketing or finance. Gradually, however, they have shifted their activities toward more and more project-based courses, consultancy, and in-company development and coaching assignments. Even the Swedish Employers Confederation with their prepackaged do-it-yourself kits found that, because initially they had not provided any follow-up to sales, many of the kits had served as decoration for the offices of small businessmen; consequently, the Confederation began to look for ways to link sales of the kit to some effective in-company training and development activity. Agencies have gradually, and in some cases reluctantly, shifted away from a center-periphery learning model. [13] That is, they have come to realize that the problem is not one where they, at the center, are the source of all wisdom about small-firm management and simply need to find suitable mechanisms for communicating their knowledge to the owner-manager peasants out in the peripheral "sticks" somewhere. Rather, the agency role is more that of a catalyst, promoting learning and self-development within individual firms and among individual owner-managers and providing resources and expertise that can be called upon when required, and perceived to be required, by owner-managers. In such a system agencies may share a number of new problems. These will include such questions as the motivation and goals of owner-managers, the relevance of operational management techniques in the small-company context, the use of specific rather than general material in training programs, the high cost of servicing individual management training and development needs and questions surrounding the measurement of the effectiveness of different kinds of management training and development activity.

Training agencies need, therefore, to ensure that the emphasis in the training and development of small-firm owner-managers and managers is shifted away from general external training courses toward a more active, in-company involvement of those training advisory staff and consultants who know the backgrounds and problems of the managers and their firms and who are continually available to offer practical help as well as advice. Training agencies could also usefully consider extending the range of their training and development services to cover all aspects of manpower utilization with particular attention to the managerial manpower resources of small firms. They could strive to offer their client firms a manpower

advisory service, rather than solely a training advisory service.
Such a manpower service, as well as dealing with training matters,
might cover such items as direct recruitment and selection assistance to firms, career information and publicity on career opportunities, help with company manpower forecasting and planning, and
guidance on industrial relations matters, on issues concerning manpower productivity, on job design and work organization, and on the
possible applications of organizational development programs within
small companies.

Even given the limited financial motivations of many owner-
managers, there is considerable scope for improving the economic
performance of small firms and the utilization of the human and
physical resources they employ. Our attempts in Chapter 8 to quantify the training and development needs of small-firm owner-managers
and managers, and to compare those needs with the level of training
activity actually taking place, indicated a serious deficiency in training activity in the small firms studied. At the same time as encouraging an increase in the quantity of management training and development in the small-firm sector, we suggested that it is necessary to
ensure that the training available is suitable in content to the particular requirements of small firms and their owner-managers and managers. It is our view that considerable potential economic benefits
remain untapped in the small-firm sector, that these benefits can be
released by the development of the skills of small-firm owner-
managers and managers, and that effective development programs
must be largely client-centered, that is, highly specific to the industry, company, and job of the individual manager. Of the many
difficulties faced by external training and development agencies in
dealing with small-firm clients, therefore, among the most crucial
will be those surrounding the motivations, expectations, perceptions,
and attitudes of owner-managers both in respect to their work and in
terms of their perspectives on external agencies. We have seen in
Chapter 5, for example, how some management training and development needs stem from specific company weaknesses. This was
particularly clear when considering the profitability and growth and
the financial and cost structures of many small firms. It is important to know, however, the extent to which company weaknesses are
recognized by small-firm owner-managers and what their perception
is of the strengths and weaknesses of their firms. In general we saw
that owner-managers were more aware of company strengths than of
company weaknesses and saw their strengths lying in many areas,
and their weaknesses as being highly specific to a few areas only.
In addition, a number of owner-managers, while recognizing specific weaknesses in their companies, believed that such weaknesses
arose primarily through factors outside their control and that,

consequently, there was no action that they themselves could take to strengthen their companies' performance in the weak areas. Such "external" factors were generally the current levels of demand, the state of the capital market, or the state of the labor market. Even where needs are perceived by owner-managers, there may not be the will to tackle them in an energetic way.

Similar problems arise in terms of the perceptions that owner-managers have of external agencies. In the United Kingdom, for example, small companies tend to have a particularly ambivalent attitude toward governments and government agencies. On the one hand they make great play with their resentment of any kind of outside interference in their affairs, with the growing burden of the civil service and the "bureaucrats" on their backs, with what they see as ever-increasing demands from government departments and other bodies for form-filling and paperwork. But at the same time many small firms in Britain feel they have been neglected by successive governments. They resent interference, therefore, but want help. The difficulty has been that too much of the so-called interference has not been seen by the small-firm clients to be related in any way to their specific problems. Industrial Training Boards in the United Kingdom reflect this interference-help ambivalence of small companies, particularly in the area of management training and development. Most small companies are very much aware of the management problems they face and do want relevant help with their problems. But they frequently find that management education and training programs available externally to the firm are too sophisticated for their particular needs and so they look upon them as irrelevant and a waste of time. The need, however, for outside counsel and assistance is clear in a number of areas. In the context of management succession problems, for example, Christensen observed that, without guidance and advice from individuals who are not a part of his daily operating team, the small businessman typically relegates the succession problem to the category of "things to be done next week."[14] He suggests, however, that, while the value of outside counsel to the small businessman can be demonstrated, the medium may be as important as the message. Informal counseling arrangements in particular appeal to the owner-manager, especially if the arrangements are such that the owner-manager has personally taken the initiative in developing his own source of help and retains full independence to accept or reject suggestions made. Christensen's research indicates that the agencies in the United States that have proved most successful in working with small businesses have had a number of common characteristics. First, they have given special attention to the problems of small companies; second, there has been a willingness on the part of the staff of the agency to spend enough time with the small-firm owner-managers to have a substantial knowledge of the specific situation in the company over a period of time; and, third, they have avoided giving the appearance of overwhelming the small businessman with a barrage of experts. If the agency allows the owner-manager to remain independent in making his decisions and yet can provide help from someone long familiar with him and his company then his usual reluctance toward taking advice and assistance from outside the firm can be overcome.

SUMMARY

Education, training, and development processes in the small firm need to be person- or job-specific, be geared to the educational levels and abilities of the owner-managers and managers taking part, be conducted in as informal an atmosphere as possible, concentrate on "learning by doing," and build on the experiences of the owner-managers and managers themselves. Courses with the traditional teacher-learner structure will have little part to play in such processes, except as information inputs on technological matters and on management techniques and as part of any general educational process. In the context of the small-firm owner-manager, therefore, the variety of management training and development methods available needs to be viewed with three assumptions in mind: (1) that the greatest need is for the development of job-specific programs; (2) that such programs must be geared to the development of those entrepreneurial skills associated with successful small business management; and (3) that it will be necessary to find education, training, and development methods that minimize the demands made on the working time of owner-managers and managers.

The kind of management training and development methods likely to prove more appropriate in the small-firm context are case studies, problem-solving and decision-making exercises, business games and simulations, intercompany exchange assignments, project work, problem clinics, Ex-Ex groups, and in-company coaching. Other useful methods are self-appraisal and self-development techniques that involve the owner-manager in recognizing his own training needs and taking appropriate action. Most of those agencies working in the field of small-firm management training and development have only limited financial resources available and consequently need to shift as much responsibility as possible onto the owner-managers and managers themselves and to guide them toward self-development situations. The role of many training agencies is primarily a catalytic one, being concerned with the development of

management systems and techniques or with the dcvclopment of
tailor-made training course methods, before passing them out to
those who will be involved in the detailed running of a range of
training and development activities geared to the needs of small
firms. The concern of all agencies should be with the promotion of
individualized and small-group training and development practices
for owner-managers and managers of small firms and with the
spread of client-centered environment and experience-based learning systems.

NOTES

1. K. B. Mayer and S. Goldstein, The First Two Years:
Problems of Small Firm Growth and Survival, Small Business Ad-
ministration Research Series No. 2 (Washington, D.C.: Small
Business Administration, 1961).

2. A. S. Glickman, C. P. Hahn, E. A. Fleishman, and B.
Baxter, Top Management Development and Succession: An Exploratory Study (New York: Macmillan, 1968).

3. P. F. Drucker, "Management's New Role," Harvard
Business Review 47, no. 6 (November-December 1969): 49-54.

4. See L. R. Sayles, Managerial Behavior: Administration
in Complex Organizations (New York: McGraw-Hill, 1964).

5. S. M. Lipset and R. Bendix, "Social Mobility and Occupational Career Patterns," American Journal of Sociology, January
and March 1952, pp. 366-74 and 494-504.

6. This description of the Swiss Ex-Ex groups is based on:
H. J. Pleitner, "Small Business Management Development by the
Swiss Research Institute of Small Business," unpublished paper
presented to the International Seminar on Small Business Management Development in Europe, Irish Management Institute, Dublin,
1971.

7. See Employment of Older Workers (Paris: Organization
for Economic Cooperation and Development, 1965).

8. C. R. Christensen, Management Succession in Small and
Growing Enterprises (Boston: Harvard University Graduate School
of Business Administration, 1953).

9. Ibid.

10. See A. C. Filley, "Today's College Graduate and Small
Business," in Studies in Managerial Process and Organizational
Behavior, ed. J. H. Turner, A. C. Filley, and R. J. House
(Glenview, Ill.: Scott, Foresman, 1972), pp. 461-65. Filley haz-
ards the prediction that in the future a greater percentage of college
graduates will start or operate small businesses and that this will

lead to more active recruitment and employment of graduates in the small-business sector.

11. Information based on: O. Bergh-Hanssen, "Management Training at the Technological Institute in Denmark," unpublished paper presented to the International Seminar on Small Business Management Development in Europe, op. cit.

12. Information based on: H. Hauge, "Activities of the Norwegian Government Institute of Technology," unpublished paper presented to the International Seminar on Small Business Management Development in Europe, op. cit.

13. See D. A. Schon, Beyond the Stable State (London: Temple Smith, 1971).

14. Christensen, op. cit.

14

SOCIAL AND
ECONOMIC POLICIES
FOR SMALL BUSINESS

In Chapter 4 it was argued that small companies will continue to have a number of important economic roles in advanced industrial societies, roles that will differ between industrial and business sectors and between national economies. It was suggested that different stages in the industrialization process coexist within any economy and that small-business survival is inevitable and necessary to economic development. The research studies, described in Part II, have indicated that there is scope for improving the economic performance of small firms and for helping them to make better use of the resources they employ. Chapter 13 described the education, training, and development processes that might appropriately be used to release the unused potential of owner-managers and discussed the problems facing agencies working with such an objective in view. There the emphasis was primarily on development from within the small firm, accepting the goals of each enterprise primarily in the terms defined by their owners.

In this chapter we will try to look at small firms in a broader context. Discussed will be the problems involved in establishing, from a national or governmental point of view, the place of small businesses in the social and economic structure of a country and the kinds of policy objectives that we feel governments should pursue in respect of small enterprises. This inevitably takes us into questions of external stimuli and controls that may be applied by governments to the small-business sector, into questions of manpower policy and their social implications, into questions of financial policy and their impact on the behavior of owner-managers, and into the complex relationship between entrepreneurship and economic development. It is necessary to make clear, therefore, that these are not areas in which we lay claim to any special expertise nor do we attempt to do more than skate over the surface of the problems that exist, in practice no doubt falling through thin ice on numerous occasions. What we do hope, however, is that we are able to achieve a better integration of theoretical perspectives on the small-business sector with the realities revealed by our study of owner-managers.

SETTING THE OBJECTIVES

Perhaps the major difficulty in discussing the objectives that any elected government might most sensibly pursue in the context of small business is the difficulty of disentangling the question from its political overtones. Small businessmen are not slow to act vociferously and cohesively to protect their interests and constitute a political lobby that is usually mobilized in defense of a free-enterprise system and against government interference of any kind. In Britain, for example, the Smaller Businesses' Association listed 11 "good reasons" for the continued existence of small businesses:

1. They preserve the FREE ENTERPRISE nature of our country.

2. They show a larger return on investment due to the GREATER EFFICIENCY of the smaller businesses.

3. INDUSTRIAL DISPUTES are practically unknown in smaller businesses.

4. They preserve and encourage REAL COMPETITION in the face of mergers and monopolies and this helps to keep prices down.

5. They provide a large and diversified source of CONTENTED EMPLOYMENT for people at all levels from operator to manager.

6. They are the principal source of NEW IDEAS and INVENTIONS.

7. The resilient factor in the economy is the smaller business. It adapts itself more quickly to CHANGING MARKET CONDITIONS, and neither needs or calls for government support.

8. A large number of independent businesses decreases the likelihood of EXCESSIVE CONCENTRATION of economic and political power.

9. If small businesses cease to exist, many major industries would be in SERIOUS DIFFICULTIES, (e.g., 70 percent of every British car comes from a subcontractor).

10. They provide an efficient reservoir of FUTURE management.

11. They are an encouragement to the best and the most enterprising ENTREPRENEURS to risk their own capital--for their own profit, but to the inestimable national good.[1]

As we have seen, the evidence to support such assertions, rather like the much-vaunted independence of the small businessman, is in many cases more mythical than real. Nevertheless it would seem that policies pursued by governments are as likely to be formulated on the basis of the myths as on the realities, a practice which in itself perpetuates the myths. The British Conservative party, for example, is able to appeal both to the established traditional conservative businessman of our literary medieval stereotype and to the individualistic radical entrepreneur of the classical economic model. In Britain it is clear, on the basis of the little evidence that we have of the party affiliations or voting behavior of owner-managers, that the majority of small businessmen are supporters of Conservative government. Since, as we have seen, many owner-managers come from manual occupational backgrounds and from socioeconomic situations in which a pattern of Labour party support would probably be the norm, we must assume that the upward social mobility associated with small business ownership leads to a greater identification with middle-class political attitudes and beliefs. It becomes difficult, therefore, for Conservative administrations to pursue policies that might contradict the preservation of existing mythologies about the small-business sector, even though the realities of the economic situation of many small firms might dictate such policies. Thus attempts by Conservative administrations to control or regulate or stimulate the small-business sector must be dressed up as self-help projects, or as measures to redress the balance between large and small firms, or as in the best long-term interests of small businessmen themselves.

But political parties on all sides are likely to be equally imprisoned by their inherited stereotypes of the small-business sector. A traditional plank of a number of European democratic socialist parties has been public ownership, through nationalization, of companies operating in certain key areas of the economy. In all probability, to extend such a policy to small enterprises would be absurd and unworkable, yet generally no alternative policy or rationale is formulated to deal with the small-firm sector.

> There exists among European intellectuals [says Jean-Francoise Revel] a certain aristocratic

disdain for the lower middle class, and for the
small businessman in particular. It is the disdain of the clerk for the tradesman, and of the
socialist for the small "proprietor"--even if
the latter is actually nothing more than a hired
manager. After the referendum of April 27,
1969, in which a large number of intellectuals'
votes had contributed to the downfall of Gaullism,
a certain number of leftist spokesmen expressed
contempt for this victory (which had put an end
to eleven years of autocracy) on the grounds that
it represented "the triumph of the shopkeepers."
This phrase of itself is sufficient indication of
how the French Left, particularly among its intellectuals, is devoid of democratic sentiment.
When a university professor, or a Parisian
journalist, makes a neighborhood grocer the
target of his attacks on the grounds that the latter is representative of the capitalist class, he
is not only being odious on the moral level; he
is also making a political blunder--a blunder
which will assure that the petite bourgeoisie
will swing permanently to the Right in times of
economic difficulty. It is obvious that reality is
being sacrificed to ideological considerations
when, in countries in which the middle classes
constitute the largest part of the social scale and
are often a decisive factor in cultural evolution,
the middle classes are excluded from the revolutionary table of organization. Ideology requires
that the revolutionary class be composed exclusively of industrial workers--and ignores the fact that
these workers are themselves part of the middle
class.[2]

While the thesis of working-class embourgeoisement lacks a sound
empirical base,[3] the disdain of the socialist theoretician for the
petite bourgeoisie is part of a long-standing tradition, a tradition
that persists in spite of both the evidence of the professed aspirations of many industrial workers to enter the ranks of the self-
employed, and the demonstrable difference in socioeconomic status
between the little-business owner-operator or small-business owner-
manager and the entrepreneur or capitalist of classical economic
theory.

But what, then, are the factors that need to be borne in mind
when considering the role of small enterprises in the social and

economic fabric of a nation? In our view there are four key points.
First, small firms cannot be ignored, either socially or economically. From an economic point of view, significant physical and productive resources are tied up in small companies. In total they represent an important asset within an advanced industrial economy even if,
in the United Kingdom, it is an asset that is both underdeveloped and
depreciating. The potential economic contribution of small firms
may be curtailed by the limited administrative and entrepreneurial
skills and abilities of their owner-managers, or by their lack of economic motivation. It is also likely to be curtailed or stimulated by
the kind of climate created by government policy. In Britain inadequate appreciation and understanding by successive governments of
how the small firm fits into overall social and economic development
has resulted in a lack of systematic attempts to formulate policies
relevant to the small firm's needs and objectives that incorporate
any vision of alternatives to the status quo in the relationship between
the business sector of the society and the culture of the society.
From a social point of view, by which we mean the point of view of
the kind of society that is created rather than the means whereby it
is created--although economic means and social ends are inevitably
intertwined--the small firm fulfills a number of important functions
within an industrial society. For example, it creates career opportunities for those without extensive formal educational qualifications
and an outlet for their energies and abilities, in many cases it provides the owner-operator and owner-manager with a psychological
contract of a more satisfactory kind than he could find as an employee,
and it preserves in some instances a set of values increasingly relevant to organizations of all sizes. Second, new enterprises should
be encouraged. If we are correct in concluding that founder-managed
small businesses are in general more profitable than inheritor-
managed enterprises, then there is obvious economic logic in pursuing policies that stimulate the development of new enterprises rather
than policies primarily geared to the preservation of the old. Similarly many of the psychological ties between the owner and his work,
which we described in Chapters 10 and 11, are stronger for founders
than for inheritors. Third, enterprise continuity is important but
family inheritance is not. Consequently, policies toward small
business should be concerned with developing managerial skills
within the enterprise, with discouraging any automatic transfer of
ownership from founders to inheritors, and with finding methods to
facilitate the introduction of fresh administrative and entrepreneurial
skills into small companies. The continuity that is being sought,
therefore, is continuity of employment for those who work in the firm
rather than continuity of ownership for the founding family. Fourth,
neither the waste of economic resources nor the stifling of individual
psychological growth are in the long-term interests of society.

Nevertheless there is undoubted conflict between the economic goal of the most efficient use of productive resources, measured in terms of the ratio of outputs to inputs in any productive process, and the social goal of individual development and growth through work. Our assumption, underlying the further discussion of policy measures that follows, is that the individual should not be unwittingly used, or coerced into use, as a means to ends over which he has no control and that any business enterprise has to account, to its members and to the community at large, both for its social function and for the social and psychological consequences of its internal processes.

MANPOWER POLICIES AND THE SMALL FIRM

Our assumptions about the key points underlying the formulation of more realistic and better integrated social and economic policies for the small-firm sector have a number of implications in the area of manpower policy. In particular they highlight problems surrounding the nature of ownership and decision-making in small enterprises, problems of managerial succession and continuity, and problems concerning the relationship between the individual and his work. It is to these problems that we now turn.

The idea of the "typical" employee being merely a cog in a vast industrial machine, or a cipher in a large impersonal bureaucracy, has had the weight and authority of many years of sociological research to support it and give it momentum. As a result, studies of the relationships between people and their work--behavioral studies, motivational studies, organizational studies-- have been almost exclusively undertaken in large organizations and a whole range of elaborate theories have been built around their findings. In fact the "typical" employee is just as likely to work in an organization that, in terms of numbers of people, is smaller than the secondary school he attended. He probably knows most of the other people in the firm passably well and is possibly related to one or more of them. It may even be that he likes his work and finds satisfaction in the job itself and in the progress of the firm as a whole. As we have seen in Part II, in the small firm formal communications systems are often of relatively minor importance and face-to-face contacts between the owner-manager and his employees may be frequent. In the small firm the managerial process is ostensibly a more visible process than in the larger organization, more visible, that is, to the members of the organization itself. The employee does know who the boss is--warts and all. It is necessary, therefore, to modify some of the arguments that have grown up around the notion that the typical modern industrial worker

is "alienated" from his work, that he is an isolated self-estranged
individual lacking any sense of membership in an occupational or industrial community, without commitment to the work itself or to
other members of the work organization, feeling controlled and
manipulated by others or by an impersonal system or technology
whose domination he cannot modify, treating work as a purely instrumental activity with no intrinsic value of its own, one of "a galley
of automatons locked in dreams."[4] The notion of the alienated employee cannot, however, be completely dismissed in the context of
the small firm. There would appear to be three major strands in
the alienation argument, an economic strand that emphasizes the
economic division of interest between capital and labor and the
corresponding powerlessness of the individual employee, a sociological strand that emphasizes the meaninglessness and normless-
ness of work tasks consequent upon the highly specialized division
of labor in large-scale enterprises, and a psychological strand that
emphasizes the self-estrangement, personal isolation, and inadequate
psychological contracts that result from using the individual employee
as a tool, as a means to others' ends. In the small firm, individual
job design may not be so psychologically inadequate as in many large
organizations and the management structure not so imposing or re-
mote. Nevertheless the economic division between employer and employed remains, tempered in some cases by the proximity of one to
the other and the possibilities for each of influencing the other's
thinking, exacerbated in other cases by the owner-manager's capri-
cious exercise of his authority and by his retention to himself of all
major decision-making functions in the firm. We would suggest that
a cornerstone of any manpower policy for small enterprises should
be efforts to widen the basis of ownership of the small firm as a
framework for greater involvement and participation by all members
of an enterprise in its decision-making processes. In such a way
the psychological benefits that owner-managers at present enjoy in
relation to their work situations could be spread. The extension of
"felt" ownership rights provided by increased participation in
decision-making would need to be supported by an extension of legal
ownership rights that, in turn, could be provided either by some
scheme of employee shareholding control or by company legislation
that eliminated the legal dominance of the shareholders in the corporate structure.

    There are a number of other aspects of manpower policy where
small businesses face more tangible problems. We have already
discussed, in Chapter 13, management recruitment and succession
problems and the need to develop management training and development programs geared to the needs of small companies. If management succession problems are to be handled with the objective of

providing for the continuity of the enterprise rather than for the transfer of ownership from generation to generation of owning families, then methods have to be devised to provide guidance on occupational choices for the relatives of owners. In Spain, for example, a number of proposals have been put forward to deal with the problems of the continuity and evolution of the family firm. These include the creation of advisory boards, or other deliberative bodies at top level in the firm, which would include a nonfamily executive and a management expert from outside the firm; the establishment of policies on the education, training, and development of those children of the owners' families who have the inclination, motivation, and necessary aptitudes and abilities to enter the business; the establishment of groups of managers from family firms who get together with management experts in order to present, study, and propose solutions for family-firm problems common to their organizations; and the formation of groups within which managers from family firms can discuss the subject of the education, occupational choice, and professional training of their children.[5] Such policies are geared, therefore, not only to providing management continuity for the small firm but also to keeping out unsuitable family members who may be attracted or coerced into the business.

One of the research reports commissioned by the Bolton Committee of Inquiry on Small Firms also made a number of recommendations designed to raise the level of management skill in the small company, to enlarge the pool of entrepreneurial and administrative skills on which small firms could draw, and to spread the opportunities for developing new enterprises, recommendations largely ignored by the committee itself in its own report. The research report concluded, on the basis of its analysis of a sample of small firms, that the small firm in Britain

> is still overwhelmingly proprietorially and family managed with 76 percent of chief executives having a significant stake in the business but recruited from extremely narrow bounds and typically without formal qualifications. The sector is in relative decline, with high mortality and very marked variability in growth rates. Some 50 percent of firms are adversely affected by declining or static markets or technological or economic change which rendered the small firm relatively less viable. Management ability, as evidenced by new markets and products, is the main factor differentiating the fast and slow growers, while the founder-managed firms

> showed outstanding growth despite the total ab-
> sence of formal qualifications and in many
> cases no direct prior experience of the industry
> concerned. [6]

The authors of the report go on to argue that their data suggest that
the small firm provides an important field of opportunity and advancement for individuals who, because of lack of qualifications, would
have little chance of comparable opportunities in the professions, in
government service or in large companies; that the small firm is to
an exceptional degree adversely affected by a combination of declining or static markets and technological or economic change; and that
the growth and efficiency of the small-firm sector is materially influenced by the inflow of new and better management to offset the
relatively poor performance of traditional managements. Three
recommendations are made in the research report to improve the
social and economic efficiency of the small-firm sector: (1) the establishment of a small-firm management training center; (2) the establishment of a related recruitment and placement center for small-
firm management; and (3) tax reforms to facilitate the participation
in or acquisition of small firms by new management: "These proposals all have as their central objectives more efficient exploitation
of the pool of entrepreneurial/managerial talent on which the efficiency of the small firm sector would appear to depend, while at the
same time enhancing the career opportunities open to this particular
sector of the nation's labour force." [7]

MOTIVATION FOR ENTREPRENEURSHIP

Proposals that involve some external stimuli to the foundation,
growth, or development of small businesses, either directly through
government policies or indirectly through the work of government or
quasi-government agencies, inevitably come up against the belief
that small businessmen, in Britain at least, are totally hostile to
outside help or interference, a belief based as we have seen on the
notion of the small businessman as an independent entrepreneur
jealously protecting his economic freedom of action. Thus the Bolton
Committee, commenting on what it sees as the declining social status
of the entrepreneur and the demoralization consequent upon the
small businessman's loss of confidence in the mastery of his fate,
suggests that the "malaise of small business . . . appears to be
compounded of three elements: resentment caused by a long term
and irreversible decline in the small businessman's ability to control his environment; a sense of persecution caused by the detrimental

side effects, deliberate or not, of the activities of Government; and
frustration at the delays and impediments arising from the sheer
multiplicity of official regulations and requirements."[8] In countries
other than Britain, however, there has been less reluctance to "interfere" with the small-business sector by offering advisory and
other services. In the United States, for example, the Small Business Administration was set up in 1953 as a federal agency wholly
occupied with the administration of policies intended to promote the
interests and increase the efficiency of small firms. The Small
Business Administration for many years provided long-term loans,
generally well below commercial rates, to small enterprises, an
activity subsequently replaced by a loan guarantee scheme and by
Economic Opportunity Loans to racial minorities and the underprivileged. The Small Business Administration also provides a
wide range of advisory services, mostly free, including direct in-
company counseling on technical or management problems, the provision of courses and seminars and the publication of numerous
pamphlets and books on management techniques for small-firm
managers. Rather ironically, therefore, the U.S. government has
gone to considerable expense to underwrite traditional values of
free enterprise and personal independence, thereby further increasing the erosion of those values. In Japan too, the Small Business
Promotion Corporation, an agency financed by the government, en-
courages the formation of small-business cooperatives and mergers
among small firms by providing them with cheap credit, consultancy
services, and training, and another government-financed agency,
the Small Business Finance Corporation, provides small companies
with long-term funds at low rates of interest. In France money

> is given from public funds for training and tech-
> nical aid of small firms in business. In Belgium
> a subsidy of 50 percent for the first day of a con-
> sultant's time and 25 percent for the second day
> is paid via the Trade Association; in Germany a
> subsidy of 50 percent to 75 percent of a set scale
> of consultant's fees is given to shops with a turn-
> over of less than £100,000 per annum. Ireland
> gives a subsidy of 50 percent of consultancy fees
> and Denmark gives the same up to a maximum of
> £250,000 per annum. . . . In comparison with
> these services, the small man in Britain stands
> in splendid isolation from the various forms of
> advice and aid available in other countries.[9]

The sanctity of the entrepreneur's independence as a basis for
policy formulation has, therefore, to be questioned, not only on the

grounds that it is a distortion of the socioeconomic reality of the situation in which most small businessmen operate, but also on the grounds that in a number of countries the small-business sector has received direct government support with, as far as one can judge, beneficial consequences. It becomes necessary to distinguish the motivation for entrepreneurship, which as we saw in Chapter 10 where we described the variety of aspirations and expectations of owner-managers is a diverse and somewhat confused subject, from the means by which entrepreneurship or owner-management of a small firm is made possible. The paradoxical situation can exist, and probably does exist, in which people who in all honesty believe they are motivated by the desire to be independent, are prepared to accept the very aid and assistance, from government, from creditors, from commercial finance houses, that denies their independent status under the guise of providing it. Perhaps it is not surprising that it is in Britain that the more conservative philosophy of the family business with its fear of external capital and religious suspicion of usury lingers on. This was the tradition in which the Victorian cabinet-maker James Hopkinson, who describes his small shopkeeper parents as "strictly moral people of the owe no man anything class Firm upholders of Church and state and <u>Tories</u> to the <u>back bone</u>,"[10] was brought up.

A further aspect of the importance that the question of entrepreneurial motivation has for the role of government in the small-business sector lies in the likely response of small businessmen to financial inducements, particularly those offered by the tax system. In Britain it has been frequently suggested that the tax system acts as a disincentive to new enterprise and is an important factor in the decline of the small-firm sector. The Bolton Committee, for example, while recognizing that there has never been any convincing demonstration of the relationship between effort or risk-taking in business and changes in taxation levels, nevertheless subscribes to the view that there is some direct, if long-term, relationship between taxes and the motivation of the small businessman:

> We have seen that small businessmen are by no means entirely motivated by the desire for wealth; they are also activated by many other motives, chief among them being the desire for economic independence. Nevertheless a man considering whether or not to start a business must weigh the potential financial benefits--the possibility of earning and accumulating a great deal more money than he could in most forms of employment--against the risks not merely of earning less than he otherwise might but

> also of bankruptcy. High and progressive rates
> of tax certainly reduce the rewards of success
> and may increase the risk of failure. They must
> therefore, in the long term, diminish the attrac-
> tions of self-employment. [11]

This may appear to be sound economic logic but is based, as we saw
in Chapter 11, on a flawed model of the decision-making processes
surrounding new business entry. If, as empirical studies suggest,
the behavior of as few as one in ten owner-managers conforms to
such a rational economic model, then the whole argument about tax
incentives or disincentives to risk-taking is irrelevant to a large
proportion of the small-firm population. You cannot effectively tax
into or out of existence what is essentially a product of a variety of
cultural and psychological factors. It is likely that even the 10 percent who conform to the more traditional economic model of business
behavior do so, not in that their decision to enter the ranks of the
self-employed is solely the result of economic variables, but in that
their choice of business venture and their approach to the setting up
of their enterprise is more rational in economic terms. Similarly
one must reject as unproven the Bolton Committee's view that taxes
on capital, especially estate duties, "seriously affect the motivation
of the small businessman" and that "many entrepreneurs are very
largely motivated by the wish to leave a thriving business and a
secure future for their families."[12] H. G. Wells' industrialist
William Clissold had this to say of that particular viewpoint:

> It is a venerated assumption among lawyers and
> suchlike preservers of antique psychology, that
> men work and organise great industries in or-
> der to "found families." I cannot imagine how
> anyone with the most rudimentary powers of ob-
> servation can repeat so foolish a statement. I
> doubt if any big business man or any big financial
> man for the last hundred years has done what he
> did for the sake of his family. Far more was it
> for the sake of the business. In former times of
> insecurity one may have looked to one's sons and
> connexions by marriage to hold together the es-
> tate one had created, but even then I believe the
> care was mainly for the estate. And nowadays,
> though sons or nephews may often prove con-
> genial junior partners, a really vigorous busi-
> ness man is much more likely to care for a
> capable stranger than for a disintegrative
> son. . . .

> No energetic directive people are deeply in
> love with inheritance; it loads the world with in-
> competent shareholders and wasteful spenders;
> it chokes the ways with their slow and wasteful
> lives; it is a fatty degeneration of property. [13]

The question of the motivation for entrepreneurship also has
a bearing on the viability of spreading the basis of small-firm ownership and of the wider participation in decision-making processes
that we have advocated. If the sole motive for self-employment was
a desire for independence, then any requirement that an enterprise
be set up on the basis of collective member ownership and control
would presumably provide a serious obstacle to the development of
new enterprises. As we have seen, however, a wide variety of
goals may be pursued by small-firm owner-managers and a wide
variety of motivations and aspirations may be present when the decision is made to found a new business. It may well be that for
many of those motivated toward new business ventures, the actual
corporate form or structure of the venture is likely to be a matter
of indifference. On the one hand there are those monocratic new
businesses that are extensions of the individual identity of their
founders, in which the "I-am-the-firm" and "It's-my-money" syn-
dromes are paramount. On the other hand there are those kinship-
based oligarchic enterprises, like the firm founded by four brothers
described in Chapter 6, where ownership is not concentrated in one
pair of hands and where some kind of collective decision-making
takes place. Certainly our experience during the fieldwork part of
the research program was that independent monocratic owners were
more likely to complain of the isolation of their position than were
oligarchic owners likely to complain of lack of personal autonomy
and the need for consultation with other owners prior to decision-
making. At the same time one must recognize the divisive effects
that family ownership can have in the management of a second-
generation firm in which the aura, authority, and ability of the
founder are no longer present to keep incompetent family fingers
out of the corporate pie. It would be misguided to suggest that any
one set of policy measures is going to achieve the objectives that
we have described. Nevertheless we find no reason to suppose,
and have seen no empirical data to suggest, that cooperative forms
of enterprise, entrepreneurial collectives, or other business
structures that combine member ownership and control, would be
antithetical to the self-development of the creative individual.

THE PROVISION OF FINANCE FOR
SMALL-BUSINESS ENTERPRISES

The management of finance is, as we saw in Chapter 8, a common area of training need for many owner-managers. It is also generally accepted that the availability of finance poses problems both for would-be entrepreneurs and for established small businesses. It is argued that small businessmen often lack the necessary capital to buy new plant or machinery, to modernize their existing facilities or extend their premises, or to tide them over short-term crises. Thus, for example, the London Chamber of Commerce, in its evidence to the Committee of Inquiry on Small Firms, reported that "many firms pointed out that had more capital been available they could have expanded both the range and scope of their activities in several directions."[14] A central theme of much of the other evidence submitted to the committee, especially the evidence of employers' associations, was that, in Britain, the percentage of business revenue that was removed by taxation made it extremely difficult to expand a small company by ploughing back profits. As a consequence small firms were increasingly dependent on external sources of finance.

As we have seen, the idea of raising money by selling a share in the business, with the associated belief that this implies that control will have to be relinquished by the owners, is repugnant to many owner-managers. Many small enterprises have started up with a little capital from personal or family savings. Even though such personal and family cash may not take the small businessman much beyond fairly modest premises, a few employees, and an output that falls short of the demand for his product, external finance of all kinds was found by the Bolton Committee to comprise "a very small proportion of the total capital employed in the small firm sector . . . long term loans together with bank loans and overdrafts accounted for about 14 percent of the total assets of the firms in our sample survey, compared with 19 percent for quoted companies. These average figures are misleading, however, since in the case of small firms they conceal extremely wide dispersions--from nil borrowing in a very large number of the smallest and static companies to very heavy borrowing indeed among the fastest growers."[15] Other studies have suggested both that the claimed problems that small businessmen face in financing their ventures are exaggerated and that they tend, when they do have recourse to external finance, to seek or find the wrong kind of money. Thus, for example, a survey of 15,500 companies, 95 percent of which had fewer than 50 employees, undertaken by the U.S. Department of Commerce in 1954, showed that 56 percent of the companies had no desire for outside financing and a further 24 percent had obtained all the financing they wanted. Thus, commented Paul Donham, "an amazing 80 percent were able to meet their financial needs either internally or from existing outside sources."[16] He goes on to argue that the remaining 20 percent are obviously the companies around which the financial problem is centered, the financial needs of small companies that have no dreams of expansion beyond their present markets, products, or geographical areas being adequately met from existing sources of funds. Of this 20 percent the vast majority (95 percent) sought loan capital and only a few (5 percent) sought more equity funds even though, says Donham, their needs were for money that would become a permanent part of their expanding enterprises. This prevalence of small companies that desire growth to seek to finance that growth with loan money reflects, he suggests, the demand for outright legal control that is "almost a fetish" with many entrepreneurs--"there are even a large number who insist on holding 100 percent of the equity on grounds that they cannot be bothered by any interference from 'outsiders.'"[17]

Mayer and Goldstein also argue that small companies are misguided in their approach to the raising of external finance. They found three principal errors in the approaches small businessmen made to the financing of their new enterprises. Some owners were undercapitalized in that they attempted to set themselves up in business without sufficient money to provide an initial stock in trade; some, having spent all of their liquid money at the opening of their businesses, had insufficient working reserves to carry them over the time required to build up the sales necessary to support the business; and others relied too heavily on borrowed capital and found that their new business could not carry the burden of debt:

> It is often assumed [say Mayer and Goldstein] that
> a major problem facing small business enterprise
> is the unavailability of bank credit. But only a
> few of the owners in the sample who tried to ob-
> tain loans from financial institutions were unable
> to get them. The major difficulty lay, not in the
> inability to obtain a loan, but in the fact that the
> loans granted were all short-term. Those owners
> who relied too heavily on this source of capital
> found that they had to make heavy payments of
> interest and capital at a time when the business
> could least afford this burden. The whole prob-
> lem thus has two aspects. From one point of
> view, small firms, lacking adequate equity capi-
> tal, have no reasons for existence and should not

be encouraged. The other point of view holds
that since persons opening such firms will try
anyhow, and since many will at least be able to
make a living if they have some capital at their
disposal, they ought to be helped through long-
term loans.[18]

In Britain, too, the reliance, of those small firms that do seek outside finance, on bank credit creates financial problems for them,
especially as such credit is so subject to government policies re-
stricting or facilitating lending. "There is no doubt," said the Midland Bank in discussing the question, "that Treasury directions in
the nature of credit 'squeezes' imposed in recent times tend to affect
the small trader more oppressively than his larger industrial coun-
terpart."[19]

It is evident, then, that most small firms do not seek external
finance because they do not need it; that some that do need it refuse,
"through ignorance, prejudice or moral scruples,"[20] to seek it; that
some that seek it are not sufficiently credit-worthy to get it; and
that those that get it most probably get the wrong sort. The opportunities for government policy to influence the small-firm sector
through the provision of financial aid to new enterprises or to expanding small firms would appear, therefore, to be limited. In
addition it is necessary to be suspicious, given what we presently
know about the motivation of small businessmen, of the efficacy of
any government policies based on the rationale of economic man, on
the belief that financial incentives and inducements are the only spur
to action and that small businessmen in particular will respond to
any opportunity of greater financial reward. Nevertheless, government financial policies toward small firms could have some impact
on the attainment of those social and economic objectives we have
outlined, particularly for small growing enterprises. In our view
the revenue from high estate duties and surtax could be used by government to finance cheap long-term venture capital at low interest
rates to small enterprises that were set up initially, or subsequently
incorporated, as copartnership, coownership, cooperative or
community-based ventures, or with any other structure that guaranteed the kind of member ownership and control that we believe a desirable objective of social policy. The provision of finance by government for small business enterprises would be designed, therefore, not only to discourage traditional family inheritance and encourage first-generation entrepreneurs, but also to influence the
form of ownership and control in small enterprises, an influence
that could be reinforced by some differential corporate taxation
policy designed to favor ventures having an approved form of

corporate structure. The availability of cheap long-term finance
could also be used as a focal point for advising prospective entrepreneurs on the viability of their embryo enterprises and for providing them with training in the entrepreneurial and administrative
skills they may require.

That such interventionist policies can have important social
and economic effects is clear from the groupement policy of the
French government in the 1960s, which, although different in kind,
was not different in principle from our proposals. In the early 1960s
the French government introduced a new scheme to encourage small
firms, particularly those located outside the major industrial centers. A six-year tax holiday was offered to any group of enterprises
that were prepared to start up a new joint company, the tax holiday
being subject to the company's meeting certain standards of management and financial control. Within ten years about a hundred of
these Societes Conventionees had been set up in various parts of
France, involving over 1,000 small and medium-sized firms. Some
started as joint marketing companies, some as joint purchasing companies, some to develop a bright idea, but they all tended, said a
reviewer of their success, "to act as much-needed yeast in the usually rather lumpish French provincial economy."[21] Most were small
companies that could see no prospects for growth in their intensely
local trade, that could not afford any fancy marketing or promotional
devices, and that had little to look forward to in the Common Market
but the ever-increasing competition of the multinational combines.
They were companies such as those in the little Normandy village of
Tinchbre

> which, for obscure historical reasons, is the
> centre of the French garden tool industry. In
> 1960 there were eight tiny firms in the village,
> with total sales of less than £1 million, and com-
> peting so hard they were rapidly starving each
> other to death. Meanwhile, they were exporting
> nothing, and the German firm of Wolf was rapid-
> ly eating up the whole of their traditional market.
> With the aid of a groupement deal, they set up a
> joint purchasing company, cut their gross costs
> by 7 percent in the first year (worth five times
> the cost of hiring a director, a buying specialist,
> two secretaries and setting up the deal), took a
> small stand at the Frankfurt Fair, sold 20 per-
> cent of their whole annual output on the first day,
> and by 1964 had pushed their joint turnover over
> £5 million, with a fifth going overseas. . . .

> The gospel of the groups had been, for France,
> one of the most economical and successful bits
> of regional aid ever devised. The net cost of
> the whole 12 year operation, which has gener-
> ated or saved upward of 50,000 jobs, has been
> less than £20 million. [22]

SOCIAL AND ECONOMIC DEVELOPMENT POLICIES

An interesting aspect of the French groupement idea, as of community development projects in both Denmark and Ireland, is that regional economic development is geared to the growth of small enterprises rather than exclusively to attempts to attract large enterprises into designated development areas. It has been suggested that in Italy, for example, the influx of new industries from the north to the south has served to undermine the economic health of the traditional local small artisan and family-based firms. Large sums of money have been spent in taking new industries southward only to find that in spite of this massive investment, mainly by the state, industrial employment in the south has remained relatively static and the forced emigration of southern Italians to the industrial cities of the north, or to other Common Market countries or abroad, has scarcely been slowed. In the United Kingdom, too, regional development policies have been based primarily on the assumption that the overriding policy objective was to attract large enterprises into areas of unemployment or underutilization of existing resources, such enterprises being seen as focal points around which small dependent satellite suppliers and servicing enterprises would spring up. It is clear that it may well be as appropriate economically, and more important socially, to build up in these areas the local small business communities in such a way as to minimize the risks to the local economy of the failure of one or two major enterprises. In this respect the problem of finding the best balance between the introduction into an area of external capital and technology and the development of the indigenous skills and resources of the area itself is not dissimilar to the problems of balancing external aid and internal self-development faced by many developing countries.

It seems possible that governments could also exercise some degree of influence on the location choices of existing small enterprises. Even though entrepreneurs may originally set their enterprises up within commuting distance of their homes, there is a considerable amount of location changing by small companies, particularly by those that are growing. During the course of our descriptive survey, for example, owner-managers were asked whether there had been any changes during the previous five years in the geographical location of their companies and, if so, what were the main reasons for changing location during that period. Of the 50 companies, 15 had changed their location once in the previous five years and two companies had changed twice. Of the highly profitable companies, all four had moved locations during the previous five years; so, in contrast, had 7 out of the 20 low-profitability firms. The relationship between company growth and location change was more clear cut. About half of the companies that were classified as expanding or expanding rapidly made location changes compared with only a quarter of the static and contracting firms. If this pattern of location change were repeated throughout the small-firm population it would mean that, in any one year, around 7 percent of all small firms would be involved in a move of location with all the possible disruption, lost production, and personnel change involved. Among the firms surveyed the principal reasons for moving site given by the owner-managers were the compulsory purchase of the firm's existing premises and the lack of sufficient space in existing premises to cope with expansion. Other reasons included the desire to concentrate production facilities in one place, the availability of a more convenient site locally, and the loss of premises through fire. Studies of industrial location decisions have emphasized the importance both of positive features in the new location, such as the availability of labor and better access to raw materials or to markets, and of negative features in the existing location, such as lack of space and restrictions on physical expansion, as prime motivators to move location.[23] Our data would seem to indicate that the motivation to move is largely a function of the internal company situation and that most government policies on industrial dispersal only affect decisions on where to move and not decisions on whether to move.[24] The message, however, is clear. Many small firms need guidance on their general site requirements and assistance in anticipating and overcoming the problems they will encounter in moving from one location to another. Where a government has policies on industrial dispersal and regional development, such policies, if they are to have any impact on small enterprises, must necessarily incorporate mechanisms for providing this kind of guidance and assistance to small firms.

While large firms are obviously more amenable than small firms to direct government influence and control, there are, nevertheless, a number of areas in which specific government policies toward the small-firm sector can have some impact. Various organizations who submitted evidence to the Bolton Committee made, for example, suggestions as to ways in which British government policies might be changed or new policies introduced to aid the establishment and growth of small enterprises. These suggestions included such matters as the reservation of a proportion of government contracts for small firms, special investment grants to encourage the growth of technologically based small companies, subsidized management consultancy arrangements, the provision of regional information and advice bureaus, export incentive schemes, and encouragement for small firms to develop cooperative arrangements for buying, marketing, and research activities. The likely impact of such policies will, of course, depend very largely on the prior technical and economic conditions that exist in an industry or a society and on cultural and social factors. Cooperative ventures, for example, may not be appropriate in contexts where the success of small enterprises is dependent upon a high degree of product or market differentiation and specialization. In the United States, government research and development contracts stimulated the growth of the "Route 128" complex of science-based enterprises near Boston and, to a lesser extent, the growth of small businesses in the Palo Alto Peninsula of California. For such direct government initiation to bear fruit, however, it is necessary for the local community to develop an environment sympathetic to the fledgling entrepreneur. Creating a business climate conducive to new enterprises and their growth may require a variety of social and economic facilities in a community, from appropriate financial and banking services to the provision of courses in entrepreneurship at local educational institutions.

> If the first new companies are successful, then their success begins to change the environment. These new firms are likely to be better incubators, that is to have higher spinoff rates, than the older firms which their founders left. Their success may begin to convince others that entrepreneurship is feasible and rewarding. Potential investors may be encouraged or created by the success of the new firms; financial consultants and venture capital firms may then develop. Future founders then find a more promising environment than those who went before . . . a self-reinforcing process takes place, in that past entrepreneurship makes future entrepreneurship more likely, and, in time, a high rate of entrepreneurial activity may develop. [25]

Our studies and speculations have been concentrated around the problems of growth and development of the small-firm sector in relatively advanced industrial economies. Finally, however, it is important to recognize that the problems of such economies may be very different from the problems of stimulating entrepreneurship in developing countries. The founding of technology-based enterprises in the United States may depend on social processes that precipitate skilled and qualified manpower into their own entrepreneurial ventures, one such process being those periodic crises which displace research and development personnel from large organizations onto the labor market. The problems of establishing new growth enterprises with a strong scientific or technological base, of differentiating the nature of the entrepreneurial function within such enterprises, of stimulating a ready supply of entrepreneurs, of providing an appropriate climate for entrepreneurship, are very different problems from those facing developing countries, where, suggests Peter Kilby, the nature of the entrepreneur's function

> seems to differ considerably in a number of respects from that in nineteenth-century Europe and America. These differences stem from a single source--the existence of a very large stock of proven technical innovations in the advanced economies which has not yet been applied in the developing economies. Thus, original technological innovation, which was frequently the heart of nineteenth-century industrial entrepreneurship, is not an activity for which there is now much call. . . . The backlog of unapplied production techniques and the existence of large, well mapped out import markets means that perceiving truly new economic opportunities, the carrying out of fundamental, pioneering innovations of the type envisaged by Schumpeter are largely irrelevant. On the other hand, the operational problems of matching advanced technology with qualitatively ill-fitting local factors of production are considerably greater than in the nineteenth century. To obtain adequate financing, to adapt techniques and organization, to maximize factor productivities and minimize unit cost, to improvise substitutes for nonavailable skills and materials--these tasks on the production side will more often than not represent the critical entrepreneurial function in the modernizing economy of the twentieth century.[26]

SUMMARY

The social and economic contribution that small enterprises make to any economy cannot be ignored by policy-makers. A number of objectives should be pursued. These should include the encouragement of new enterprises, the development of managerial skills within them, and the widening of their ownership and control. While improving the economic performance of the small-firm sector, and making more effective use of the manpower resources employed in the sector, are important aims, they should be seen in their social context. Thus consideration of questions of ownership and decision-making, of managerial succession and continuity, and of the psychological contract between the individual and his work, need to inform policy-making and to be incorporated into the criteria by which the merits of alternative policies will be evaluated. In Britain it is necessary to encourage an increased number of new entries into the small-firm population, to pay special attention to the needs and problems of founder-run companies, to promote greater innovation and experimentation by small enterprises, and to develop entrepreneurial skills within organizations of all sizes. Small firms should also be seen as a mechanism through which provision can be made for the creation of a wider range of occupational choices for the educationally underprivileged and an opportunity for the development of their abilities.

Policies that might be advantageously pursued fall into a number of categories. Proposals that have been advanced in Britain on the manpower side include the establishment of a small-firm management recruitment, placement, and training center and tax reforms to facilitate the participation in or acquisition of small firms by new management. On the financial side it has been suggested that government should link the provision of long-term loans at low interest rates to particular forms of small-business ownership and control, laying emphasis on collective and cooperative ventures. It is argued that such a policy would not be antithetical to the motivation for entrepreneurship or the self-development through business enterprise of the creative individual. Other areas in which government can have some impact on small companies are through regional development and industrial location policies, through the stimulus afforded by government spending power, and through the development in particular communities of an infrastructure of facilities and services that create a favorable climate for entrepreneurship. The exact choice of a set of policy measures to achieve the objectives specified will, however, depend on social, cultural, and economic factors specific to the country or economic sector under review.

The "search for the source of dynamic entrepreneurial performance has much in common with hunting the Heffalump," says
Peter Kilby. Certainly in the course of our research we have come
across both entrepreneurial Heffalumps and owner-manager Woozles
and a variety of species of each. Some of these species have been
close to extinction, others have already been transformed into the
mythological creatures of a mediaeval bestiary; in such cases we
have merely been able to speculate on the meaning of skeletons and
fossils. In other cases we have identified our prey more clearly,
described its habitat, observed and analyzed its behavior, understood a little of its way of life, and then returned to our ruminations.
We have recognized no single role for small firms in advanced industrial economies, no single overriding entrepreneurial function, no
single set of entrepreneurial motivations, no simple prescriptions to
guarantee new enterprise growth or to ensure a ready supply of entrepreneurial skills and abilities. Hopefully, however, we have il-
luminated rather than obscured our chosen area of study, identified
some of the factors that contribute to its complexity, prompted some
thought both among policy-makers and practitioners, and raised
more questions than we have been able to answer.

NOTES

1. "Britain's Smaller Businesses Threatened," pamphlet
by the Smaller Businesses' Association (London, 1969).

2. J-F. Revel, Without Marx or Jesus (New York: Doubleday,
1971).

3. See J. H. Goldthorpe et al., The Affluent Worker in the
Class Structure (Cambridge: University Press, 1969).

4. R. Fraser, ed., Work: Twenty Personal Accounts
(Harmondsworth: Penguin Books, 1968). For discussion of the
question of alienation see especially, M. Seeman, "On the Meaning
of Alienation," American Sociological Review, December 1959, and
R. Blauner, Alienation and Freedom (Chicago: University of Chicago
Press, 1964).

5. Information based on unpublished paper presented by
Joaquin De Arquer, Professor of Human Behavior in Organizations,
University of Navarra, to the International Seminar on Small Business Management Development in Europe, Irish Management Institute, Dublin, 1971.

6. Merrett Cyriax Associates, Dynamics of Small Firms,
Committee of Inquiry on Small Firms, Research Report No. 12
(London: HMSO, 1971).

7. Ibid.

8. Small Firms--Report of the Committee of Inquiry on Small Firms (The Bolton Report) (London: HMSO, 1971), para. 9.13.

9. M. Hall, The Small Unit in the Distributive Trades, Committee of Inquiry on Small Firms, Research Report No. 8 (London: HMSO, 1971).

10. J. Hopkinson, Victorian Cabinet Maker, The Memoirs of James Hopkinson 1819-1894, ed. J. B. Goodman (London: Routledge and Kegan Paul, 1968).

11. Small Firms, op. cit., para. 13.6.

12. Ibid., paras 13.7 and 13.69.

13. H. G. Wells, The World of William Clissold, Book 5, Section 9 (London: Ernest Benn, 1926).

14. Evidence Submitted to the Committee of Inquiry on Small Firms (London: Chamber of Commerce, 1970).

15. Small Firms, op. cit., para. 12.3.

16. P. Donham, "Whither Small Business," Harvard Business Review, March-April 1957.

17. Ibid.

18. K. B. Mayer and S. Goldstein, The First Two Years: Problems of Small Firm Growth and Survival, Small Business Administration Research Series No. 2 (Washington, D.C.: Small Business Administration, 1961).

19. "The Committee of Inquiry on Small Firms," Midland Bank Review, February 1970.

20. Small Firms, op. cit., para. 12.3.ii.

21. P. Wilsher, "Scots can learn from French groupies," Sunday Times, September 26, 1971.

22. Ibid.

23. See, for example, W. F. Luttrell, Factory Location and Industrial Movement (London: National Institute of Economic and Social Research, 1962).

24. See, for example, "Industrial Dispersal," Planning 31, no. 485 (London: Political and Economic Planning, February 1965).

25. A. C. Cooper, "The Founding of Technology Based Enterprise," (Milwaukee: Center for Venture Management, 1971).

26. P. Kilby, "Hunting the Heffalump," in Entrepreneurship and Economic Development, ed. P. Kilby (New York: The Free Press, 1971). For an alternative view of the kind of innovation required in the context of a developing country, see E. F. Schumacher, Small is Beautiful (London: Blond and Briggs, 1973), and G. McRobie, "Technology for development--small is beautiful," Journal of the Royal Society of Arts, March 1974, pp. 214-24.

THE DESCRIPTIVE SURVEY

This survey was conducted among furniture companies employing from 25 to 75 persons. While the fixing of precise limits in
terms of size as measured by employees is obviously arbitrary, the
intention was to concentrate on companies that would be large enough
to have some sort of management structure but not so large as to
prevent the owner from exercising personal and detailed control of
the major activities of the business should he so wish. Statistics
from the British Furniture and Timber Industry Training Board indicated that, in November 1969, 358 furniture firms were of the size
required. Consequently, early in December 1969 each of these companies was sent a standard letter addressed to the managing director.
This letter set out briefly the aims of the project and asked for an
indication of interest in the study. By early January 1970, 169 companies, 47 percent of the total, had replied to this letter, 127 of
these, or 36 percent of the total population of 358, expressing interest in the study. This was felt to be a surprisingly good response
but meant, as in almost any research program, that a considerable
degree of self-selection had taken place before any sample could be
constructed.

The time available for field work in the project meant that the
sample of firms selected for study would have to be limited to about
50, or 13 percent of the total population. On the basis of analysis of
the industry sector, size, and regional characteristics of the 358
companies in the population, a sample requirement was constructed.
The 127 companies expressing interest in the study were then similarly classified and, where numbers allowed, selected at random to
match the sample requirement.

The next stage was to telephone the managing directors of
each of the 50 companies selected by the stratified random sampling
process in order to give them some more information about the
project and to explain what they would be letting themselves in for
by agreeing to take part. At the same time this telephone call was
used to establish that the company concerned was a fully autonomous
and independent unit, not part of a larger concern, and that it fell
within the industrial and size parameters required, and also to
identify the number of managers and supervisors employed by the
firm. If the managing director was still prepared to go ahead and
the company satisfied the selection criteria, then a date for visiting

the firm was arranged. As a result of these calls five companies were eliminated, two because they were part of large groups, one because the managing director decided not to go ahead, and two were abandoned because it proved impossible to pin down the managing director to making a decision one way or the other. In each case a replacement company with similar industry, size, and regional characteristics was selected as a substitute, again on a random basis. In spite, however, of the careful preparation of the ground with the managing directors of the selected companies, three firms had to be dropped from the selected sample after visits had been made. In two cases the companies proved to be subsidiaries of larger groups and in one it was immediately obvious to the researcher that the necessary cooperation would not be forthcoming. The three firms excluded after visits were replaced in the same way as the five excluded after the initial telephone contacts. This means that 8 of the 50 companies in the selected sample were replaced during the course of the project. The characteristics of the sample interviewed and of the survey population are set out in Table A.1. As can be seen the sample interviewed matched the survey population fairly closely in terms of the size and industry characteristics of companies and in terms of their regional distribution.

While contacts were being made with companies and a sample selected for participation in the project, work was carried out on the design and testing of a questionnaire. Earlier work with small companies had made it clear that much of the information required would probably not, with the exception of balance sheet and profit-and-loss account data, be recorded anywhere in the firm. Most of the information on a manager's education, experience, and training would, for example, have to be gleaned from an interview with that manager and, similarly, much of the information about the company would have to be obtained directly from discussion with the managing director. The possibility of collecting sufficient reliable data by means of a postal questionnaire was discounted.

Two phases were involved in the preparation of a questionnaire. The first step, in November 1969, was to visit a number of small companies and talk, in an unstructured way, with the managing directors about the development of their businesses and their current operations. These visits were made in the Leeds area and covered such topics as the history and development of the firm, its structure of ownership and control, its financial structure and performance, and its current operations and problem areas. The second step, in December 1969, was to draw up and test a pilot questionnaire. This was tested with three companies that were sufficiently different in size and organization structure to indicate the relevance of the questionnaire both to the smallest firm likely to take part in the main project and to the largest. In the light of this pilot study a number

of changes were incorporated into the design of the questionnaire to
be used in the main survey. These included bringing together all the
items concerned with information on the company so that they could
be dealt with prior to the interviews with individual managers. At
the same time a number of questions on control procedures were
eliminated since it was felt they would provide little useful information unless dealt with in far greater depth than the time available, or
the general purpose of the survey, warranted. As much of the information as possible was then precoded and the layout of the questionnaire revised in order to allow easy access to coded data for computer analysis. This was carried out in conjunction with a local
computer programming service.

TABLE A. 1

Descriptive Survey Population and Sample Interviewed

	Percent Population (n = 358)	Percent Sample Interviewed (n = 50)
By industry sector		
Cabinet furniture	73.7	70.0
Upholstered furniture	17.9	20.0
Bedding	8.4	10.0
By size of firm		
25 to 49 employees	64.2	66.0
50 to 75 employees	35.8	34.0
By region		
London and South East	34.4	34.0
Eastern	6.7	6.0
Southern	14.2	16.0
South Western	3.1	2.0
Midlands	6.4	4.0
North Midlands	5.9	4.0
East and West Riding	7.3	12.0
Scotland	6.4	8.0
Wales	2.0	2.0
North East	9.5	8.0
Northern	4.2	4.0

Source: Compiled by the author.

The first company in the main survey was visited on January 21, 1970, and the fiftieth company was visited on June 24, 1970. The main survey reports were completed by the end of September 1970.

DEVELOPMENT OF THE COSAR METHOD

Prior to the commencement of the depth study three preliminary studies, each lasting for around one week, were carried out in order to test the appropriateness of different methods of analyzing the work of the small-firm owner-manager. In the first of these preliminary studies three techniques were used. Initially the owner-manager was the subject of random observation and the two observers involved recorded anything that seemed of particular interest or significance but they did not attempt to record everything nor did they record on the basis of a prepared framework. Next the owner-manager was the subject of continuous observation and in these periods all his actions, contacts, conversations, and decisions were recorded insofar as this was physically possible. Finally the owner-manager's activities were sampled at fixed time intervals and recorded. This system of activity sampling was tried on the basis of 5-, 10-, and 15-minute intervals with recordings on precoded forms which the observers drew up and modified as the work proceeded. In order to operate this system without constantly interrupting the owner-manager for descriptions and explanations of what he was doing, it was found necessary to keep the owner-manager under continuous observation even though only recording his activity at selected intervals. Continuous observation, therefore, became a necessary condition for understanding the owner-manager's actions and making a meaningful activity record at the specified times. In terms of the appropriateness of different time intervals for activity sampling, the first preliminary study concluded that something in the region of six to eight observations per hour was the most workable arrangement. With 5-minute intervals difficulties were experienced in making accurate recordings with sufficient detail and with 15-minute intervals the observers were not fully occupied. The importance of this first study was, then, that it demonstrated the kind of information that could be gained from detailed analysis of the way in which an owner-manager spent his time and the advantages and disadvantages of different analytical methods.

Building on the methods developed in the first of these preliminary studies, the second study set out to give some indication of the way in which a small-firm owner-manager spent his time over a short period in order both to indicate some of the difficulties involved in analyzing managerial work and to show some of the uses to which such an analysis could be put. Prior to the commencement of this second study, therefore, a number of questions were formulated. These questions included:

1. What is the content of the owner-manager's job and what is the purpose of the various activities and tasks being carried out?
2. What is the frequency of various activities and tasks and the degree of difficulty involved in carrying them out?
3. To what extent is the owner-manager engaged in solving problems and making decisions and with what degree of success?
4. How often does the owner-manager initiate activities rather than respond to the demands of others? What sources of information are open to him and how does he use them?

As can be seen these were primarily questions about the content and nature of an owner-manager's work rather than about methods of analysis. In this second study, then, the observer, while using the continuous observation and sample activity recording method developed in the first study, attempted to identify, where possible,

1. examples of problem-solving behavior and decision-making;
2. the use of information in decision-making and problem-solving and the sources of the information used;
3. the consequential work load stemming from the initiation of activities and tasks;
4. the volume, duration, and nature of telephone calls and other communications activity;
5. examples of sequences of behavior and the linkages between tasks;
6. the nature of the skills, experience and training being used by the owner-manager in the course of his work.

The third of these preliminary studies attempted to take the analysis a stage further. The methods used were those developed in the two previous studies with the emphasis now placed less on the methodology of analyzing managerial work and more on the application of such an analysis to the identification of management training needs. What the third study was concerned with was, therefore, not the representativeness of the behavior observed, but the usefulness of a sample of behavior as a focus for discussion of the problems of a business and the training needs of its management. At the same time samples of behavior would provide some objective evidence, albeit of a limited general validity, against which notions of difficulty in particular areas of a company's operations might be tested and defined. The use of similar methods in a number of situations might

then eventually make it possible to build up comparative data across
a number of companies, thereby providing some crude kind of behavioral interfirm comparisons. The pattern of the owner-manager's
activities that emerged during this third preliminary study provided
some fruitful leads for discussing with the owner-managers a number
of problems posed by the development of the firm and, in particular,
a number of the difficulties he faced in his own job. Because this
study was an attempt to indicate the practical applications of the research methodology developed, specific recommendations to deal
with some of the problems and difficulties identified were made to
the owner-manager at the conclusion of the study.

The basic research method developed in these short preliminary studies and carried forward into the larger depth study was,
therefore, the method of continuous observation with sample activity recordings (or the COSAR method). There are a number of
limitations to the method and problems associated with its use.
COSAR is, for example, a method that is largely restricted to the
analysis of the work of one person at a time, although it can be
used with a group of people engaged in similar work in one well-
defined area where there is little or no movement from that area.
It is a method that involves difficulties in transferring the activities
observed into some useful classification of tasks or functions. For
example, telephoning is an observable activity. It can then be
classified as part of a current task, the task being, say, ensuring
an appropriate supply of upholstery covers for next Monday's production requirements. Such tasks can in turn be classified on a
functional basis, and in this case the function might be called purchasing, or stock control, or planning and programming. What is
observed is an activity, the content of that activity may be called a
task, and the purpose of that task a function. As can be envisaged,
the reliability of any set of observations is reasonably high on an
activity classification and progressively less reliable as those activities are transferred into tasks and functions. Yet it is the identification of tasks and functions that is important, particularly in
the training context. What the three preliminary studies provided
was material for agreement about the way in which specific activities and tasks were to be classified on a functional basis.

A further major problem in analyzing managerial work is that
the work cycle is not a short one. Thus, whereas in a week's observation of many operative jobs each activity and task making up
the job may recur many times, with management and supervisory
jobs some tasks may only be carried out once a week (for example,
calculating weekly bonus earnings), once a month (checking the
month's purchases and sales), or once a year (preparation of annual
budgets). Similarly the pattern of activities over any given period

will not be a regular one; particular items may crop up, there will
be a flurry of activity, perhaps extending over several days, and
then the matter will lie dormant for weeks or months before any
further observable action takes place. This means that any observation study of managers at work involves only a sample of their activity and one can only guess the extent to which the period selected
for study is representative of their work as a whole or the extent to
which activities repeat themselves on a predictable, if long-term,
cycle. It is obviously not feasible to observe a manager at work
over the full period of his work cycle, even assuming there is such
a cycle and that its length can be identified. Too short a period of
observation is likely, on the other hand, to be a very inadequate
guide to the relative frequency of different tasks and functions, although it may throw light on their difficulty and criticality. However, on the basis of the studies carried out it becomes increasingly clear that, in the analysis of managerial work, frequency is probably the least important dimension of any function and that much
more attention needs to be paid to the dimensions of difficulty and
criticality.

In using the COSAR method a further problem may arise connected with the physical barriers to observation of managers at
work. Not only do many owner-managers of small firms work extremely long hours but work goes on in a variety of places that may
not be accessible to the observer: over lunch with customers or
suppliers, for example, or at home in the evening. Similarly there
may well be some difficulty involved in keeping track of the manager's movements: In any one day he might, for example, spend
time in the factory, in the office, and out visiting suppliers. In two
of the preliminary studies no tracking difficulties of this kind arose,
primarily because most of the owner-managers' time was spent
within their factory or office locations and the observer was able to
travel with them when external visits were made and to take lunch
with them. In the other preliminary study there was only one occasion when the observers were specifically excluded from part of the
owner-manager's work activity. This arose when a visit was made
to discuss the claims of the Inland Revenue with the company's accountants. Unfortunately, it is, of course, just those areas of activity that may be considered too confidential to admit outside observation that may be most critical to the success of the business
and present the greatest problems to the owner-manager. The conclusion drawn, however, from the preliminary studies was that
tracking difficulties would not be so great as to undermine the usefulness of the COSAR method.

Nevertheless, it is obvious that the carrying out of any detailed analysis of managers at work involves both careful preparation

with the manager concerned and a willingness on his part to put himself out to a considerable degree, something that in itself will distort the more normal pattern of his activities. It also involves a realization on the observer's part that, even given the high degree of cooperation necessary from the manager concerned, there is a threshold beyond which toleration of continuous observation will not stretch and should not be asked to stretch. The most appropriate approach may be, therefore, a series of continuous observation periods of, say, three days at a time spread over several months. But such a spread to a study raises a further difficulty. One of the aspects of managerial work that is of particular interest in understanding the skills being used by managers is the duration of sequences of activity, the way in which one episode triggers off another and the way in which two activities, separated by a considerable time lapse, may be related to the solution of one particular problem. In continuous observation studies problems can be followed through their various stages over perhaps a period of some days or weeks. A break in the observation period means that the track is temporarily lost and has to be filled in from the manager's memory of events rather than from observation of what in fact occurred. If critical sequences of behavior last longer than the observation-tolerance period, then the usefulness of the information collected by the study may be severely limited.

In practice the owner-managers involved in the preliminary studies apparently did not find the COSAR method onerous and saw no reason to believe that longer periods of observation would have proved intolerable. Other studies confirm the view that most people positively enjoy a detailed interest being taken in their work. This is likely to be particularly so with owner-managers of small companies who, in many cases, find little opportunity to discuss their business (and personal) problems in detail simply because they carry many of their responsibilities and problems alone. With managerial work the distortion of activity that will arise through the presence of an observer cannot be measured and controlled and must be considered as one further variable in an already complex situation. The action research approach would appear, therefore, to be an appropriate one in this context. The observer in such a study is involved in a developing situation and is going to make, whether he desires it or not, some impact on that situation even if only by providing a sounding board for some of the ideas and proposed decisions of the owner-manager.

THE DEPTH STUDY

Twelve small owner-managed firms were involved in the depth study. Two of the firms were timber businesses and the other ten were companies in the furniture industry, manufacturing a range of products from reproduction upholstery to contract cabinetmaking and sports goods. Most of the firms were approached as a result of interest expressed during the descriptive survey interviews and a number were approached directly by the researcher. The kind of research methods envisaged for the depth study made it imperative that the owner-managers involved should have some commitment to and interest in the objectives of the project and, consequently, prospective participants tended to be owner-managers who had already established some contact with the research program or with the activities of the Furniture and Timber Industry Training Board. As a result very few of those owner-managers approached declined to take part in the depth study. Many, in fact, saw it as an opportunity that might provide useful information on the operation of their firms and on their own managerial performance. The 12 firms did not, therefore, constitute a sample in any sense, nor was it ever the intention that they should do so. Nevertheless, the companies involved in the depth study were not all of a kind. They covered a range of product groups, they varied in size (the smallest being a timber business employing 13 staff and the remaining 11 firms all employing from 25 to 80 employees with a median of 40 employees), in location, in generation of ownership, and in financial performance. Among the 12 companies were firms of high profitability and rapid growth and static firms with poor profit records. In terms of financial performance they were, however, better than the average revealed by the descriptive survey. This was both a deliberate function of the research design, since it was thought desirable to study the work of the more successful owner-managers, and an inevitable consequence of the selection process. It seems probable that, in mounting any depth study of this kind, the owner-managers of relatively successful firms will be more ready participants than the owner-managers of firms with poor performance records. While, however, the expectations of owner-managers are obviously an important variable in determining their willingness to participate in research programs, the study did not probe those expectations in any detail.

Three research methods were used in the depth study. They were interviewing, the examination of available records and data kept by each company, and developments of the COSAR method already described. In studies of small firms problems always arise in the collection of statistical information. As anticipated, the 12 small firms in the depth study kept very few written records or statistical analyses, the main source of historical information being balance sheets and profit and loss accounts. Eight of the 12 companies gave the researcher access to this financial data. Other sources of data included budgets, sales charts, production records, personnel records, stock records, and invoices. In the context of the depth

study the main value of such data, which was often of an extremely
rudimentary kind, lay in its usefulness as a basis for checking and
reinforcing some of the information provided by the owner-managers
in interviews.

The observation part of the research was focused on the work
of the owner-manager who was managing director of the firm under
study. During the depth study a large amount of general observation
took place. This included walking around factories, accompanying
the managing director when he was visiting customers and suppliers,
attending meetings with salesmen, sitting in on conversations with
employees and other managers, and even attending a funeral. Much
unstructured interviewing took place on these occasions. General
observation also yielded information on premises, customers, suppliers, employees, conditions of work, management styles, and,
especially, on the personality and life-styles of the 12 managing
directors. While this kind of observation was very useful, it did not
enable the researcher to describe managerial activities and tasks in
any statistical way. In order, therefore, to answer the question,
"How does the small-firm managing director spend his time?" some
much more precise measure was required.

Attempts to classify the nature of managerial work are not new
but, as Sune Carlson in Executive Behaviour pointed out, "most of
the writing is not even concerned with results in the form of observed
and classified facts, but merely with generalisations from limited
experience and with principles . . . which are in most cases nothing
else but opinions."[1] A number of attempts in the past to provide
factual records of the division of management time have used "diary
analysis" techniques.[2] These usually involve administering structured time sheets to managers, who fill the time sheets in over a
specified period. These techniques have a number of advantages
over observation by an individual researcher. As Rosemary Stewart
points out, they greatly increase the number and distribution of
managers who can be covered, and they increase the length of time
for which they can be studied.[3] In addition the classification of activities is made by the respondent, who knows better than any observer what he is doing, and all time can be recorded, whereas, as
we have seen, an observer may be excluded from confidential discussions. Bearing these not inconsiderable advantages in mind, a
pilot project in "diary analysis" was carried out among lecturers in
the Department of Administration at the University of Strathclyde.
Each of six participants received a "diary," with columns for time,
the activity being pursued, the subject or function with which it was
concerned, and the place it occurred. A separate sheet for telephone
calls was also administered. Participants filled in these sheets for
a period of one week, at the end of which time they were gathered in

and analyzed on an individual and an aggregate basis. The results exposed four of the weaknesses in the diary analysis methods of studying people's jobs. First, because of lack of commitment to the objectives of the exercise, respondents may fail to complete the forms. Second, respondents may be very inaccurate in their recording of events. For example, several different topics may be discussed in one self-recorded interaction, but the respondent may include only one of these in his diary entry. Third, short episodes, especially interruptions, may tend to be overlooked or completely forgotten. Finally, the allocation of topics to different subject or functional headings tends to differ between different people, whereas an observer can impose some consistency in classification. What tends to emerge from diary analysis methods is, then, an inaccurate picture of work activity, which appears on diaries as much less fragmented than it really is. As a result diary analysis methods were not considered to be sufficiently accurate for the purposes of the depth study of the work activities of small-firm owner-managers. Instead, the researcher "trailed" managing directors of seven firms for periods of either three or four days, using a modification of the COSAR method.

The process of continuous observation of the way in which managers spend their time has the one big disadvantage that it severely limits the scope of the investigation. But in this study scope was deliberately sacrificed for depth and consistency. Seven of the 12 managing directors were, therefore, studied for a total of 214 hours and a total number of 2,146 work episodes were recorded. Each episode was timed to the nearest minute, and the following information about each was noted:

1. The place where the episode occurred.
2. The observable activity taking place during the episode (for example, writing, talking).
3. The contact with whom the episode took place, if any.
4. Whether the episode was initiated by the subject himself or by his contact.
5. The function with which the episode was concerned (for example, sales, production).

In addition, all telephone calls were analyzed separately, mainly to assess the effect of the telephone on the small-firm managing director's work pattern. An attempt was also made to analyze in some detail any decision-making activity that could be identified. It is necessary, in the context of the use of the COSAR method in this study, to sound a cautionary note. In each case the COSAR study of the managing director's work lasted only a few days. What we have, therefore, are samples of activity and behavior that may not be representative. This must be borne in mind when interpreting the results. Similarly, although much of the material collected was amenable to statistical treatment, reservations both about the selection of firms and about the selection of behaviors subtract from the value of any elaborate statistical analysis. Therefore this was not attempted and the material presented from the depth study is not primarily statistical in form. Quantitative methods are, however, used to indicate basic information about the activities of the managing directors studied and to provide illustrative material. As well as the basic information that continuous observation of the work of seven managing directors yielded, the COSAR study was also of use as a vehicle for gathering information on other aspects of managers' work. Continuous observation reveals managers in a great many situations and this in turn yields information on management styles, personalities, problems, skills, and deficiencies. It can reveal how they deal with other people, their thought processes in decision-making, and their priorities. The importance of observation methods of the COSAR kind may be, therefore, that having some simple recording procedure to follow provides an acceptable method of entry to the work situation of the person or group being observed. In other words, it makes it seem that the observer too has some work pattern to follow and is not merely watching in an apparently aimless way. Whether the observer's having such a work tool to hold onto is more comforting for the observer or the observed is a matter of conjecture. What is clear in retrospect from the depth studies is that methods like COSAR provide opportunities to get under the skin of work situations. Their advantage may be, therefore, not so much that they provide some crude quantitative measures of work activity, but that they present an opportunity for an observer to be exposed over a period of time to different work behaviors. Such exposure would seem to be a necessary prerequisite if understanding of, and insight into, work behavior is to be an end-product of a research program.

NOTES

1. S. Carlson, Executive Behaviour: A study of the workload and working methods of managing directors (Stockholm: Strombergs, 1951).

2. For further discussion, see, for example, T. Burns, "Management in Action," Operational Research Quarterly 3, no. 2 (June 1957): 45–60; G. Copeman, "Where does the time go?" Business, October 1961; J. H. Horne and T. Lupton, "The Work Activities of 'Middle' Managers," Journal of Management Studies 1, no. 2

(February 1965): 14-33; Rosemary Stewart, "The Use of Diaries to Study Managers' Jobs," Journal of Management Studies 2, no. 2 (May 1965): 228-35; and D. L. Marples, "Studies of Managers--A Fresh Start?" Journal of Management Studies 4, no. 3 (October 1967): 282-99.

    3. Rosemary Stewart, Managers and Their Jobs (London: Macmillan, 1967).

BOOKS AND PAMPHLETS

Acton Society Trust. _Management Succession_. London: Acton
Society Trust, 1956.

Allen, C. _Small Firm Survey 1970_. London: Industrial and Commercial Finance Corporation Ltd, 1970.

Allen, L. L. _Starting and Succeeding in Your Own Small Business_.
New York: Grossett and Dunlap, 1968.

American Institute of Certified Public Accountants. _Management
Information Systems for the Smaller Business_. New York:
AICPA, 1969.

American Society of Mechanical Engineers. _Small Plant Management: A Guide to Practical Know-how Management_. 2d ed.
New York: McGraw-Hill, 1960.

Anyon, G. J. _Entrepreneurial Dimensions of Management_. Philadelphia: Livingston, 1973.

Aris, S. _The Jews in Business_. London: Jonathan Cape, 1970.

Arnold, T. W. _The Folklore of Capitalism_. New Haven, Conn.:
Yale University Press, 1938.

Baker, A. W. _Personnel Management in Small Plants_. Columbus:
Ohio State University, 1955.

Banks, R., ed. _Managing the Smaller Company_. New York:
American Management Association, 1969.

Basil, D. C. _Organization and Control of the Smaller Enterprise_.
Minneapolis: University of Minnesota Press, 1959.

Bates, J. A. _The Financing of Small Business_. 2d ed. London:
Sweet and Maxwell, 1971.

Bayliss, B. The Small Firm in the Road Haulage Industry. Committee of Inquiry on Small Firms, Research Report No. 1. London: HMSO, 1971.

Bennis, W. G. Changing Organizations. New York: McGraw-Hill, 1966.

Berna, J. J. Industrial Entrepreneurship in Madras State. London: Asia Publishing House, 1960.

Bernstein, L. and Paskin, S. A Business of your own. London: Mercury House, 1971.

Bjerkoe, E. H. The Cabinetmakers of America. New York: Doubleday, 1957.

Blum, A. A. Industrial Relations and the Small Firm. Bulletin No. 34. Ithaca, N.Y.: New York State School of Industrial and Labor Relations, July 1960.

Boswell, J. The Rise and Decline of Small Firms. London: Allen & Unwin, 1973.

Boyson, R. The Ashworth Cotton Enterprise: The Rise and Fall of a Family Firm, 1818-1880. Oxford: University Press, 1970.

Broom, H. N. and Longenecker, J. G. Small Business Management. 3d ed. Cincinnati, Ohio: South-Western, 1971.

Bruce, M. M. Human Relations in Small Business. Small Business Administration Management Series No. 3. Washington, D.C.: Small Business Administration, 1969.

Bunn, V. A. Buying and Selling a Small Business. Washington, D.C.: Small Business Administration, 1969.

Burlage, C. L. The Small Businessman and his Problems. New York: Vantage Press, 1958.

Calder, G. H. et al. Small Business Counselling: An Evaluation of Techniques. Salt Lake City: University of Utah Bureau of Economic and Business Research, 1964.

Carlson, S. Executive Behaviour: a study of the workload and working methods of managing directors. Stockholm: Strombergs,
1951.

Carroll, J. J. The Filipino Manufacturing Entrepreneur. Ithaca,
N.Y.: Cornell University Press, 1965.

Caves, R. American Industry--Structure, Conduct, Performance.
Englewood Cliffs, N.J.: Prentice-Hall, 1964.

Cawelti, J. G. Apostles of the Self-made Man. Chicago: University
of Chicago Press, 1965.

Christensen, C. R. Management Succession in Small and Growing
Enterprises. Boston: Harvard University Graduate School of
Business Administration, 1953.

Church, R. A. Kenricks in Hardware: A Family Business, 1791-
1966. Newton Abbott: David and Charles, 1969.

Clark, D. G. The Industrial Manager--His Background and Career
Pattern. London: Business Publications, 1966.

Clarke, P. Small Businesses: how they survive and succeed.
Newton Abbott: David and Charles, 1972.

Clements, R. V. Managers: A Study of Their Careers in Industry.
London: Allen and Unwin, 1958.

Cochran, T. C. and Miller, W. The Age of Enterprise. New York:
Macmillan, 1958.

Cochran, T. C. and Reina, R. E. Entrepreneurship in Argentine
Culture. Philadelphia: University of Pennsylvania Press, 1963.

Collingridge, J. and Ritchie, M. Personnel Management: problems
of the smaller firm. London: Institute of Personnel Management, 1970.

Collins, O. and Moore, D. G. The Enterprising Man. East Lansing:
Michigan State University Press, 1964.

_____. The Organization Makers. New York: Appleton-Century-
Crofts, 1970.

Committee of Inquiry on Small Firms. Small Firms--Report of the
    Committee of Inquiry on Small Firms (The Bolton Report).
    London: HMSO, 1971.

Confederation of British Industry. Britain's Small Firms: Their
    Vital Role in the Economy. London: CBI, 1968.

The Consumer Council. Furniture Trade and Consumer. London:
    HMSO, 1965.

Copeland, M. J. The Executive at Work. Cambridge, Mass.:
    Harvard University Press, 1952.

Copeman, G. H. Leaders of British Industry. London: Gee and
    Co., 1955.

Cox, J. G. Scientific and Engineering Manpower and Research in
    Small Firms. Committee of Inquiry on Small Firms, Research
    Report No. 2. London: HMSO, 1971.

Creedon, J. D. Counselling Services for Small Businesses. New
    York: Credit Research Foundation, 1966.

Cyert, R. M. and March, J. G. A Behavioral Theory of the Firm.
    Englewood Cliffs, N.J.: Prentice-Hall, 1963.

Dahmen, E. Entrepreneurial Activity and the Development of
    Swedish Industry, 1919-1939. Homewood, Ill.: Richard D.
    Irwin, 1970.

Dailey, C. A. Entrepreneurial Management. New York: McGraw-
    Hill, 1971.

Dale, A. G. et al. Simulation Training for Small Business Execu-
    tive Development. Austin: University of Texas Bureau of
    Business Research, 1963.

Davies, J. R. and Kelly, M. Small Firms in the Manufacturing
    Sector. Committee of Inquiry on Small Firms, Research
    Report No. 3. London: HMSO, 1971.

Denny, E. Signposts to Staff Management: A Brief Guide for
    Managers of Small Businesses. London: Institute of Per-
    sonnel Management, 1970.

Department of Employment and Productivity. Report of the Committee on the Training Problems of Small Firms. London: DEP, June 1968.

Drucker, P. F. The Practice of Management. New York: Harper, 1954.

Dwyer, D. J. and Chuen-Yan, L. The Small Industrial Unit in Hong Kong: Patterns and Policies. Hull: University of Hull, 1967.

Economists Advisory Group. Financial Facilities for Small Firms. Committee of Inquiry on Small Firms, Research Report No. 4. London: HMSO, 1971.

_____. Problems of the Small Firm in Raising External Finance-- The Results of a Sample Survey. Committee of Inquiry on Small Firms, Research Report No. 5. London: HMSO, 1971.

Economist Intelligence Unit. A Study of the Furniture Industry and Trade in the United Kingdom. London: EIU, 1958.

Emery, F. E., ed. Systems Thinking. Harmondsworth: Penguin Books, 1969.

English, A. R. Financial Problems of the Family Company. London: Sweet and Maxwell, 1958.

Etcheson, W. W. and Robb, J. F. A Study of Business Terminations. Seattle: University of Washington, 1962.

Fang, H. D. Small Industry in Singapore. Singapore: Nanyang University, Institute of Business Studies, 1971.

Flink, S. J. Equity Financing for Small Business. New York: Simmons-Boardman, 1962.

Ford, I. Buying and Running Your Own Business. London: Business Books, 1970.

Fortune, eds. Adventures in Small Business. New York: McGraw-Hill, 1957.

Fowler, F. P. and Sandberg, E. W. The Relationship of Management Decision-Making to Small Business Growth. Washington, D.C.: Small Business Administration, 1964.

Fram, E. H. What You Should Know About Small Business Marketing. Dobbs Ferry, N.Y.: Oceana Publications, 1968.

Freeman, C. The Role of Small Firms in Innovation in the United Kingdom Since 1945. Committee of Inquiry on Small Firms, Research Report No. 6. London: HMSO, 1971.

Galbraith, J. K. The New Industrial State. London: Hamish Hamilton, 1967.

Gide, C. and Rist, C. A History of Economic Doctrines. 2d ed. Translated by R. Richards. London: George G. Harrap, 1948.

Glickman, A. S.; Hahn, C. P.; Fleishman, E. A.; and Baxter, B. Top Management Development and Succession: An Exploratory Study. New York: Macmillan, 1968.

Godfrey, E. P.; Fiedler, F. E.; and Holl, D. M. Boards, Managers and Company Success. Danville, Ill.: Interstate Press, 1959.

Golby, C. W. and Johns, G. Attitude and Motivation. Committee of Inquiry on Small Firms, Research Report No. 7. London: HMSO, 1971.

Goldthorpe, J. H.; Lockwood, D.; Bechhofer, F.; and Platt, J. The Affluent Worker: Industrial Attitudes and Behaviour. Cambridge: University Press, 1970.

Gough, J. W. The Rise of the Entrepreneur. London: Batsford, 1969.

Granick, D. The European Executive. London: Weidenfeld and Nicholson, 1962.

Grundy, M. Tax and the Family Business. 4th ed. London: Sweet and Maxwell, 1970.

Grunewald, D. What You Should Know About Small Business Management. Dobbs Ferry, N.Y. Oceana Publications, 1966.

Haas, R. M. et al. Long Range Planning for Small Businesses. Bloomington: Indiana University Bureau of Business Research, 1964.

Hailes, W. D. and Hubbard, R. T. Small Business Management. Albany, N.Y.: Delmar Publishers, 1965.

Hall, M. The Small Unit in the Distributive Trades. Committee of Inquiry on Small Firms, Research Report No. 8. London: HMSO, 1971.

Hawkins, E. D. et al. Entrepreneurship and Labor Skills in Indonesian Economic Development: A Symposium. New Haven, Conn.: Yale University, Southeast Asia Studies, 1961.

Heal, A. The London Furniture Makers from the Restoration to the Victorian Era, 1660-1840. London: Batsford, 1953.

Hebden, J. and Robinson, R. V. F. The Small Firm in the Motor Vehicle Distribution and Repair Industry. Committee of Inquiry on Small Firms, Research Report No. 9. London: HMSO, 1971.

Henke, R. Effective Research and Development for the Smaller Company. Houston: Gulf Publications, 1963.

Hill, P. Towards a New Philosophy of Management. London: Gower Press, 1971.

Hillebrandt, P. Small Firms in the Construction Industry. Committee of Inquiry on Small Firms, Research Report No. 10. London: HMSO, 1971.

Hoad, W. M. Cases in Small Business. Ann Arbor: University of Michigan Bureau of Business Research, 1968.

_____ and Rosko, P. Management Factors Contributing to the Success or Failure of Small Manufacturers. Ann Arbor: University of Michigan Bureau of Business Research, 1964.

Hofstadter, R. Social Darwinism in American Thought. Philadelphia: University of Pennsylvania Press, 1944.

Hollander, E. D. et al. The Future of Small Business. New York: Praeger, 1967.

Holmes, R. The Ownership of Work: A Psychological Approach. London: London School of Economics and Political Science, Department of Social Psychology, November 1966.

Hosmer, W. A.; Tucker, F. L.; and Cooper, A. C. Small Business
    Management: A Casebook. Homewood, Ill.: Richard D. Irwin,
    1966.

India Techno-economic Survey Team. Report on Small Industry Op-
    portunities and Policies in Fiji Islands. New Delhi: Ministry
    of External Affairs, Economic Division, 1969.

Institute of Directors. Finance Problems of the Smaller Company--
    An Institute of Directors Guide to the City. London: Institute
    of Directors, November 1967.

International Labour Office. Services for Small-Scale Industry.
    Geneva: ILO, 1961.

Jepson, A. M. What to Do with a Family Company Now. 2d ed.
    London: Butterworths, 1969.

Jewkes, J.; Sawers, D.; and Stillerman, R. The Sources of Inven-
    tion. London: Macmillan, 1958.

Kaplan, A. D. H. Small Business: Its Place and Problems. New
    York: McGraw-Hill, 1948.

Katona, G. Psychological Analysis of Economic Behavior. New
    York: McGraw-Hill, 1951.

Kaufman, A. Small-scale Industry in the Soviet Union. New York:
    National Bureau of Economic Research, 1962.

Kelley, P. C.; Lawyer, K.; and Baumback, C. M. How to Organize
    and Operate a Small Business. 4th ed. Englewood Cliffs,
    N.J.: Prentice-Hall, 1968.

Kilby, P., ed. Entrepreneurship and Economic Development. New
    York: The Free Press, 1971.

King, D. Training Within the Organisation. London: Tavistock,
    1968.

Kinnard, W. N. and Malinowski, Z. S. How Urban Renewal Projects
    Affect Small Business. Washington, D.C.: Small Business
    Administration, January 1961.

Kirzner, I. M. Competition and Entrepreneurship. Chicago: Uni-
    versity of Chicago Press, 1973.

Klatt, L. A. Small Business Management: Essentials of Entrepreneurship. Belmont, Calif.: Wadsworth, 1973.

_____, ed. Managing the Dynamic Small Firm: Readings. Belmont, Calif.: Wadsworth, 1971.

Krooss, H. E. and Gilbert, C. American Business History. Englewood Cliffs, N.J.: Prentice-Hall, 1972.

Lanzillotti, R. F. Pricing, Production and Marketing Policies of Small Manufacturers. Pullman: Washington State University, Bureau of Economic and Business Research, 1964.

Lasser, J. K. How to Run a Small Business. 3d ed. New York: McGraw-Hill, 1963.

Latham, B. Timber, its Development and Distribution, A Historical Survey. London: Harrap, 1957.

Lawyer, K. Small Business Success: Operating and Executive Characteristics. Cleveland: Western Reserve University, 1963.

Leon, E. L. Personnel Management Guides for Small Business. Washington, D.C.: Small Business Administration, 1961.

Lewis, R. and Stewart, R. The Boss. London: Phoenix House, 1958.

Liles, P. R. New Business Ventures and the Entrepreneur. Homewood, Ill.: Richard D. Irwin, 1974.

Lund, P. and Miner, D. Three Studies on Small Firms. Committee of Inquiry on Small Firms, Research Report No. 11. London: HMSO, 1971.

Lynn, K. S. The Dream of Success: A Study of the Modern American Imagination. Boston: Little, Brown, 1955.

Lynn, R., ed. The Entrepreneur--8 Case Studies. London: Allen and Unwin, 1974.

McClelland, D. C. The Achieving Society. New York: The Free Press, 1967.

McGuire, J. W. Factors Affecting the Growth of Manufacturing
    Firms. Seattle: University of Washington, Bureau of Busi-
    ness Research, 1963.

_____. Theories of Business Behavior. Englewood Cliffs, N.J.:
    Prentice-Hall, 1964.

Marting, E. , ed. Management for the Smaller Company. New York:
    American Management Association, 1959.

Matthews, T. and Mayers, C. Developing a Small Firm. London:
    BBC Publications, 1968.

Mayer, K. B. and Goldstein, S. The First Two Years: Problems
    of Small Firm Growth and Survival. Small Business Adminis-
    tration Research Series No. 2. Washington, D.C.: Small
    Business Administration, 1961.

Mayes, L. J. The History of Chairmaking in High Wycombe.
    London: Routledge and Kegan Paul, 1960.

Meeting the Special Problems of Small Business. New York: Com-
    mittee for Economic Development, 1947.

Merrett, A. J. and Lehr, M. E. The Private Company Today. An
    Investigation into the Economic Position of Unquoted Companies
    in the United Kingdom. London: Gower Press, 1971.

Merrett Cyriax Associates. Dynamics of Small Firms. Committee
    of Inquiry on Small Firms, Research Report No. 12. London:
    HMSO, 1971.

Metcalf, W. O. Starting and Managing a Small Business of Your Own.
    Washington, D.C.: Small Business Administration, 1962.

Miller, E. J. and Rice, A. K. Systems of Organisation. London:
    Tavistock, 1967.

Miller, R. E. Innovation, Organisation and Environment. Quebec:
    Institute of Research, University of Sherbrooke, 1971.

Miller, W. , ed. Men in Business: Essays in the History of Entre-
    preneurship. Cambridge, Mass.: Harvard University Press,
    1952.

Moos, S. Aspects of Monopoly and Restrictive Practices Legislation in Relation to Small Firms. Committee of Inquiry on Small Firms, Research Report No. 13. London: HMSO, 1971.

Morse, F. C. Going into Business for Yourself. Austin, Texas: F. C. Morse, 1965.

Morton, J. Three Generations in a Family Textile Firm. London: Routledge and Kegan Paul, 1971.

National Academy of Sciences. Research Management and Technical Entrepreneurship: A U.S. Role in Improving Skills in Developing Countries. Washington, D.C.: NAS, 1973.

National Economic Development Office. Management Recruitment and Development. London: HMSO, 1965.

Newman, W. H. and Logan, J. P. Management of Expanding Enterprises. New York: Columbia University Press, 1955.

Nichols, T. Ownership, Control and Ideology. London: Allen and Unwin, 1969.

Numas (Management Services) Ltd. Tackling the Problems of the Smaller Firm. London: British Productivity Council, 1968.

Oliver, J. L. The Development and Structure of the Furniture Industry. Oxford: Pergamon, 1966.

O'Neal, F. H. and Derwin, J. Expulsion or Oppression of Business Associates: "Squeeze Outs" in Small Enterprises. Durham, N.C.: Duke University Press, 1961.

Organization for Economic Cooperation and Development. Problems and Policies Relating to Small and Medium-Sized Businesses. Analytic report drawn up by the Industry Committee of the OECD. Paris: OECD, 1971.

Panglaykin, J. and Palmer, I. Entrepreneurship and Commercial Risks; The Case of a Schumpeterian Business in Indonesia. Singapore: Institute of Business Studies, Nanyang University, 1970.

Parris, A. W. The Small Business Administration. New York: Praeger, 1968.

Perrow, C. Organisational Analysis. London: Tavistock, 1970.

Peters, R. S. The Concept of Motivation. London: Routledge and
    Kegan Paul, 1958.

Petrof, J. V.; Carusone, P. S.; and McDavid, J. E. Small Busi-
    ness Management: Concepts and Techniques for Improving
    Decisions. New York: McGraw-Hill, 1972.

Pfeffer, I., ed. The Financing of Small Business. London: Collier-
    Macmillan, 1967.

Phillips, J. D. Little Business in the American Economy. Urbana:
    University of Illinois Press, 1958.

Pickering, J. F.; Greenwood, J. A.; and Hunt, D. The Small Firm
    in the Hotel and Catering Industry. Committee of Inquiry on
    Small Firms, Research Report No. 14. London: HMSO, 1971.

Pickle, H. B. Personality and Success: An Evaluation of Personal
    Characteristics of Successful Small Business Managers. Small
    Business Administration Research Series No. 4. Washington,
    D.C.: Small Business Administration, 1964.

Preston, L. E., ed. Managing the Independent Business. Engle-
    wood Cliffs, N.J.: Prentice-Hall, 1962.

Proxmire, W. Can Small Business Survive? Chicago: Henry
    Regnery, 1964.

Ringstrom, N. H. Case Studies in Business Success and Failure.
    Washington, D.C.: Small Business Administration, 1962.

Rischin, M., ed. The American Gospel of Success: Individualism
    and Beyond. Chicago: University of Chicago Press, 1965.

Robinson, R. I. Financing the Dynamic Small Firm: Problems of
    Promotion, Survival and Growth. Belmont, Calif.: Wadsworth,
    1966.

Rodgers, W. Think. A Biography of the Watsons and IBM. London:
    Weidenfeld and Nicholson, 1970.

Roe, G. Profitable Marketing for the Smaller Company. London:
    Directors Bookshelf, 1969.

Rotch, W. Management of Small Enterprises--Cases and Readings. 2d ed. Charlottesville: University Press of Virginia, 1967.

Sadler, P. J. and Barry, B. A. Organisational Development. London: Longmans, 1970. Chapter 2, The special problems of the family firm.

Safier, F. Small Business Wants Old-Age Security. Washington, D.C.: Senate Small Business Committee Print No. 17, 1943.

Sanzo, R. Ratio Analysis for Small Business. Washington, D.C.: Small Business Administration, 1970.

Sayich, Y. A. Entrepreneurs of Lebanon. Cambridge, Mass.: Harvard University Press, 1962.

Sayles, L. R. Managerial Behavior: Administration in Complex Organizations. New York: McGraw-Hill, 1964.

Schabacker, J. C. Cash Planning in Small Manufacturing Companies. Small Business Administration Research Series No. 1. Washington, D.C.: Small Business Administration, 1960.

Schein, E. H. Organizational Psychology. 2d ed. Englewood Cliffs, N.J.: Prentice-Hall, 1970.

Schon, D. A. Beyond the Stable State. London: Temple Smith, 1971.

Schumacher, E. F. Small is Beautiful. London: Blond and Briggs, 1973.

Schumpeter, J. A. Capitalism, Socialism and Democracy. 4th ed. London: Allen and Unwin, 1954.

Segal, M. Sales Management for Small and Medium Sized Businesses. West Nyack, N.Y.: Parker, 1969.

Shenfield, B. E. Company Boards: Their Responsibilities to Shareholders, Employees and Their Community. London: P.E.P., 1971.

Shetty, M. C. Small-scale and Household Industries in a Developing Economy. Bombay: Asia Publishing House, 1963.

Small Business Administration. Delegating Work and Responsibility. Washington, D.C.: SBA, 1967.

_____. Executive Development in Small Business. Small Business Administration Management Series No. 12. Washington, D.C.: SBA, 1955.

_____. How to Find a Likely Successor. Washington, D.C.: SBA, 1968.

_____. Safeguarding Your Business and Management Succession. Washington, D.C.: SBA, 1965.

_____. The Small Manufacturer and His Specialized Staff. Washington, D.C.: SBA, 1954.

_____. Suggested Research Topics. Washington, D.C.: SBA, 1961.

Small Business Finance Corporation, Tokyo. Outline of Small Business Finance Corporation. Rev. ed. Tokyo: SBFC, 1967.

Smith, A. D. Small Retailers: Prospects and Policies. Committee of Inquiry on Small Firms, Research Report No. 15. London: HMSO, 1971.

Staley, E. and Morse, R. Modern Small Industries for Developing Countries. New York: McGraw-Hill, 1965.

Stanworth, M. J. K. and Curran, J. Management Motivation in the Smaller Business. Epping, Essex: Gower Press Ltd, 1973.

Stekler, H. O. Profitability and Size of Firm. Berkeley: Institute of Business and Economic Research, University of California, 1963.

Steindl, J. Small and Big Business. Oxford: Blackwell, 1945.

Steinmetz, L. L.; Kline, J. B.; and Stegall, D. P. Managing the Small Business. Homewood, Ill.: Richard D. Irwin, 1968.

Stepanek, J. E. Managers for Small Industry: An International Study. Glencoe, Ill.: Free Press, 1960.

Stewart, R. Managers and Their Jobs. London: Macmillan, 1967.

Still, J. W. A Guide to Managerial Accounting in Small Companies. Englewood Cliffs, N.J.: Prentice-Hall, 1969.

Supple, B. E., ed. The Experience of Economic Growth. New York: Random House, 1963.

Sutton, F. X.; Harris, S. E.; Kaysen, C.; and Tobin, J. The American Business Creed. Cambridge, Mass.: Harvard University Press, 1956.

Swayne, C. and Tucker, W. The Effective Entrepreneur. Morristown, N.J.: General Learning Press, 1973.

Tamari, M. A Postal Questionnaire Survey of Small Firms: An Analysis of Financial Data. Committee of Inquiry on Small Firms, Research Report No. 16. London: HMSO, 1971.

Thompson, W. An Analysis of Environmental and Managerial Factors in the Success or Failure of Small Manufacturing Enterprise. Iowa, Bureau of Business and Economic Research, September 1963.

Todd, D. The Relative Efficiency of Small and Large Firms. Committee of Inquiry on Small Firms, Research Report No. 18. London: HMSO, 1971.

Torbert, F. Personnel Management in Small Companies. Los Angeles: University of California Institute of Industrial Relations, 1959.

United Nations. Technical Co-operation for the Development of Small-scale Industries. New York: United Nations, Department of Economic and Social Affairs, Center for Industrial Development, 1967.

Venables, P. F. R. and Williams, W. J. The Smaller Firm and Technical Education. London: Parrish, 1961.

Warner, W. L. and Abegglen, J. C. Big Business Leaders in America. New York: Harper, 1955.

Weiss, E. B. Death of the Independent Retailer. New York: Doyle Dane Bernbach Inc., 1963.

Weston, J. F. The Financing of Small Business. New York:
     Macmillan, 1967.

Wickesberg, A. K. Organizational Relationships in the Growing
     Small Manufacturing Firm. Minneapolis: University of
     Minnesota, 1961.

Wilkie, R. and Deeks, J. The Training and Development of Small
     Firm Owner-Managers and Managers. Bradford: Institute of
     Scientific Business, 1973.

Williams, R. Culture and Society, 1780-1950. London: Chatto and
     Windus, 1958.

Willman, G. C., ed. Planning and Co-ordinating Administrative
     Management Courses for Small Business Owners. Washington,
     D.C.: Small Business Administration, 1961.

Woodruff, A. M. and Alexander, T. G. Success and Failure in
     Small Manufacturing. Pittsburgh: University of Pittsburgh
     Press, 1958.

Wyllie, I. G. The Self-Made Man in America: The Myth of Rags to
     Riches. New Brunswick, N.J.: Rutgers College, 1954.

Zimmer, B. C. Rebuilding Cities: The Effects of Displacement
     and Relocation on Small Business. Chicago: Quadrangle
     Books, 1964.

Zwick, J. A Handbook of Small Business Finance. Small Business
     Administration Management Series No. 15. Washington, D.C.:
     Small Business Administration, 1965.

                              ARTICLES

Alexander, A. P. "Industrial Entrepreneurship in Turkey: Origins
     and Growth." Economic Development and Cultural Change,
     July 1960, pp. 349-65.

_____. "The Supply of Industrial Entrepreneurship." Explora-
     tions in Entrepreneurial History, Winter 1967, pp. 136-49.

Allen, L. L. "Executive Self-Selection in Small Businesses." Man-
     agement of Personnel Quarterly 4, no. 2 (Summer 1965).

Atkinson, J. W. "Motivational Determinants of Risk-Taking Behaviour." Psychological Review 64 (1957): 359-72.

Aves, E. "The Furniture Trades." In Life and Labour of the People of London, edited by C. Booth. London: Macmillan, 1893.

Baumol, W. J. "Entrepreneurship in Economic Theory." American Economic Review 58, no. 2 (May 1968): 64-71.

Becker, S. W. and Gordon, G. "An Entrepreneurial Theory of Formal Organisations." Administrative Science Quarterly 11 (1966): 315-44.

Belshaw, C. S. "The Cultural Milieu of the Entrepreneur: A Critical Essay." Explorations in Entrepreneurial History, February 1955, pp. 146-63.

Bendix, R. and Howton, F. W. "Social Mobility and the American Business Elite." British Journal of Sociology, December, 1957, pp. 357-69.

Bird, M. M. "Major Problem Areas as Perceived by Presidents of Small Manufacturing Firms." Academy of Management Journal 16, no. 3 (September 1973): 510-15.

Blau, P. M.; Heydebrand, W. V.; and Stauffer, R. E. "The Structure of Small Bureaucracies." American Sociological Review 31 (1966): 179-91.

Blomstrom, R. L. and Fearon, H. "An Analysis of the Functional Work Assignments of Managers in the Small Manufacturing Firm." Journal of Small Business Management 3 (January 1965): 3-15.

Bossard, J. H. S. "The Law of Family Interaction." American Journal of Sociology 50 (1945): 292-94.

Boswell, J. "Corporate Planning in Small Manufacturing Firms." Journal of Business Policy, Spring 1971.

Braybrooke, D. "The Mystery of Executive Success Re-examined." Administrative Science Quarterly 8 (1963-64).

Brown, H. G. "Career Patterns of Foundry Managers." Paper presented to the annual conference of The Institute of British Foundrymen, June 1960.

Browne, M. N. and Haas, P. F. "Interindustry Effects of Centre Firms on Perifery Firms." Journal of Small Business Management 11 (October 1973): 44ff.

Buozen, Y. "Determinants of Entrepreneurial Ability." Social Research, Autumn 1954, pp. 339-64.

Burns, T. "Management in Action." Operational Research Quarterly 3, no. 2 (June 1957): 45-60.

Chalkidis, G. "Obstacles in the Road to Higher Productivity in the Furniture Industry." An Economic Review for the Furniture Industry, 1964-65. Stevenage: Furniture Development Council, 1966.

Chamberlain, J. "The Businessman in Fiction." Fortune, November 1948.

Charlesworth, H. K. "The Uncertain Future of Small Business." M.S.U. Business Topics 18, no. 2 (Spring 1970): 13-20.

Charm, S. D. "Organizing the Owner-Manager's Job." Management Aids Annual, No. 7. Washington, D.C.: Small Business Administration, 1965.

Cochran, T. C. "Entrepreneurial Behaviour and Motivation." Explorations in Entrepreneurial History 2, no. 5.

_____. "The Entrepreneur in Economic Change." Explorations in Entrepreneurial History, Fall 1965, pp. 25-38.

Collins, O. F.; Moore, D. G.; and Unwalla, D. "The Enterprising Man and the Business Executive." M.S.U. Business Topics 12 (Winter 1964): 19-34.

Connellan, L. and Deeks, J. S. "Management Development and the Small Firm." Industrial and Commercial Training 4, no. 6 (June 1972): 284-85.

Cook, S. "Training and the Small Firm." Personnel Management 3, no. 2 (February 1971): 40-41.

Cooper, A. C. "Entrepreneurial Environment." Industrial Research, September 1970.

_____. "R and D Is More Efficient in Small Companies." Harvard Business Review, May-June 1964.

Coulthard, L. "Boardroom Pay in the Smaller Companies." The Director, September 1968, pp. 394-97.

Crozier, D. "Kinship and Occupational Succession." Sociological Review, March 1965.

Davis, R. D. "Small Business in the Next Decade." Advanced Management Journal 31, no. 1 (January 1966).

Davis, S. M. "Entrepreneurial Succession." Administrative Science Quarterly 13, no. 3 (December 1968): 402-16.

Deeks, J. S. "Educational and Occupational Histories of Owner-Managers and Managers." Journal of Management Studies 9, no. 2 (May 1972): 127-49.

_____. "Job-Specific Management Training: An Experimental Approach." Industrial and Commercial Training 4, no. 4 (April 1972): 176-82.

_____. "The Owner-Manager: Some Training Perspectives." Industrial and Commercial Training 2, nos. 6, 7, and 8 (June, July, and August 1970): 265-69, 326-30, and 386-91.

_____. "The Small Firm--Asset or Liability?" Management Decision 10, no. 1 (Spring 1972): 52-70.

Deutermann, E. P. "Seeding Science Based Industry." Business Week, May 1966, pp. 3-10.

Donnelly, R. G. "The Family Business." Harvard Business Review 42, no. 4 (July-August 1964): 93-105.

Drucker, P. F. "Entrepreneurship in Business Enterprise." Journal of Business Policy 1 (Autumn 1970).

_____. "Management's New Role." Harvard Business Review 47, no. 6 (November-December 1969): 49-54.

Easterbrook, W. T. "The Entrepreneurial Function in Relation to Technological and Economic Change." In Industrialisation and Society, edited by B. F. Hoselitz and W. E. Moore. Paris: UNESCO, 1963.

Elley, A. J. S. "Hard on the Small Company." Professional Administration, February 1974, pp. 12-16.

Emery, F. E. and Trist, E. L. "The Causal Texture of Organisational Environments." Human Relations 18 (1965).

Filley, A. C. "Today's College Graduate and Small Business." In Studies in Managerial Process and Organizational Behavior, edited by J. H. Turner, A. C. Filley, and R. J. House. Glenview, Ill.: Scott, Foresman, 1972.

Fink, Rychard. "Horatio Alger as a Social Philosopher." Introduction to H. Alger, Ragged Dick and Mark, the Match Boy. New York: Collier Books, 1962.

Foley, E. C. "Unskilled Managers--the Major Barrier to Small Business Success." Journal of Small Business Management 3 (July 1965): 13-15.

Foster, G. "What the Small Business Really Needs." Management Today, February 1966.

Friedlander, F. and Pickle, H. "Components of Effectiveness in Small Organisations." Administrative Science Quarterly 13, no. 2 (1968): 289-304.

Fry, R. H. "The British Businessman 1900-1949." Explorations in Entrepreneurial History 2, no. 1 (1948).

Furniture Development Council. "A Review of the American Household Furniture Industry." An Economic Review for the Furniture Industry, 1968-69. Stevenage: FDC, 1970.

Gibbons, M. and Watkins, D. S. "Innovation and the Small Firm." R and D Management 1, no. 1 (October 1970): 10-13.

Gilbert, X. F. "Is Time-Sharing for Small Businesses?" European Business, Summer 1970.

Golde, R. A. "Practical Planning for Small Business." Harvard Business Review 42 (September-October 1964): 145-55, 158, 161.

Goldstein, S. and Mayer, K. "Patterns of Business Growth and Survival in a Medium-Sized Community." Journal of Economic History, June 1957, pp. 193-206.

Gordon, R. A. "The Executive and the Owner-Entrepreneur." In Reader in Bureaucracy, edited by R. K. Merton et al. Glencoe, Ill.: Free Press, 1952.

Grabowski, D. J. "Labor Relations and the Small Employer." Personnel Journal 41, no. 3 (March 1962).

Graham, D. D. N. and James, M. J. "Working Week-ends. The EITB Tackle Management Training in the Smaller Firm." Industrial Training International 4, no. 1 (January 1969): 22-25.

Graves, D. "Vive la Management Difference." Management Today, April 1971.

Grose, D. D. "The Small Business Administration Prepares for the Future." Journal of Small Business Management 12, no. 1 (January 1974): 13ff.

Grusky, O. "Corporate Size, Bureaucratization and Managerial Succession." American Journal of Sociology 67 (1961): 261-69.

Hall, D. and Amado-Fischgrund, G. "Chief Executives in Britain." European Business, January 1969.

Hall, D.; de Bettignies, H-CI.; and Amado-Fischgrund, G. "The European Business Elite." European Business, October 1969.

Harrod, R. F. "Price and Cost in Entrepreneur's Policy." Oxford Economic Papers, No. 2 (May 1939).

Hartmann, H. "Managers and Entrepreneurs--A Useful Distinction." Administrative Science Quarterly 3 (1958-59).

Hornaday, J. A. and Bunker, C. S. "The Nature of the Entrepreneur." Personnel Psychology 23 (1970): 47-54.

Horne, J. H. and Lupton, T. "The Work Activities of 'Middle' Managers." Journal of Management Studies 1, no. 2 (February 1965): 14-33.

Ijiri, Y. and Simon, H. A. "Business Firm Growth and Size." American Economic Review 54 (1964): 77-89.

Indik, B. P. "Some Effects of Organization Size on Member Attitudes and Behaviour." Human Relations 16 (1963): 269-84.

Jarman, L. E. and Tillman, A. W. "Industrial Training and the
    Very Small Company." Industrial Training International 3,
    no. 5 (May 1968): 210-13.

Jenks, L. H. "Approaches to Entrepreneurial Personality." Ex-
    plorations in Entrepreneurial History, 1950, pp. 91-99.

Jephcott, J. "The National Plan and the Furniture Industry." An
    Economic Review for the Furniture Industry, 1964-65.
    Stevenage: Furniture Development Council, 1966.

Kleiman, E. "Wages and Plant Size: A Spillover Effect?" Indus-
    trial and Labour Relations Review, January 1971.

Kocka, J. "Family and Bureaucracy in German Industrial Manage-
    ment, 1850-1914: Siemens in Comparative Perspective."
    Business History Review 45, no. 2 (1971): 133-56.

Krentzman, H. C. and Samaras, J. N. "Can Small Businesses Use
    Consultants?" Harvard Business Review 38, no. 3 (May-June
    1960): 126-36.

Laloine, M. "Small-scale Industry in the Modern Economy."
    International Labor Review 84 (October 1961).

Lawrence, S. "Personnel in Small Firms." Personnel Management
    4, no. 9 (September 1972): 24-27.

Lee, D. J. "Very Small Firms and the Training of Engineering
    Craftsmen." British Journal of Industrial Relations, July 1972.

Lees, D. and Chiplin, B. "The Economics of Industrial Training."
    Lloyds Bank Review, April 1970, pp. 29-41.

Levinson, H. "Conflicts That Plague Family Businesses." Harvard
    Business Review 49, no. 2 (March-April 1971): 90-98.

Lewis, G. F. "A Comparison of Some Aspects of the Backgrounds
    and Careers of Small Businessmen and American Business
    Leaders." American Journal of Sociology 65, no. 4 (January
    1960): 348-55.

Liebenstein, H. "Entrepreneurship and Development." American
    Economic Review 58, no. 2 (May 1968): 72-83.

Liles, P. R. "Who Are the Entrepreneurs." M.S.U. Business Topics, Winter 1974, pp. 5-14.

Lipset, S. M. and Bendix, R. "Social Mobility and Occupational Career Patterns." American Journal of Sociology, January and March 1952, pp. 366-74 and 494-504.

Lumsden, A. "The Small Business Syndrome." Management Today, January 1968.

Lupton, T. "Small New Firms and Their Significance." New Society, December 21, 1967.

McConnell, D. "Entrepreneurial Planning." Management Decision 9, no. 1 (Spring 1971).

McNulty, J. E. "Organizational Change in Growing Enterprises." Administrative Science Quarterly 7 (1962): 1-21.

McRobie, G. "Technology for Development--'Small Is Beautiful.'" Journal of the Royal Society of Arts, March 1974, pp. 214-24.

Mansfield, E. "Entry, Gibrat's Law, Innovation, and the Growth of Firms." American Economic Review 52 (1962): 1023-51.

Markland, R. E. "Role of the Computer in Small Business Management." Journal of Small Business Management 12, no. 1 (January 1974): 21ff.

Marples, D. L. "Studies of Managers--A Fresh Start?" Journal of Management Studies 4, no. 3 (October 1967): 282-99.

Mayer, C. S. and Flynn, J. E. "Canadian Small Business Abroad." Business Quarterly 38 (Winter 1973): 33-45.

Mayer, K. B. "Business Enterprise: Traditional Symbol of Opportunity." American Journal of Sociology, June 1953, pp. 160-80.

_____. "Small Business as a Social Institution." Social Research 14 (September 1947): 332-49.

_____ and Goldstein, S. "Manual Workers as Small Businessmen." In Blue-Collar World, edited by A. B. Shostak and W. Gomberg. Englewood Cliffs, N.J.: Prentice-Hall, 1964.

Mills, A. E. "Environment and Size of Firm." Journal of Manage-
     ment Studies 1, no. 1 (1964): 1-25.

Mohr, L. B. "Determinants of Innovation in Organizations."
     American Political Science Review 63, no. 1 (1969): 111-26.

Monsen, R. J. "Ownership and Management." Business Horizons
     12, no. 4 (August 1969).

Mosson, T. M. and Clark, D. G. "Some Inter-Industry Compari-
     sons of the Backgrounds and Careers of Managers." British
     Journal of Industrial Relations 6, no. 2 (July 1968).

Muerst, J. S. and Wiggins, J. S. "How a Small Company Attracts
     and Keeps Above-Average Employees." Personnel 41 (January-
     February 1964): 40-41.

Musgrave, P. W. "The Educational Profiles of Management in Two
     British Iron and Steel Companies with Some Comparisons,
     National and International." British Journal of Industrial Re-
     lations 4, no. 2 (July 1966).

Neilsen, E. H. "Contingency Theory Applied to Small Business Or-
     ganisations." Human Relations 27, no. 4 (April 1974): 357-79.

Newcomer, M. "The Little Businessman--A Study of Business
     Proprietors in Poughkeepsie, New York." Business History
     Review, Winter 1961, pp. 476-531.

Ohlin, G. "Entrepreneurial Activities of the Swedish Aristocracy."
     In European Social Class: Stability and Change, edited by
     B. Barber and E. G. Barber. New York: Macmillan, 1965.

Palmer, M. "The Application of Psychological Testing to Entre-
     preneurial Potential." California Management Review 13,
     no. 3 (Spring 1971).

Papanek, G. F. "The Development of Entrepreneurship." Ameri-
     can Economic Review 52, no. 2 (May 1962): 46-58.

Peterson, R. A. and Berger, D. G. "Entrepreneurship in Organi-
     sations: Evidence from the Popular Music Industry." Admin-
     istrative Science Quarterly 16 (March 1971): 97-107.

Pfeiffer, P. "Why Small Businesses Fail." Management 21 (January 1974): 33-35.

Pondy, L. R. "Effects of Size, Complexity and Ownership on Administrative Intensity." Administrative Science Quarterly 14, no. 1 (1969): 47-61.

Revans, R. W. "Human Relations, Management and Size." In Human Relations and Modern Management, edited by E. M. Hugh-Jones. Amsterdam: North-Holland, 1958.

Roberts, E. B. "Entrepreneurship and Technology." Research Management 11, no. 4 (1968).

_____. "What it takes to be an Entrepreneur . . . and to hang on to one." Innovation, No. 7 (1969).

_____ and Warner, H. A. "New Enterprises on Route 128." Science Journal, December 1968.

Rosenbluth, G. "The Trend in Concentration and Its Implications for Small Business." Law and Contemporary Problems 24 (Winter 1959).

Sabata, G. de. "Computer Applications for Small Business." Advanced Management Journal 34, no. 1 (January 1969): 51-55.

Sadler, P. J. and Barry, B. A. "Action Research in a Small Firm." Journal of Management Studies 5, no. 3 (October 1968): 316-37.

_____. "Organisational Characteristics of Growing Companies." Journal of Management Studies 4, no. 2 (May 1967): 204-19.

Samuels, J. M. and Smyth, D. J. "Profits, Variability of Profits and Firm Size." Economica, 1968.

Sawyer, J. E. "Entrepreneurial Studies: Perspectives and Directions, 1948-1958." Business History Review 32, no. 4 (1958): 434-43.

Schabacker, J. C. "The Special Case of Small Business as L. T. White Saw It." Journal of Small Business Management, October 1970.

Schleh, E. C. "How Is Management Related to Company Size?"
    Advanced Management Journal 30 (January 1965): 59-65.

_____. "Six Managerial Pitfalls for a Growing Company."
    Management Review 62 (September 1973): 3-14.

Soltow, J. H. "The Entrepreneur in Economic History." American
    Economic Review 58, no. 2 (May 1968): 84-92.

Stait, N. "Management-by-Objectives and the Small Company."
    Enterprise 1, no. 4 (1971).

Stanford, M. J. "Forecasting for New Enterprises." Journal of
    Small Business Management 12, no. 1 (January 1974): 36ff.

Stanworth, J. and Curran, J. "Profile of the Small Business."
    Enterprise 1, no. 7 (1971).

Stauss, J. H. "The Entrepreneur: The Firm." Journal of Politi-
    cal Economy 52, no. 2 (June 1944): 112-27.

Steinmetz, L. L. "Critical Stages of Small Business Growth: When
    They Occur and How to Survive Them." Business Horizons 12,
    no. 1 (February 1969): 29-36.

Stewart, R. "The Use of Diaries to Study Managers' Jobs." Journal
    of Management Studies 2, no. 2 (May 1965): 228-35.

Swaisland, A. E. H. "Furniture's Small Firm Problem." Personnel
    1, no. 10 (September 1968): 32-34.

Talacchi, S. "Organisation Size, Individual Attitudes and Behaviour:
    An Empirical Study." Administrative Science Quarterly 5
    (1960): 398-420.

Tilles, S. "Survival Strategies for Family Firms." European
    Business, April 1970, pp. 9-17.

Trow, D. F. "Executive Succession in Small Companies." Admin-
    istrative Science Quarterly 6 (1961-62).

Turner, J. H. Entrepreneurial Environments and the Emergence of
    Achievement Motivation in Adolescent Males." Sociometry 33
    (1970): 147-65.

Venables, E. C. "Success in Technical College Courses According to Size of Firm." Occupational Psychology 39, no. 2 (1965): 123-34.

Wendt, P. F. "Deciding on Location for a Small Business." Journal of Small Business Management, January 1972.

Wheelwright, S. C. "Strategic Planning in the Small Business." Business Horizons, August 1971.

White, L. T. "Management Assistance for Small Business." Harvard Business Review 43 (July-August 1965): 67-74.

Whyte, W. F. and Braun, R. R. "Heroes, Homework and Industrial Growth." Columbia Journal of World Business, Spring 1966.

Wittnebert, F. "Bigness versus Profitability." Harvard Business Review, January-February 1970.

Wortman, M. S. and Reif, W. E. "An Analysis of the Industrial Relations Function in Small Manufacturing Firms." Journal of Small Business Management 3, no. 4 (October 1965).

Yamamura, K. and Rosovsky, H. "Entrepreneurial Studies in Japan: An Introduction." Business History Review 44, no. 7 (1970): 1-12.

achievement motivation, 19-25, 43, 185, 190, 199
action research, 274-75
adhocracies, 235
administrative abilities and skills, 17, 146, 220-29, 255, 257, 260-61, 264, 266, 271, 293-94, 296, 304
administrative activities, 135
administrator, 214-18, 220, 224, 226
agricultural industry, 56
alienation, 294-95
American business elite, 16, 31-32
anarchic firm, 237
antiintellectualism, 44-45, 191
Austrian Regional Economic Chambers, 282
automation, 68

bankruptcy, 12
bargaining and negotiating skill, 18, 223-24
behavioral theory of the firm, 9-10, 249
Big Business, 38
boosterism, 43-45
bureaucracy, 230, 294
business analysis package, 282-83
business culture, 10-12, 27
business morality, 38, 43, 47, 50-53
business school graduates, 278, 279-80
business success, 16-20, 24, 34, 48, 194-95

Cash planning, 212-13

career opportunities and choices, 118, 292, 296, 310
career patterns, 24, 113-15, 121-22
center-periphery learning model, 283
Central Training Council (U.K.), 57
child-rearing practices, 22
climate for entrepreneurship, 308, 310
cognitive style, 242, 246, 259
Committee of Inquiry on Small Firms (the Bolton Committee), 56-67, 146, 186, 189, 296-302, 307
communications, 156-61, 211, 223-24, 234, 248, 261, 264, 294
community-based ventures, 304, 306
community development projects, 305
competitiveness, 10, 13, 50, 186-87
computers and the small firm, 68
Conservative party (U.K.), 291
consultancy and advisory services, 147, 150, 190, 220, 274, 278-83, 297-98, 304, 307
Continuous observation methods (COSAR), 153, 316-24
cooperatives, 298, 301, 304, 308, 310
coownership and copartnership, 304
corporate executive, 46-48
corporate structure, 301, 304

cost control, 87, 141, 143, 153
craft industries and enter-
    prises, 64, 68, 73, 86,
    188-89, 306
craft skill, 85, 198, 199, 232
craftsmanship, ethics and tra-
    ditions of, 50, 88, 187-90,
    198, 205
craftsmen who establish their
    own businesses, 86, 185
craft training, 131, 254
creativity, 17
credit control, 89, 148
crisis, function of in small
    firms, 247, 260
critical incident technique, 136
cross-cultural comparisons,
    10-13, 21, 51, 95
cultural stereotypes, 67-68,
    186-89, 192, 202, 291
customer relations, 43, 88,
    198

decision-making behavior, 9-
    10, 18, 58, 99, 196-98,
    212, 224-25, 260-61, 295
decision-making process, 58,
    220-25, 240-50, 299, 301
delegation, 151, 156, 219,
    223-24, 233-34
design, 87, 90-91, 140, 141,
    143, 149, 199
diary analysis techniques,
    322-23
distribution management, 90
dynamic conservatism, 247

Economic Opportunity Loans,
    298
economies of scale, 60-61,
    64
educational processes in the
    small firm, 254-55, 258,
    259
electronics industry, 65

employee shareholding, 295
engineering industry, 56
entrepreneur, 214-18; business
    environment, 17, 19, 191,
    214, 249, 308; cultural con-
    text, 11-12, 191, 203; en-
    ergy, 13, 17, 22, 43, 174,
    222; functions, 4-8, 13, 22,
    186, 214-15, 308, 311; goals,
    7-10, 17, 23-24, 185-86,
    195, 198, 199, 205, 219; life
    cycle, 219; personality char-
    acteristics, 16-19, 196; re-
    muneration, 5-6, 23-24, 65,
    84, 219
entrepreneurial: activities,
    135; attitudes, 48; behavior,
    9-10, 22, 38, 48, 192, 205;
    collectives, 301; ethics, 48-
    54, 186, 192; innovation, 257-
    58; motivation, 16-17, 20,22
    24, 185-86, 196, 206, 297-
    301, 310-11; philosophy, 218-
    19, 227; skills, 126, 146,
    220-29, 234, 249, 255-61,
    266, 286, 293, 296, 305, 310-
    11; stereotypes, 186-90, 291
entrepreneurship courses, 308
environmental predictability,
    209, 213-14, 219
environmental turbulence, 236-
    37, 245, 249 (see also, un-
    certainty)
estate duties, 300, 304
ethics of self-interest, 50, 190
experience-exchange groups,
    266, 272-73, 279, 286
export incentive schemes, 308

family background and business
    success, 16-17
family firm, 11-12, 92, 93, 99-
    103, 115, 125, 131, 140,
    188, 217-18, 276-77, 296,
    299, 301, 306

family inheritance, 293, 300–
    301, 304
family relationships: intrusion
    of business into, 31, 99,
    205, 277; organization
    structure and, 99
financial capitalism, 37
financial management, 87, 88,
    139-43, 148, 153
financial ratios, 83
financial resources and provi-
    sions for small firms,
    302-306
flexibility and adaptability,
    18, 88, 91, 190, 234, 245,
    250, 290
flexible work structures, 258
founders of new enterprises:
    expectations and motivations
    of, 193-98; origins of, 77-78
Furniture and Timber Industry
    Training Board (U.K.), 75,
    130, 313, 321
furniture industry, 12, 50-51,
    65, 73-75, 79, 84, 90, 95,
    188

genius entrepreneur, 17
ghetto manufacturer, 12-13
goal-seeking behaviors,
    244-45
government: contracts for
    small firms, 308; loans
    and subsidies to small
    firms, 297-98, 304-307,
    310
groupement policy of French
    government, 305
group management services,
    278-79
group training methods, 275
group training schemes, 278-
    79, 282

handicraft enterprises, 69,
    280-81

heroic entrepreneur, 13, 37
heuristics, 245, 260
honesty, 49, 53

incremental learning behavior,
    18
independence of the small busi-
    nessman, 13, 16, 20, 29, 46,
    49, 54, 58, 63, 66, 176-77,
    186-87, 190-92, 195, 196,
    202, 205, 258, 291, 297-99,
    301
individualized training methods,
    272, 274, 287
individualism, 10, 23, 30, 34,
    41, 186, 190-91, 214
industrial concentration, 60, 63,
    66, 69, 73
industrial democracy, 248
industrial location decisions,
    306-307, 310
industrial relations, 191, 283,
    290
Industrial Training Boards,
    279, 282, 285
industrial trusts, 38
informal learning processes,
    250, 275
information cues, 18, 242, 249
information processing, 18,
    224-25, 237-42, 249, 264
innovation, 6-7, 12, 18, 22,
    63-67, 90, 190, 199, 223,
    234, 237, 248, 257, 261,
    290, 309-10, 312
interbusiness financing, 149
invention, 65
investment grants, 308
Irish Management Institute
    Small Business Division, 282

job analysis, 230-31
job descriptions and specifica-
    tions, 230, 256
job design, 284, 295
job-rotation training, 131, 254

job-specific training, 134, 255, 259-60, 264, 271-72, 274, 280, 286

joint marketing and joint purchasing companies, 305, 308

Jutland Technological Institute, 281

kinship and employment in small firms, 13, 93-96, 114-15, 197-98, 301

labor market, 86-87, 148, 179, 309

Labour party (U.K.), 291

leadership, 7, 10

learning by doing, 112, 259, 286

learning by experience, 259

learning systems, 246-50, 259, 274-75

lend-lease, 148

little business, definition of, 58-59, 192

loans and sources of finance for small firms, 302-304, 310

London Chamber of Commerce, 302

loneliness of the man at the top, 30, 177

long-range planning, 22 (see also, planning)

long-term perspectives and objectives, 209-10, 224, 242, 243

management development: in the large company, 121, 256-58; in the small firm, 112, 120-21, 126, 135, 147-50, 223, 231, 246-47, 254-58, 276-80, 285-87

management processes, 223-24 249, 294; adaptive, 214, 220, 237, 243; predictive, 209-15, 220, 237, 272

management shareholding, 92

management structure, 57-58, 295

management succession, 96, 99, 143, 148, 243, 256, 276-78, 285, 295, 309

management tools and techniques, 219, 222, 261, 266, 272, 276, 283

management training index, 150

manager, large company: age, 123-25; career patterns, 104, 113-15, 121-22; education, 104-13; functions, 7, 11, 57-58; length of service, 118-21; mobility, 115-20

managerial: behavior, 9-10, 217; goals, 10, 187; prerogatives, 217; skills, 147, 149, 151, 220, 223-29, 261, 264, 266, 276, 293, 310; tasks and task specialization, 151-53, 242

man-job relationship, 230-32, 249, 256-57

manpower advisory service, 283-84

manpower utilization and productivity, 283-84, 310

manpower policies and the small firm, 283-84, 294-97

manufacturing industry, 60, 61, 64, 212

market differentiation, 69, 84-86, 308

market environment, 58

marketing and sales management, 40-41, 100-101, 139-44, 147-48, 154, 305, 307-308

matrix organization, 234

mechanization, 68

Midland Bank, 304

money making, 33-35

monocratic companies, 96, 301
monopoly, 85
motivation: theories of, 199;
  to learn, 258 (see also,
  achievement motivation)
multinational companies, 59,
  67-69, 305

Norwegian Government Institute
  of Technology, 281-82
Norwegian Ministry of Education, 281
nouveau riche, 11, 32, 48

objective setting, 209 (see
  also, planning, and short-
  term perspectives and objectives)
office administration, 87, 101,
  153, 156
oligarchic companies, 96-97,
  301
oligopoly, 85
open adaptive systems, 231,
  234-38, 246-50, 255
opportunism, 29, 50, 78-79,
  185, 214-15, 221, 241-42,
  249
optimism, 12, 22, 43, 277
organization charts, 97, 230
organization man, 46, 48,
  166-67
organizational abilities, 22
organizational goals, 7-10, 13,
  203-205, 236-37
organizational development,
  143-48, 234-35, 248, 284
orientations to work, 199-202
owner-manager: age, 123-25,
  141, 143; attitudes toward
  borrowing, 191-92 [em-
  ployees, 175; external agencies, 285; government, 146,
  178, 190-91, 285, 291;
  growth, 191-92, 197; large
  firms, 191; training, 145-

47, 258; work, 189-93, 199,
  202]; career patterns, 113-
  15, 197; career profiles, 121-
  126; decision-making activities, 59, 224-25; definition
  of, xvii; education, 104-12;
  functions and activities, 59,
  154-58, 223, 231-32; goals,
  86, 186, 197, 199-206, 246;
  health, 88, 141, 143; hours
  worked, 153-54; initiation of
  activities, 158-61; interpersonal contacts at work, 158-
  59; length of service, 118-21;
  life-styles, 175-78; long-
  term problems, 143-45; management styles, 154, 161-78;
  mobility, 115-19; motivation,
  86, 186, 189-98, 199, 205,
  246; orientation to company,
  86, 141, 143, 185, 199, 215-
  16, 266; physical work, 58,
  198; politics, 177-78; remuneration, 144, 177-79,
  198; short-term problems,
  140-42; social status, 177;
  strategies and tactics, 18;
  task difficulties, 138-40, 146;
  task specialization, 151-52;
  training needs, 126; training
  received, 128-34; work episodes, 153-57, 161; work
  profiles, 161-78; work satisfactions and dissatisfactions,
  198-202
owner-operator, 59, 192, 193-
  98
ownership and control, 92-93,
  187, 214, 216, 301, 304, 310
ownership, psychological consequences of, 214-18
ownership rights: felt rights,
  216-17, 248, 295; legal
  rights, 216-17, 248, 295

paperwork, 30, 99-100, 139,
    141, 143, 149
participation in decision-
    making, 248, 295, 301
partnership, 30-31, 92
paternalism, 47, 167-68
patrician companies, 97
perseverance, 18, 28, 196
personal and business finances,
    194-95
personnel management and em-
    ployee relations, 47, 100-
    101, 139-48, 198
personnel recruitment and
    selection, 87, 135, 140,
    148, 230, 284
petite bourgeoisie, 292
planning, 141, 209-14, 220,
    224, 242-45
policy-making, 101, 211, 213,
    224, 226, 245, 261
political attitudes and beliefs,
    291-92
power and authority, 11, 36,
    42, 48-49, 204, 215, 217,
    219, 227, 230, 248, 295,
    301
pricing policy, 9, 186
private enterprise system,
    186, 217-18, 290
problem clinics, 266, 272,
    278, 286
problem-solving, 23, 99, 136,
    222, 224-25, 242, 260-61
problem-solving ability, 17,
    225
product diversification, 77-
    78, 84, 147
product, identification with
    by owners, 30
product specialization, 60,
    85, 308
production management, 87,
    89-90, 139-43, 148-49,
    153, 154

professionalization of manage-
    ment, 104
profit maximization, 7-10,
    185-87, 198, 204-206, 215
profit motive, 8, 11, 23, 194-95
profit-sharing, 179
programmed learning methods,
    266
promotion opportunities, 111-14
Protestant Ethic, 34, 204, 206,
    218
psychological contract, 216-18,
    248, 293, 295, 310
public relations, 40-41, 51-52
purchasing, 87, 141, 143, 153,
    305, 308

qualified staff in small firms,
    65, 107-10
quality control, 86-87, 141,
    143, 153

rags to riches, 17, 28, 36, 38,
    81
recruitment and placement cen-
    ter for small-firm manage-
    ment, 297, 310
regional aid and development,
    305-307, 310
regional information and advice
    bureaus, 307
respectability, 29, 39
retail price maintenance, 190-91
retail trade, 60, 61
retailing methods, 88-89, 100,
    147
risk-taking, 5-6, 11-13, 17, 22,
    44, 186, 191-92, 198, 218,
    243, 261, 291, 299-300
robber barons, 33-39, 48
routine work, 30, 139, 141,
    143, 156, 222, 260-61

salesman entrepreneur, 40-45
science-based small enter-
    prises, 307

scientific management, 230
security, 11, 28, 177, 187
self-appraisal techniques, 275, 286
self-employment, 24, 58, 192-93, 195-96, 299-300
self-help, 28, 34-35, 38, 45, 291
self-improvement, 28, 32-33
self-learning and self-development, 275, 282, 286, 301, 310
self-made man, 27-34, 37-38, 43, 48-49, 196
self-reliance, 10, 13, 16, 28, 186-87, 190
self-renewing organizations, 248
short-term perspectives and objectives, 51, 209-13, 242, 243-44, 260
Small Business Administration (U.S.), 272, 298
Small Business Finance Corporation (Japan), 298
Small Business Promotion Corporation (Japan), 298
Smaller Businesses' Association (U.K.), 290
small firm: definition, 56-59; economic contribution, 60-61, 63-67, 293; environment, 221; functions, 66-67; management training center, 297; marketeers, 64; organizational characteristics, 214, 222, 227, 230-34, 256-57; organizational goals, 203-205; profitability, 64-65, 197, 213; satellites, 64, 306; specialists, 64, 67, 188-89; survival, 67-69, 196, 205, 213
small-firm sector in developing countries, 308-309

small-firm sector in industrialized countries, 59-60, 61, 66-67, 289, 308-309, 311
small firms in the furniture industry, 84; barriers to entry, 85; cost structure, 83; financial structure, 80, 83, 84; growth, 82-83, 133, 143-45; organization structure, 96-99, 151; profitability, 80-82, 85, 133, 179, 197; site requirements, 149; strengths and weaknesses, 86-88, 284; survival, 143-45, 188-89; working conditions, 189
small group training methods, 266, 272, 286
social and economic development policies, 289, 292-93, 306-309
Social Darwinism, 34, 204
social mobility, 20, 23-24, 31-32, 38, 195-96, 291
social responsibility, 28, 43-44, 49, 51, 204-206, 220, 293-94
social status, 195-96, 220, 297
Societés Conventionées, 305
sociotechnical systems, 236-37
span of foresight, 245, 250
starting a new business, 100, 193-98
stewardship of wealth, 34, 49
stock control, 87, 140-41, 143, 149
strategy and strategic behavior, 18, 209-10, 213, 221, 244-45, 249, 277
strategic skills, 220-221
supply of entrepreneurs, 309
survival of the fittest, 17, 34-35, 50
Swedish Employers' Confederation, 282
Swiss Research Institute of Small Business, 272

systems theories, 234-38, 249

tactics and tactical behavior,
    18, 210, 213, 221, 244-45,
    249, 277
tactical skills, 220-21, 260-61
task differentiation, 237
task difficulty, 135-36, 138-40
task frequency, 135-36
task-related training, 136
tax incentives and disincentives,
    299-300, 302, 305
tax planning, 149
tax reform, 297, 304, 310
taxonomy of managerial skills,
    223-29
technological change, 60, 63-
    64, 65, 67-69, 75, 193,
    246, 296
Technological Institute (Copen-
    hagen), 280-81
technology-based enterprises,
    309
thrift, 16, 28, 29, 53, 188
tolerance of ambiguity, 248
trade unions, 99, 177-78, 204

training, 87, 102, 134-35, 138-
    50, 197; agencies and ad-
    visory services, 147, 150,
    280-87; development con-
    tent, 259-66; framework,
    135-38; methods, 126, 137,
    266-76; needs, 126, 136-
    38, 147-50, 259-66; of
    older workers, 258, 275;
    targets, 149-50
troubleshooting, 170-71, 223-
    24, 241, 261

uncertainty, 6, 9, 18, 22,
    218-19, 243, 245
understudy training, 131,254
U.S. Department of Commerce,
    302
usury, 192, 299
utilitarianism, 204

voting behavior, 291

will-to-win, 36-37, 43
work organization, 283-84
working-class embourgeoise-
    ment, 292

ABOUT THE AUTHOR

JOHN DEEKS graduated in Economics from Cambridge University, England, in 1963 and completed postgraduate studies in Personnel Management at the London School of Economics and Political Science the following year. After working with an engineering company in North London he returned to the London School of Economics as Tutor in Personnel Management and a member of the Building Management Research Unit studying the problem-solving behavior of managers in the U.K. construction industry. During this period he also carried out contract research in the construction and petroleum industries and was an Industrial Relations Adviser to the Prices and Incomes Board.

In 1968 Mr. Deeks joined the Furniture and Timber Industry Training Board in High Wycombe, England, as Research Officer and head of a new research division being established within the organization. His main concern in the following years was with the management training and management development problems of small firms. In addition to his own researches and publications in this area he has conducted a variety of conferences and seminars for the owners and managers of small companies.

Born in Edinburgh, Scotland, in 1940, Mr. Deeks moved to New Zealand in 1972 where he lives with his wife and three children in Auckland's North Shore and is Senior Lecturer in Business Studies at the University of Auckland's Centre for Continuing Education.

THE CRISIS IN CAMPUS MANAGEMENT:
Case Studies in the Administration of
Colleges and Universities
George L. Mauer

PUBLIC PERSONNEL MANAGEMENT: The
Heritage of Civil Service Reform
Jay M. Shafritz
Foreword by Dale S. Beach

MANAGING MULTINATIONAL CORPORATIONS
Arvind R. Phatak

FAMILY BUSINESS GROUPS IN ECONOMIC
DEVELOPMENT: The Case of Nicaragua
Harry W. Strachan

HOTEL SECURITY MANAGEMENT
Harvey S. Burstein

MANAGEMENT OF TRANSPORTATION CARRIERS
Grant M. Davis,
Martin T. Farris, and
Jack J. Holder, Jr.

2